Goldfield

Goldfield

The Last Gold Rush on the Western Frontier

BY SALLY ZANJANI

Swallow Press / Ohio University Press
Athens

Swallow Press/Ohio University Press books are printed
on acid-free paper ∞

97 96 95 94 93 92   5 4 3 2 1

Library of Congress Cataloging-in-Publication Data

Zanjani, Sally Springmeyer, 1937–
    Goldfield : the last goldrush on the western frontier /
by Sally Zanjani.
        p.   cm.
    Includes bibliographical references and index.
    ISBN 0-8040-0960-0. – ISBN 0-8040-0961-9 (pbk.)
    1. Goldfield (Nev.) – Gold discoveries.   2. Goldfield
(Nev.) – History.   I. Title.
F849.G8Z36   1992
979.3'35 – dc20   92-12093
                                              CIP

For the two Georges,
THE GOLD RUSHER OF 1906
AND HIS NAMESAKE TODAY

Table of Contents

Acknowledgements

———————————◆•◆•◆———————————

This book had its genesis in the stories my father, George Springmeyer, told of joining the rush to Goldfield as a young man. Before his death a quarter century ago, he made the boom days live before my eyes, provided me with an invaluable internal compass that serves as a corrective against erroneous interpretations, and left me with an abiding sense of what the last great gold rush meant to those who took part in it.

In the years since I listened to my father's stories, I have accumulated a great many additional debts. I am grateful to other former Goldfielders who generously shared their time and their memories with me, especially Joseph Fuetsch, John Koontz, Roberta Childers, Robert Douglas, and Catherine and James McKenna. Material I would otherwise have missed was made available to me through the generosity of several colleagues, Phillip Earl, Eric Moody, Robert Nylen, William Metscher, David Millman, Karen Gash, Elizabeth Raymond, William Breault, S. J., and Don Bufkin. Other colleagues at the libraries and historical societies where I sought assistance provided much aid and many courtesies. Special mention should be made of Lee Mortensen and Erik Lauritzen, Nevada Historical Society, Lori Davisson, Arizona Heritage Center, Tom Lugaski, Mackay School of Mines, Jeffrey Kintop, Nevada State Division of Archives and Records, Michael McQuade, Oregon Archives Division, and Janet Wadley, California State Archives. Ora Roper, Norah Adams, and other officials in the Esmeralda County courthouse and Naoma Lydon and Donna Motis at the Nye County courthouse went far beyond the call of duty in responding to my requests for old records. Guy Rocha was kind enough to read the manuscript and give me the benefit of his valuable advice. The map showing locales mentioned in the text was designed and drawn by Patricia DeBunch.

A portion of this book, in somewhat different form, first appeared in *Western Historical Quarterly* as "To Die in Goldfield: Mortality in the Last Boomtown on the Mining Frontier," v. XXI (February, 1990), 47–69, copyright by the Western History Association. I wish to thank the editors for permission to reprint material from their pages and also extend my thanks to the editors of *Montana The Magazine of Western History*, the *Nevada Historical Society Quarterly*, *Nevada* magazine, and *The Nevadan*, where other portions of the book have appeared. The support of the Nevada Humanities Committee for part of the research underlying this project is gratefully acknowledged.

Prefatory Note

The discovery of Goldfield, Nevada, in 1902, along with the earlier discovery of Tonopah in 1900, marked the revival of mining in Nevada. Mining production, which had escalated after the discovery of the Comstock Lode in 1859, dropped to almost nothing with the decline of the Comstock in the 1870s. Without continued mining production, the state entered what proved to be a twenty-year depression period that ultimately led some observers to suggest that Nevada be deprived of its statehood. Nevada was saved from further abuse by the new discoveries in the southern part of the state.

The Tonopah boom was moderate, as was the early development at Goldfield. Then in the winter of 1904 a rich gold strike at Goldfield set off a boom reminiscent of the earlier days of the Comstock rush. Within a short time Goldfield was the largest city in Nevada. The boom, however, did not last and Goldfield, confronted with a major labor dispute, was headed for oblivion.

It is this basic story of discovery, boom, and bust that Professor Zanjani recounts. Hers, however, is not the ordinary history of a boom mining camp. It is a social documentary of Goldfield as it moved from discovery, through its boom period and into decline. Based on a massive research effort, *Goldfield* is more than just a recitation of facts. Zanjani gives the reader a detailed look into the lives of the people of Goldfield as they worked, played, ate, slept, and died during the various phases of the camp's history. I know of no other mining boom camp that has been covered in this fashion. It is a unique story, well-told by a literary craftsman. It is, in the opinion of this writer, a classic of its kind.

RUSSELL R. ELLIOTT

PART ONE

The Development of the Mines

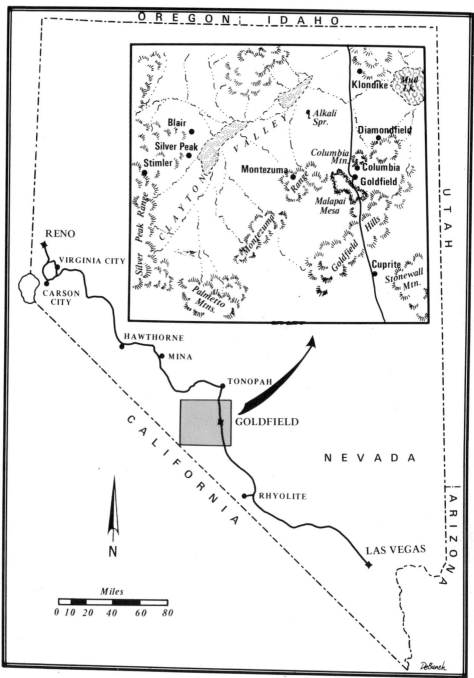

Goldfield and its surroundings in the boom days

I

Tom Fisherman's Gold

THE DISCOVERY, 1901–02

"An Indian came up loaded down with float rock that was yellow with gold." Frank "Shorty" Harris

---

The wind was raging as Harry Stimler and William Marsh drove their buckboard south from Tonopah that December day in 1902. They'd found out the hard way that they'd never get rich working leases in the Tonopah mines. To cash in on the real money, you had to be first on the ground in a new strike. Now the chance was theirs. Jim Butler was ready to grubstake another search for the Indian's gold. Thanks to Butler and Tom Kendall, they had enough food for about a week and a worn-out buckboard pulled by a horse and a mule. Maybe it was just as well that Stimler's wife Queen wasn't the kind of woman to go out prospecting with her husband, being fonder of bright lights and romantic late suppers and wine rooms than camping in the desert. Even though it troubled Stimler's mind to wonder what she was doing, and with whom, the grub would go further without her. What mattered now was the gold float they had seen in the hands of the Indian, Tom Fisherman.

The trouble was that the Indian sometimes talked around the wrong people, especially when he had been drinking. Already he'd promised Butler to show "Shorty" Harris where the gold float came from. Then, when Harris and his partner, "Stuttering" Parker, got ready to start out with a grub stake from Butler, the Indian was too sick—or too drunk—to go. Instead he drew what Harris called "a lot of funny looking maps." That was a year ago last summer, and Harris hadn't come back into town yelling bonanza, so there was reason to hope that maybe those funny looking maps confused him enough to make him miss the spot. You couldn't be sure though. Even a prospector with as little talent for the calling as Harris might get it all straightened out in time, if he stayed out in the desert long enough mulling over the Indian's chicken scrawls. Neither could you be sure, in a town crawling with prospectors hungry for the next big strike, who else Fisherman might have told.

So Stimler and Marsh had known they better trail the Indian back to his camp, even though the icy wind was cold enough to have come straight from the snow-capped peaks of the Sierra Nevada. On a clear day the mountains could be seen towering on the far western horizon, range after range, but this was no such day. The wind raised fine particles from the glittering white expanse of the Clayton playa that lay to the southwest and whirled the gray sand from beneath their feet into an eye-stinging, skin-pitting, nose-clogging sandstorm, through which their buckboard creaked slowly forward.

From time to time, between the blasts, Stimler caught a glimpse of Fisherman's shadowy figure far ahead on an old horse. Did he know they were behind him? They'd gotten him good and liquored up back in Tonopah, hoping that if Stimler talked to him just right, reminding him that Stimler's own mother was Shoshone, which made him almost one of the tribe, then maybe he'd tell them where he got the gold float. But Fisherman had dropped into the same old game he'd played with them for over a year, both drunk and sober, half telling, acting like he was just about to tell, yet somehow never quite telling. Damn old Tom anyway! Did the man have some stupid hope that by pulling those rocks from his ragged pocket and dropping a few hints in his slow broken English he could go on forever, stringing out the booze and the grubstakes for one year after another? Or was it some crazy blanket Indian idea about not tearing up the breast of mother earth with mines? Stimler didn't know, but once they realized Fisherman didn't mean to tell, they laid on the whiskey extra, so he'd be too blind drunk to notice them trailing him out of town.

A sand-laden blast of wind lashed across Stimler's face. He wouldn't have minded hunkering down along with the elf owls, the woodpeckers, and the lizards in the shelter of one of the big shaggy joshua trees and pulling his blanket over his head to wait out the storm, but unless Fisherman stopped, they had to keep going. Marsh, his plump ruddy young face pallid with dust and his red hair frosted nearly gray, pointed out some landmarks looming through the unnatural twilight of the storm—in the southwest the long flat-topped rosy sandstone mesa called the Malapai, to the east an abrupt triangular hill. Stimler nodded. The Indian must be camping at Rabbit Spring. If that meant his gold was somewhere close by, they'd better get it out of him fast. Why, any fool could stumble right onto it here, only a few miles from the old wagon road swinging south from Belmont to Montezuma. Some miner out prospecting from a nearby camp might come across it. Even now Harris might be drawing closer to the spot. Others might be out there too, hidden from their view in the fog of whirling sand.

When they pulled into the Indian's camping place, Fisherman didn't put up much resistance. Stimler almost wished he'd fought back more, but it might be that even Tom could add enough to tell that one whiskey-staggered Indian was no match for two men. Or maybe he just figured he'd played out his string as far as he could and the game was up.

Afterward Fisherman led them slowly to the north end of the hill and showed them the gray quartz that panned gold. Maybe it wasn't so yellow with the stuff as those rocks Tom had been showing around town, but it was unmistakably gold. Real gold at last! And Stimler knew there had to be even more at the spot the gold float had washed down from. After he'd scrambled around the mountain for awhile with Marsh looking for the source, Fisherman silently showed them how the bits of gray quartz led step by step to a rock ledge twenty feet wide. Under the weathered surface, it might be pure gold. Their fortunes were made! Now Queen would look at her husband with new eyes. She'd have to, when she found out she just happened to be married to one of the richest nabobs west of the Rockies. He decided to name one of the claims he was staking after her—call it the May Queen. That ought to please her some, especially after it turned into a glory hole. He turned to the Indian.

"What do you call this place, Tom?"

"Gran Pah," said the Indian. It was the only word he said. Stimler had nothing to do with Indian stuff. He was white like his father, and anybody who called him "injun" was going to have a fight on his hands. Still, against his will, a few words of his long dead mother's tongue stuck in his mind. He thought Gran Pah meant big water, or something like that, in Shoshone.

"Hey, Bill, what do you say we let Fisherman name our camp?" he yelled over to Marsh. "He calls it Gran Pah."

Marsh, kneeling beside the ledge and dry panning the gold, looked up. His dust-masked face cracked into a grin. "Sounds crackerjack to me," he said. "This camp's going to be the grand-daddy of all the gold camps, so Grandpa it is."

The Indian gave no sign that he had heard. "Look, Tom, I'm sorry we had to be so rough on you," said Stimler. "You're the best. I mean it, the best prospector I ever saw. First you

*put old Butler onto Tonopah, now this Gran Pah of yours,
and likely there's even more gold out there somewhere. But you
got to quit keeping it to yourself. Next time you make a strike
you got to bring it to me right away. I'll make us all rich. I've
been watching these big promoters in Tonopah. I could sell a
mine to the Easterners for plenty, just like they do. But you
got to come to me right away, pronto. You savvy?"*

*Fisherman said nothing. He squatted, bent over, back to
the wind, his half-closed black eyes staring dully as though they
saw through Stimler and beyond him to some faraway place.
Stimler knew the Shoshone called Fisherman a man to whom
the earth talks. That was how he always found the silver and
gold, so the story went, by sitting still and listening till the earth
told him her secrets. It made sense to Stimler—Indian sense
anyway. After all, how else could a dumb blanket Indian hunt
out the gold better than all those mining engineers who'd been
to school and were supposed to know all about science and
geology? He stole another look at Fisherman, squatting impas-
sively while the dust whirled around him like the smoke of an
Indian funeral pyre. Was he listening to something Stimler
couldn't hear? Years later, when the mines had closed, the mills
stood silent, and a booming city named Goldfield had come
and passed from this place, Stimler was to remember those
hooded eyes and wonder just what the earth had said to Tom
Fisherman that day.*

Neither Stimler, nor Marsh, nor anyone else would have been
entirely sure in what county Rabbit Spring lay, for until then it had been
a desert watering hole of no importance, except to an occasional thirsty
traveler and to rancher John Chiatovich. When the old Yugoslav rancher's
cattle occasionally wandered far to the east across the playa and beneath
the sheltering flanks of the long mesa, Chiatovich used it as a watering
place, without ever uncovering the hidden treasure in its environs. Later,
when Rabbit Spring became a spot of the utmost importance, officials would
determine that it lay just over the line from Nye County in Esmeralda.

It was a geographic boon sorely needed in that desolate and impoverished
domain, stretching eastward from the California border through the heart
of central Nevada and southward into the Death Valley region. One of
the original counties created at the time Nevada territory was organized
in 1861, Esmeralda was described by early historian Myron Angel as a
"barren, unknown waste,"[1] and vast stretches of it remained a barren

unknown waste throughout the nineteenth century. Near the eastern Sierra, where rivers coursed downward to green the valley meadows, lay lands that could sustain a few pioneer ranchers and their families. But to the southeast, after the river ended in Walker Lake, came broad valleys of sand and sage, where no streams trickled, little rain fell, and the blue pools ahead glimpsed by thirsting travelers proved to be only mirages on the burning sands. Mountain ranges rimmed these valleys, the long chains that rib Nevada from north to south, lavender, in the distance, sometimes weirdly striated in rose, cream, and black as the traveler draws nearer, wooded with piñon and juniper, and culminating on the west in the jagged snow-capped cliff of the Sierra that bars the rain clouds from this parched land.

After Nevada received statehood in 1864, the legislature carved Nye County out of Esmeralda, reducing Esmeralda to a domain of little more than seven thousand square miles. During these early years, the square miles considerably outnumbered the people, the bulk of Nevada's population being concentrated near the western border of the state around the Comstock. Following the same pattern, Esmeralda's small population was similarly skewed on the western side of the county around the short-lived, tumultuous mining camp of Aurora and the pioneer ranchers in the Mason and Smith valleys. The legislature later altered county boundaries to award these arable lands to neighboring Lyon County. What remained for Esmeralda was the desert, those sand valleys and piñon-covered hills where few but the occasional prospector cared to venture, the land of terror commonly known as the "black belt." Pioneer Nevadans left that world to the Shoshone, who knew, and had known for centuries past, how to survive in a barren land on lizards and piñon nut soup.

How a county in which no emerald was ever mined, or even seen, came by the name of Esmeralda is a point shrouded in a certain obscurity. The usual story has been that prospector J. M. Corey, one of the discoverers of Aurora in 1860, named the district Esmeralda in the mistaken belief that he had encountered emeralds as well as gold and silver quartz. However, it has also been suggested by M. B. Aston in an early county history that Corey probably had in mind "some beauty who answered to that musical word, as it is a common name for girls with green eyes." [2] Aston tactfully refrained from mentioning that Esmeralda was one of those names with a romantic aura, such as Juanita and Rosalind, that ladies of easy virtue in the nineteenth century often assumed for professional purposes. This raises the distinct possibility that the mistake over the discovery of emeralds was a mere fairy tale used to discreetly veil the circumstance that a piece of territory originally the size of a small nation had been named through a prospector's fond recollections of a soiled dove with green eyes. In retrospect, it seems rather a pity that the move to name the entire state Esmeralda failed and the neutral name Nevada, meaning snow-capped, with no scandalous overtones, narrowly won the day.

For nearly forty years the eastern reaches of Esmeralda County remained a region in which few green-eyed girls of either stern or easy virtue were likely to venture. Lieutenant George Wheeler, struggling southward with his surveying party in 1871, called it "hitherto unexplored."[3] To the north and east of Rabbit Spring, mining camps sprang up in the 1860s and 1870s at Belmont, Tybo, Hot Creek, and other localities; to the south and west, during the same years, mining commenced at Candelaria, Silver Peak, Sylvania, and the Lida Valley. In 1867, when silver miners began their excavations only six miles away from Rabbit Spring at Montezuma, the excitement brushed amazingly close by. Mining continued intermittently for two decades, and the camp grew large and stable enough to warrant a post office. Yet none of the prospectors roaming the desert in those years uncovered the fabulous secret waiting beside present Columbia Mountain. By 1890, instead of developing, the region appeared to be reverting to a desert wasteland. Even in the best of times, none of these camps in the "outlying regions," as they were sometimes termed in such centers of civilization as Reno and Carson City, had approached the bustling population and high prosperity of the Comstock. By the close of the century, most were defunct or tottering along on a low level of operation. Belmont was literally blowing down and crumbling away. Aurora was a ghost town, with a handful of inhabitants becoming petrified in their own eccentricities; the county seat had been moved to Hawthorne at the southern tip of Walker Lake. Scattered throughout the region, abandoned headframes and stopes, deserted cabins, and rusting machinery stood like monuments to a lost civilization. The already scanty populations of Nye and Esmeralda trickled away, leaving less than 3,500 people in an area of over twenty-five thousand square miles. Most of these were mining men tied to an old hope beyond all reason, county officials scratching a bare living from the public treasury, and ranchers chained to barren lands and unwilling to abandon the only way of life they knew. The Carson and Colorado Railroad, despite its ambitious name, had penetrated no closer than Candelaria, several days' journey northwest of Rabbit Spring by wagon and team. Like the old overland trails, with the hamlets that developed along their routes, the continental railroads passed far to the north and south of this great interior no man's land.[4]

The desperation of the nineties was by no means confined to the few remaining pioneers in no man's land. From the Oregon border to the Colorado River, the entire state was caught in the downward spiral of a deepening depression. Even the mighty Comstock, the primary source of Nevada prosperity from the beginning, had plunged into borrasca. There was some discussion in happier climes on whether the United States Constitution provided a means by which this sorry shell of a state, bereft of population, situated on a desert where agricultural production was destined to remain minimal, and now obviously stripped of the mineral wealth that had provided her sole reason for existence, should not be divested of the honors of statehood.[5]

All this was to be altered by a piece of ore brought into Belmont by rancher and sometime prospector Jim Butler on May 19, 1900. Unable to afford an assay, Butler turned to a friend, Tasker Oddie, an affable young New Yorker who had recently moved to Nevada. Oddie also lacked the necessary few dollars for an assay, but he persuaded an Austin science teacher, Walter Gayhart, to perform one in exchange for a part interest in the future claim. Gayhart's assay, showing 640 ounces of silver and $200 worth of gold to the ton, proved so rich that Oddie and Gayhart were anxious to stake a claim at once; the cautious and phlegmatic Butler, by contrast, considered himself a rancher, with prospecting firmly pigeonholed as an occasional diversion. Numerous tasks demanded his presence at the ranch, then there was hay to be harvested. Not until three months later on August 25 did he get around to locating the claim. In this casual and desultory way, the mining camp of Tonopah was born, Nevada's twentieth-century mining boom commenced, and the iron grip of the long depression was at last broken.[6]

The folklore of Butler's momentous discovery, as told and retold in the ensuing years, has invariably emphasized its accidental nature. Butler recounted that he was on his way from Belmont to Klondike when one of his burros wandered off. While pursuing the stray burro, he came across the vital ledge of ore by chance. Some, however, have cast doubt on the veracity of Butler's account and suggested that he owed his strike to the Indians. A story persists among the local Shoshone that Butler wheedled the secret from his Indian mistress. Perhaps a number of Indians knew of the site. P. E. Keeler, in his history of Nye County, suspiciously observed that Butler spoke perfect Shoshone, had grown very friendly with the Indians, and had diverged far from the logical route to his announced destination when he made his great strike. Keeler also recounts that Tom Fisherman (whom he calls Charlie Fishman) secured a grubstake from a Silver Peak assayer known as Van to prospect some ledges composed of black quartz, a variety of ore later to become well known as Tonopah's distinctive feature. Fisherman returned without staking any claims for Van—perhaps he had never seriously intended to do so—and laconically reported that he had panned only one color. When Van paid a visit to Tonopah several years later, he encountered Fisherman working a single jack drill in one of the mines. The Indian greeted him and pleasantly remarked that this was the spot where he had found the black quartz, a piece of news which sent the assayer hastening back to Silver Peak in a rage of disappointment over the fortune so narrowly missed. Author William Caruthers was another to hear the intriguing rumor that the Indian informant who directed Butler to the Tonopah site was Fisherman.[7]

If any truth lay in this underground story, the Indian stood at the very source of the great boom that transformed Nevada's rags to riches. He

In this 1905 photo, Harry Stimler's dark good looks reflected his Shoshone forebears (Nevada Historical Society)

William Marsh about two years after he struggled through the desert sandstorm with Stimler to stake the first claims in the future Goldfield district (Nevada Historical Society)

was an illiterate Shoshone, born in 1868 about fifty miles southwest of Rabbit Spring in the Fish Lake Valley, between the crumpled canyons of the Silver Peak range and the lofty summits of the White Mountains, towering ten thousand feet and more into the piercingly blue desert sky. Keeler calls him "intelligent and restless." He had a wife named Minnie and a small son whom he brought along when he went prospecting at Rabbit Spring. His greatest discoveries, probably beginning with Tonopah, belonged to a decade of prospecting trips on horseback while he was in his thirties. Grandpa in 1901–02 was followed by the Gibraltar Mine in the Bullfrog district, where prospector Shorty Harris and his partner of the moment Ed Cross found a bonanza in 1904 to compensate for the one he had earlier missed through confusion over Fisherman's funny-looking maps. The last was Nivloc (originally named Stimler) in the Silver Peak range in 1907, a discovery Fisherman brought to Harry Stimler.[8]

The Stimler-Fisherman relationship remains one of the central mysteries at the core of Goldfield's discovery. Unlike many of the prospectors fanning out into the central Nevada desert from Tonopah, Harry Stimler was a native Nevadan with deep roots in the westering experience. His father, Henry, had traveled west as a youngster to the California gold fields in a wagon train guided by the famous mountain man Jim Bridger. Young Stimler, a gifted musician, used to play an accordion by the campfire in the evenings. When the wagon train reached Wyoming, the Indians were so charmed by his music that they bore him away to their camp to play for them and loaded him with gifts.

In California Henry Stimler peddled vegetables and eggs in the gold camps along the Sierra and eventually ended up in Belmont, where he worked as postmaster and storekeeper and played his fiddle at the pioneer dances. Perhaps the Shoshone woman he took as his wife in the 1870s found his music as enchanting as did the Indians for whom he gave a command performance as a boy. Before her early death, his Shoshone wife bore him two children: Charlotte, in 1877, later the wife of central Nevada rancher John Nay, and Henry Christian in 1879.

Young Harry, a handsome youth with the dark liquid eyes and broad features of his Shoshone mother, grew up in the Smoky Valley and Belmont, where he grew friendly with a red-haired freckle-faced young man from Austin named William Marsh. Soon after Christmas in 1900, Harry joined the rush to Tonopah. Since he was "no miner," as his sister candidly recalled, he talked his way into a job as cook at the Tonopah boarding house. The boarders soon noticed that Harry was no cook either, and his sister, Lottie, took over the job. Late in 1901 he married the slender fair-haired Queen Eleanor Whitford, described in the *Tonopah Bonanza* as a Los Angeles teacher and an "accomplished singer." The wedding was a first, both for Tonopah and for its justice of the peace, who had never attended a wedding other than his own and endeavored to concoct a suitable ceremony. For the next year, Harry worked in the Tonopah mines and scraped together a living in various ways, while keeping an eye open for the main chance.[9] After a prospecting party led by Shorty Harris failed to locate the site of Tom Fisherman's gold, Stimler at last had his opportunity.

Exactly what happened in the desert that day will never be fully known, obscured like those three figures in the mist of blowing sand. Marsh's family absolutely deny that force was used against Fisherman, and the subsequent relationship between Fisherman and Stimler seems more amicable than might be expected between the victim of a beating and his assailant. Perhaps, if rumors that Stimler was related to Fisherman through his Indian mother were true, Fisherman led him to Rabbit Spring on the strength of that relationship. Yet Fisherman had earlier dealt with Harris, and the story the old-timers tell about the beating refuses to die.[10] This much is certain: through Fisherman, Stimler and Marsh gained a chance at one of the greatest Nevada bonanzas since prospectors uncovered silver on the Comstock lode more than forty years earlier. But working in the Tonopah mines had failed to make a miner of Stimler, and at heart Marsh was still a rancher, who knew a good deal more about tending to a sick calf than tracing a vein of rich ore. The golden opportunity the two young men held in their hands that December day in 1902 would slip through their fingers during the year that lay ahead.

II

Al Myers' Gold

THE EARLY YEARS, 1903–05

"The homes of mud or canvas—like
The dice of fortune's throw—
Are scattered on the ups and downs
Of rush and fever row.
And fifty hundred men are there,
And twenty hundred mules,
And twenty dozen gambling halls,
And twenty hundred fools."
From "Nevada's New Mining Camps"
by Phillip V. Mighels, 1905

Al Myers opened his eyes after an uneasy doze, ran his fingers over the thinning black hair matted sweatily to his skull, and looked at the triangle of sky outside his tent. Still the same cursed, perfect blue, without a cloud to dull the edge of the relentless sun. Still the same unmarred stillness, without a bird song or a barking dog to scratch its hard surface. Sometimes when he listened to that stillness long enough it seemed to pound like thunder, and he wondered if he was going as crazy as Woods. So he tried not to listen. The scanty puddle of shadow under the joshua tree told him it wasn't much past noon. If he went out now to swing his pick at the hard quartz on the hillock, he'd be thirsty enough in half an hour to drink Rabbit Spring dry all by himself. Better to wait another three or four hours, at least. He shifted onto his back, closed his eyes, and reached far toward sleep.

It wasn't working, even though the pounding heat and the time he'd spent shoveling in the coolness of early morning should have tired him enough to bring several hours of good dreamless sleep. Since the others had given up and pulled out, he was alone without a human voice to interrupt his siesta, yet the old man was with him in the tent as real as when he'd headed out for Alaska nine years ago. This was one of the days when Myers felt certain that out there, somewhere, the old man was still alive.

For years he had been equally certain that the old man was dead, and there were times when he thought so still. "I'll let you hear from me at the coast point from which I set sail for Alaska," the old man had said when he left Cripple Creek, hell-bent to make a fortune at last. Month after month, year after year, Myers and his brothers and sisters had waited for the old man's letter. Even his mother had been waiting, though she wouldn't admit it, after all the quarrels that made her leave the old man way back before he caught the gold fever. All that came back from the North was the old man's partner, Robert Woods, with the cryptic story that they had lost track of each other in Seattle, when the old man decided to go out with a hunting and trapping expedition.

For a long time, Myers had accepted that. Then, in 1899, federal agents came hunting for Woods on counterfeiting charges, and a suspicion that had festered in Myers' mind like a sliver in the thumb became a certainty. Woods was a crook. And a man who would stoop to counterfeiting would hardly stick at murder, would he? No wonder the old man had never written before he set sail, nor sent notice of a change in plans. Woods had killed him for the two thousand dollar stake he brought with him.

Myers had no proof, no body, no witnesses, just a screaming hope that it wasn't in the old man to abandon his family without a word, but somehow he secured a warrant for Woods' arrest on a murder charge and rode out with the deputy to serve it. They had arrived too late, just after Woods' arrest for counterfeiting, and were told that murder would have to wait its turn. Myers had not minded much, confident that the lawyers would either grill the truth out of Woods on the witness stand or he himself would wrench it out afterward with his own hands. But Woods had escaped in a way that Myers never imagined. After his conviction for counterfeiting and before the murder trial could begin, Woods had gone stark raving crazy. The officers had to take him away and lock him up in a nut house in Washington. No one would ever get the truth out of him now. Still, Myers felt the old man was avenged. If it was Woods' bad conscience that drove him clear out of his mind and tortured him day after day in the crazy house like a man on the rack, there was a rough kind of justice working. Myers had drawn a measure of comfort from that.

Then the mysterious letter that kindled their hope and pain all over again had come to Mother from Flagstaff. Signed with the name Martin, the letter simply said the old man had died in

Flagstaff, after working there for awhile. Myers had not been able to find any trace of the old man in Flagstaff, nor of anyone called Martin either. The hell with it, Myers told himself sometimes. Whether it happened out in the snow with a party of trappers, or in a Seattle back alley with Woods, or down in Flagstaff, anyway you wanted to call it the old man was dead and gone. The trouble was, Myers didn't believe it. He didn't believe there was a Martin either. The conviction was growing on him that the old man had written that letter himself so they'd quit waiting for him to come home. "Gone west" was what people called it when a man was so shamed to return empty-handed that he just decided to disappear. Myers could picture the old man down and out, arrested as a vag and kicked around by a tough sheriff in some jerkwater town. There were many days when Myers wished the letter had never come.

He opened his eyes to look outside. Not yet awhile. He wished he could take the skimpy shadow under the joshua and stretch it out. Up where he had started his cut in the thinnest part of the detritus on the ridge, the signs looked good, and he had to know whether he really had hold of a stringer. Or was it just another comb of barren quartz? Admit it, he thought, the better part of the reason you're so sure the old man wrote that letter is how close you've come to writing one yourself— just a chip off the old block. All your years of mining and prospecting have brought you to your present pinnacle of success, fifty cents in your pocket and your trunk in soak for seventeen bucks. You've reached Last Chance Gulch, and there's just about three ways left for you to go. You can go west like the old man, go crazy like Woods, or go blast that ridge down to the good shipping-grade ore. If you can hit gold, your whole life will turn around. Instead of writing a letter home announcing your own death, you can end the hard times for everyone. You can hire detectives and comb every mining camp in the west until you find the old man. If he hears the news that his son made a big strike, maybe he'll even come out from hiding of his own free will. You'll finally know for sure. With gold, you can do anything. Maybe, thought Myers as he ducked outside the tent and shouldered his pick, you can even raise the dead.

━━━━━━━━━━━━━━⯈•●•⯇━━━━━━━━━━━━━━

In a burst of euphoria, Stimler and Marsh had named the new district Grandpa, retaining the name that Fisherman had given it, Gran

Pah, a Shoshone word meaning "the land of much water." According to Aston, Grandpa appealed to Stimler and Marsh because it sounded the bold assertion that of all the central Nevada mining camps with Indian names ending in pah (a spring), such as Tonopah, their district would prove to be the old man, the greatest and the richest of them all. It was to be a long time before anyone took that claim very seriously, and even Stimler and Marsh appeared to disbelieve it at times. Though the assays on their first samples showed gold, the values were so low at five to twenty-five dollars a ton that Butler and Kendall lost interest in backing the venture. As was already evident when Butler procrastinated over locating his own Tonopah claim and delayed over sending a second set of prospectors after the Indian's gold, his interest flagged easily.

Shortly after Christmas Stimler and Marsh succeeded in securing a new grubstake, this time from Harry Ramsey, and returned to the Grandpa district to continue the legally required location work on their claims. This involved considerable labor because it entailed not only the construction of location monuments consisting of rock cairns four feet high on each claim, its corners, and its sidelines, but also the excavation of a ten-foot shaft on the ledge through which the newly discovered vein presumably ran (diggings in the softer earth nearby failed to meet the legal requirement). In addition, ten days or one hundred dollars worth of annual work were required to retain an unpatented claim, which meant that New Year's Eve tended to be a scene of frenetic activity in mining districts. A patented mining claim could, of course, be held in perpetuity like a homestead without annual location work, but few prospectors could afford the initial patenting fee or the yearly taxes on a patented claim; as a result, most claims, like those of Stimler and Marsh, remained unpatented. The two prospectors also commenced work on a tunnel to crosscut the main ledge fifty feet below the surface. Historian Hugh Shamberger is probably right in suggesting that Stimler and Marsh later relocated some of their claims, the last of which were dated August 26, 1903, and altered the dates of others, because they failed to complete all the location work within the ninety days required by law before the claim became void. Of the thirty claims that they reportedly filed, only nineteen have thus far been confirmed.[1]

Mining camp newspapers being ever liberal in dispensing hyperbole whenever the faintest whiff of a strike reached the editor's nostrils, the labors of Stimler and Marsh surfaced in print in the February 21, 1903, issue of the *Tonopah Bonanza*. The new district, the *Bonanza* declared, was "about to spring to popular notice by reason of its almost marvelous extent and solid worth independent of any display of 'specimen' gold ores." The truth was, however, that months were to pass before Grandpa sprang to popular notice even briefly, and afterward it was long to remain dwarfed amidst news reports of other mining excitements that would ultimately prove of little worth.

Charlie Taylor, the Nova Scotian prospector, in 1905 two years after he staked several of Goldfield's richest mines (Nevada Historical Society)

The next milestone in the history of Goldfield occurred in late May when prospector Charlie Taylor came slowly riding in on an aged gray horse that appeared about to collapse under the combined weight of his rider and a barley sack containing a few loaves of bread and two cans of corned beef. Taylor was then a husky handsome man of forty, with a broad face, blond hair, and frank, open features. Born in Nova Scotia, he had commenced his prospecting career at twenty-one in the gold fields of British Columbia, evidently with no great success. The press later described him as "by no means an ignorant man" who had devoted much time to the study of phrenology and hygiene. He drifted on to San Francisco. When he heard of the discoveries at Tonopah, Taylor was in Bodie nursing his brother, Harrie, also a prospector, through a serious illness. Although all the promising claims in Tonopah had been staked by the time he reached the district in the summer of 1902, he stayed on to prospect the surrounding country. On May 17 he decided to try his luck at Grandpa.

Stimler and Marsh were more than pleased to see Taylor. Their own claims had been safely located and recorded, though some of those they considered unimportant had been permitted to lapse. The arrival of another prospector might mean that at last someone could be convinced of the value of Grandpa and their claims could be sold for a good price. In fact, they were anxious to encourage Taylor. After he had made camp in the arroyo below the Sandstorm claim and declared that the ground looked good to him, they offered him the Jumbo, one of their lapsed claims. With that casual piece of generosity, Charlie Taylor received a piece of ground destined to become one of the premier mines of the district and to eclipse the Marsh and Stimler claims. Taylor also located the Florence of future fame, as well as several less important claims. [2]

Two more arrivals reached Grandpa within the next few days, including the plump-faced thirty-one-year-old prospector with lively dark eyes, a long straight nose, and thin black hair already receding from his forehead who would one day be known as the "father of Goldfield" — Alva Myers. With his partner, Bob Hart, Myers secured a grubstake from a group of Tonopah businessmen and decided to look the district over on their way to the new copper strike at Cuprite thirteen miles farther south — at least, Myers decided to. With Hart grumbling at his heels about wasting their time in a worthless spot, he chipped a few chunks from a ledge and began to examine the ground with great interest. An experienced miner who was raised in Cripple Creek and had prospected extensively in Idaho after his service in the Spanish-American War, Al Myers knew a good deal more about geology and ore formations than did the amateurs Stimler and Marsh. "We'll stake here," he told Hart, indicating an area some distance from the Marsh and Stimler claims.

"Stake, hell!" said Hart. "This is no good. Let's go to Cuprite, where we started for."

"We started for a mine," said Myers. "This is going to be it." The claim that Myers and the reluctant Hart staked, along with nine others, was the famous Combination, named for the combination of backers who had put together their grubstake. [3]

Alva Myers, the "father of Goldfield," after his mining discoveries transformed him from a penniless prospector to a millionaire (Nevada Historical Society)

Soon afterward one of these new residents of Grandpa (news reports do not identify the finder) struck a rich outcropping that assayed at $175. This, combined with improved assays of about sixty dollars a ton on the Stimler and Marsh claims, catapulted a horde of Tonopah prospectors into the district during the last week of May. Some one hundred claims were filed on the periphery of Grandpa alone, and investor interest quickened to the point that Stimler and Marsh succeeded in selling their quarter interest in seventeen of the claims for ten thousand dollars, plus shares in the stock of the future corporation. The buyer was Winnemucca banker and Southern Pacific railroad agent George Nixon, a balding mustachioed middle-aged man with a sharp birdlike nose, intent gray eyes, and large political ambitions. Nixon had recently been investing in the Tonopah district in conjunction with a floating assortment of partners that ranged from Death Valley borax king Chris Zabriskie to George Wingfield, an Oregon cowboy turned gambler, who ran a game in a Tonopah saloon. However, Nixon began to doubt the value of the claims in the new district. After an initial payment of five hundred dollars, he requested an extension of his option.

Stimler and Marsh were equally uncertain whether the possibility that Nixon might eventually decide to exercise the option was their only real hope of seeing any cash returns for their six months of hard labor at Grandpa. Stimler had sold an eighth interest in his claims to William Douglass on June 1, but no other buyers appeared seriously interested. Marsh later told the pioneer newspaper editor Carl Glasscock that on impulse they decided to consult a Tonopah clairvoyant advertising "Spiritualistic Medium; Palm and Card Reading; Your Past and Future Made Clear; Mining Information and Advice." It was the last of these promises that particularly attracted them. The medium's message, far from being shrouded in a fog of cloudy ectoplasm, proved to be loud and clear. "You own a rich mining claim. Someone wants to buy it from you. You are doubtful. There is no need for you to worry. The option will not be taken up. The property will come back to you. Later you will sell it for a great deal more money than you are offered now."[4]

Though Stimler and Marsh took this advice and declined to extend the option, it began to look as though the clairvoyant was dead wrong. Lack of funds forced them to dispense with the services of the seven miners who had been set to work developing their claims. The prospectors who had hastened to Grandpa grew discouraged under the warming summer sun and drifted away to pursue rumors of grand bonanzas in other places. Many had scratched at the surface by now, but the secret of Rabbit Spring still lay locked in the rocky ground under the joshua trees.

By mid July even Stimler and Marsh had departed. The only tent remaining at Grandpa was that of Myers. Long since deserted by Hart, the doubter convinced that Grandpa was worthless from the first day he set foot in it, Myers doggedly continued his efforts to develop the Combination. When Taylor offered to sell him two of his best claims for seventy-five dollars each, Myers' desperate efforts to borrow the money in Tonopah ended in failure. Taylor then offered him the Florence for a bargain basement price of twenty dollars, but having pawned his trunk months ago, even that was more than Myers possessed; indeed Myers' principal backer responded by attempting with equal lack of success to sell Taylor thirty-five of the Myers claims in the heart of the district for seven hundred dollars. Taylor, unable to unload his claims on the only man who retained any faith in Grandpa, undertook a final effort to develop the Jumbo. In return for a half of his remaining interest in the Combination, Tom Murphy agreed to lend a hand in Myers' efforts to develop the claim. A handful of other prospectors, including Stimler and Marsh, returned to Grandpa as summer waned. [5]

Myers, for his part, was not discouraged, but he was dead broke and for some time had been endeavoring to sell the Combination to Lucien Patrick, an eager-faced young mining promoter, with a bulging forehead and wide mouth, who had recently arrived in Nevada after the frustration of his efforts to secure investments in British Columbia and Thunder Mountain. On July 3 Patrick had made a quiet inspection of Grandpa while enroute to Tokop with a Chicago investor. At least, it was quiet in the sense that all hands were absent for the Fourth of July celebration in Tonopah and no one could talk up a storm over the solid gold virtues of the district as an investment opportunity. Instead the din was provided by band after band of wild horses galloping into the camp throughout the night in search of a drink at Rabbit Spring. "There must have been five hundred of those fuzztails," Patrick later said. It was a real "wild horse night." [6]

In mid September Patrick went out with Myers for a second inspection, but again rejected the Combination because Myers had not yet uncovered anything better than thirty-dollar ore, which would yield no profit after transportation costs. However, Myers had gained a new source of development funds. Harry Ramsey, a Texas cowpuncher, gambler, fighter, and one of Myers' original grubstakers, was a true believer in the new district, tirelessly urging Senator Nixon to turn his mining investments in that direction. Recently Ramsey had done well enough on the Fraction claim in Tonopah to buy out several of the other backers and to finance a short tunnel into the Combination ridge where Myers had made his cut. New samples from twenty feet below the surface showed ore shoots running at fifty-two dollars and, better yet, $250. The great ore body Goldfielders would later call the "glory hole" had been struck. Now Patrick was definitely interested, and not at all deterred by the absence of ready capital available to him.

He told Myers and Ramsey that he was now prepared to pay their thirty thousand dollar price. Ramsey said that was the old price—the new one was fifty thousand dollars. Myers insisted the Combination was now worth one hundred thousand dollars. After long and hard negotiations, Ramsey and two of the other part owners persuaded Myers to accept seventy thousand dollars. However, not a single piece of paper for writing an agreement could be found within the scattered tents at Grandpa. Patrick, aware that other investors were extremely interested and eager to close a deal, spotted a bag of rice in the grub box. He dumped out the rice and wrote the agreement on the sack with an indelible pen. On his way back to Tonopah to secure the signatures of the remaining part owners of the Combination, Patrick passed attorney Key Pittman and John McKane, representative of eastern financier Charles Schwab, enroute to inspect the Combination. Thirty minutes after the agreement was signed on the rice sack, McKane offered Myers and Ramsey $125,000 for the claim.

Though the offer came moments too late, Patrick's grip upon the Combination was not yet entirely secure. When October 26, the day when the first payment was due, came around, no money had arrived from the consortium of Chicago capitalists whom Patrick represented. Between anxious trips to the telegraph office, Patrick attempted to float a loan at the bank; with a similar object in mind, he approached Tasker Oddie, whom a portion of Butler's original Tonopah claim had served to transform in the span of three years from an impecunious attorney without the price of an assay in his pocket to a wealthy and respected investor. As the day wore on, Oddie and his partners offered to take up the option. Patrick decided to check the telegraph office one last time before signing the agreement. On the street, to his immense relief, he met a messenger boy waving his money order.[7] Three years and many dividends later Patrick's consortium was to sell the Combination for more than $2,500,000.

Meanwhile, reports of Myers' $250 ore and investor interest had aroused such excitement that Tonopah was "menaced with spontaneous combustion," and for the second time that year, "a motley caravan struggling helter skelter, in a long line of sweltering dust" headed south toward Grandpa. As the 1905–06 annual issue of the *Goldfield News* recalled it: "Hundreds of men who had joined in the first rush in May and staked claims by the score, but failed to do the location work within the 90-day period required by law, were thrown into foaming paroxysms at the thought of the riches that had slipped through their hands . . . The first consideration with all delinquents who retained their senses, was to get to Goldfield and protect their titles."[8] These fears were by no means groundless, for subsequent litigation revealed that Myers and other prospectors had been standing by, ready to relocate a likely looking claim the day after the period for location work expired in late August. Moreover, when a prospector arrived at Grandpa to do his location work and had difficulties in finding the claim so hastily staked during the first rush, some were not above pointing him in the wrong direction.

The *News* description of the new stampede continued: "Men rushed for the livery stables. Wives sprang to the duty of hustling grub and water. . . . All Tonopah (thus it seemed) stampeding for Goldfield—the road lined with hurrying, scurrying caravans of wagons and drays and carriages, and men ahorseback and men afoot and men pushing their outfits on wheel-barrows, for to be sure such insanity is not limited to those able to pay for a ride. . . ."

Inevitably, the mania abated. "The enthusiasts saw the billions of their crazy hopes dwindle to millions, the millions to thousands, and the thousands to the price of a meal."[9] Nonetheless, on the afternoon of October 20, 1903, seated in the benign sunshine upon piles of shingles and scattered building materials, the thirty-six enthusiasts remaining in Grandpa after the stampede had run its course organized themselves into a mining district. Claude M. Smith, a former California school teacher, was elected recorder—and unwittingly presented with what would soon become Nevada's most lucrative public office—due to a general belief that his small frail physique was better suited to recording claims than to digging them; fittingly, the assemblage elected Al Myers as its president by acclamation.

After some discussion, the founding fathers selected Goldfield as both the name of the proposed town and the mining district, evidently because it dangled greater promise before potential investors than a jocular name like Grandpa. W. H. Harris, who wanted to honor his hometown, Goldfield, Colorado, had been urging the name for some time, and Myers, a former resident of Cripple Creek, also favored the idea. The name was accepted with the proviso that Harris forego a final "s" by which he had hoped to imply a plethora of fields of gold. Had it been possible to foretell that Goldfield, Colorado was shortly to become notorious as the site where miners would be imprisoned in bullpens during union strife, a name with different connotations would no doubt have been chosen, because the meeting was solidly pro-union. This was evident in the only overtly political segment of the organizing resolution, a declaration setting the scale of wages and hours in the new district at four dollars for eight hours. The meeting had the authority to set wages at the top level for the period because federal statutes empowered each mining district to make its own laws, provided they were congruent with state and federal law.

Aston has noted that of these thirty-six signers, twenty-six were miners or prospectors, or in the process of learning these occupations. In addition, the group included three surveyors, an assayer, a doctor, a druggist, a teacher, a merchant, an attorney, and a cowboy. The average age was thirty-three, with Stimler the youngest at twenty-four and Harris the oldest at sixty. Seventy-five percent were unmarried. Only three were native Nevadans, the rest tracing their origins to fourteen other states and three nations. The backflow of previous mining booms could be discerned in the California backgrounds of seven and the Colorado antecedents of four, and the continuing importance of the Irish in Western mining was affirmed by the Irish ancestry of nearly half. Although the man who would one day control the district was absent, being instead engaged in counting and stacking the silver dollars on the table before him as he ran his game in the shadowed gloom of a Tonopah saloon, a retrospective story in the Goldfield press listed a handful of others present but not signing, among them Lucien Patrick, the skulking black-clad Jackson Lee ("Diamondfield Jack") Davis, future aspirant for the title of the toughest gunman in Goldfield, and one woman, Dr. Frances Williams, a mine promoter whose stern grandmotherly appearance belied her unscrupulous dealings. [10]

Although the population of Goldfield would not again sink as low as it had during the summer weeks when Al Myers was the sole resident, the new camp was not yet fully launched. From the comfortable perspective of success four years later, the state press could satirize the pretensions of the October organizational meeting in the remoter reaches of the desert: "At a meeting of snakes, skunks, and toads this afternoon it was decided that our ledges go neither up nor down, that there are no nssures [fissures] nor contacts in the district, that the place is unhealthy, overbuilt, and ephemeral, that nobody will never come here nohow nor won't find nothing neither." And could also suggest that mining developments in the district had been somewhat exaggerated: "The Badger Hole has attained a depth of two feet, where a strong lead of hardpan has been encountered. Work has been temporarily suspended on the coyote diggings. Since the arrival of the last consignment of dried greasewood surface improvements on the Trader Rat Nest are being rushed." [11]

Yet mining developments elsewhere than the Trader Rat Nest were beginning to take on substance. The Combination shipped Goldfield's first load of ore in late November. Despite the high cost of hauling ore by mule teams to the Carson and Colorado railroad depot at Candelaria, the Patrick investment group made enough profits during the first year to meet their payments on the mine, as well as all expenses and improvements. McKane, having lost the race for the Combination, had acquired an interest from Taylor in the Jumbo and commenced development. In January the district's first incorporated mining company, the Goldfield Gold-Mining Company of Nevada, was formed, and Patrick, John ("January") Jones, and Zeb Kendall leased the January and February claims. This was the first of the great leases that were to play the major role in Goldfield's early development.

On the theory that the Combination ledge ran westward into their adjoining ground, the Patrick group drew an imaginary line from the Combination and began surface crosscutting. In short order, they struck broken quartz, beneath which lay the hidden vein they sought. Ore shipments from January commenced the following month and returned a net value of $310,000 to the operators during 1904. Around the first of June, the Sweeney lease on the Florence and several leases on the Jumbo began to ship. The arrival of a narrow-gauged railroad at Tonopah in July halved the freighting distance for the long mule teams hauling caravans of loaded ore wagons from the mines, and transportation costs decreased. By the end of the year, several leasers had commenced small shipments. The Nevada State Bureau of Mines and other sources have estimated total production for 1904 at around $2,350,000. [12]

In the late summer of 1904, the Sandstorm, one of the three original claims staked by Stimler and Marsh, came into its own through the efforts of a newly arrived mine promoter from Denver. J. P. Loftus, a middle-aged mining man with mournful eyes, a thick brush of a mustache, jughandle ears, and a center part in his thin fair hair, arrived to find Goldfield "on the bum." In fact, despite the facade of success that Loftus always contrived to present to the world, his own situation might have been described in similar terms. He had recently confided to a young friend, *Goldfield News* editor James O'Brien, that business problems at his Denver firm, the Big Five mining corporation, had him "jumping sideways to keep from being walked on" and would presently demand "an entire change of front." These problems devolved upon a lawsuit by an angry investor that was forcing the Big Five into receivership. By the time he vamoosed from Denver, Loftus was compelled to privately acknowledge that "men of standing in the mining world. . . . shake their heads knowingly when my name is mentioned." Nonetheless, he harbored a mine promoter's characteristically buoyant belief in his own future and that of the central Nevada mining region. [13]

Just then mining developments in the Goldfield district offered little to warrant such optimism. Although development had started on the January and Sweeney leases, the Jumbo was at low ebb, and Goldfield mining stocks were being traded for drinks or bacon and beans. The Sandstorm had yet to show pay ore. Six months after the first rush to Goldfield, Stimler had lost all faith in the clairvoyant's psychic powers and sold his portion of the Goldfield claims to Nixon for the rock bottom price of one thousand dollars. The more patient Marsh eventually sold his for a larger but still modest sum, which he divided evenly with Stimler. Thereafter, the two young prospectors who had been the first to stake claims in the district would play no significant part in Goldfield mining. Nixon later cut Wingfield in on the deal. In August 1904, they incorporated the Sandstorm and other Stimler-Marsh claims into the Sandstorm Mining Company, and an assortment of leasers commenced work. [14]

As he rode past the leasers at the Sandstorm, Loftus noticed a dark clean-cut young man with chiseled features smashing ore samples with a mortar, then carefully panning them in a tub of water. In response to Loftus's questions, Jim Davis explained that he was pocket hunting. Max Junghandel, a former Prussian army officer and a distinguished mining engineer who held the fifth of six verbal leases on 150 foot sections of the Sandstorm, had vaguely promised Davis a one-eighth interest if he could trace the gold float to its source and determine the best spot to mine. Subsequent conversations between Loftus and Davis over several days culminated in a night meeting in Davis' tent, where the miner lit a candle and pulled forth from a sack buried in his blankets an ore sample so yellow with gold that even a mining investor like Loftus, rarely at a loss for words, found himself speechless. It was clear that Davis had succeeded in his mission. He agreed to accept a quarter interest if Loftus could purchase the lease from Junghandel.

Prolonged dickering between Loftus and Junghandel ensued, as Junghandel feigned interest in the proposition of a rival prepared to double Loftus' two thousand dollar offer but unable to pay cash. While these discussions were in progress, Davis rode out to the Sandstorm, where he was much disturbed to find an experienced prospector dispatched that morning by Junghandel. The man was about to blast pop holes just twenty inches from the ledge Davis had traced. As soon as the dust settled, the secret buried in Davis' blankets might well be exposed. In a desperate attempt to stave off this imminent disaster, Davis tied his horse close by, sauntered over to the prospector, and casually inquired whether he would mind postponing his blasting until the horse could be taken away. No doubt to Davis' surprise, this thin stratagem succeeded and the prospector agreed to wait. Davis then made himself scarce for two hours, by which time he figured that Loftus had either succeeded in buying the lease or the deal was off.

This assumption proved correct. The lease had been sold to Loftus, and no one was more pleased about it than Junghandel. With the air of the conqueror, he strode into the Northern Saloon, laid Loftus' check upon the bar, and called his friends to join him in champagne. "Come on, boys," he said. "I haf yust a sucker caught who had more money dan egsperience. Suckers are plenty ven you know how to find dem."[15]

Loftus spent most of the next three months securing written confirmation of the lease from Wingfield and Kendall and buying all the Sandstorm stock his broker could lay hands on. These stocks were held in such low esteem that he managed to acquire 120,000 shares at only seventeen to twenty cents a share. So vast was the indifference toward the Sandstorm that all this was accomplished without creating a ripple in the stock market. In December Loftus, with a shotgun across the pommel of his saddle, rode guard on the first shipment of highgrade ore from the Sandstorm and returned with a check for seventeen thousand dollars, nearly nine times the price he had paid for the Junghandel lease. And that was just the first shipment. Within six months, Sandstorm stock climbed to three times or more the price that Loftus had paid. The Loftus-Davis lease, subsequently extended by the company when the vein apparently pinched out, produced more than a quarter of a million dollars worth of ore in less than two years. Quite apart from what it accomplished for Loftus, Davis, and the owners of the Sandstorm, the lease was a success story that did much to instill greater public confidence in Goldfield. [16]

As mining developments expanded, the town of Goldfield began to take shape upon the spot where Al Myers' tent had lately stood in splendid isolation amidst the joshua trees. In late August 1903, Harry Ramsey brought in the first all wood structure, a portable twelve by fourteen foot contraption that could be trundled around on a two-horse wagon. It had already seen service as a saloon during the early days of Tonopah but was now demoted to the lowly status of a kitchen. The social center of the camp was Goldfield's first saloon, a frame-walled, tent-roofed structure; its opening night was celebrated as a landmark event in the history of the camp, which those present insisted proprietor R. A. Dunn should observe by providing free drinks to all comers. Shortly after the opening of the saloon and the organizational meeting, Myers, Patrick, Ramsey, and several others chipped in ten dollars apiece to have a townsite surveyed. Town lot sales lagged, however, and the farsighted investor who bought a choice lot at the fifty dollar price that still prevailed in the spring of 1904 would see it climb to thirty-five thousand dollars inside three years.

By New Year's 1904, Dunn's tent saloon had been joined by two others, and some of the less essential accoutrements of a town were in place. Goldfield boasted a post office, a telephone line under construction, three weekly stages to Tonopah, a lumber yard, and livery stables. A butcher and a blacksmith opened for business, as well as assayers, bakers, stores, and restaurants. The visitor could seek accommodation in one of three small, primitive hotels, or if he decided to join the four hundred inhabitants, take up residence in a tent, an adobe, or perhaps a cave-like dugout in the hillside. Although considerable depopulation apparently occurred during the spring, the parents of twenty children petitioned Esmeralda County for the establishment of a school. With crime in the new camp soaring, other needs were even more pressing. The county commissioners in distant Hawthorne acknowledged that Goldfield needed a jail—and soon. The need for a church was evidently less critical, but Goldfield's women endeavored to raise funds for the construction of a hall where religious services of several denominations could be held. By early 1905 various sources estimated the population of the Goldfield district at between six and ten thousand, four banks had commenced operations, electricity had been brought in from Bishop, California, and construction had started at several custom mills. In September 1905, another milestone arrived. Goldfielders draped the O'Keefe stagecoach in black and decorated it with a banner that read "At Rest"—the railroad had reached the city, and the day of the stages and mule teams was waning. [17]

Yet neither the growth in the population and infrastructure of the town nor the rise in mining production signified that Goldfield had as yet come

Columbia Mountain looms in the background of this 1905 Goldfield street scene (Larson Collection, Nevada State Museum)

into its own. A deep and persistent mistrust continued to surround the district, leading many to dismiss her bonanzas as surface pockets or flashes in the pan while seizing upon her failures as certain proofs of worthlessness. The wildcatting of Frances Williams and other equally unscrupulous stock promoters undoubtedly contributed to this attitude. Another more fundamental element, however, was the complex and confusing geology of the Goldfield ore deposits.

To the trained eye of the geologist, Goldfield rested over a mile high at the base of low hills on the edge of a rolling plain where dacite and andesite quartz had erupted some twenty-two million years ago during a period of massive volcanic activity to form a low dome over older metamorphic sediments. Columbia and Vindicator mountains, though they superficially appeared to have thrust up through the volcanic rock, were really ancient masses of shale hard enough to withstand the erosion process that had littered the quartz dome with patches of gravelly debris, giving the hills the appearances of drowning sand castles and adding to the difficulties of early mining engineers in their attempts to locate the gold-bearing zones.

As the pattern underlying the irregularities of ore deposition in the district gradually became clearer, mining engineers realized that most of these valuable zones lay within a thousand feet of the surface where the quartz layer had been broken by faults, some—but not all—of which contained gold deposited by ancient hot springs percolating upward through the fissures. The quartz along these faults had formed comb ridges where the initial discoveries at the Combination and Jumbo were made. Nevertheless, most of the ridges curling haphazardly through the district turned out to be barren of pay ore. Geologists eventually determined that two major faults intersected in a "Y" shape creating a narrow ellipse three-quarters of a mile long and a few hundred feet wide. This area, later known as the "golden horseshoe," contained the richest mines in Goldfield. Inside the golden horseshoe smaller fractures intersected almost at right angles, but tracing the sinuous course of the main quartz ledge system still proved to be a complicated task. So violently had the heaving earth buckled the quartz layer that feeders leading to ore bodies were exceedingly hard to locate or follow. Once miners uncovered a body of ore, the shape varied so widely, from plate to spindle, that estimates of future reserves were little better than wild guesses. *Mining and Scientific Press* judiciously cautioned the mining world on the puzzling inconsistencies that continued to defy logical explanation during the early years: this district contained veins of gold neither "persistent nor well defined" in outcroppings of quartz described as "irregular, straggling, branching and apt to disappear suddenly." Accompanying drawings of these "vagaries" showed scattered archipelagoes of pay ore. [18]

An ancillary difficulty lay in the character of the Goldfield ore, imperfectly understood because this hard gray quartz did not resemble anything the early miners had previously worked and even pay ore was not always recognized. Much of the ore from the dump that an early leaser on the Jumbo had discarded as worthless was later found to average over $175 a ton. Amidst all this confusion over the character and deposition of Goldfield ores, the largest doubts centered on the continuation of rich ore at greater depths. Strong arguments that the district contained nothing more than surface deposits could only be disproved by future development, and as late as the summer of 1905, F. N. Fletcher, a prominent Goldfield attorney and mining investor, prudently advised the public at large, "The future of the camp is still a mooted question . . . Wise mining men whose opinions are best worth having are not indulging in any loud prophesying as yet." [19]

The 1905 mining production figure of $1,888,139, a substantial decrease since the preceding year, did little to allay these doubts. The market in Goldfield stocks had remained disappointing throughout the autumn of 1905, because even after the arrival of the railroad, transportation and smelter treatment charges per ton still hovered around thirty dollars on ore with an average value of one hundred dollars. [20] Yet declines in production and geologic caveats could deter only sensible men, and the myth of Goldfield was spreading in defiance of all sense and reason. Throughout the nation and the world, the dream of a new bonanza tugged at the popular imagination.

Travelers to Goldfield poured in by train, by stage, by horse, by mule, by wagon, and on foot. Orin Merrill, a young eastern tenderfoot arriving in 1905, has vividly described the train trip south from Reno to Tonopah. His train was so full of men bound for Goldfield that many had to stand in the aisles all 244 miles—and sixteen hours—of the way. As he listened to their excited talk of five thousand, hundred thousand, and million dollar deals "in such a general way as though it were an everyday occurrence," Merrill wondered how a man like himself with "merely his little shoe string" could get in on the game. When he learned that many of these men had recently been as down-at-the-heels as he, his optimism revived, providing a necessary balm to the discomforts of the journey. Merrill found the railroad "one of the most abominable stretches" in the United States, with "dinky" engines and a "mountainous and uneven" roadbed. [21]

Passengers arriving from Los Angeles and points south enjoyed even less speed and comfort. The stage trip seventy miles north from Rhyolite took two days. *Mining and Scientific Press* advised those readers attempting the journey on their own in the spring of 1905 that water was scarce, hay expensive, and due to extensive washouts, "the desert roads—never good at best—are now in deplorable condition." Readers were sharply warned: "It is no new thing to meet with hardship and discomfort on a mining stampede in a country well timbered and watered, and where life is endurable, if food can be obtained at all, but a stampede across a desert amid rugged and verdureless hills, through deep sands or floundering in the clayey muck of a desert sink, is quite a different matter—and those who have not had experience on the desert undertake a risky task when they attempt to cross . . . to the Goldfield region of Nevada." [22] Nonetheless, many fortune seekers disregarded all warnings. The desert roads heading north were "lined" with dead horses and mules, and wagon outfits of every imaginable description could be seen along the way bound for Goldfield.

Throughout these alternate periods of burgeoning hope and general despair that characterized the early years, Al Myers, now informally known as "the father of Goldfield," continued to live and work in the district. In return for a part interest, he had agreed to do the location work on a pair of claims that Thomas Ramsey and Con Crook had relocated in late August and christened the Mohawk 1 and 2, the last of which would one day prove to be the richest ground in Nevada. These and other holdings, coupled with his share in the Goldfield townsite and his investments in other districts such as Wonder and Tuscarora, eventually made him a millionaire. But Myers remained a miner to the core of his being, more interested in developing a mine than in manipulating mining stocks. He was not careless with other people's money, despised charlatans and chicanery, and showed no sign of the ruthless drive to power that characterizes an industrial titan. He was, in short, too decent a man to reign supreme in Goldfield. [23]

No results ensued from the extensive effort Al Myers mounted in 1905 to find his missing father.

Vincent St. John's Gold

THE BOOM YEAR, 1906

"The opening struggle is now upon us: the gauge of battle has been given. . . . There is no time to be lost. Our enemies are moving with all the power at their command. We must be up and doing with a heart for any fate." Vincent St. John

The red banners billowed in the stiffening January wind as the parade turned into Ramsey Street. Goldfield's combined union, the Western Federation of Miners and the Industrial Workers of the World, was marching through the streets to protest the impending trial of union leaders Big Bill Haywood, Charles Moyer, and George Pettibone in Idaho and to commemorate the Russian revolutionaries shot down in St. Petersburg on "Bloody Sunday." Vincent St. John, marching arm in arm with the other union leaders in the front rank, noted with an approving glance that the doors of every business they passed, right down to the saloons, were locked shut. That was how it should be. The union had ordered the city closed down, and the union's word was law. Now it was the employers who sent negotiating committees to shuffle their feet with hats in hand while awaiting the union's pleasure, instead of the other way around. By God, but that tasted sweet.

It had all come so easy that St. John himself couldn't quite believe it. Down deep he thought they'd have to fight for it the way they'd always had to do. Strike. Try to hold on for weeks and months. Organize the soup kitchens. Watch the children grow thinner and more ragged. Try somehow to pull enough hope out of himself to shore up the flagging spirits. Watch the weak ones start to drift off and try to hold them. Tell them again and again, "An injury to one is an injury to all, we've got to stand together," saying it so many times it turned into sounds without meaning.

In those times, he held fast to the vision of the new world union men could build standing side by side. There'd be no more men crushed in the mines because the bosses figured timbers cost more than human life. No more children sent down to

work in the dark tunnels when they should be playing out in the sun. No more women driven by the desperation of their poverty to the cribs on the line. A world without hunger and want. But first he had to make them believe that all the wealth of the earth belongs to the men who labor for it.

St. John had been through the bad times in Cripple Creek. When the thug deputies and the scabs moved in and his men started to give up on the strike, he struggled to hold back the tide. Blast through the hard rock of their souls, down through the layers of discouragement and defeat, and try to find their pride. Show them dynamite can be used for other things than blasting ore in a magnate's mine. Give them guns. Station them behind the rocks and trees like Indian warriors in an ambush. Teach them how to fight.

For a short glorious time, his boys had held their own before the union was smashed and St. John had to hit the road along with the rest. Then, under an assumed name in the Coeur d'Alene, he'd been through a good deal more of the same. In all his years of mining and organizing for the union, he'd almost come to believe that nothing was real unless you fought for it the hard way. But Goldfield had been served right up to the union like free lunch in a saloon, here it is and take what you want. It was all so easy. Almost too easy, thought Vincent St. John.

In the crowd by the side of the street, some of the boys were shouting to him and waving a red banner that read, "If they pack the jury to hang our men, we will pack hell full with them." St. John answered with a grin and a raised fist. At least, the Idaho arrests had fired them up like nothing ever had before. For years St. John had been warning them that a battle with the mine owners was coming and it wasn't going to be a pink tea affair. The trouble was that the boys had been poor so long that it didn't take much to satisfy them. Give them steady jobs, halfway decent wages, and a pork chop for Sunday dinner, and they'd get lulled into going along with the AFL lackeys of the capitalist class. They'd forget there was nothing except the One Big Union to stop the mine owners from cutting wages, stretching hours, and blacklisting anyone who sounded an objection. They'd forget that Sunday dinner and everything else are the rightful due of the laborer who sweats for it. They'd forget the master class and the working class. They'd even forget the revolution.

St. John's hand curled around the gun in his pocket at the thought of his enemies the bread and butter unionists, men with small dreams that reached no farther than a pork chop in the belly. Traitors! Didn't they see how the mine owners were using them? Or didn't they care? Every day more men came over to his side, but there were some, like that half crazy Paddy Mullaney from Cripple Creek, who thought he was poison. St. John sometimes thought that if he could ever get a solid grip on this union of hard-nosed working stiffs running the world would come easy.

Running the world? With the red flags snapping in the wind, the cheering crowds calling out to the "Saint," his nickname among his friends, and the legions of the union, more than three thousand strong marching at his back as he entered Union Hall, it suddenly seemed possible. Why not? It wasn't just a promise. It could happen, not in the distant future, always just over the horizon, but right now, right here, today. Have you gotten so used to running out of town ahead of the guns that you can't recognize victory when you see her, thought St. John? Has she got to grab you by the arm like a girl in the tenderloin? Take her, Vince. This city is yours. You've built the one big union here in Goldfield, with every wage worker inside, from the miners, and the waiters, right down to the hookers.

Now you can spread into the other camps. When you control the economy, you control the state. Isn't that what you've always preached? And this state's got so few people that you can do it, with union men of your own kind pouring into every camp from the Colorado River to the Idaho border. When you've won the state, every man in America who sweats for his bread will see what you can do and take heart. One state after another will fall, and you'll have all the gold of Goldfield in the union treasury to make it happen. The revolution is here, in your own day and time.

As Vincent St. John stepped out on the balcony of Union Hall, the shouting and cheering swelled to a crescendo. The street was packed with people, as far as he could see into the city, and into the world beyond. The cheers intermingled with tramping feet as the parading men marched forward, arm in arm, rank on rank, to take their places before him. Yet even as St. John held out his arms to them, an old sense of danger, too well learned to be undone, prickled the back of his neck. There was something that made him uneasy in the sound of marching feet.

Nineteen-six was Goldfield's banner year. The peak in mining production lay four years in the future. But 1906 was the year of the largest increase—more than threefold—over a previous full year of production. It was the year when technical discussions on the vagaries of Goldfield ore depositions and doubts concerning their continuation at depth were brushed aside in a burst of spectacular development. Most of all, it was the year when the exuberant spirit of bonanza reached the peak. In 1906 the rush to Goldfield quickened into a stampede, and the population of the district soared from the grand total of thirty-six recorded three years earlier to twelve or fifteen thousand. Although it was no longer possible to locate a new claim, buy the Florence for twenty dollars, or acquire a lot in the heart of town for next to nothing, Goldfield was now the place where everyone believed he could make a fortune—in leasing, in stocks, in highgrading, in dance halls, in saloons, in lawyering—and union men dreamed of the millenium to come. All things still seemed possible to all men in the last great bonanza.

Passengers arriving from the south came upon Goldfield abruptly after the road crested the Goldfield Hills; those approaching from Tonopah to the north would see a forest of head frames gradually emerge in the dusty distance. As the visitor drew nearer, he would note a few large and substantial buildings and new frame houses, but most of the population continued to live in tiny cabins and in tents. If he was lucky, he might get a bed at the Esmeralda Hotel—at least, he would get it for a six-hour shift, with blankets only and no change of bedding. Venturing forth onto the plank sidewalk, he would see a bustle of activity in the deeply rutted street before him—an army of prospectors preparing to head back into the hills with strings of burros, eighteen or twenty horse teams hauling large freighting wagons heaped with cargo, four-horse stages meant to carry eight or ten passengers but sometimes stuffed with sixteen plus baggage, newfangled automobiles carrying four passengers and terrifying every mildly excitable horse on the street. So frantic was the rush that passengers for Goldfield without advance reservations often had to wait in Tonopah for a week before they could get a seat on any passenger conveyance.[1]

The feature that most clearly set Goldfield apart from other camps, however, was the density of the crowds. Merrill noted that people were packed into the saloons as thickly as "bees in a hive." George Springmeyer, a young attorney arriving in the late autumn of 1906, found the sidewalks and streets so jammed with people that he could only move by inching gradually along with the crowd. Merrill was struck by both the varied origins of the men around him and their buoyant optimism. Even those who had lost everything in one gamble or another voiced "nothing but praise" for Goldfield.[2]

The mines that were the foundation of this vast excitement were in 1906 essentially the same ones known since the organization of the district in 1903, although their ownership was still undergoing considerable change. The excitement lay in learning through expanded development exactly what they contained and getting a share in it by participation in a lease, a stock purchase, or perhaps a little highgrading. Though over five thousand claims had been located in the Goldfield district by late 1905, the mines that proved the richest and accounted for over 95 percent of production were familiar names located inside the golden horseshoe just east of the city: the Combination and the Combination Fraction, both Al Myers' discoveries, the Florence, Jumbo, and Red Top, all located by Charlie Taylor, the January, and the Mohawk. The first working mine in the district, the Combination, continued to ship ore at a steady rate under the ownership of the Combination Mines Company; little development had as yet been undertaken on the Combination Fraction, which remained in the hands of Myers and Murphy. By the time the one-year lease held by Jones, Patrick, and their associates on the January expired in early 1905 and the Goldfield Mining Company took over operations, $350,000 worth of ore had been produced; Shamberger has concluded that by the close of 1906 total production from the January over the two years of its working existence had reached at least one million dollars. [3]

By contrast, the value of the Mohawk was not yet evident in early 1906. Lying between the base of Columbia Mountain and the Combination Fraction, the Mohawk had initially been located as the Tennessee and Berkeley claims by R.C. (Con) Crook and the two Texans, Harry and Thomas Ramsey during the first stampede to Grandpa in May 1903, when all the principal mines were staked. Late that summer the claims were relocated as the Mohawk 1 and 2 and the Slim Jim Fraction, and Myers received an interest in return for doing the location work. In early 1904, acting through his friend Harry Ramsey, Nixon acquired Con Crook's interest in the Mohawk and a host of other Goldfield claims for five thousand dollars, his largest investment in the district up to that time. Later that year he organized the Goldfield Mohawk Mining Company with Ramsey, Myers, and others who still held substantial shares in the claims. Apparently George Wingfield, who became president of the company in 1905, received a share sometime after the initial formation of the company and took a more active role after Nixon's departure for Washington D.C. in 1905 to assume a seat in the United States senate and Ramsey's early retirement to the Bay Area in 1906. [4]

For some time after Wingfield ascended to the presidency of the company, it appeared that the Mohawk might well be the worst of Nixon's central Nevada investments. The outcroppings appeared barren. Shallow shafts in various locations yielded no results, and several leasers gave up in disgust. In January 1906, even in the city where hope forever shimmered on the horizon like the mirages above the glittering expanse of the Clayton Playa, no one was likely to guess that inside six months the Mohawk would uncover a bonanza that was to put every mine in Goldfield in the shade.

The future of the Jumbo and the Red Top, the two mines remaining under the aegis of Charlie Taylor, appeared equally uncertain but for a quite different reason. Leasers on the Jumbo had produced $1,690,000 worth of ore in 1904, making it the premier mine in the district; by the end of the year, however, the Jumbo was entirely closed down by litigation, as Taylor struggled for control with former friends and backers, and closed it was to remain during most of 1905. His opponents succeeded in placing the Jumbo in receivership, but Taylor emerged from the Nevada Supreme Court the eventual victor.

During the same period, James Ford, the owner of a Tonopah livery stable, multiplied Taylor's legal troubles by suing for a half interest in all Taylor's Goldfield claims on the ground that he had grubstaked Taylor to the aged horse on the back of which his historic prospecting trip to Goldfield in May 1903 was made. Few livery stable owners were to realize as high a profit from their animals as did Ford. Diamondfield Jack Davis had presented him with twenty-one thousand dollars and a large share of stock in return for the loan of an old mule named Maud during his prospecting trip to Goldfield in the autumn of 1903, possibly implanting the notion in Ford's mind of a means to secure even larger returns. Ford eventually scaled down his demands to a mere half of the Jumbo, but Taylor showed no inclination to settle. While he admitted borrowing an old gray horse from Ford's son Claud in return for a half interest in a mining claim, Taylor denied locating the Jumbo on the trip made on Ford's horse and contended that the claim he located for Claud Ford had been abandoned when Ford refused to pay his portion of the assessment work. The court characterized Taylor's defense as "evasive and deceptive," since no location notice was presented in evidence to show that Ford had actually received a half interest in any claim outside the Jumbo group. Nonetheless, the roster of Goldfield pioneers who bore witness on Taylor's behalf apparently carried the day for him, and in December 1905, the United States Circuit Court finally dismissed Ford's loaned horse suit against Taylor, clearing the way for the resumption of full-scale operations on the Jumbo.[5]

Scarcely had these difficulties been settled when Taylor found himself embroiled in a new set of legal problems on the Red Top. Taylor had held the presidency of the Red Top Company from the beginning, and development had been relatively slow paced, in keeping with his conservative policy of gradually demonstrating the value of a mine with a view to eventual sale, rather than gutting its bonanzas for quick profit. The Red Top's main ore shoot was not opened until February 1905, and its total production up to November 1906 reached only $308,516, though it was generally regarded as a mine with great potential.

Both future potential and immediate production fell under the pall of litigation in late March 1906, when months of rumor culminated in a sensational expose in the San Francisco press. Former deputy United States surveyors confessed to special federal investigators that they had conspired with Taylor to defraud the United States government; in defiance of legal restrictions against using their government positions for profit, they had located the Red Top and turned it over to Taylor in exchange for a half interest in the claim. Taylor's friends indignantly argued that the then impecunious prospector had merely paid the pair in stock for surveying work on his claims done on their own time. Taylor's own explanation was never made public. Despite his position as locator of three of the richest mines in Goldfield, in addition to the less valuable Atlanta group, very little is known about him. He and his brother and close associate, Harrie, were taciturn Canadians. They do not seem to have been the sort of hail-fellows-well-met about whom amusing anecdotes circulated in the press. They did not linger on after the Goldfield boom to give their reminiscences to Glasscock or anyone else in the twilight of their years.[6] As the months slipped by, Taylor held on to his title to the Red Top with the same aggressive tenacity with which he had held control of the Jumbo, and when the moment for the big sale for which he had been preparing arrived, James Ford, owner of the old gray horse once lent to Taylor, may have drawn a certain grim satisfaction from the results.

The one group of claims that Taylor had not retained would soon prove the richest of all his fabulous finds—the Florence. This group consisted of the Florence and Red King claims, located in May 1903, and the Cornishman and Firelight, located three months later at the same time as the Red Top. It was the Florence that the dead broke and desperate Taylor had once offered to Myers for seventy-five dollars. Myers had been too insolvent to take advantage of the offer, but another prospector arrived in Goldfield with the October rush who showed a keen interest in the Florence and had a good deal more cash on hand. He was an awkward man, ill at ease in good clothes, with a bushy black mustache and dark-shadowed eyes under heavy brows. Anyone in the camp would probably have viewed Tom Lockhart as the least likely man to succeed, almost an ill-omened figure. Unlike such young men as Stimler and Myers, he had twenty years of failure behind him.

For the better part of all those years, with a faith that passeth all understanding, Colorado railroad man A.D. Parker had grubstaked Lockhart's prospecting without receiving a dime of return for his investment. Then Lockhart joined the rush to Tonopah in 1901 and located a piece of the subsequent Tonopah Extension. In camps where shared endeavor was the rule and nearly everyone had a brother, a partner, and

Tom Lockhart in 1905, after years of fruitless prospecting had ended with the purchase of the claim that made him rich at last, the fabulous Florence (Nevada Historical Society)

possibly several, or at least a hired Indian to help out, Lockhart's lonely efforts appeared almost comical. Hour after hour, day after day, he clambered up and down his mining shaft to fill the bucket at the bottom and hoist it with the windlass at the top. However, he succeeded in establishing the value of his claim to the satisfaction of eastern financier Charles Schwab, who bought it for twenty-eight thousand dollars. According to Glasscock, "When, a few days after the sale, he learned that Schwab had been prepared to pay fifty-six thousand dollars, Lockhart wailed to a jeering world that he had lost twenty-eight thousand dollars in that hole." Glasscock estimates that the Tonopah Extension was eventually to yield over three million dollars in dividends to its owners.[7]

In contrast to most of the Goldfield crowd, who bore their losses philosophically in the easy-come-easy-go way of gamblers, this experience seems to have seared Lockhart to the depths of his soul. He arrived in Goldfield determined not to repeat it, too late to locate a good claim but with the cash to make some purchases. Not much was afterward heard of his first acquisitions that December—the Sunset, Native Son, and Native Daughter—and even less of his last ones, the Red Rock claims, but they brought him in touch with Charlie Taylor. Along with these other deals, Taylor sold Lockhart and Parker a half interest in the Florence for a mere $3,500. Early in 1904 the Sweeney lease, in which Wingfield and Nixon held shares, commenced operations on the Florence that were to produce six hundred thousand dollars in the course of the following year.

As these developments haltingly proceeded, Lockhart was the first to grasp the value of the mine. Moving swiftly at an early point when Wingfield still lacked faith in the Goldfield district, Lockhart succeeded in inducing other stockholders to sell him an additional tenth of the Florence for twenty-five thousand dollars, for which he paid an initial ten thousand dollars and met the next ten thousand dollar payment with his royalties from the Sweeney lease. In this way, Lockhart and Parker gained control of the Florence and held it with the clamped iron bite of chuckwalla lizards. The annals of Goldfield were replete with stories of men who sold out early for a fist full of dollars, or sold somewhat later for higher sums still far below the value of their holdings, but never was the name of Tom Lockhart to be added to that dolorous litany.

The lion's share of the wealth of the Florence, which would produce over six million dollars from 1904 through 1908, was Lockhart's and Parker's. No offer of purchase was seriously entertained, although Wingfield, who, belatedly realizing his mistake, became the largest stockholder after Lockhart and Parker, undoubtedly made several. While his new status as a mining millionaire enabled Parker to complete his ascent from railroad section hand to vice president of the Colorado and Southern Railway, his passion for the bonanza he had awaited for twenty years was as great as Lockhart's, and accounting was his particular pleasure. Unlike many absentee owners who took little interest in the mining operations from which they skimmed their profits, Parker constantly scrutinized the accounts with such rigor and attention to minute detail that he was said to know the disposition of every last miner's candle in the Florence.[8]

The Florence, like every other mine in the golden horseshoe except the Combination, had been developed through the leasing system, under which at least one hundred companies worked the Goldfield district. Leasing companies incorporated in the same way as mining companies, and some of the larger ones sold stock for development purposes. A leasing company's only asset was its right to operate a mining company's ground for the period of the lease, usually six months to a year, for which the leaser paid the mining company a royalty generally set at 20 to 25 percent of gross production. If he found pay ore, the leaser could anticipate profits ranging from about 15 percent to half of gross production. In the event of a strike or lockout, depending on the provisions of their contracts, extensions generally enabled the leasers to recoup only a part of the time lost. Several leasers, like those on the Sandstorm, frequently operated on different sections of a mining property at the same time.

In Goldfield, as had earlier proven true in Tonopah, the great advantage of the leasing system was that the energy and acumen of the leaser in "keeping his nose to the streak" developed the mines more quickly and thoroughly than lackadaisical absentee ownership. The leasing system particularly suited the erratic nature of the small rich ore deposits in Goldfield's curling comb ridges; under these conditions, as *Mining and Scientific Press* noted, "systematic exploration is less successful than constant watching of signs and changes understood by experienced miners."[9] Because locating Goldfield's pay ores was a less than exact science, leasers often toiled in vain until most of their time had elapsed, making the last weeks a rush of frenetic activity. The operators of the famous Reilly lease on the Florence, for instance, only struck pay ore in their last ninety days, during which they hoisted nine hundred thousand dollars worth of gold.

Historian Rodman Paul has observed that the California gold region underwent a rapid transition from the early democracy of the prospecting stage, in which opportunity was open to everyone, to industrial capitalism, in which the prospector-entrepreneur became an miner-employee in a large scale enterprise owned by distant investors.[10] It might not be too much to suggest that the leasing system, because it required little or no capital, extended the phase of democratic opportunity in Goldfield by several years and injected into the development process the energies of competitive individual entrepreneurship. At the same time, the activities of the busy horde of leasers had profound and unforeseen effects. Not only did their discoveries transform the owners of barren prospects into wealthy and powerful mine owners, but also their paramount interest in uninterrupted production created a climate in which the radical unions could thrive and organize. Thus, in a rapid telescoping and distortion of the ordinarily slow and regular progression of economic stages, the two titans of the industrial age, capital and labor, both arose from the ceaseless burrowings of a multitude of leasers only a short step removed in the industrial scale from the prospectors of '49.

Also, and by no means incidentally, the system offered large risks and larger opportunities to the leasers themselves. Leasing provided a method through which men without financial resources could gain a share in an enterprise by their willingness to labor on a lease, as did Frank Athern, a miner on the Sweeney lease. Athern and his three friends were at work for Sweeney, Wingfield, and their associates when an initial lead yielding up to eight hundred dollars to the ton at the surface of the Florence abruptly disappeared. The work force sunk the shaft fifty feet and cut drifts along the vein in both directions, but uncovered no values above ten dollars a ton. In the situation of general despondency that ensued, Athern proposed that he and his friends would locate the elusive body of ore in return for a half share in the Sweeney lease. His employers accepted the offer, Athern hit the high-grade ore within a few days, and four working miners gained a half share in a six hundred thousand dollar lease.[11]

Some might have been so unkind as to suggest that Athern already well knew where to look, for the practice of concealing a rich streak until a new lease or a share in an existing lease had been secured was one of several aspects of leasing that drew occasional criticism. On the other hand, leasers were sometimes reproached for blindly "gophering around"—which actually may have been as good a method of uncovering Goldfield ores as any. Other criticisms related to the leaser's haste to obtain the maximum profit within the short time allotted to him. The welter of litigation in which mining companies charged leasing companies with failing to remove waste rock from the interior workings, improper timbering, or overstepping the boundary lines of their leases suggests that leasers often fell into careless practices in their rush to gut the mines. Another common complaint was that, rather than risk a strike by the union, leasers preferred to turn a blind eye to highgrading, the theft of rich chunks of ore by the miners. This widespread practice would eventually become a serious point of contention between ownership and the union.[12]

Both the strengths and the weaknesses of leasing were nowhere better exemplified than in Goldfield's richest and most famous lease, the Hayes-Monnette. On September 1, 1905, a portly, balding, middle-aged mining engineer named George W. Hayes obtained a lease on a 373×700-foot section at the southern end of Mohawk No. 2. Although Hayes had reputedly acquired a fortune before he turned twenty-one from mining in Arizona and Mexico, little of it had survived to finance his explorations of the Mohawk. In a matter of weeks, he was out of funds and obliged to take in a partner, former Cripple Creek mining operator M. J. Monnette, who looked enough like Hayes to be his twin. Apparently the slimness of his wallet resembled Hayes' condition as closely as did his breadth of girth, because in short order the pair found themselves bereft of money and forced to appeal to two visiting Chicago capitalists, Harry Benedict and J. W. Smith.

Despite Monnette's role as Smith's representative on his Goldfield investments, the Chicagoans were clearly unimpressed by the proposition. The absence of any ledge or promising surface indication, combined with the circumstance that no valuable ore had as yet been found in the Mohawk—or even in its immediate neighborhood—lent little credence to the belief of Hayes and Monnette that their hole in the ground pointed toward a hidden bonanza. Primed though these investors were for the risks of Goldfield mining, it seemed like "just too long a shot." Smith and Benedict shook their heads and boarded the train for San Francisco.

Then, after the train had proceeded nearly one hundred miles through the desert, a sudden and inexplicable mutual impulse led them to change their minds and dispatch a wire back to Goldfield. On October 26, 1905, they bought a half interest in the Hayes-Monnette lease for five thousand dollars.

This infusion of capital enabled Hayes and Monnette to continue digging for another six months, but finally their faith in the Mohawk drained away, along with their funds. After a gloomy conference in mid April, they agreed upon a final effort closer to the surface in an area they had earlier abandoned. Dispirited, dead-broke, and devoid of the last vestiges of belief in his Goldfield prospects, Monnette departed on the train for Colorado Springs. Before he reached Ogden, Utah, however, a messenger rushed onto the train with a telegram from Hayes announcing a great strike in the Mohawk. Monnette remained unconvinced. Although a few stringers and small veins had been cut in the last several months, each gleam of hope that pay ore was at last opening up had quickly been rubbed out on the barren rock of the Mohawk. Monnette continued his journey. But at every stop, another batch of excited telegrams from Hayes announced that the strike was not only promising but beyond all expectations. Eventually, Monnette turned back. He arrived in Goldfield to find himself a very rich man.

In a small chamber like Aladdin's cave, miners working on an ore shoot thirty feet wide were knocking down sulfide ore so weighty and rich that assays were superfluous. With the naked eye, a man could see its dull yellow color in the flickering candlelight. No sorting was necessary because none of the ore was waste. No walls indicating the outer boundaries of the ore body had yet been struck, nor had the direction of the ledge been determined. Within fifteen days, Hayes and Monnette shipped thirty-five thousand dollars worth of ore from an opening the size of a small room. Because they soon realized that all of this fabulous bonanza could not be exploited before the clock ran out on their lease, they subleased a section of their ground to the Frances-Mohawk Company. Subsequent minor subleases reduced the Hayes-Monnette territory to a 373×250 foot section.

During the months remaining after pay ore was struck on April 17, these two bonanza leases, the Hayes-Monnette and the Frances-Mohawk, produced just over six million dollars, more than 85 percent of production from all Goldfield mining operations during 1906 and 30 percent of production by all leasers during the five-year period 1904–08. In less than eight months during the fiscal year 1906–07, these two bonanza Goldfield leases had yielded more gold than any mine in the Americas, Europe, or Asia except Mexico's Esperanza. On the $3,940,000 production of the Hayes-Monnette lease alone, according to a breakdown given to the press, transportation and treatment costs consumed roughly $677,000, labor and machinery around $500,000, and royalties to the Mohawk Company something above $700,000, leaving more than $2,000,000 in profits for the owners and stockholders. [13]

During this period, the small gleaming Aladdin's cave that Monnette had seen upon his return magnified to three huge caverns one hundred feet high and sixty feet wide, from which a rapidly expanding work force hoisted 28,800 tons of ore—"a dross of gold to set the blood surging," in the words of an excited newspaper reporter. [14] At one point, the superintendent boasted that he was raising as much ore with sixty men as Cripple Creek's famous Portland Mine could do with six hundred, partly because almost every chunk of rock was shipping grade ore. While Hayes and Monnette did little timbering, they denied sacrificing safety in their haste to seize the bonanza and pointed to the fact that the most serious accident in the period of their lease resulted in only the loss of a fraction of one miner's finger. In the last days, no effort was spared to speed production. When the final whistle blew, fifty-seven carloads from the Frances-Mohawk lease alone were rolling north on the railroad tracks just outside Goldfield, and mountains of milling ore remained heaped around the dumps and the shaft awaiting transport. Seven months later leasers were still profitably working the ore discarded on the Hayes-Monnette dump.

While Hayes-Monnette ore averaged around $132 a ton (casting some doubt on a recent estimate that the average for Goldfield ore ran as high as two hundred dollars a ton), some was too rich to be shipped in the ordinary way. One day in mid November an express wagon apparently bearing thirteen white sacks of flour drew up at the entrance to the John S. Cook bank. Although no armed guards were in evidence, the unloading of the mysterious sacks for storage in the bank vault created great excitement among the volatile crowd in the street because the knowledgeable had quickly surmised the presence of ore too valuable to be slung into railroad cars with the regular shipments. In fact, the sacks contained an estimated forty dollars of gold to the pound, nearly sixty thousand dollars

The Mohawk Mine, scene of the Hayes-Monnette bonanza (Larson Collection, Nevada State Museum)

worth of gold for the wagonload. On January 7, 1907, the special 47¾ ton shipment of Hayes-Monnette ore from the bank vault completed its journey to the Selby smelter in San Francisco under the watchful eye of Wells Fargo guards and Hayes himself; the shipment yielded a return of $574,958 from 609.61 ounces of gold and 75.38 of silver to the ton and according to Selby officials set a record as the richest shipment for its weight ever received by a smelter.[15]

These spectacular developments sent the bonanza spirit soaring. The massive Hayes-Monnette headframe became a kind of shrine pointed out to visitors as the premier landmark of the city. Other leasers whipped out their tape measures and scrambled for a share of the luster shed by Hayes-Monnette: "Do you want some of this Mohawk gold?" full page newspaper ads inquired — "This will be your last chance to get in on the ground floor;" "Our shaft is but 285 feet from the Hayes-Monnette Mohawk lease hoist."[16] Mining men like Lucien Patrick who had formerly basked in the glow of public admiration as fortune's favored sons acknowledged that their operations simply weren't "in it" when compared to Hayes-Monnette. Newspaper editors never previously at a loss for hyperbolic language declared that "new words" would be needed to adequately describe the wonders of this "marvel of all mines." The level of popular expectations shifted so far up that displays of ore with assays that would once have aroused tremendous excitement on the street no longer stirred the least interest; as the *Goldfield News* put it, to create any comment these days, a piece of ore "ought to have the government stamp on it, and none of the feathers of the eagle should be missing."[17] Even the management of the Mohawk Company became infected with the bonanza spirit, at least to the extent of offering to hoist fifty tons of Hayes-Monnette ore left waiting at the last whistle as a courtesy before the company began operations on the ground.

The most cavalier gesture, however, was that of George Hayes himself. At 3:00 A.M. on an October morning, five masked men had emerged from the darkness at the Hayes-Monnette shaft house. Forcing the engineer to open the locker, they loaded its contents, seven sacks of high grade ore worth one thousand dollars apiece, into an express wagon and made their escape. After a somewhat desultory search failed to recover the stolen ore, Hayes abandoned the effort with the casual remark, "What's the use of worrying over a little thing like that? There's more of that stuff below, and more than we can hoist."[18]

If grand larceny seemed too trivial a matter to worry Hayes, it may be correctly surmised that any points of potential friction with the miners' union, including highgrading, fell into the same category, even though union miners reportedly paid high commissions to secure jobs on the Hayes-Monnette, with the particular fringe benefits that work in Aladdin's chamber afforded. Since early 1904, the camp's union movement had been dominated by the Western Federation of Miners (WFM), although two small and aggressive American Federation of Labor (AFL) locals, the carpenters and typographers, also gained a foothold. Conditions in Goldfield, where ownership was dispersed among several major companies and most production remained in the hands of a host of leasers hellbent for maximum production during a limited time period, had been conducive to accommodation with the union. Wages remained high at four dollars a day, the eight-hour day prevailed, and any difficulties were speedily resolved.

In 1906 this harmonious situation began to change. The WFM had suffered a series of harsh blows since its formation among the miners of Butte, Montana in 1893, and these struggles began to alter its character. The union emerged from a crushing defeat at Cripple Creek not only a tough and militant organization but an increasingly radical one. The WFM was the moving spirit behind the 1905 formation at a Chicago convention of the Industrial Workers of the World (IWW), an organization of revolutionary anarchists dedicated to organizing the entire working class in "One Big Union." In 1906 the first IWW locals in Goldfield began pressing their ideals toward realization under the aegis of the miners' union. Despite a lockout by the mine owners, the WFM supported the IWW in a dispute with the influential Goldfield and Tonopah *Sun* newspapers. The matter ended with the sale of the *Goldfield Sun* and the amalgamation on

September 10 of the Goldfield WFM and the town workers organized by the IWW into the single all-embracing unit envisioned by syndicalists like Vincent St. John. Ironically, the mine owners were said to favor the labor merger in the belief that the IWW radicals would be submerged and out voted by the conservative majority of miners in the WFM.[19]

By Christmas this was beginning to look like a gross miscalculation. The miners demanded a dollar a day in wage increases, and the first major strike in the district began. After brief resistance, the mine owners capitulated. When Vincent St. John stepped out on the balcony that January day in 1907 at the "Bloody Sunday" parade, he could look back over a year in which Goldfield's miners' union had pushed forward as the fastest growing and most powerful local in the WFM. The One Big Union was virtually a reality, marred only by the continued presence of the AFL locals.[20] Over the short span of that bonanza year, while no one was paying much attention, the union giant had emerged full grown and begun to flex his muscles and dream a revolutionary dream.

Aside from what the union radicals called the "Revolution in Our Day and Time," other grandiose schemes were afloat around the golden horseshoe. One of the possibilities that captured attention from time to time was the consolidation of the principal mines of the district. Speculation about such a move tended to center on the famous Eastern financier Charles Schwab, who had been an active player in the Greenwater mining district in California. But even as reporters questioned Schwab, another man, waiting in the shadows, was doubtless hatching his own scheme, though hampered by the circumstance that the needed capital lay nowhere within his reach. This was George Wingfield, until recently a minor figure eclipsed by larger operators in the district. A waspish description from his arch rival, stock promoter and con artist George Graham Rice, born Jacob Herzig, is worth quoting: "At that time Mr. Wingfield was about thirty years old. Of stinted, meager frame, his was the extreme pallor that denoted ill health, years of hardship, or vicious habits. His eyes were watery, his look vacillating. Uncouth, cold of manner, and taciturn of disposition, he was the last man whom an observer would readily imagine to be the possessor of abilities of a superior order. In and around the camp he was noted for secretiveness. He was rated a cool, calculating, selfish, sure-thing gambler-man-of-affairs—the kind who uses the back stairs, never trusts anybody, is willing to wait a long time to accomplish a set purpose, keeps his mouth closed, and does not allow trifling scruples to stand in the way of final encompassment. Among stud-poker players who patronized gaming tables in Tonopah, Goldfield and Bullfrog, he was famed for a half-cunning expression of countenance which deceived his opponents into believing he was bluffing when he wasn't. In card games he was usually a consistent winner."[21]

Wingfield's early moves in the Goldfield district showed no great perspicacity. At a time when the Florence, Jumbo, and Combination were available for little more than pocket change, Wingfield purchased none of them, and also turned down the Goldfield townsite when it was offered to him by Myers. He made some acquisitions, reportedly received as payment for gambling debts from prospectors who played at his table in the Tonopah Club, but most were claims of negligible value like the Burnt Hill, Silver Cup, Gold Coin, and Bull Con. In fact, his most valuable acquisitions in the district resulted from George Nixon's enthusiasm over Grandpa.

Rumor had it that the Nixon-Wingfield association commenced when Wingfield, then a youthful cowboy and "something of a shambler," walked into Nixon's Winnemucca bank, slammed his diamond ring on the counter, and demanded a twenty-five dollar loan ("There's the rock. Loan or not. It's up to you"). The banker, while mildly amused by Wingfield's assumption that banks were the same as pawn shops, liked the young cowboy's boldness, and Wingfield became one of several friends who acted with Nixon in his central Nevada mining investments—but by no means his only associate. Nixon appeared to place greater confidence in Harry Ramsey and Tonopah banker John Cook. [22]

Although historians have generally assumed that Nixon was the passive partner in the investment relationship with Wingfield, and after Nixon's election to the senate in 1904 this no doubt became increasingly true, newspaper reports, Esmeralda county records, and private correspondence show that Nixon did a good deal more than sit in his Winnemucca bank and reap the benefits from Wingfield's investments. In June 1903, while Wingfield was busying himself in the dead-end camp of Cloverdale, Nixon visited central Nevada and became greatly excited over the Grandpa district, bonding the Stimler claims and bringing samples home with him to display. It was Nixon who finally purchased Stimler's portion of the Sandstorm group of claims in December, after Stimler had been ground down to a rock bottom price, Nixon who purchased a large and lucrative share of the Florence, which he subsequently divided with Wingfield, and Nixon who purchased the Mohawk and a host of other Goldfield claims through Harry Ramsey and formed the Mohawk Company in July 1904 at a time when Wingfield's name did not appear among the original incorporators.

These purchases in the Sandstorm, the Florence, and especially the Mohawk were to prove the source of the partnership's fortunes in Goldfield, but Wingfield as yet had little inkling of the district's significance. In early 1904 he offered to sell Jack Hennessey, his gambling partner in the Tonopah Club, a half interest in all his Goldfield claims for one thousand dollars, an offer which Hennessey with equal lack of foresight refused. During much of that year, Wingfield directed his primary efforts elsewhere in such ephemeral camps as Silverbow. Not until the autumn of 1905 had he belatedly seen where his future lay and moved his office from Tonopah to Goldfield. [23]

To a conservative investor without Wingfield's gambler's instincts, his position at that point might not have appeared overly promising. His share of the Sweeney lease and royalties from the Sandstorm, coupled with the winnings from his gaming table in the Tonopah Club, his other mining stocks, and the resources allocated to their investments by George Nixon had enabled him to stay in the Goldfield game and acquire a sizeable cash stake. The partnership held the major interest in both Goldfield's premier bank, the John S. Cook, and the Tonopah Banking Corporation. They also controlled several Goldfield mining companies of the second rank, such as the Sandstorm, Columbia Mountain, Kendall, Blue Bull, and Laguna, as well as a great deal of stock in marginal Goldfield mines. To this was added the favorable circumstance that Nixon's ascension to the United States senate in 1904 had lent a new prestige to their partnership and might eventually be turned to good account with Eastern investors. As Nixon frankly wrote to Wingfield during his campaign, "While my politics may keep me away from there more than I would like, it will not hurt the combination later on, eh?"[24] Nor did it.

All the same, it could not be denied that all the mines securely stacked in Wingfield's pile of chips appeared nearly worthless. The Sandstorm was no longer producing well; most of the others had never produced, despite numerous gopher holes sunk by hopeful leasers; all the properties yielding steady revenues remained beyond his grasp. Had he a mine like the Florence in hand, he could have parlayed his worthless mining companies into hundreds of thousands and his ace mine into millions. Without it, he seemed destined to remain a minor personage on the Goldfield scene, dwarfed by such figures as Al Myers, John McKane, and January Jones, whose doings crowded the pages of the newspapers, a man who had done as well as anyone could be expected to do with such mines as the Conqueror for assets but had missed out on the really big money. It was then, in what had appeared to be the most worthless of Wingfield's many barren mines, that Hayes and Monnette struck bonanza.

At last Goldfield's shrewdest gambler had drawn the high card he needed, and at the end of October, with royalties from Hayes-Monnette and the other Mohawk leasers piling in at an ever-increasing rate, he made his move. While even more royalties would have accrued with the passing months, several factors argued for immediate action. Given the rate at which Hayes and Monnette were gutting the Mohawk, it was far from clear how long the bonanza would last, and public confidence in the provable worth of the mine now invariably called the "great Mohawk" was essential to his plan. Moreover, a lawsuit had commenced between the Mohawk and the Combination. If the Mohawk lost, Combination leasers Ish and Sheets could legally follow the vein they were working into the Mohawk. Already they had dug an inclined shaft into Mohawk ground and Wingfield had been forced to station armed guards to protect his ore.

George Wingfield at the time of his rise to power (Nevada Historical Society)

Even if the leasers eventually lost, both mines might be closed while the issue was adjudicated, entirely choking off the flow of royalties. A mining engineer hired by Wingfield and Nixon to examine the geological formations at issue recommended not only the purchase of the Red Top and the Jumbo, but also the January and February mines owned by the Goldfield Mining Company. And that was not all. Other investors with large plans of their own were rumored to be on the verge of acquiring some of these properties. Last, but not least, Charlie Taylor, an unlucky gambler, had reputedly suffered a series of heavy losses at the gaming tables. According to the usual story, as soon as Wingfield and Nixon reached a decision, they hastened to Taylor's house and rousted him out of bed to hear their proposition. Taylor himself later said that Wingfield and Nixon had long held a verbal option on the Jumbo which he agreed to honor when payment fell due. Another version holds that Charlie Taylor unwisely sat down to a game of poker with George Wingfield.[25]

In any case, the outcome was the same. On October 24, 1906, Wingfield secured an option to purchase Taylor's controlling interest in the Jumbo and the Red Top for a total price of $1,330,000. Donald Mackenzie, one of the principal owners of the Frances-Mohawk lease, had reportedly acquired a short-term option on these properties two days earlier, but for reasons that remain mysterious, he abstained from exercising it, though he was known to have the cash in hand. On November 13 Wingfield and Nixon organized the Goldfield Consolidated Mines Company with a capitalization of fifty million dollars. Five million shares of stock were issued at a par value of ten dollars, and stock transfers were announced among its constituent mines, the Mohawk, Jumbo, Red Top, Laguna, and Goldfield Mining. The last of these, purchased about the same time as the Red Top and the Jumbo, was no longer productive; Laguna had scarcely any underground workings, had evidently never shipped ore, and had allegedly been acquired by Wingfield in payment for a gambling debt; both were unquestionably overvalued at two million dollars in Goldfield Con's prospectus. *Mining and Scientific Press* later observed that if Goldfield Con's capitalization figure had been realistically related to the proven ore reserves and the selling prices of the constituent mines merger stock would have been worth a great deal less. Goldfield Con is a "great mine," the editor soberly concluded, "but in the exuberance of their speculative activities the promoters have overcapitalized it."[26] A more realistic capitalization figure would probably have been in the twenty-five million dollar range.

Now Wingfield moved to gain control of the Combination itself. He may have been briefly dismayed to learn that an option to purchase the controlling interest had been taken by Charles Botsford, a New York investor; a half interest in the Botsford option had been acquired by Jim Davis, the young prospector Loftus had found crushing ore samples on the Sandstorm two years earlier, now a successful mining investor with the cash that Botsford lacked. In return for a large share of stock in Goldfield Con and a place on the directorate, Davis agreed to step aside, and Botsford also allowed himself to be persuaded. By December 15 Wingfield was able to enter into a contract for nearly all stock in the Combination for a total purchase price of $2,580,000, a million dollars of it due on January 20 and the rest in two remaining payments in March and May. To assist in meeting these obligations, Nixon, on December 28, secured a million dollar loan at 6 percent interest from New York financier Bernard Baruch.

One of the little known aspects of the Combination deal—and it is considerably at odds with the reputation that Wingfield and Nixon enjoyed as shrewd and prescient businessmen—is that less than two years earlier they had sold the half interest they held in the Combination, no doubt at the minimal prices that still prevailed in early 1905. Had they foreseen the value of the mine and simply retained their holdings instead of being compelled to buy back Combination stock at much higher prices, no million dollar loan would have been needed. But that ill-advised sale belonged to an era of financial stringency that predated the fabulous discovery of Hayes and Monnette. As Nixon later candidly acknowledged, "I can tell you he [Wingfield] and I had some pretty hard sledding. . . . but in the end the good old Mohawk pulled us out."[27]

On the safe assumption that the undisclosed purchase price of Goldfield Mining was minimal, it will be noted that the properties Wingfield had purchased for the merger he had capitalized at $50,000,000 had cost him less than $5,000,000—in fact, a good deal less, since the Combination stock-holders agreed to accept all but a tiny fraction of the $1,580,000 payments due to them in Goldfield Con stock in lieu of cash. In connection with the Combination transaction, stock sales yielding more than $7,000,000 were anticipated. Company reports show that as compensation for these wearing exertions in the winzes and stopes of finance Wingfield awarded $2,500,000 worth of stock in Goldfield Con to Nixon and himself.

The great merger was accompanied by what Rice, perhaps with a shade of envy, termed a "stock-market campaign for higher prices that stands unprecedented for audacity and intensity in the history of mining stock speculation in this country since the great boom of the Comstock." The press noted that at the Goldfield stock exchange collarless, coatless, hoarse, and perspiring brokers massed about the caller, "frantically buying and selling." Behind them surged "semi-suffocated humanity packed in like sardines." Rice's description was even more vivid: "Outside of the exchange the stridulous, whooping, screeching, detonating voices of the brokers that kept carrying the market up at each session could be heard half a block away. Later, did you find your way into the crowded board-room, the half-crazed manner in which note-books, arms, fists, index fingers, hats and heads tossed and swayed approached in frenzy a scene of violence to which madness might at once be the consummation and the curse."[28]

The Goldfield Mining Stock Exchange, where the shouting of frenzied brokers, packed together like sardines, rattled the windows, and curbside trading often continued in the street after regular sessions (Larson Collection, Nevada State Museum)

The mining stock craze ballooned to such a level that even the Goldfield press, usually the first to applaud any favorable development in the stock market, sounded a "note of warning" against indiscriminate purchases: investors were paying stiff figures for stock in mines that had "never developed a pound of ore," and a day of reckoning was bound to come. [29]

Such warnings proved useless, as stock prices soared under Wingfield's guiding hand. A little more than two years earlier when Wingfield was still running his game in the Tonopah Club, Nixon had urged the young gambler to "cut out the cards" and devote himself to mining stocks because "you can do better than any of those lobsters." Events in the stock exchange would shortly prove the prescience of Nixon's assessment. Jumbo stocks, which sold for 73¢ in 1905 and $1.42 in an already inflated market during the September before the merger, leapt to $5.20 on November 9 two weeks after the merger story hit the newspapers; Red Top followed a similar progression from 41¢ to $1.60 to $4.95; Mohawk, which had been listed as merely a "prospect" on the exchanges prior to the Hayes-Monnette strike, rose from 17¢ in 1905 to $3.75 during September, 1906 to $17.75; even

Laguna, unlisted in 1905, and Goldfield Mining lofted from 41¢ in September to $2.10 after the merger and 72¢ to $1.90 respectively. Much of this rise was characteristic of a mining stock craze. Thirty years earlier, during the "Sierra Nevada Deal" on the Comstock, it was the stocks worth the least that appreciated the most.[30]

A great deal was later made of the fact that since Taylor's agreement with Wingfield had been purely verbal he might have reneged as the market skyrocketed, but Taylor had no more inclination to stand in the way of Wingfield's plans than did Mackenzie, Botsford, or Davis. Taylor would nonetheless have noted that the difference between the two-dollar price at which he had sold his shares of Jumbo and Red Top to Wingfield and their price on the stock market two weeks later was $2,049,000, a sum more than one and a half times larger than the entire purchase price of his stock.

Because Goldfield Con allowed a period during which the stockholders of the constituent companies could exchange their stock for Goldfield Con stock and some stockholders resisted making the exchange, shares in the constituent companies continued to be separately listed and traded on the stock exchanges for more than six months. Rice believed that Wingfield, who was always personally present at the exchange in the thick of the fray, utilized this system to unload large blocks of his Mohawk stock at the time when it had more than quadrupled in value, as well as profitable chunks of Jumbo and Red Top.[31]

Whatever the truth of this charge, Wingfield would have needed a far duller head for mining stocks than anyone supposed he possessed if he had failed to profit when all boats in the stock exchange rose with the swelling tide. Wingfield, or Nixon, held the presidency of no less than five Goldfield mining companies other than Goldfield Con (Columbia Mountain, Conqueror, Kendall, Milltown, and Sandstorm) and undoubtedly retained large holdings in companies they had originally organized such as the Blue Bull and May Queen, as well as substantial miscellaneous holdings. Stocks in these companies, with the exception of Sandstorm, had sold for only twelve to eighteen cents in 1905, when they sold at all. During the November stock craze, the most sluggish of these mining stocks nearly doubled in price while the most volatile skyrocketed by more than 500 percent.[32] There can be little doubt that Wingfield was in the process of amassing an enormous personal fortune in the stock market at the same time that he was organizing the most productive gold mine in America. But Vincent St. John and his anarchist legions were on the march.

At the close of the great boom year, the highest stakes game George Wingfield had ever played was not yet over.

IV

George Wingfield's Gold

THE DECLINE, 1907–1910

"Oh, Casey, it's cheers for Wingfield,
Who's buying the foam just now—"
And George's smile was a quiet smile,
And his bow was just a bow.

"He's a kindly man," says Casey,
"And the shrewdest that iver was,
And he spends his time in this heated clime,
A gathering golden fuzz."
—from "Fireman's Night" by Willard P. Hatch,
Goldfield News, July 28, 1905

Inside the Goldfield Con office building, light from a single table lamp with a fringed silken shade caught the deep reds of the intricately figured oriental carpets, the polished gleam of the massive hand-carved mahogany desk, and the dull sheen of the silver dollars on the desk, but the man who sat behind it, his white hands busy with the dollars, remained in shadow. At his table in the Tonopah Club during the early days, George Wingfield had learned to swiftly, ceaselessly stack the dollars as he ran the game, and he had found that it aided his thinking. Back then he'd had to do it all at the same time—run the game, stack the bets, and keep thinking every minute. Worry over how to get his old horse and buggy off the delinquent tax list. Figure how fast the prospector across the table could be made to go broke and start paying off with shares in his claim. Read in his hard greedy eyes and stubbled face just how much he had and how far he'd go. Play him along. Listen, all the while, to the voices buzz around the room, telling crazy prospectors' stories of rich stringers, glory holes, gold-spangled picture rock, ore that ran thousands to the ton—most of their glory holes weren't worth deuces. Christ, sometimes the guff in the Tonopah Club had hung thicker than the cigar smoke and whiskey fumes. He'd watched and waited, knowing that hidden somewhere in all those miles of worthless desert there had to be another

Tonopah. Somehow he'd never doubted that he was going to get his hands on it. Too bad he hadn't guessed it was going to be Goldfield.

Truth to tell, he'd made his mistakes back in the Tonopah Club days, like going heavily into those bum camps of Cloverdale and Lone Mountain when every mine in Goldfield could have been his for pocket change. By God, he could even have had the Florence and left that beetle-browed old Tom Lockhart humping around the desert with his hard luck stories for the rest of his days, instead of obstinately blocking the way to control of the district. A pity that Lockhart, cursed tight-fisted Scot that he was, didn't gamble like Charlie Taylor. With a vicious swipe, the pale hand sent stacks of dollars sliding into a heap.

Funny, thought Wingfield, how all those good-for-nothing claims he had picked up back in the Tonopah Club days were made to pay off in the stock market as if they were first-rate mines. Turned into pure gold in a way that fool crowd of desert rats in the Tonopah Club had never dreamed of when they went stampeding off in droves after every new boom. They'd never understood how a worthless hole in the ground could be made to pay in the stock market. Not an inkling. If they'd spent less time holding their breath over the assays and studied over the stock quotes instead, they'd be worth more than a shot of tangleleg whiskey today.

All the same, Wingfield liked to throw a few dollars their way now and again, when they tipped their battered hats to him in the street and edged up respectfully, trying to trade on old times. A top-heavy stack tumbled down as he put a final dollar on top. His busy hands slid over the table, gathering the dollars together again.

Laughter and drunken voices from the dark street outside drifted up through Wingfield's second story window. "Hallelujah, I'm a bum," they were singing. "Hallelujah, bum again. Hallelujah, give us a handout to revive us again." The song of the IWW. Was it intended for him? Wingfield stiffened, then relaxed again as the voices grew fainter and the singers passed down the street. They wouldn't dare. He'd turn them into bums alright. Sooner than they knew those Wob reds were going to be cadging handouts on street corners. Wingfield sometimes thought that left to themselves, the union dogs might kill each other off with no assistance from him. But it would take time, and there was always a chance that something like this scrip issue would line the conservatives up with the radical crowd. Besides, it would be a lot less amusing.

For an instant, Wingfield's hand left the sliding pile of dollars to caress the gun in his pocket. It was almost time to go ahead with the last part of his plan. One of the keenest pleasures he knew was shoving a gun in a man's belly and watching the reaction. Pulling the trigger wasn't part of the game, but only Wingfield knew the rules. A man would start to sweat and turn pale, breath quivering, eyes bulging out of his head like a strangled jack rabbit. Sometimes they begged. You could feel them turn to jelly in your hands. And whenever you passed them in the street in the days afterward, you could savor the taste of knowing they knew you'd made them crawl. Wingfield smiled as his hands flew among the dollars. It was time now, in a manner of speaking, to shove a gun in the belly of the union.

On December 6, 1907, federal troops rolled into Goldfield. In response to a coded telegram from the mine owners, Nevada governor John Sparks had requested their presence to maintain order in the face of "domestic violence and unlawful combinations and conspiracies," by which was meant another strike by the miners' union. Local officials, who had not asked for military assistance, the union, and the populace were taken by surprise. Aside from the usual crowds and carousing, the city was entirely at peace. [1]

Actually, the peace of the city had seemed more precarious in the spring. The self-defense shooting of restauranteur John Silva by union organizer Morrie Preston in a picketing dispute aroused fears of union violence. These later seemed confirmed when a jury convicted Preston of murder after hearing testimony that the shooting was an assassination planned by the union; perjured testimony and special prosecutors hired by Nixon and Wingfield had helped to accomplish this result. The public hysteria surrounding the shooting had already enabled Wingfield to unite Goldfield's long-divided mine owners and leasers in a lockout against the union and to make the newly organized Goldfield Business Men's and Mine Owners Association the de facto government of the city. As the lockout dragged on, a force of Goldfield Con company guards patrolled the streets, and Wingfield issued an ultimatum to the union: "Compromise be damned. The Goldfield mines will stay closed down until hell freezes over before we open them to let a lot of anarchists tell us how to run our property." After thirty-eight lean days of soup kitchens and hardship, the union capitulated to Wingfield's demands. [2]

The influence of the radicals in the miners' union continued to wane over the ensuing months. St. John rose to speak in his calm matter-of-fact style at union meetings, never allowing the heckling to ruffle him and waiting patiently as his enemies tried to hiss him off the platform, but the radicals failed to win the support of other members in their drive to end the employment of non-union watchmen in the mines. An August strike over the establishment of change rooms to halt highgrading in the Mohawk ended three weeks later with the change rooms still intact. The union rejected the radicals' demand for a sympathy strike in support of fellow unionists on strike at the power company supplying Goldfield. That fall most of the radical leaders under indictment as conspirators in Silva's murder agreed to leave the district in return for dismissal of the charges against them.

A fusillade of bullets, rather than a deal with the district attorney, effectively removed the most unyielding of their leaders. On November 5 a heated argument in front of the Palm Grill between Vincent St. John and Paddy Mullaney, a more conservative union rival, culminated with Mullaney whipping out his revolver and shooting St. John in the left wrist and upper right arm, crippling him for life. St. John subsequently departed to receive medical treatment in Chicago and to become secretary and general organizer of the IWW at the national level. Besides the wounds inflicted on St. John, Mullaney's flying bullets had injured two innocent passers-by. One of them, a miner with several children, suffered the amputation of a leg as a result of his wound. Nonetheless, Mullaney was never prosecuted for assault. Eventually returning to his old stamping grounds in Cripple Creek, he suddenly went so violently beserk that the combined efforts of four strong men could scarcely restrain him. [3]

Less than two weeks after the St. John shooting, Goldfield Con announced that, due to the cash shortage accompanying the October financial panic, the miners would be paid in scrip, with no guarantees of eventual redemption in cash. Opposition to scrip, or "worthless paper," as many miners called it, speedily dissolved all differences between radicals and conservatives in the union. The vote for a strike to begin on November 27 was unanimous. Not until later did anyone realize they had just dealt Wingfield exactly the card he needed to complete his inside straight.

On December 2 the mine operators association cancelled its agreements with the union and a committee led by Wingfield called upon Governor Sparks on the pretext of selecting a smelter site. In fact, they agreed upon a signal. As soon as the coded telegram from the mine owners arrived on December 5, Sparks telegraphed his request for troops to the president. Shortly afterward Roosevelt began to doubt whether Goldfield was actually plagued by domestic violence and dispatched a presidential commission to investigate. Their report provided a clear post mortem on the real reason for the military presence at Goldfield: "The action of the mine operators warrants the belief that they had determined upon a reduction in wages and the refusal of employment to members of the Western Federa-

This young soldier stood ready for action when federal troops were dispatched to Goldfield in 1907 (Larson Collection, Nevada State Museum)

tion of Miners, but that they feared to take this course of action unless they had the protection of federal troops, and that they accordingly laid plans to secure such troops, and then put the programme into effect."[4]

Over the next four months the miners' union died a lingering death. Under the military umbrella, the mine owners cut wages, introduced an illegal card system, and began recruiting scabs from neighboring states. Humble offers from the once proud and powerful miners' union to purge its ranks of radicals and to negotiate on virtually any terms were rejected out of hand. Dwindling groups of union men stood clustered on the streets in the bitter winds of winter. Although a few impatient operators broke ranks by seeking compromise with the WFM or circumventing the reduced wage policy with bonuses, Wingfield managed, by and large, to maintain unity against the union.

In February union pickets continued to threaten scabs and obstruct labor recruitment, and the arrival of certain "traitors to the working class" could still spark a brawl in the Mohawk Saloon where WFM men did their drinking. However, that saloon melee was their last. On April 3, 1908, less than one hundred members, a tiny emasculated remnant of a union that just a year earlier had numbered more than three thousand, accepted the inevitable and decided to call off the strike.[5]

The "Revolution in Our Day and Time," as the radicals had called it, was not the only dream that trickled away in the gravelled sands of Goldfield during the winter of 1907–08. Stock prices had been dropping with little surcease since the speculative frenzy of November 1906, and the day of reckoning drew inexorably nearer. As *Mining and Scientific Press* had predicted in a discussion on the "two extremes" of financial chicanery, "Gold mining in Nevada is likely to suffer as much from the inflation of stocks representing splendid mines as she has suffered from the sinking of money into worthless schemes."[6]

The crux of the problem lay in the ballooning of mining stocks, led by Goldfield Con, to levels far beyond their real value and the willingness of the public to plunge on risky investments in the hope of huge returns. Moreover, the financial practices prevalent in Goldfield exacerbated the situation. Rice recalled that while the market was rising the John S. Cook bank, in which Nixon and Wingfield held a large interest, "stimulated speculation and managed to spread a feeling of security" by loaning 60 to 80 percent of the purchase price for shares of Goldfield Con.[7] Many borrowers and margin traders took advantage of this opportunity to buy the stock and pledged it as collateral for further purchases. In addition, while awaiting orders from their clients, Goldfield brokers sometimes used the clients' funds to play the market. Also the system of thirty-day stock contracts (introduced on the theory that the delivery of stocks over long distances required thirty days after each transaction) gave brokers a time period that many used to gamble with their clients' stocks as they pleased.

And these, be it noted, were the practices among some of the more reputable brokerage firms. No scruples whatever restrained the "wild-catters" in their scramble for the investor's dollar, and the skyrocketing prices of Goldfield securities during November furnished them with a convincing argument with which they gulled investors throughout the United States.

As stock prices slumped, dangerously overextended brokers in Goldfield and San Francisco started to go under, beginning with Rice's L. M. Sullivan Trust Company in early January 1907—an inauspicious omen for the coming year. Among the Goldfield fraternity, few brokers were not heavily in debt to the Cook bank, and fewer still managed to meet their obligations after they had exhausted their margins and the bank demanded payment. By July a plethora of firms, including the once wealthy and respected Kenneth Donnellan and Company, had succumbed, taking with them untold sums in investor dollars, and the suicides were beginning. Eastern market letters gave wide coverage to the suicide of a San Diego investor who had made large purchases in Nevada mining securities, sending shivers through the Goldfield stock exchange. Worse was still to come.[8]

"SHOT TO PIECES" read the Goldfield News following the October financial panic. Conqueror (7¢), Columbia Mountain (18¢), Kendall (8¢), and other Wingfield companies had dived down to the pre-boom levels of 1905, or lower, accompanied by a host of wildcat mines. On November 30 Goldfield Con, issued at $10 a share a year earlier, struck rock bottom at $3.80. The Goldfield press, though always eager to avoid "knocking" the camp, acknowledged that the decline in Goldfield stocks over the past year averaged 65 percent, and many had fallen 80 percent or more. Transactions at the Goldfield exchange alone had shriveled from 2,580,000 stocks worth $1,180,000 during the top week to 280,000 worth $30,000. As Rice recalled, "The carnage was awful." Losses to American investors as a whole can not be fixed with certainty, but Rice, whose figures appear to be generally accurate, estimated them at $150,000,000.[9]

During Goldfield's remaining time, the impossible mirage of wealth glimpsed during the bonanza year was never seen again. By the end of 1910, Conqueror, Kendall, and other Wingfield companies, as well as a host of wildcat properties, had dropped off the stock boards entirely, wiping out every dollar invested in them, and the market had withered to the point that only 17,200 Goldfield shares were traded in a typical day. Of eighty-four Goldfield mining stocks listed on the exchange in December 1906, only sixteen were still quoted four years later. Although Goldfield Con recovered to $8.25 a share at the peak of production and ultimately paid a total of $29,780,000 in dividends, this amounted to only $8.20 per share, and those who had bought stock at the $10 price at which it was issued were never to recoup their investment. The day was at hand when, as Tom Lockhart had once warned, you "couldn't sell a twenty-dollar gold piece for fifteen cents" if it came from Goldfield—"people would say it was bored full of holes and then plugged."[10]

Possibly it was fitting that none of the original fraternity of prospectors whose boundless hopes against all odds had created the camp continued to play a significant role in Goldfield mining after the bonanza spirit was shattered in the crash of 1907. Marsh was rounding up cattle at his ranch. Stimler had turned himself into a mine promoter, but despite the tips on new bonanzas received from Tom Fisherman, he never succeeded on the scale of brokers like George Graham Rice and Donald Mackenzie. Taylor had apparently exited the Goldfield scene after the sale of the Jumbo and Red Top—and in considerably greater style than he entered it less than four years earlier on the back of the old gray horse borrowed from Ford.

Al Myers' mood turned increasingly black as he saw the camp he had once known changing into a different kind of place. In 1906 he declared that he would be willing to wipe his shoes on "Goldfield's doormat" if someone would make him a fair offer for his holdings; he sold his shares in the Mohawk for four hundred thousand dollars to the first man who took him at his word, only to see them more than quadruple in value within six weeks with the organization of Goldfield Con. All the same, Myers had gained a fortune beyond the reaches of his imagination in the dead-broke summer of 1903.

Sometimes he seemed hellbent to squander it by extravagances that aroused comment, even in the free-spending climate of Goldfield's flush times. In Long Beach, California, he built a palatial mansion with such luxuries as solid gold doorknobs. His heavy gambling became legendary, and a crowd of awed spectators would follow his balding dapper figure from one saloon to the next to watch him lay five hundred dollars on each turn of the roulette wheel. His younger brother Ed came down from Wyoming to share in his good fortune and started down the path that would end, after the investments made on Al's money and reputation had all gone bad, with a suicidal bullet fired into his brain as he stood before the mirror in his room in the Esmeralda Hotel.

In late June 1908 the press reported the sale of Al Myers' last holding in a major Goldfield mine, the Combination Fraction, to Wingfield. A familiar scenario then began to unroll: a fabulous strike was announced in the Fraction; its stock trebled in value, then plunged, all in less than six weeks. Not long after the break, Wingfield acquired the holdings of Myers' old partner, Murphy, and took control of the property. Despite general expectations that the Combination Fraction would be added to Goldfield Con, with which it was contiguous, it remained in Wingfield's vest pocket, suggesting that his object was not the greater glory of Goldfield Con but the personal mastery of the district. In 1909 Goldfield Con miners uncovered one of Goldfield's last and greatest bonanzas, the Hampton stope, inside the mine that Al Myers had almost singlehandedly turned into the first producer in the camp—the Combination.

Myers did not linger to witness all of these developments. In early August 1908, five years from the summer when he had stayed on in his tent after other prospectors lost heart, he unloaded the last of his Goldfield stocks, the Commonwealth, and made good his threat to wipe his feet on the doormat. When the "father of Goldfield" stepped on the train, en route to his mansion by the sea, it was the end of an era. [11]

In other ways as well, the old era was drawing to a close. The leasing system was declining in importance, though the change did not show immediately. Goldfield leasers still numbered over two hundred in 1907 and accounted for more than half of total production during the four-month period on which figures are available. Moreover, several spectacularly successful leases followed the final whistle at Hayes-Monnette. The Little Florence (thus named for its original owners, Stephen and Theodore Little) topped the production list with $1,840,000, of which the operators paid out $430,000 in dividends. At the close of 1908, the leasers grew militant enough to organize in an effort to win more favorable terms from the mine owners, the railroads, and the power company, and the press opined that the entire district would have been "deader than a mackerel" during the preceding year without their activities. [12] Some would remain until the very end. All the same, as Goldfield Con company operations loomed larger in production from 1909 onward, the golden age of leasing had unmistakably passed.

As leasing gradually died away, so too did the boom spirit once fired by the great expectations of the leasers, with their fervent talk of rich stringers, picture rock, free gold, rich float, pay shoots, three hundred dollar ore, and fortunes to be made tomorrow, or at least inside the next sixty days before their time ran out. When, at last, their time had really run out, no more to be renewed or shifted to a new piece of ground, even more promising, they would swear, than the last, Goldfield was never the same. No man harbors the dream of making his fortune in a company town.

A sharp reduction in the number of miners at work in the district predictably accompanied the decline in individual entrepreneurial activity by leasers. In February 1908, two months after Wingfield smashed the union, only seven hundred miners were employed, suggesting that the replacement of the WFM with scabs was proceeding more slowly than management acknowledged. However, in mid 1909, when the period of adjustment had long passed, no more than 1,065 miners were at work in the district—probably half the number employed three years earlier during the great boom. This precipitate decrease, at the same time that production was on the upswing, undoubtedly reflected shrinkage in the investment funds that had financed extensive exploration prior to the stock crash. [13]

While the prospector's dream of finding a new bonanza died away, mine owners constructed better milling facilities to improve the yield of existing bonanzas and to extract a profit from low-grade ores that had been scorned in palmier days. In the spring of 1905, operations had commenced in Goldfield's first two mills, the Gardner mill, a ten-stamp operation located at the base of the Malapai Mesa and supplied with water from deep wells, and the Combination mill, a ten-stamp operation owned by the mine of the same name and operated with spring water. At the latter mill, mining engineer Francis Bosqui performed the critical experiments in working Goldfield ores. Goldfield, as the last great gold mining boom, benefited from half a century of metallurgical experience in the bonanza West, including the introduction of the cyanide process that had revolutionized milling during the preceding decade. Nonetheless, Goldfield ores presented special problems. To begin with, the quartz was exceptionally hard and flinty with soft pockets of alunite that necessitated special devices in the mill because the pulp could not be easily filtered after crushing the ore. Although most of the gold particles streaked through the gray quartz like dull gilt paint were fine, Bosqui found that dry crushing followed by agitation in a cyanide solution left a small but valuable percentage of coarse gold undissolved in the tailing.

After some six months of experimentation, Bosqui devised a two-fold system so controversial that he was compelled to hotly defend it against his critics in the engineering field. He reduced the quartz by wet crushing (advocates of dry crushing to the contrary not withstanding), followed by treatment on amalgamation plates to recover the coarse gold (over protest from the proponents of cyaniding without amalgamation), concentration, and cyaniding to recover the fine gold. With these methods, Bosqui recovered about 95 percent of the gold values from ores treated at the Combination mill. During the following summer, the district's milling capacity further expanded with the opening of the Nevada-Goldfield Reduction Company, a twenty-stamp operation with a cyanide mill capable of treating 100 tons a day and a sampler with a 450 ton daily capacity. Among the handful of other independent mills that attempted to operate in the district (and, in Goldfield's typical style, sometimes made wildly fanciful claims concerning their efficiency in gold extraction), the large crushing and sampling plant operated by the Western Ore Purchasing Company was the most important. [14]

When a pipeline from the Lida-Magruder Mountain region to the south finally brought plentiful water to Goldfield in the autumn of 1907, milling ceased to be constricted by inadequate water supplies. The day after Christmas, 1908 operations commenced at the new one hundred stamp nine hundred thousand dollar Goldfield Consolidated Company mill, a shining white asbestos structure descending in six terraces down Sandstorm Hill. During its ten years of activity, this mill, where Bosqui also served as consulting metallurgist, was to treat nearly three million tons of Goldfield Con ore with gold values of $48,580,000 by essentially the same system of amalgamation, concentration, and cyaniding that Bosqui had devised at the Combination. The last major mill built in Goldfield was the Florence, which commenced operations in January 1909. Drawing its water supply by gravity from Indian Springs, the Florence mill had forty stamps capable of processing 160 tons a day at the peak of its operations, and Lockhart boasted that it could profitably work relatively low grade ores.

When rumors began to circulate that the new Florence mill was shivering at the seams because it had been precariously constructed over an old stope, Lockhart believed they were orchestrated by Wingfield in an effort to "hammer the stock down so he can pick it up at a beggarly price."[15] Nonetheless, the Florence mill operated with great success until it was destroyed by a fire of mysterious origin in 1911. Instead it was Wingfield's Combination mill that tumbled two hundred feet into the recently excavated Hampton stope on the fourth level of the Combination, killing three men, in the autumn of 1909.

The attempt to beat down Florence stock may well have been a vengeful footnote to the failure of a grand plan that could be glimpsed skimming like the shadow of a hawk over the surface of Goldfield events during the early months of 1908. In late January Lockhart and Parker turned down a $6,300,000 offer, the largest ever publicly made for a Goldfield mine, from Frank Oliver, manager of the Little Florence lease and former superintendent of the Florence, who presumably had good reason to know the value of the mine he was endeavoring to buy. On the other hand, Oliver may have been acting for an unseen consortium with larger plans. Within a week rumors were rife that Goldfield Con was on the verge of taking over the Florence and the Combination Fraction. According to the San Francisco press, Myers and Lockhart had been invited to a New York meeting with Wingfield and Eastern capitalists interested in the venture. This was partially confirmed when Myers did in fact obey the summons to New York in March and apparently agreed to sell the Combination Fraction. Lockhart, however, remained obstinately at his office in Goldfield, declared that the Florence was not for sale to Goldfield Con or anyone else, and unceremoniously dropped Wingfield from the position on the Florence board of directors that was the normal perquisite of a large stockholder. This raised a good many eyebrows in Goldfield.

Although Wingfield gained the Combination Fraction, which would soon prove a valuable and productive mine, from the truncated transaction in New York, he may have planned to repeat the grand financial coup of 1906 with a new roster of mines. But Lockhart, since the days when he used to clamber his lonely way with antlike diligence up and down the Tonopah Extension shaft, had become well known for a "tenacity of purpose" that neither a campaign of unrelenting pressure nor six million dollars could budge. Time would show that the offer was a generous one. Though the Florence had yielded more than that sum by the close of 1908, Lockhart was soon reduced to working such limited bodies of low grade ores that the Florence was not to produce another six million dollars before it went into receivership in 1916.[16] But perhaps production figures were beside the point. The Florence was still Tom Lockhart's mine.

After the frustration of Wingfield's reputed plan to secure both the Florence and the Combination Fraction, no significant mergers were accomplished in the district, nor did Goldfield Con make any major new acquisitions. During the labor tensions of 1907, Bernard Baruch paid a visit to Goldfield, where he was much impressed by Wingfield's gun-toting wild West appearance: "He was carrying five revolvers and had four Pinkerton detectives. . . . He was afraid of nothing." However, the shrewd Eastern financier was not sufficiently bemused to buy Goldfield Con at $7.75 a share. Instead of exercising his stock option, he agreed to accept two hundred thousand shares of Goldfield Con treasury stock (thus valued at five dollars a share) plus a small cash sum as repayment for the loan.[17]

In time Nixon evidently tired of strutting around Goldfield with what Rice termed the "pride and gravity of a Spanish grandee" and transferred his shares in Goldfield Con to Wingfield in exchange for Wingfield's interest in banking ventures other than the John S. Cook bank in Goldfield. Nearly five years earlier Nixon had enthusiastically confided to a friend that he was "in at Goldfield with both feet." Now he was out the same way, and Wingfield was the one hailed by newspaper reporters and the toast masters of testimonial banquets as the "Napoleon" and the "King of Nevada Mining and Finance." At the end of March 1909, he could dash off a triumphal telegram declaring, "I have took over everything."[18]

While the output from the Florence and the leasers declined, new bonanzas were discovered in the Combination and the Mohawk. These two mines were proving the backbone of Goldfield Con's "empire of opulence." At the close of its first year of operations Goldfield Con announced an extraordinary production figure of $6,300,000. The stockholders were growing restive because a mere $355,000 of this sum had been paid out in a single 10¢ dividend; this represented a small ratio of dividends to production by the standards of most mining companies in the period—the Red Top, for example, had paid a dividend under Taylor's management after producing less than 2,500 tons of ore and the owners of the Reilly lease had paid out a whopping 78 percent of production in dividends. No one in Goldfield was likely to wonder long over the identity of the unnamed individual whom Lockhart sharply told the press had used his stock market manipulations and his niggardly dividends to "rob widows and orphans";[19] in his own operations, Lockhart adhered to the stodgy idea that the business of mining companies was producing ore rather than promoting stock.

Goldfield Con cited several reasons, none especially persuasive, for post-poning dividends. Apparently no need arose to postpone Wingfield and Nixon's commission, the value of which was more than six times greater than the entire dividend payed to the stockholders during the first year of operations.

The attempt to untangle the obfuscations and discrepancies in Goldfield Con's 1907 annual report led Thomas A. Rickard, the editor of *Mining and Scientific Press*, to throw up his hands in disgust, while clearly imply-ing that the figures on yield per ton and profit in relation to production defied credibility—this was, after all, the same company that had casually published an eight hundred thousand dollar error in its original prospec-tus. Thus, a measure of uncertainty continues to surround the comparative figures in *Mining and Scientific Press* showing that Goldfield Con was the most productive gold mine in America in 1907, surpassing the mighty Homestake, and the second richest gold mine in the entire world.[20] It was a brief moment of glory, destined soon to pass, for the vast low-grade deposits of the Homestake would continue producing at a steady rate long after the rich but comparatively small bonanzas of Goldfield had been gutted away.

Accurate figures on the total production of the Goldfield district are difficult to determine because newspaper reports were spotty and produc-tion was frequently underreported to the state authorities to avoid pay-ment of bullion tax and exaggerated to the stockholders for purposes of promotion, as well as being fractionated among a multiplicity of leasers. Despite these difficulties, J. P. Albers and J. H. Stewart of the Mackay School of Mines, University of Nevada, Reno, have arrived at production figures for the district which show a tremendous leap in the boom year of 1906, in which production more than trebled to $7,040,000, and a sharp drop below $5,000,000 in 1908 after the destruction of the miners' union. During the years following the great boom, the fortunes of Goldfield Con, the source of more than 80 percent of the ore produced in Goldfield from 1909 through 1918, were increasingly the fortunes of the district. Annual production peaked at $11,210,000 in 1910, but jubilant press predictions of $21,000,000 a year from the new bonanza of the Hampton stope proved entirely unrealistic.

In 1912 the downward slide began, with a sharp drop to $6,410,000, a 40 percent decline from the previous year, bringing production once more below the level of 1906. Although by 1908 Goldfield Con pumped thirty-five thousand gallons of water per day from its workings, drainage caused fewer problems than in such localities as Tombstone and the Comstock. Production declined for one essential reason—the exhaustion of Goldfield's limited bodies of ore. The "final and lasting era of golden prosperity" opti-mistically proclaimed by the Goldfield press in 1908 had lasted less than four years.

In the years following 1912, production showed a steady downward progression, 1918 being the last year it ever surpassed one million dollars. After the Goldfield Con mill closed in 1919, small scale operations averaging less than three hundred thousand dollars per year continued through 1941, subsequently becoming occasional and miniscule. Albers and Stewart conclude that the production of the entire district from the outset through 1960 was $89,700,000, 94 percent of it during the fifteen-year period 1904–19. Shamberger contends that the total figure should probably be closer to one hundred million dollars. If the widely exaggerated figures on the Hayes-Monnette lease are a representative sample, however, Goldfield's production figures may instead require revision in a downward direction. Although a definitive tabulation of dividends poses similar difficulties, Goldfield Con reports and figures Shamberger has derived from a variety of sources on the 1904–08 period provide a rough indication that dividends ran close to 50 percent of production. [21]

While the numbers on the Goldfield ledgers remain a little smudged, the figures on the human landscape stand out with absolute clarity, and all are dwarfed by the newly crowned "King of Nevada Mining and Finance." The first generation, Myers, Taylor, Stimler, and the rest had abdicated in Wingfield's favor. Subsequent contenders exited after they made their bundles. Hayes, for one, within a year of telling the press he had no intention of leaving Goldfield because "the camp has been good to me," departed to become the president of a Los Angeles gas company, while Monnette embarked upon a protracted cruise of the Mediterranean and the Orient. No one else matched Wingfield's relentless drive toward mastery of the district. Highgraders he pursued like an avenging nemesis, even after the unions were crushed beneath his heel. When he felt that county officials failed to pursue the campaign with sufficient vigor, he publicly reminded them that Goldfield Con was the county's largest taxpayer and they would thus be well advised to exercise themselves in his interests. [22]

Enemies and rivals he crushed with a ruthless hand, though some fought back tenaciously, as Lockhart had done. Rice, for instance, believed that Wingfield and Nixon had a hand in the downfall of his brokerage company. He withdrew to Reno and for about two years published the *Nevada Mining News*, the pages of which crackled with savage attacks on Wingfield and Nixon, so angering Wingfield that a fist fight with *News* editor Merrill Teague ensued in the streets of Reno. Even after the promotions of his latest brokerage company landed Rice in the federal penitentiary for mail fraud several years later, he continued to insist that his financial misdeeds were mere petty peccadillos in comparison to Wingfield's grand "raid" on the stock market. Such criticisms were rarely printed in Nevada outside the pages of Rice's short-lived publication, but they sometimes appeared elsewhere and evoked the same kind of explosive reaction from Wingfield. In 1907 Wingfield allegedly secured more favorable coverage by striking the editor of the *San Francisco Examiner* in the face at a San Francisco restaurant and challenging him to a gun duel.[23]

In his duel with Donald Mackenzie, one of the principal owners of the Frances-Mohawk lease, Wingfield brandished law suits as effectively as six guns. He successfully sued Mackenzie's mining and brokerage company on the ground that the terms of the lease had been broken. Afterward the presiding judge declared to Mackenzie in court, "A verdict of this kind could hardly result otherwise than as a surprise, and the defendant naturally feels that justice has been outraged." Although Mackenzie won a partial victory on appeal and countersued on the ground that Wingfield's suit had been a malicious action brought with the "sole purpose" of crushing him, Wingfield had already succeeded in destroying his credit and attaching the assets of his business, once lauded in the press as the "largest and most successful" in the region.[24]

Those who abstained from the cardinal crimes of rivaling, opposing, or criticizing Wingfield might be treated with lordly generosity, as the miners standing humbly in the street outside his window after his return to Goldfield with a new bride were showered with silver dollars. Later, as the boss of Nevada's bipartisan political machine, he would help to raise certain favored friends from the "old Goldfield crowd" to positions of power. With his new wealth and influence came all the trappings of the dynast, the private hunting grounds in northern Nevada, the fashionable new residence overlooking the Truckee River in Reno, the far-flung interests in mines, banks, ranches, and hotels in Nevada and California, the thorough-bred horses at his stock farm, and Maude Murdoch, the daughter of a San Francisco banker, as his beauteous new bride, acquired after May Wing-field, the humbler consort of the Tonopah Club days, had been discarded.

Although Wingfield sometimes made a triumphal visit to Goldfield, he had discarded the city with his mistress of former days. As Diamond-field Jack Davis, Wingfield's former lieutenant, put it, "His motto is to use anyone that he can and then throw them aside like a broken branch."[25] By the end of 1908, there were no more great deals yielding millions to be made, no more marching union revolutionaries to be crushed, and no more frenzied throngs at the stock exchange to be swayed. Now that he had scraped Goldfield into his pile of winnings, the game was over. George Wingfield rose from the table and left.

PART TWO

Life in the Last Boomtown

V

This Godforsaken Spot

THE SETTING AND THE CITY

"Goldfield is a sadly hideous aggregation of tents, huts, shacks, adobes, frame houses, and three good stone buildings. The climate is, perhaps, the worst in the world. For three months it scorches the life out of you; freezes and chills you for another three, and blows what's left of you into dust for the remaining six." Parmeter Kent in Goldfield Gossip, 1906

New arrivals often reacted to Goldfield with shock. After all, this was still the same fearful desert that had repelled exploration and settlement for half a century. Poet Mighels called it a place "where the desolations meet." A homesick Coloradan thought Goldfield had "too much sky and not enough water"; he soon headed back for the wooded green slopes of home. Another newcomer, no stranger to harsh conditions after living in many frontier locales, saw Goldfield as "the end of the world."[1]

In time many gold rushers became accustomed to the strangeness and saw the beauty in "the end of the world." Southwest of the city was the Malapai Mesa, level as if smoothed with a carpenter's plane and rosy hued in the light of late afternoon. In the Clayton Valley, beyond the ridges to the west, lay the sugary white expanse of a dry lake, punctuated in the distance by low coal-black volcanoes. Far beyond the Clayton Valley and the jagged blue silhouette of the Silver Peak range on its western rim, the snowy wall of the high Sierra rose on the horizon. Fred Wamsley, a British visitor, described his changing reactions to this desolate and hallucinatory desert scenery: "At first they [the physical surroundings] are formidably and strangely repellant, then they are endurable, and then they come to hold you with a weird fascination. The flat expanse of desert, the glaring, burning hues of the earth and sky, the utter desolation of the barren mountains seem to be softened and blended in a more pleasing mood the more you see of them, and yet there is always that awed feeling of a soul lost on the waste."[2]

The effect would have been less exotically desolate for Wamsley to contemplate if Goldfield had been more generously endowed with greenery. Perhaps at the outset it was. A newspaper account of the inital strike calling the area "well wooded," unless mere error or hyperbole intended to encourage the new district, long puzzled historians until they found stumps suggesting that piñons and junipers may have grown in this region before the early settlers chopped them down for fuel and timber. The Wheeler survey's description of timber "abundant all over the mountains" near Montezuma also points to a time of piñon-and juniper-studded slopes. However, Goldfield's most distinctive flora still punctuates the landscape—the joshua tree, a shaggy giant yucca, from nubbin-size to forty feet in height, with twisting arms tipped by sharp-daggered leaves. Tonopah, only thirty miles north, lay in the sagebrush land of the Great Basin desert, but Goldfield was situated just inside the northern border of the Mohave desert where joshuas abounded. These peculiar trees, besides providing homes to earlier inhabitants such as elf owls, ladder-back woodpeckers, lizards, and packrats, furnished the new arrivals with fuel for their campfires. To eyes accustomed to the more symmetrical shapes of deciduous trees, the joshua seemed a peculiarly ugly creation. In the melodramatic prose of visiting journalist Winifred Bonfils: "It is like a weazened, cruel, avaricious old man turned into a Joshua tree for his sins and condemned to stand bent into all manner of contorted miseries in the gray-parched sagebrush, with great misshapen fists stretched to the brazen sky in one last gesture of eternal despair."[3]

Though usually less evident to the casual observer than the joshuas, animal denizens of several varieties subsisted on the barren sands of the Mohave. The rarest sight was the region's small herd of camels, turned loose after freighting operations on the Comstock and the railroads to fend for themselves in an unfamiliar land. Travelers occasionally glimpsed the ghostly shape of a camel at a waterhole in the desert to the east before the last of the band died out. The mustangs that had pounded through the fledgling camp on the night of Patrick's 1903 visit had been forced to concede their traditional watering place at the spring to the new settlers, but they still abounded on their old ranges in the deserts to the north and east and occasionally lured a freighter's horses to heed the call of the wild and gallop away from their sleeping master by night to join the band. A growing population of burros descended from prospectors' pack animals showed fewer qualms than the mustangs about venturing near the city, especially in the vicinity of their favorite grazing ground, the local dump, which they shared with those adaptable scavengers, the coyotes. On nights when they pointed their noses to the moon and howled, large numbers of coyotes made their presence audible on the outskirts of the city.[4]

A more subtle and troublesome visitor was the pack rat, or trade rat (not a true rat but a burrowing rodent of another genus), who conducted raids from his burrow at the base of the joshua and somehow managed to penetrate the most tightly built cabin and the most stoutly closed cupboard. Goldfielders did not view the conical piles of debris or neatly sorted nails left on the floor by this silent ghostlike visitor as sufficient compensation for the edibles he removed. They also voiced complaints about a host of other pests of both the flying and crawling variety, and not everyone shared *Goldfield Gossip* editor Parmeter Kent's enthusiasm for the "aristocratic" and "beautiful" lizards of the region, buff-colored creatures with carmine splotches. In the best traditions of mining camp tall tale journalism, Kent went on to inform his readers that this "royal family" of lizards ruled the Malapai, where they dined on hummingbird eggs and rode about on the backs of plain black lizards they had enslaved to serve them – no doubt some readers believed him.[5] Other Goldfield reptiles, such as the rattlesnakes that not infrequently slithered through their old haunts, evoked no one's enthusiasm; children learned early to watch where they walked. The extreme heat of August also seemed to foster an unusual abundance of tarantulas, vinegarones, and small, dark-brown, bloodsucking flies in the city and its environs.

These natural inhabitants of the desert came better equipped to cope with the climatic conditions than the new human arrivals. United States Weather Bureau data from the early 1960s at Goldfield shows an arid climate with annual precipitation slightly under six inches and moderate temperatures averaging slightly less than thirty degrees Fahrenheit in January and in the mid seventies in July, with extremes from ten below zero to one hundred degrees. Nonetheless, press reports make clear that Goldfield's boom coincided with a series of winters far harsher than these averages would suggest, and also indicate that to those who experienced it unalleviated by modern comforts and conveniences, the heat of summer could often prove enervating, or even perilous.

By June the Goldfield bon ton eagerly contemplated prolonged summer vacations at Lake Tahoe or California ocean resorts, society women fanned away the afternoons with languid games of bridge or whist, and the *Goldfield News* acknowledged that the "heat is too intense for anyone to be energetic."[6] One unenthusiastic visitor from Los Angeles compared the summer weather to Dante's inferno with the lid off. The stagecoach south to Bullfrog began making its run by night and fruitless petitions from flushed and suffering passengers urged the railroad company to adopt a similar schedule. Ice cream and soda water were in great demand – and no wonder, since on a hot day in the desert a man's physiology demands more than a gallon of liquid refreshment or he will slowly weaken, his blood thickening and his heart laboring, until he dies from dehydration.

Beyond the city limits, the desert held mortal dangers for those venturing away from well-traveled roads. Some who lost themselves amidst the myriad ranges and valleys of that barren wasteland never returned at all. Some returned without their wits, like the English girl who had thought she would like to try prospecting as a lark. Another young woman attempted to walk from Los Angeles to Goldfield and was found by a train crew near the tracks in a delirium, her hair streaming in the wind. Others barely managed to survive by any succor the desert provided, as did the young man who subsisted for five days by chewing cacti and lizards until a rescue party found him.[7]

The experience of Goldfielder Andrew Murphy provided a harrowing illustration of the perils that waited on the waterless sands outside the city. While transporting supplies to Ellendale, a mining camp about forty miles to the northeast as the crow flies, Murphy turned his horse-drawn wagon onto an unfrequented shortcut. Only five miles east of Tonopah, his rented horse stopped in the traces and refused to pull the wagon another step. Filling his canteen from the water barrel in the wagon, Murphy headed on to Tonopah Wells ten miles farther ahead. Within a few miles, his water ran out. Soon he was ravaged with thirst from the blazing sun and the whirling dust that filled his eyes and mouth. To his dismay, the well was dry.

He decided to wait out the day at the dusty well and head straight back to Tonopah by night without returning to his wagon. All night he traveled without reaching his destination, and with the return of the scorching sun, his thirst became a torment. Eventually, he realized that he had lost all sense of direction and walked in a great circle without drawing any nearer to Tonopah. Seeing a little trail, he lay down across it in the hope that some traveler might find him, but by nightfall, not a single human footstep had broken the vast silence.

Fortunately, the night was clear enough for Murphy to figure the direction where Tonopah lay by the north star. As he plodded slowly onward the next day, the horse behind him, he could think of nothing but his thirst. The wind blowing dust in his face felt like the fumes of a lime kiln, through which he could scarcely draw breath. He kept seeing a mirage of a cool blue pond and imagining that he heard the gurgling trickle of water. At times the mountains seemed to chase around him like the rim of a gigantic flywheel. Both Murphy and the horse repeatedly stumbled and fell on the sandy ground. Somehow, though his strength was rapidly failing, he struggled on through another night.

At dawn Murphy saw smoke smudging the skies from the chimneys of Tonopah and knew he was saved. He pitched across the threshold of the first dwelling in his path, but his throat and tongue were too parched and swollen to whisper the word "water." No matter. Someone understood what he needed, and, little by little, lest too much should kill him, the sweet, cool drops trickled down his throat. Unfazed by his experience in the desert, Murphy slept for most of two days, then set out once more in search of his abandoned wagon.[8]

Despite perils such as these, Goldfielders clearly preferred the heat of a desert summer to the rigors of the winter. Then occasional snowstorms whipped into blizzards by the region's characteristically strong winds could pile a foot of snowfall into four- to six-foot drifts, stranding wagons and the new autos that the affluent were beginning to use for desert travel, armed with a curious confidence that any wagon road, however rugged, would also serve for an auto. Stories of travelers lost in the desert, unable to distinguish the road in the drifted snow, plagued by sinister packs of howling coyotes, and huddled, frostbitten, over tiny fires of damp brush as they fought the deadly slide into unconsciousness began to replace hot weather sagas such as Murphy's in the press. One unfortunate miner dwelling near an outlying Goldfield mine froze to death in the snow only fifty feet from his cabin. Others found their dwellings imperfect protection against the elements. Springmeyer sometimes awoke of a morning in his tent cabin to find his blanket laden with a thick comforter of snow blown inside by the howling winds. He was, however, luxuriously sheltered in comparison to those forced to spread their "Tucson blankets" on the frozen ground because no accommodations were to be had at the height of the great boom.

A series of unusually severe winters, culminating in 1906–07, multiplied the hardships of cold weather. Goldfield pioneers recalled that on Christmas, 1904 the wind had blown like an icy hurricane for the entire day. The winter of 1905–06 commenced in November with a two-day blizzard, closing down the mines, halting construction, and packing every saloon in the city with men seeking shelter from the storm. "Shortly before midnight Sunday," the *Goldfield News* recounted, "the north wind rent his ice shackles and bursting forth from the frozen fastnesses of the Arctic swept over the desert in a veritable fury. His advent was announced by a shower of hail whose patterings resembled the rattle of drums punctuated by the shrill fifeings of the blast . . ." New Year's Eve brought another blizzard, with temperatures sinking to ten below zero, which no doubt seemed balmy to those miners just down from the Klondike but struck many of those bundled in their blankets outdoors as decidedly chilly.[9]

The winter of 1906–07 repeated the pattern, commencing with a heavy snowstorm around the first of December, which coincided with such a scarcity of fuel that Goldfielders were soon chopping up stolen telephone poles for their fires or paying the price of gold-bearing quartz for a few fragments of coal. Anne Ellis, a miner's wife, tall, rangy, and fair-haired, with a long face, a nose to match, and a wide generous mouth, recalled: "There is a real famine and people suffer. Coal and timber are stolen from the mines; a car of coal is taken right off the tracks, and guards are put to take care of it."[10] In those days of hardship, grain for stock was even scarcer than flour, and many baked bread for their horses. As the season progressed with two months of almost continuous rain, sleet, snow, and fog, miners refused, even for the highest pay, to venture forth into the snow to do the annual assessment work at claims a short distance from town. The most aged among the local Shoshone called that winter the worst in living memory.

The thaw that inevitably followed the snows turned Goldfield's unpaved streets into a "sea of slime" that "bespatters and bedraggles all beholders." The *Goldfield Tribune* called it "mud of the oozy, unctious order that sticks to everything; mud that proves a most elusive footing, that slips and squeezes itself from under your understandings when you think that you have secured a firm foothold." In many places this "porridge-like mixture" had inundated the board sidewalks and humorists claimed that it reached such depth in the streets that a Renfro auto sank away without a trace. The *Goldfield Chronicle* suggested that those in need of mud baths to relieve rheumatism would find them readily available in any part of the city.[11]

March weather was usually fitful, with balmy sunshine one day, snow the next, and recurrent high winds lasting into midsummer. These gusts could be strong enough to send the tent dwellings in which many Goldfielders resided skipping across the sands with their owners in pursuit or to topple the one ton masonry gable over the entrance to the Goldfield high school, whipping bricks inside the building until the roof partially collapsed. One of the most memorable among these playful desert zephyrs ripped a board-floored Ramsey Street tent house loose from its moorings. Onlookers watched the house sail majestically through the dust clouds, as an explosion resounded from the interior and flames licked through the cracks. The wind presently deposited the house on the ground some distance from its original location with most of its furnishings destroyed.

The most common and unpleasant effect of Goldfield's winds, however, was not whisking houses through the skies but blowing the pervasive dust everywhere and into everything. It powdered the butcher's meat, sifted into the sugar bin, drove the housewife to despair, and salted the diner's meal with a gritty crust. "Dust, dirt, grit, grime, and powdered muck everywhere," lamented the *Goldfield Chronicle*. "Dust! clouds of it—and no water wagon. Clogging, choking, contaminating dust, that clogs the keys of the typewriter, makes the writer choke and contaminates the water so that he is forced, Oh so much against his will, to drink other fluids, and much thereof!"[12]

As *Goldfield Gossip* editor Parmeter Kent (alias Sidney Flower) rightly noted, the city taking shape through this veil of dust lacked the architectural charm of a Bisbee or a Virginia City. Panoramic photos of Goldfield show a barren vista devoid of any sprig of a tree, a sprinkling of headframes at the mines northeast of the city toward Columbia Mountain, and a handful of large public buildings reminiscent of barns or stone forts. Buildings of stone blocks quarried near Rabbit Spring from the same formation as the Malapai Mesa included the courthouse, several schools, and a cluster of business buildings, most notably the three-story Nixon building on Columbia Street and the four-story Nye building. Local boosters took great pride in the permanence and large investments embodied in these buildings and constantly pointed to their solid gray and light brown facades as proof that Goldfield had developed from a mere fly-by-night mining camp, easily taken apart and carted away in a few wagons like so many in the region, into a real city with all the accoutrements of civilization.

THE WORLDS GREATEST GOLDFIELD
AS THE PHOTOGRAPHER SAW IT.

*This 1907 Goldfield panorama shows rapid evolution from the tents scattered like dice on
the desert three years earlier to a real city, with tall buildings clustered in the downtown area
and an increasing number of permanent homes (Larson Collection, Nevada State Museum)*

Among these large landmark buildings, the one with the most esthetic
merit and the largest price tag was the new Goldfield Hotel, completed
in 1908 and still standing today on the same site at Crook and Columbia
streets where its more modest predecessor burned in 1906. Its blueprints
came from the drawing board of Reno architect George Holesworth, who
also planned the Nye building. The proud owners had some cause to advertise this $350,000 four-story red brick wonder, with the gracious white-
railed balcony above the entrance, as the "most elegantly equipped hotel
between San Francisco and Denver." Its mahogany trimmed lobby was
resplendent with gilded columns, black leather upholstery, and globular
chandeliers; its dining room displayed floors of tiny black and white mosaic
tiles, potted palms, and heavy white linen tablecloths; its bedrooms had
brass beds, red carpeting, and velvet draperies. In short, it offered heretofore
unknown amenities to a populace long accustomed to making do with
tent houses and Tucson blankets, and not a few young bachelor professionals gladly availed themselves of the opportunity to board at the new

hotel. The press reported a million dollars worth of new buildings, including the Goldfield Hotel and the Hippodrome Theater, under construction during 1907.[13]

The humming bustling hub of the city's life was not, however, the Goldfield Hotel but rather the "four corner saloons," the Palace, the Northern, the Hermitage, and the Mohawk, standing a block away at the intersection of Crook and Main streets. The Palace, a two-story stone structure dating from 1904, had an exterior indistinguishable from an office building and, in addition to the usual fittings of a drinking establishment, contained the office of Goldfield sheriff William Ingalls, one of its original owners. At least in reputation, the Palace was somewhat overshadowed by its famous neighbor in the frame building across the street, the Northern, constructed by two adventurers just down from the great rush to the Klondike, E.S. ("Kid") Highley and future fight promoter Tex Rickard. Photos of the Northern show a gloomy but spacious tunnel-like interior, where a dozen bartenders poured drinks around the clock at the sixty foot bar, as roulette wheels spun and dice rolled in the gambling hall. Of course, Goldfield had "saloons without number," as one shocked visitor reported, in addition to the famous drinking parlors at the four corners.[14] More sordid and disreputable establishments, such as the Red Top and the Ajax, clustered on lower Main Street, as well as dance halls, hurdy-gurdy houses, and rows of cramped cribs. Still farther up the gulch toward the Malapai huddled the well-guarded "hop joints" where "lovers of the poppy" repaired to satisfy their cravings. Since church construction lagged considerably behind the saloons, spires only appear in the photos of later days.

In many respects, the truest mirrors of the Goldfield way of living were neither the churches, the saloons, the much vaunted stone buildings, nor even the Goldfield Hotel but rather the private dwellings, from primitive to posh. Although the press regarded the growing host of "dobes" and miners' shacks as a great advance over the tent city and the cave dwellings of the early days, much of the populace was as inadequately housed as their mining camp predecessors decades earlier on the Comstock. Large families from aged grandparents to infants often crammed themselves inside one or two small rooms, and for no small cost. Among the newspapers' scanty selection of classified advertisements for homes, prices appear fairly steep for the time period. In 1907 a three-room adobe cost $2,500, a dwelling frankly described as a "shack" $750, and a tent-roofed cabin rented for $25 per month. Although the new residences being erected by the Goldfield elite cost a good deal more, they scarcely reached palatial proportions by the standards of more gracious cities. During the building boom of 1906, a fire department survey found 176 houses, mostly bungalows costing from $1,000 to $15,000, in the process of construction. Sewall Thomas, a young mining engineer, described the architectural styles as "castles off the Rhine (and glad to be off), Spanish Renaissance, Norman-French, Elizabethan;

Dugout houses in early Goldfield (Larson Collection, Nevada State Museum)

also Mormon, Paiute, and Renaissance Sourdough."[15] Colonials seem to have been much in vogue. The largest and most ornate homes were the $15,000 residence, with an electric heating system, stove, and lights, belonging to H.T. Bragdon, president of the local stock exchange, and George Hayes' 64×60 foot, twelve-room, two-story bungalow—destined to be scarcely occupied before its owner departed to make his permanent home elsewhere.

Like the silver kings of the Comstock years, Goldfield's mining millionaires showed a disposition to build their mansions in more civilized and fashionable cities. No doubt the prevailing view that Goldfield was the place for a man to "stand the inconveniences for awhile, make his wad, and then duck out," as visiting Denver attorney Orrin Hilton advised,[16] did much to forestall the emergence of ornate residential architecture in the city. Moreover, so much has perished in the fires and floods of later years that only a few of the structures so enthusiastically heralded at the time of their construction survive today.

Though the residences of the elite elicited admiration, humbler dwellings displayed more individual eccentricity. These included bottle houses in which the gold rushers turned to materials plentifully at hand and cemented empty bottles, gleaming like saucers, in thick walls of gray adobe. Another type of dwelling derived from the discards abounding in a mining camp was the barrel house. A 1903 photo shows one about four vertical barrels wide and two high, the bottom layer deeply embedded in the dirt, with the second row stacked on top, end to end, and capped with a crude roof. *Goldfield News* reporter W. P. De Wolf found many such productions by amateur home builders "bizarre and picturesque." However, the dwelling regarded as the most original in the city was the abode of Glen Rogers, described in the press as an "old time sport." Not everyone who noticed the huge block of stone that had tumbled down from the Malapai would have envisioned it as a possible domicile, but Rogers did. He hollowed out the boulder to make a home and planted a small truck farm beside it, protected with windbreaks and watered from a well. [17]

Rogers' flourishing lettuce and parsnips were nearly as remarkable as his boulder shell house because most Goldfield horticultural experiments ended in utter failure. Aspen, balm of Gilead trees, and eucalyptus planted by a Goldfielder homesick for leafy shade all succumbed to the desert environment sooner or later, as did the fifty young cottonwoods planted by the city. A Goldfielder pulling up weeds amidst the sickly stunted potatoes in his backyard was admonished by a passing friend, "Let 'em grow, man, let 'em grow. Anything green that'll grow in Goldfield deserves to be encouraged." This argument had undeniable merit, since efforts to nurture lawns fared as badly as experiments with potatoes and trees. According to Parmeter Kent: "One man, a saloon keeper, wrestled with a small patch this summer, but he had to cover up each blade during the day and water it all night. About eighteen blades have come through all right. Only a saloon keeper could afford the experiment." [18]

While Goldfield construction had its delays and cost over runs (the Goldfield Hotel cost at least fifty thousand dollars more than originally planned), it was particularly notable for its speed. At the height of the boom, the busy cacophony of hammering and sawing went on all day, Sundays included. Lumber could not be shipped in fast enough during 1906–07. Ten- to twelve-car freight loads of mine timbers piled in each day and new headframes, despite their height and heavy timbering, appeared to go up overnight. When the railroad imposed a freight embargo to hasten the removal of shipments piling up at the tracks, the owners of the *Goldfield News* ordered the structural steel for their new building shipped in by Wells Fargo express, a luxurious gesture that Wells Fargo announced was the only instance when its speedy but high-priced facilities had been used to transport tons of heavy constuction materials.

It was not unusual for the smaller buildings to go up in a single day—and show it. Stevens and Redart took just one Sunday to erect a new Main Street store, counters and all, to replace the tent in which they had formerly done business. De Wolf observed, "As a Sunday diversion building a house holds the attention with the intentness of a baseball game and the hours fleet away unnoticed the while the builder marvels at the results of his handicraft." Chilly October nights, reminding Goldfielders that the rigors of another winter would soon blow in from the north, spurred a great wave of home building. The desire for more privacy may have lent a certain added incentive. As De Wolf slyly noted, at night the exteriors of tents alit within "present a series of interesting shadow pictures for the edification of the passer by."[19]

During the building boom, downtown real estate values rose even more rapidly than new construction projects. For example, a corner lot on Ramsey and Columbia streets sold for fifteen thousand dollars in November 1906, twenty-five thousand dollars in February, 1907, and thirty-five thousand dollars in April, while less choice locations also doubled or tripled in price. Though the press abstained from covering such matters, the depreciation in real estate after the boom collapsed was without doubt equally spectacular. Construction never started on the eight-story "skyscraper" planned by New York investors, and other projects erected in flush times quickly closed down. One of these, the Casey Hotel, greatly admired at the time of its completion in June 1907 for its lobby music stand, its elevator, and its thirty-six suites with private baths, remained open for only a year and a half.[20]

As long as the great boom lasted, both valuable downtown real estate and less choice residential lots, as well as a host of mining claims, became the objects of numerous wrangles, sometimes legal but more often physical. Claim jumping, though never so widespread as some sensational accounts suggested, was not an entirely unknown practice in early Goldfield, as an occasional brevity gleaned from the newspapers reveals. Without comment, the press noted that "armed forces" were patrolling the Ohio Mine to hold the claim jumpers at bay, that claim jumpers had partially succeeded in their efforts to wrest the Bulls and Bears claim from its former owners, and that a prominent attorney had desisted from a claim jumping attempt after having "his nose pulled." New Year's Eve was generally the scene not only of drunken revels but also of frenetic activity, as the owners of several hundred claims hastened to complete the annual assessment work the law required before the stroke of midnight and new contenders lurked in the darkness awaiting the hour when the claims would be up for grabs. The latter group sometimes included claim jumpers hired by the owners to procure their own claims and sell them back for a nominal fee. Goldfielders anticipated violence at these annual events, and exactly what transpired in the wintry darkness of New Year's Eve was known only to the participants.

By the spring of 1904, when the value of the Goldfield townsite began to exceed that of a good many mines in the district, property disputes spread, and legal imbroglios that were to drag on for years commenced (a common mining camp phenomenon also seen in Tombstone and Aspen). One pitted Al Myers and his associates in the ownership of the principal Goldfield townsite against a group headed by future Nevada governor and United States senator Tasker Oddie. George Phenix, another Goldfield founding father, attempted to turn a profit on a worthless mining claim by dividing it into town lots, only to be swept aside by an invading horde of squatters. A group eventually embracing more than a hundred squatters sued Phenix to gain title to the land occupied by their homes and businesses. Eventually the United States land office decided in their favor.[21]

In the meantime, while these disputes wound slowly through the courts, Goldfielders undertook to settle matters by less time-consuming methods, including arson, guns, and dynamite. An "unknown party" generally assumed to be a squatter with a grievance against Phenix dynamited his combined office building and residence. One Dr. Drake, having ascertained that a neighbor's lodging house impinged on his property by six inches, erected a twenty-two-foot high "spite fence" smack dab against its wall, blocking all windows and ventilation on that side. However, Drake's method of demonstrating his displeasure was subtle in comparison to some other combatants. In her struggle to hold onto a lot, Mrs. Mary Galvin refused to be intimidated by a man who throttled her, thrust a revolver against her bosom, and burned her cabin—evidently he had not heard about the legendary mining camp gallantry toward women. In another memorable conflict, the owners of a lot continually plagued by squatters purchased a large brown bear and tethered him on their property. Henceforth, squatters gave their lot a wide berth.

As these conflicts illustrated, squatters strove by fair means and foul to erect a building upon a disputed lot because the property then became classified as "improved" land, for which the owner could eventually secure a government title. Once the structure had been erected, maintaining it on the lot could prove an equally perilous proposition. Cabins and tent houses were not infrequently wrested from their foundations and cast into the street, causing the Goldfield Tribune to observe, "If this sort of thing keeps up one may go to sleep some night in Goldfield and wake up somewhere under the Malapai."[22] Families thus forcibly evicted sometimes continued to occupy their cabins amidst the passing wagons and horsemen in the middle of the street while pondering their next move. No vacant space was safe from the squatters. At one point they grew so numerous and so bold, even attempting to pre-empt the land set aside for a new school building, that the city fathers employed a posse to forcibly dispossess them.

Among these aggressive gypsy householders, ready to pitch their tent houses wherever an opportunity presented itself and to reside in the middle of Columbia Street when the occasion demanded, such amenities as water, sewage, and sanitation received little attention, either from the careless residents or the governing officials. As a result, conditions were often abominable. Sewage from backyard privies seeped into the shallow wells. Local doctors warned against the spread of disease unless householders cleaned the filth from their back yards. Garbage collectors persisted in depositing their loads just outside the city to avoid a trip to the dump. Meat in the uncovered butcher wagons slowly wending their way from the train depot to the markets arrived seething with flies and coated with the omnipresent dust. A "cleanup day" sponsored by the civic minded businessmen of the Chamber of Commerce or the Ladies Aid Society occasionally alleviated these unsavory conditions, and the rest of the time the dry desert climate undoubtedly did a good deal to protect the city from the worst results of poor sanitation.[23]

If Goldfield's desert situation conferred certain blessings, it also bestowed severe disadvantages when the need for an increased water supply became acute. The early settlers had drawn water sufficient for their needs from Rabbit Spring at the base of the Malapai and from shallow wells twenty or thirty feet deep in the downtown area, four of them free public wells equipped with buckets and windlasses. In those early days, a bath was the ultimate luxury. A 1904 visitor noted that Goldfield boasted just one public bathtub, located in a barber shop. The first private bathtub in camp was the proud possession of Lucien Patrick and his wife. On the roof of their house, the Patricks built a tank, which they supplied with water purchased by the bucketful from a water wagon and carried to the roof by a ladder. This laborious process brought them the sumptuous pleasure of running water in their bathtub and sink. Even after water and sewer pipes had been installed in most of the city, many householders continued to buy their water from wagon vendors. "Never was water so precious," Anne Ellis later recalled. "One never used more than one could help, the family all bathing in the same tubful, then using it to mop with, then pouring it, very sparingly, on a small patch of wheat planted beside the door. . . . I know of one woman who kept a boarding-house, who would boil the dishwater, then skim it, and strain it, in this way using it time and time again."[24]

As the population soared and the development of the mines required more water for milling, limited supplies from the wells and Rabbit Spring proved inadequate to the demand. Attorney Hilton voiced a common complaint when he observed that Goldfield was the only town he knew where water cost more than whiskey. Not only the quantity but also the quality of the water gave cause for lament. Parmeter Kent called it a "compound which looks like rinsing fluid, and tastes like whitewash gone bad;" he suggested that the president of the water company should be compelled to drink a pint of his product three times a day, with the certain result that he would either pass away or be converted to the necessity of purifying the water. Some idea of the ingredients likely to produce such an effect can be gleaned from an analysis of the Alkali Springs water piped into the Combination mill. Although this warm, strong-smelling, and readily foaming fluid contained large proportions of sodium and sulphate, it was considered suitable for domestic use and remained one of Goldfield's principal water sources until the autumn of 1907. [25]

During 1904 and 1905, several water companies competed in Goldfield, and the county commissioners awarded various franchises with indifferent results. The eventual victor in this struggle for supremacy was Thomas Rickey, a cattle baron, a banker, and as ruthless a capitalist as Nevada ever produced. Among his other interests, Rickey headed the soon-to-fail State Bank and Trust, in which Goldfielders and many other Nevadans lost a great deal of money. Rickey presently absorbed his competitors for the water franchise, transformed his organization from the Montezuma Company to the Goldfield Consolidated Water Company, and commenced to construct a four hundred thousand dollar system piping water from springs at Magruder Mountain thirty miles southwest of Goldfield near Lida. However, dust gathered on the promises of the Goldfield Consolidated Water Company, work lagged on the system for a year and a half, and thousands of people pouring into the city at the height of the boom were forced to subsist on a trickle of bad whitewash. The Chamber of Commerce announced an investigation into the company's franchise, and finally, in October 1907, just when the boom was about to collapse, the new system began to operate.

Although the mountain water was pure and plentiful, rates remained unreasonably high. Under the old regime, Kent noted that Goldfielders typically paid a monthly bill of fifteen dollars for domestic use (the price of two weeks room and board at a hotel in that period and the equivalent of about three hundred dollars today); with the benefit of the new system, a 1913 survey showed that the mines and mills used more than 97 percent of metered water, while householders unable to afford the high prices continued to make do with backyard privies and water purchased from wagon vendors. The cause of these high rates, the *Goldfield Chronicle* suggested, was the company's attempt to recoup expenditures 2,000 percent above the norm for the installation of a similar system in other communities. The city had gained a plentiful water supply, but water remained the same expensive luxury as in the beginning. [26]

Electricity and communications in the new camp evoked comparable complaints over high rates or poor service. Goldfield remained without illumination stronger than candles and kerosene lamps until a steam-generating power plant commenced operations in January, 1905. However, high fuel costs and limited capacity rendered the enterprise unsuccessful. In late September 1905, a hydroelectric power plant at Bishop Creek in the Sierra a hundred miles to the west supplied electricity more effectively, although not until 1909 did Goldfield's network of twenty-four street lamps function properly. The new power system, installed by the Nevada Power, Mining and Milling Company, also supplied Tonopah and other towns in the region. One of the principal directors of the power company was the same tycoon who dominated the water company, Rickey, and residents voiced the same grievances concerning the rates charged by his power company. "The people of Goldfield begin to appreciate the power of monopoly," the *Chronicle* bitterly observed. [27]

After the telephone and telegraph lines became operational in 1904–05, public protests primarily devolved upon poor service. At the height of the boom, Goldfield brokers successfully transacted a huge volume of business over Western Union on working days, but some telegrams reached their destinations at a slower pace than the regular mail or never arrived at all. Complaints about telephone service centered on a welter of wrong connections. Most of the time this was merely exasperating, but the editor of the *News* felt outraged when callers with exclusive scoops for the newspaper were connected with other parties who misused the information thus fortuitously acquired. [28]

In the telephone system, however erratic its behavior, Goldfield was the beneficiary of a modern invention unknown in the early years on the Comstock. In the field of transportation as well, Goldfield, as the last great mining boom, presented a fascinating amalgam of the old and the new. Wagons drawn by twenty-mule teams, strings of burros, and stages of a variety scarcely changed since the first Nevada mining camps sprang up nearly half a century earlier thronged the streets together with two new and fascinating novelties, the motorcycle and the automobile, while overhead the airship constructed by a reclusive desert inventor could occasionally be glimpsed floating through the night skies to the south.

During Goldfield's early days, freight wagons and stagecoaches traveled by different routes. The heavy freight wagons, hauled by teams of twelve to twenty horses or mules, traveled a sixty-five-mile road northwest to the Carson and Colorado railhead at Candelaria; the stages followed an eighty-eight-mile route, with fewer steep grades, to the railhead at Sodaville by way of Tonopah. So heavy was the traffic that draft animals were sometimes in short supply. After watching their driver struggle with a wild-eyed rambunctious team of mustangs, lately brought in from the range and incompletely initiated to harness, the more prudent passengers sometimes refused to ride in the stagecoach. Even with a team of wild mustangs between the traces, the final twenty-eight-mile stretch from Tonopah to Goldfield often passed slowly. A letter from Fred Corkill, a 1904 visitor, noted, "It is a dusty ride of six hours from Tonopah on a rig called a stage, three in a seat built for two, but anything goes here these times. . . ." [29]

After the first automobile to cross the desert, mining engineer Fred Siebert's Winston touring car, arrived at Tonopah from Sodaville in July

1903, the new invention became the rage. Establishments such as the Palace Blacksmith Shop began to advertise "automobile repairing," as well as "horseshoeing." Wealthy brokers ordered expensive autos like Henry Weber's "space annihilator," also a Winston and reputedly the winner of several prizes in an auto show prior to its delivery in 1907. Weber's Winston was a luxuriously appointed five hundred horsepower model, equipped to carry its own gas (since gas stations were still in the future) and four spare tires. It also contained special compartments for Weber's tent, his dining service, and such necessaries to a broker's sustenance as Mumm's Extra Dry champagne.

With rash confidence that an automobile could go anywhere a horse could travel, Weber and other investors set off across the desert in their cars to visit remote mining camps and new prospects. The *Goldfield Tribune* observed, "A race for the location of mining claims between two ambitious operators who have thousands at stake, may oblige the chauffeur to make a night run over unknown roads into a trackless country where any kind of an accident may happen to him. . . ."[30] Considering the appalling condition of the trails and rutted wagon routes that passed for roads, the autos seem to have performed remarkably well, only rarely becoming stuck or breaking down.

Entrepreneurs, as well as motoring enthusiasts, quickly seized upon the new invention. As early as 1905, two "automobile stage lines" carried passengers between Goldfield and Tonopah, more than halving the time consumed by the stage ride. Another auto line operated north from Las Vegas, charging forty dollars per passenger for the fourteen-hour, 124-mile trip from Las Vegas to Rhyolite and twenty-five dollars for the seventy-mile stretch from Rhyolite to Goldfield. These were prices only the affluent and the highly impatient could afford, but there were plenty of customers, close to nine thousand in less than a year's time on one of the Tonopah-Goldfield lines.

On both these routes, separate roads were constructed for the autos because horses often reared and bolted in terror from the new machines, a more even surface was less likely to turn the Mumm's Extra Dry into fizz, and automobile drivers itching to skim over the desert at speeds as high as nineteen miles an hour could scarcely bear to crawl along at a tortoise pace behind the slow-moving teams. The method of construction on the Goldfield-Tonopah auto road was primitive. After pulling a T-rail over the route to clear the brush, heavy chains were dragged over it to establish a track. Road repair consisted of occasionally hauling a pair of pipes over the route to smooth the ridges. Oddly, the course of the auto routes altered with usage, and originally straight roads gradually became serpentine. While it seems hard to imagine that these new auto routes offered much improvement over the old wagon tracks, teamsters found them irresistible, and automobile owners soon complained that freight wagons had spoiled the twenty-five thousand dollar automobile road between Goldfield and Rhyolite.[31]

A number of related firsts accompanied the arrival of the first autos. The first Goldfield auto accident was reported in February 1905, when one of the auto stages turned too sharply at Diamondfield and made a complete somersault. No one suffered any injury worse than a broken shoulder. A new malady, "chauffeur's blindness," appeared, until the motoring fraternity absorbed the lesson that dark goggles were imperative in the dust, wind, and brilliant sun of the desert. By 1907 the press was reporting the first injury of a pedestrian by a motor vehicle and the first auto theft, and the city boasted forty private cars, collectively valued at $250,000 and numerous enough for an occasional two-car collision. The way these big lurching bounding automobiles went "tearing through the town" and their "riotous, ripping, roistering" honking became such a problem in the Goldfield streets that demand developed for a speeding ordinance, a legal innovation unknown in the days when local safety ordinances centered upon the need to hitch horses.[32] The transitional nature of the times was vividly illustrated when a law officer thundered off in hot pursuit of one of these speeding automobiles—on his horse.

While the elite chugged over the desert in their fancy automobiles, Goldfield's ordinary travelers sought accommodations with a good old-fashioned form of transportation, the railroad. Other mining towns had often raised bond issues and agitated and petitioned for years in order to secure a railroad, but Goldfield quickly and easily gained rail connections to three major trunk lines. In September 1905, less than two years after the district was organized, Goldfield celebrated the arrival of the broad-gauged Goldfield Railroad (subsequently merged with the Tonopah line as the Tonopah and Goldfield Railroad); it connected to the northwest with the Nevada and California Railway (formerly the Carson and Colorado), the Virginia and Truckee, and finally the Southern Pacific system and San Francisco, principal supplier for the central Nevada region during the boom years. The Tonopah and Tidewater (operated for several years by the Tonopah and Goldfield line), linked Goldfield to the Santa Fe railroad at Ludlow, California in 1907. In the same year Goldfield gained a connection with the San Pedro, Los Angeles and Salt Lake Railroad to the south when the Las Vegas and Tonopah Railroad reached the city. In addition, Goldfield Con operated a small railroad inside the district connecting its mines with the mill and the Tonopah and Goldfield. Plans for a Goldfield electric trolley system never moved beyond the drawing boards, although the project teetered on the brink of realization for a short time.

The mining boom that followed the fabulous Hayes-Monnette strike would not have been possible without the railroad's capacity to handle a large volume of freight, but the period of political agitation that Goldfield had been spared by the speedy arrival of the railroad would belatedly arrive in the form of an era of protest over high freight rates after it became clear that railroad charges offered scant improvement over those of the old twenty-mule teams. Thomas Rickard thought the tolls levied by the railroad "tantamount to highway robbery." Aside from the general inclination to charge anything the traffic would bear in free spending Goldfield, the managers of the Tonopah and Goldfield had apparently decided to recoup their investment before the boom could collapse, and in a remote desert mining camp dependent on supplies shipped in from great distances, they had every opportunity to do so. Within three months of the jubilant ceremony of driving the golden spike, Goldfield mine owners announced a boycott to force a reduction in the railroad's exorbitant rates. While the protest brought some reductions, complaints recurred over the next two years concerning the railroad's "Shylock" policies, its long haul charges, its protracted delays, and its insistence that freight costs must be prepaid. Another source of wrangling with the railroad was slow removal of freight from the depot. At one point the Tonopah and Goldfield sought to force speedier action from its Goldfield customers by a sweeping embargo that halted one hundred freight cars loaded with Goldfield merchandise farther up the line until nearly two hundred cars standing in the railroad yard had been unloaded. Probably the major factor in the eventual reduction in rates was the arrival of the competing Las Vegas and Tonopah line, although the Tonopah and Goldfield remained dominant in total passengers and freight. [33]

The salutary effects of competition failed to produce a similar result in the prices charged by Goldfield merchants. Indeed even after freight rates dropped, storekeepers continued to charge the same prices and pocketed the difference. Thanks to such practices, Goldfield was widely regarded as an expensive place to visit, let alone live. Los Angeles judge H.A. Pierce, for example, warned prospective visitors in a press interview, "Don't go to Goldfield for your vacation unless you have plenty of money," and sourly recalled being compelled to pay $1.50·for a plate of ham and eggs. Moreover, at the height of the boom, when coal was scarcer than gold and horses ate bread for lack of fodder, goods and services could scarcely be stretched to meet the demand. While acknowledging some truth in reports surfacing in national newspapers of suffering and death in Goldfield due to these shortages in the midst of a harsh winter, the editor of the *News* tartly informed visitors who complained of the facilities that Goldfielders were "miners and not hotel keepers" and had never advertised the camp as a "resort." Nonetheless, after a conflagration at the original Goldfield Hotel in November 1906 further reduced the city's already inadequate hotel capacity, the need to provide accommodations for the hordes streaming into the city turned acute. A drive for public shelter sparked by *Goldfield Gossip* editor Parmeter Kent and underwritten by the members of the Montezuma Club resulted in the erection of a huge tent that accommodated one hundred guests, each of whom could stay for three nights at a dollar a night while finding permanent quarters. [34]

Inside six months the willingness of Goldfielders to pay liberally for their comforts—and even their discomforts—had eased the problem of short supplies and accommodations. "Gold is the magic wand that transforms everything. It brings American Beauty roses and young onions into camp. . . ." remarked the *Goldfield Review*. "You can buy anything from a bunch of radishes to a Prince Albert coat or from a balbrigan undershirt to a grand piano." The problem of high prices was solved by fiat when the Mine Owners Association decreed in the winter of 1907–08 that Goldfield prices must decrease by 20 percent and pledged its members to accomplish this result. [35] The stimulus behind this ultimatum may have been less a public-spirited concern for the consumer than the discovery, after the union had been routed, that even scab labor could not be recruited to work for reduced wages unless the cost of living went down.

Another inherent fact of Goldfield life that even the Mine Owners Association could not solve by ultimatum was the peril of a major fire of the kind that had consumed so many other mining towns. A settlement largely consisting of tents and flimsy shacks, with a limited water supply, located in a hot dry desert swept by heavy winds was in constant danger. The possibility always lurked in the minds of Goldfielders, especially those old enough to remember the great Virginia City fire of 1875, and it curtailed the tendency to cavil at the quality or price of the water supply, so long as the water company maintained pressure at the hydrants. The establishment of the first volunteer fire department in July 1904 and the enactment of strict ordinances on fire hazards from dynamite to firecrackers failed to allay public apprehensions. The persistence of these fears clearly showed in an announcement by the Hippodrome that three firemen would be on duty in the theater at all times, two back stage and one in the audience.

On July 8, 1905, late on a Saturday afternoon, the fire everyone had half expected started from a leaking gas stove in the Bon Ton millinery shop on Columbia Street. The proprietress attempted to extinguish it herself, then summoned assistance. Although firemen swiftly arrived at the scene, they were already too late. The flames were spreading, and the heat was intense. Contractor J. E. Bundy desisted from paying his construction workers in the Hotel Nevada and fled just in time, leaving two hundred dollars in gold coins behind him. He would later return to find them fused in a solid mass in the ashes of the hotel, which had burned to the ground in eight minutes from the time it caught fire. A parrot, rescued from the advancing flames by its mistress, flew back to its abandoned cage, where it croaked "Fire! Fire!" until it was incinerated.

As Goldfielders all over town began filling the buckets and washtubs with which they hoped to save their homes, water pressure at the hydrants dropped to a trickle, multiplying the difficulties faced by the firemen. In this

DFIELD NEV JULY 8Th 1905

Kegs of beer helped to save the city when the 1905 fire broke out in Goldfield (Larson Collection, Nevada State Museum)

emergency situation, Bert Ulmer of the Little Hub Saloon and his bartender started using blankets, comforters, and rugs soaked in kegs of beer to sheathe the sides of buildings. The idea quickly caught on. In a lively article, historian Phillip Earl depicts saloonkeepers who "never stood a drink in their entire lives" rolling out kegs of beer to douse the flames and soak the clothing of firefighters—perhaps the first time that Goldfield's multiplicity of saloons had served a civic purpose. The energetic application of buckets of beer saved the Oxford Restaurant. Through the beer stratagem and heroic effort, firemen and volunteers managed to confine the fire to two blocks of the downtown area, but within that section property owners lost nearly everything because only one building, a small private home, had been insured. A stale beery odor wafted from downtown Goldfield for some weeks after the conflagration. [36]

Following a major fire in Columbia a week later, Goldfield suffered no more serious fires until the holocaust that consumed most of the city in 1923, although lesser fires burning a building or two occurred frequently and the loss of such major structures as the original Goldfield Hotel and the Florence mill seriously damaged the city. The usual cause of fires was a defective stove, most often a gasoline one. Goldfield's general success in containing fires may be largely credited to the efficiency of the fire department and the vigilance of the citizenry. The firebell was Goldfield's signal for any kind of trouble, and when no bell stood handy, shooting a revolver into the air accomplished the same purpose. The instant the alarm sounded the horses at the fire station would jump from their stalls without a command to take their places at the fire wagons, waiting for the harness to drop onto their backs from above. Firemen slid down the pole, fastened the harness hooks, and jumped onto the wagon. Any who slithered down too slowly would be left behind, because as soon as firemen had climbed aboard, the big powerful horses would gallop off through the streets with no signal from their masters, seeming to know their destination by instinct.[37]

For almost twenty years, a fusillade of shots followed by the thunder of hooves in the night meant that once again the city was saved.

VI

Strange Mingling

THE POPULATION

"An indefineable attraction attaches to a mining camp and to the followers of such excitements it appeals with the same tenacity as does the odor of the poppy to the dope fiend. . . . It is an insidious disease and once the fever of it gets into the bones it cannot be eradicated, even though the victim pass years in fancied security by the home fireside."
W. P. De Wolf in the *Goldfield News*

Observers of the passing scene invariably commented upon the the wonderful variety and rough democracy of the Goldfield throng, where wealthy brokers from New York and Berlin rubbed shoulders with union firebrands and grizzled prospectors just in from the desert. Clarence Eddy, an attorney known as the "poet-prospector," found it the "most metropolitan and cosmopolitan camp of all," a "marvel of variety, color and life;" Fred Wamsley mused upon "its strange mingling of the primitive and the civilized . . . like no other town or city in the world." "Tenderfoot, gambler, clergyman, legitimate promoter, mining shark, sure thing man, panderer, courtesan, each have their place in the passing show," wrote W. P. De Wolf in the *Goldfield News*, also noting that many of the men and women crowding the rough board sidewalks were seasoned boomers "whose ears are never deaf to fortune's insistent call."[1] How suddenly the call could sound was illustrated when a gentleman on a Chicago-bound train aroused the interest of his fellow passengers by unfolding a Goldfield newspaper—four families moved to Goldfield in consequence.

Because Goldfield boomed and declined between the censuses of 1900 and 1910, educated guesses from a variety of observers provide the main clues to the size of the population. While some variation appears and it is wise to remember that the low estimates of "knockers" and "croakers" received no airings in the local press, a diverse number of observers arrived at roughly similar conclusions. Beginning with Al Myers' isolated tent in the summer of 1903, the population reached about forty (those present but not signing included) when the first pioneers organized the camp in October. It then rose from several hundred in early 1904 to a number most often estimated at six or seven thousand, and sometimes as high as ten thousand, the following year. During the great boom of 1906-07, the probable figures ran from fifteen thousand (the assessor's conclusion) to eigh-teen thousand for Goldfield proper, with an additional two thousand in Columbia and other adjacent suburbs (the appraisal of the compilers of the Goldfield city directory).[2]

In those early years, a deluge of letters descended on the editor of the *Goldfield News* from men and women of all ages and circumstances seek-ing advice on whether they should move to Goldfield. "Can a fellow get a fair sort of living out in your country, without much capital?" asked a hopeful Coloradan. An Oregon stone contractor declared that he was "thinking of comming down to Goldfield and wood like to know the streight of things." A denizen of Bearmouth, Montana sought "the following infla-mation": "What is the poplation of your town and how old is it. . . . Hop-ping to hear from you at your earilest conveiance."[3]

The all-purpose answer editor James O'Brien published in the summer of 1907 warned them, "Already there are too many adventurers." He also admonished those with poor health, little money, or scant familiarity with "rough conditions" to stay away. At the same time, O'Brien offered limited encouragement to the hardy with a stake in hand: "there never were better opportunities in the world for the right kind of people, rightly equipped, than here in Goldfield. But be sure you have some money and much health and determination and willingness to work and also know you meet up with the sharpest, shrewdest, most aggressive lot of people gathered any-where on God's footstool."[4]

After Goldfield's decline commenced, the assessor pegged the population at 12,000 in the spring of 1908, though the local postmaster still thought 15,000 a more realistic figure. The decrease soon became indisputable. By the 1910 census, Goldfield and Columbia had dwindled to a mere 5,400 people. Scanty as this figure appears, compared to the period only three years earlier when the city was bursting at the seams, in thinly populated Nevada, with only 81,900 people and no large metropolitan areas, Goldfield still retained considerable importance as the second largest city in the state, surpassed only by Reno, with a population just under 11,000. A decade later, after major mining operations ceased, Goldfield plummeted below 1,600.[5]

Despite the mingled disparities of economic and social condition that caught the visitor's eye, Goldfield's population was less racially and ethni-cally diverse than in many nineteenth-century Nevada mining camps. So completely did the tide of gold rushers inundate the indigenous Shoshone that few Goldfielders noticed the remaining Indians. One old Goldfield resident recalled Indians living in huts "up the gully" until the 1913 flood destroyed their dwellings and they permanently departed. Even before the flood, however, the Indians appear a fainter and less numerous presence than in earlier mining camps such as Belmont. Nor did Indians constitute an important part of the labor force in the mines, in contrast to the role they had played in remote mining camps such as Sylvania on the Nevada-

California border to the south. Instead they did odd jobs around the mines or vended pine nuts; Indian women worked as laundresses and sold their beautiful handmade basketry. An early photograph shows Indian wood-cutters peddling their wares from heavily laden mules in the streets of Goldfield, as they had done forty years earlier on the Comstock.[6]

Though Indians were relegated to the margins of camp life, Goldfield could not entirely ignore its debt to the Indian. Few acknowledged Tom Fisherman's primary role in the camp's discovery, but Harry Stimler, a half-breed, was widely hailed as one of the original locators and became an accepted figure in the community. Occasionally, Goldfielders showed a twinge of recognition that the original residents of Esmeralda had received little share in the city's millions—recognition coupled, of course, with that sense of racial superiority characteristic at the turn of the century. One local reporter ended his otherwise cheerful report on the fantastic floats and colorful costumes of a high-spirited Fourth of July celebration on a sombre note: "The most dramatic incident of the whole parade was the steadfast gaze of an old Indian squaw, holding a papoose, surrounded by children, watching the paleface people who have taken over their land, marching past. It typified the decadence of the Indian, with the passing of his race, and the onward march of the progress and civilization of the white race."[7]

Goldfielders' discrimination against Asians took more virulent and overt form than their treatment of Indians. In 1904 Goldfield had a large and growing Asian community, as Chinese and Japanese formerly employed by the Southern Pacific in standard-gauging on the Carson and Colorado Railroad gravitated toward the city. Alarmed by the increasing influx, Goldfield's miners and businessmen ordered all Asians to leave the city just before Christmas. The Asians immediately departed en masse, no doubt intimidated by remembrance of the Tonopah anti-Chinese riot of the preceding year, in which one was killed, many were beaten, and none of the white perpetrators were ever punished. During the ensuing years, Goldfield's "unwritten law" barring Asians was enforced with iron rigidity. The sheriff ordered any "Chink visitor" who alighted from the train to leave at once and kept Chinese witnesses brought to testify in forthcoming criminal cases in jail under guard to forestall mob attack in the streets. The sole exception to the unwritten law was a noted Japanese mining engineer, whose position as the representative of a large Japanese mining syndicate earned him a special dispensation for a brief visit—even solidly entrenched prejudice could bend a little at the behest of a large syndicate.

In 1909, when discriminatory California legislation strained relations between the United States and Japan, the San Francisco press reported that the Japanese planned to test their rights by proceeding to Goldfield and "awaiting developments." Evidently the test never materialized, and Goldfield succeeded in maintaining its policy of Oriental exclusion to the end. Instead of moving forward in the direction of greater racial tolerance,

Goldfield's "exile order" signified a large step backward from the Comstock, where a sizeable Chinatown had existed, despite much discrimination and the exclusion of Chinese labor from the mines by the union. The underlying causes of Goldfield's policy of total exclusion probably lay in three factors: the strong influence in Goldfield of the element from Colorado, where the Chinese had been banned from several mining camps; the successful and recent assertion of racism by laborers in the Tonopah anti-Chinese riot; and above all, the early dominance in Goldfield of the miners' union, whose members' fear of cheap Chinese competition in the labor market dictated Draconian racial measures. As the *Goldfield News* put it: "It is the voice of labor that says them nay and stands ready to back the deed with the word."[8]

The primary exception to racial homogeneity in Goldfield was the presence of a small but not insignificant black community comparable to its earlier counterpart on the Comstock. So low was the black population in the West in those years that even a community of this size exceeded the norm in many frontier towns; one old Goldfield resident called the black quarter "quite a settlement." Evidently local blacks did not work in the mines. Instead they filled low-income positions as service workers, household help, and unskilled laborers, as was also the pattern on the Comstock. A sizeable contingent worked as porters on the railroads. Even these jobs yielded occasional fringe benefits, however. Rumor had it that the wealthiest black in town had acquired a fortune in mining stocks through tips from brokers at the Montezuma Club where he worked as a porter. Other blacks operated a variety of establishments, including a cleaners and dyers business, a dance hall, a brothel, and probably the 3J saloon in the tenderloin. J. W. ("Ham") Hamilton, janitor for Wingfield, through whom he gained an enviable chunk of stock in Goldfield Con, owned the "Need More" dance hall, a successful establishment with bar, lunch counter, crap table, piano, and the "warmest dancing" in town from 9:00 every evening until 4:00 A.M. At the other end of the spectrum from the investor and the entrepreneurs, newspaper reports and other sources indicate the presence of some prostitutes (including the comely mulatto said to have caught George Wingfield's eye) and black involvement in an occasional petty theft but almost never in serious crime.

The opportunities abounding in the great boom evaporated too quickly to reverse the erosion of Nevada's black middle class in the late nineteenth century, traced in a recent study by political scientist Elmer Rusco, but some signs suggest the temporary presence of a vigorous community organizing for social and political purposes. A ball for blacks in Goldfield was an elegant affair, with a fine orchestra and a formal program. Beautiful women in evening dresses and men in evening clothes would arrive by cab; whites who slipped inside to see the spectacle were politely asked to leave. In addition to these glittering social events, the formation of the

Foraker Republican Club by thirty black voters signalled an attempt to secure greater political clout.[9]

As Rusco points out, newspaper use of derogatory terms such as "coon," generally not seen in the Nevada press until after 1900, suggests a period of rising white hostility shared in much of the nation. In Goldfield the Fourth of July, 1907 program offering prizes in these terms prompted an outraged letter to the *Goldfield Tribune* from E. W. Lucas: "I wish to advise all colored persons contemplating participation to refrain from so doing unless those words 'coon male,' 'coon female,' etc. are stricken out on said program. 'Tis unjust on the part of the committee to use such terms, and any descendant of Ethopia who would strive for laurels in any contest in Goldfield on the day aforesaid mentioned, puts himself in a position to be called, not a 'coon,' but a monkey reaching for hot chestnuts, because he was patted on the head and told that he was O.K." Lucas won his point, and Goldfield instead awarded prizes for the winning costumes in the grand parade to "best colored dude," and so forth. Blacks may have acted on his suggestion to boycott these competitions, since the winners were evidently impersonators in blackface, women portraying men, men as women, and most prizes won by a near professional who had "plucked the persimmons" at similar contests from Chicago to Salt Lake City.[10]

In national origins, as in race, Goldfield was more homogeneous than the Comstock. The native white, native parents census category reached 43 percent in Esmeralda in 1910, roughly double the figure on the Comstock twenty years earlier. Among the 21 percent of the county population listed as foreign born, the largest national groups were the British (England, Scotland, and Wales), the Irish, and the Canadians, followed by the Germans, a similar pattern to the Comstock, where the same national groupings loomed large. The only mention so far uncovered of Goldfield's German community appeared in the *News* when a young German mining engineer and confidence man, with a "practice of living by his wits," gambled away funds obtained for about a year from local Germans "with very little money but big hearts." The Hispanic element assumed less importance than the Germans—indeed not until 1909 was the first Hispanic baby born in Goldfield.[11]

Though numerous enough to sustain social organizations and activities, Esmeralda's foreign born gave few signs of strong ethnic consciousness. The British and Germans did not organize; the Canadians showed no cohesion, though some, such as the Taylors and Mackenzie, were among the most prominent figures in the city; only immigrants from present Yugoslavia, in the fraternal order they christened Vijonac, and the Irish, through their vigorous social organization, the Gratton Club, and to a lesser extent, the local Catholic church, displayed a continuing sense of ethnic identity. If Goldfield social life was little enlivened by the ethnic group organizations that injected such variety into Comstock social life, at least she was also spared the ethnic hostilities that broke out at the Ely copper mines and rumbled in Tonopah when older groups clashed with new immigrant miners from southern and eastern Europe. [12]

In place of the ethnic consciousness of earlier mining camps, Goldfielders instead clustered in strong state groupings based on the bonds formed through shared experiences at past mining booms, primarily in Colorado and Alaska. Californians, though numerous in Goldfield, did not seem to act together, perhaps because former residents of San Francisco or Los Angeles felt no sense of common identity. Native Nevadans were apparently few and far between and never formed a cohesive grouping. It was the Coloradans, extensively represented among mine operators, miners, and members of the bar, who were generally regarded as the largest and most influential group, right from the point when the first settlers named the camp "Goldfield" to commemorate a Coloradan's former home. Such Coloradans as Myers and Lockhart assumed preeminence from the first months of operations. Several years later the group behavior of the Coloradans was indirectly revealed when a former Montana man urged others from his state to "emulate the Colorado idea" and "stick together like glue the way the Coloradans do" by forming a Montana society. [13] Whether the Coloradans had organized a comparable society is not clear, though they did hold such events as an "All-Colorado Feast" or a "Sons of Colorado" night. So far as is known, these gatherings did not transcend the sharp rift between Colorado mine operators and miners who had faced each other in the bitter union battles at Cripple Creek. If the Coloradans had brought fraternal ties with them as they headed farther west, they had also packed along some old animosities that fed into the dispute between the mine operators and the WFM.

No such divisions sullied the fellowship among the "Arctic Brotherhood" that had stampeded down to Goldfield from the North. Its most notable members became the proprietors of the famous Northern saloon, Tex Rickard, the future boxing promoter, and Kid Highley, whose handsome wife was said to have been immortalized by poet Robert Service in one of his Alaskan epics. In 1907 former "mushers" and "sourdoughs" announced plans to establish an "Egloo." Whether they organized a formal society is not clear. Perhaps the veterans of the Klondike rush of 1897–98 merely continued to fraternize in the saloons that particularly solicited their patronage. There is little doubt, however, that their northern experience had created a strong bond between them. In his memoir of Goldfield, Henry Miles recalled the "mushers" gathering in a body to assist a member of the brotherhood accused of homicide. The sourdough button, a gold pan with the initials AB for "Arctic Brotherhood," sparkled on the lapels of many Goldfielders, and one confided proudly to Miles, "This means a lot more than any Masonic emblem." [14]

Doubtless a large proportion of the Arctic Brotherhood, like the Coloradans and all the rest, consisted of adventurous young men of the kind who had supplied the bulk of every mining boom since the first forty-niners set out across the plains. In Goldfield, they usually garbed themselves in khaki coats and breeches, which De Wolf called a "complete disguise" worn by busted prospectors, millionaires, gamblers, and clergymen alike. In winter corduroys sometimes replaced the khakis. They tucked their breeches into high-laced boots in the miners' style and wore their blue flannel shirts tie-less and open at the collar. De Wolf suggested that the tenderfeet could be easily distinguished: they wore "their sleeves rolled up well above the elbows and their shirt flaring open at the neck in exaggerated imitation of the miner, although they never swung a single jack." More experienced hands predicted the early death of these greenhorns from pneumonia "as the result of exposing such a remarkable expanse of cuticle to the mercy of the elements." Miles found an equal measure of humor in the mining promoters who had not so much as a post hole in their mines but thrust candle sticks in their high-laced boots and sprinkled their khakis with candle grease as though just returned from a prolonged tour of the most extensive underground diggings.[15]

The English novelist Elinor Glyn, on the other hand, offered no such sly criticisms after her encounter with the young manhood of Goldfield on a visit to the city. Indeed her breathless description of their "splendid" faces and physiques and "courtly" manners was enough to make the most modest tenderfoot swagger to the mirror and expose a few more inches of cuticle to the desert breezes. "The types thrilled me," said Glyn. "Infinitely better bred-looking than any I have seen elsewhere in America, and some extraordinarily good looking. . . . they might all have been princes and dukes by their manners. . . . There among them were the most complete specimens of what we call breeding in England, that indescribable balance of limb and slenderness exemplified in a race horse—lithe and lissome, and their throats coming from the unfettered blue flannel shirts, with the points of the collars sticking up and no tie, showed proportions of young gods—but purely English type." Moreover, Glyn thought these glorious specimens of manhood neither "vulgar" nor "the least bit middle class or pretentious," and she could detect "not the slightest smell of common people or 'fustian'" about them.[16] (A good deal more fustian might have pervaded the atmosphere if Glyn's visit had not postdated the days when water was so scarce that a man inquiring at a Goldfield establishment which advertised baths was given a ticket labelled number 813 and told that he would receive his turn in several weeks.)

In addition to these godlike young adventurers who so impressed the British novelist, the passage of fifty years, during which two generations had matured in the West, had undoubtedly produced a larger proportion of older men in the Goldfield population than had been present at the California placer country. In fact, some who had participated in Nevada's first mining boom on the Comstock still had enough strength and will to take part in her last. De Wolf called these oldsters a familiar sight on the Goldfield streets: "a coterie of hale and hearty old fellows, relics of the breezy, bullion days of Comstock; sturdy veterans these who have played the game for years and who risk their all on the turn of a card or the result of a round of shots with equal sang-froid, and speak of retrieving their fortunes with the same buoyancy and hope as they did in the days before the hand of time had frosted their locks."[17]

The most remarkable gentleman among the older set may well have been ninety-five-year-old Frank Healey, an Irish immigrant and veteran of the Civil War and the Comstock, as well as sundry other events, who set himself up in business as an auctioneer in Goldfield. Healey attributed his remarkable vigor and longevity to vegetarianism, refusing to worry about his debts, smoking only the best cigars, enjoying a "little drop of whiskey" without guzzling, and other good habits. Upon his arrival in town, he issued a challenge to any Goldfielder aged seventy-five or over to meet him in a mile race. Some months later when a sand twister roared down Main Street like a cyclone, sending all bystanders dashing for cover, the press reported that Healey's fast sprint into the fire house ahead of the twister would have done credit to a youngster. If none of the older residents felt able to match his fleetness of foot, Healey also declared himself ready to take on any of them in a boxing match, for which he offered to put up a five hundred dollar purse himself. Apparently there were no takers.[18]

Just as older citizens were more numerous in Goldfield than in the earliest camps, so too were children. In 1908 the school board estimated the number of school age children at 1,500 and the entire under-twenty-one age group at 5,000, which would have meant children comprised at least one-third of the town's population. Even allowing for the evident fact that some children worked instead of attending school, the fact that school enrollment never reached 700 casts some doubt on the board's estimate. Still, it is clear that children were no longer such treasured rarities as they had been among miners suffering the pangs of separation from their families in pioneer California.

Apart from reportage on school exercises, Goldfield's children most often appeared in the news in connection with their misdeeds. Under the state's new juvenile laws, law officers hauled some into justice court and placed them on probation for petty thievery or for pelting passersby with snowballs and rotten eggs and apples. Less serious pranks included hitching rides on the backs of freight wagons, at the risk of a flick from the driver's whip, sending Goldfield's large mongrel dog population howling away with dynamite cartridges exploding at their heels in celebration of the Fourth of July, and capturing wild burros at their favorite grazing ground at the city dump for some wild and ructious rides over the hills. Like children in previous mining camps, Goldfield youngsters showed some tendency to pursue the vices of their elders. In 1908 the county commissioners ordered the sheriff to suppress gambling in saloons by youths less than fourteen. Apparently a fifteen-year-old was considered an adult entitled to risk his stake as he pleased like any other man.[19]

In his careful study of childhood in the Rocky Mountain mining camps, Elliott West concludes that this attitude may have represented the survival on the frontier of an early nineteenth-century American social tradition allowing children of fifteen or even less to cross the boundary into the adult world, co-existing with the newer conception of childhood as a special stage of life requiring the protection of society through the new juvenile laws. The adult world of the mining booms was one that George McDevitt, the Goldfield "boy prospector," had entered early. Like other prospectors several times his age, he hastened forth on his own to every new mining excitement in the region, traveling "any old way he could." Before he was old enough to vote, the "boy prospector" had already made and lost his first thousand-dollar stake. Several other youthful prospectors occasionally received mention in the press.

Another child on his own in the adult world was fourteen-year-old Walter Cresswell, a Pittsburgh orphan, who arrived with three hundred dollars in hard-earned capital to open a newsstand in Goldfield, where he had heard that most newsboys were "mutts" who "don't know de game." His first view of Goldfield upon alighting from the train clearly did not measure up to young Cresswell's expectations. "Dis burg soitny looks on de bum," he was quoted as saying. "W'y we got buildings in Pittsburgh you could put de whole town into." He nonetheless expressed confidence in "coppin' out de coin" in Goldfield, and despite some resistance from the existing newsboy fraternity to this aggressive new arrival, he probably succeeded.[20] As Cresswell's story illustrated, the newsstand provided a common avenue of business opportunity for children in the city. The entertainment of this enterprising group of youngsters at holiday time, with Christmas dinners and perhaps an auto ride, was Goldfield's most deeply rooted charity.

Like children, Goldfield's women comprised a small proportion of the population in the early years and rapidly increased thereafter. The 1910 census still showed a male-female ratio in Esmeralda of slightly less than two to one, but during the height of the boom, the disparity may have approached twenty to one, according to a press estimate. So far as can be determined, the first white woman in Goldfield was Mrs. George Kernick, who prospected the district on foot with her husband. The second to arrive on the scene was Dr. Frances Williams, a tightly corseted middle-aged woman of stern appearance, with hair tightly knotted atop her head, a thin roll of bangs, and large fierce dark eyes. Perhaps it was a clear sign of the times that one of the first women in the camp, reputedly present but not signing at the organization of the district, was not a stereotypical frontier harlot, with or without a heart of gold, but rather an independent entrepreneur as tough, unscrupulous, and aggressively ambitious as any of the men surrounding her. Mining was just the latest of Williams' entrepreneurial ventures. She had entered the adult world early as a child supporting her invalid mother. Married young to a varnish manufacturer many years her senior, she bore him two children and successfully endeavored, with both account books and laboratory phials, to recoup his failing business. The couple's retirement to Florida lasted only until a killing frost ruined the crop in their orange groves. Then, at the age of forty, the indomitable Williams became a physician specializing in "electric medicine," one of the bogus sciences that endangered patients' lives in the nineteenth century, and built up a lucrative practice in San Francisco. She went on to mining promotions in California, where her husband eventually died.

By the summer of 1904, when most local mining promoters had barely started sharpening their pencils, Williams was already scooping up the first crop of dollars from gullible investors with her impressively printed prospectuses on "Affiliated Corporations," a promotion of coal lands in the barren desert some distance northwest of Goldfield, and the "St. Frances" mining company, which she grandly declared had been "incorporated pursuant to Act of United States Congress approved by the president." The *Tonopah Bonanza* subsequently questioned several aspects of the Williams Goldfield promotion, which boasted of ore contracts far in excess of any yet signed in the district and assays showing high values in silver that seemed slightly unusual for a gold camp; Williams' promises of free land and lifetime employment to investors in Affiliated Corporations also came under reportorial scrutiny. The expose of "St. Frances's" promotional mendacities created such a sensation that every issue of the newspaper sold out and Williams sued the *Bonanza* for fifty thousand dollars. The editor could at least consider it lucky that he had inflamed the Williams temper less than did Goldfield attorney Henry Lind (offense unknown), against whom Williams drew a pistol the following year. She was placed under bonds to keep the peace. [21]

Others among the contingent of pioneer women who followed came closer to the model of the sunbonneted helpmate than Williams. Though three-quarters of the original organizers of the district listed themselves as unmarried, the wives of several early settlers broke the ice on the water barrels, "smoothed the wrinkles from the grim visage of poverty," swept the snow from tent floors during the first winter, and were afterward ignored, while the men beside them basked in renown as the pioneers of Goldfield. Were these unappreciated "homebuilders" not also "partners in hardship and adversity, sterling, cheerful and generous?" inquired the society editor of the *Goldfield Chronicle* with some asperity in a retrospective article. Far from being reluctant partners in the hardships of the early days, many of these spirited housewives apparently had prodded their

Christening a mine was a festive occasion for celebrants of both sexes. The small number of women in this photo probably reflected their proportion of the boomtown population (Larson Collection, Nevada State Museum)

husbands to pull up stakes for Goldfield. Loftus, for one, wrote of his wife: "She is a brave little body and is entirely willing to cast her fortunes with me in Tonopah or Goldfield, and brings the matter up every day." Anne Ellis, one of those who had persuaded her miner husband to try his luck in Goldfield, remembered "not so many women" on the journey to Goldfield "but what there were, were more excited than the men."[22]

As Goldfield developed into a full-fledged mining community, the usual female occupations on the frontier, prostitutes, waitresses, cooks, laundresses, school teachers, nurses, clairvoyants, and so forth, were soon fully represented. Sometimes women could not be neatly pigeonholed by occupation, as when part-time prostitution by Goldfield housewives erupted into scandal in 1907 (Emmett Arnold, the young drifter who operated a lunch wagon in the tenderloin district for awhile, noted that the husbands of these women viewed prostitution as acceptable because "in the code she wasn't cheating if she collected for it"). Constable Claude Inman later estimated that at one time five hundred girls worked in the tenderloin district Goldfielders remembered as a "city onto itself." About fifty of these had been commandeered from San Francisco and forced to prostitute themselves in Goldfield bordellos under conditions approaching white slavery. But, noted the constable with satisfaction, "they all got away."[23]

Other cyprians came voluntarily. Some had been born into houses of ill repute in the "dregs of the big cities." Many others had been recruited by paid agents in San Francisco and Los Angeles who promised them high salaries for their services as entertainers, singers, and dancers at establishments similar to the elegant California hotels where cultivated patrons listened to music during the dinner hour. When they crossed the thresholds of the Goldfield dance halls, they found a different scene from the hostelries of refinement that they had anticipated. A few turned on their heels and marched indignantly to the railroad station or the district attorney's office. A good many more stayed on, attracted by high earnings for hustling drinks and dances. The story that one popular lady from Alaska earned five hundred dollars on corkage alone in a single night may have been an exaggeration, but Arnold recalled that dance hall girls often "made more than highgraders." Some eventually came to deserve the nastiest gibe in the dance halls—"she lays on her backside for every dollar she makes"—and ended up in the crude board cribs extending up the hill or in the bordellos.

The proprietresses of two of these bordellos reflected backgrounds of surprising refinement. George Springmeyer remembered the stunningly beautiful madam, with soft brown eyes and dark brown hair, whom he met in the course of his legal work as "clever and cultivated"—adjectives that an intellectual educated at Stanford and Harvard did not lightly bestow. Old timers who witnessed Goldfield's years of decline spoke of another madam, tall, blond, and "wonderful looking," not born in a brothel but a minister's daughter from a distinguished Eastern family. A crisis occurred each time the good reverend announced plans to visit his daughter at her Western home, which he undoubtedly envisaged rather differently from a red velvet draped bordello. Hurriedly the madam would pack her bags and "hightail it back East" to forestall his arrival. Apparently her family never learned the truth.[24]

It would, however, be a mistake to assume that because the town was dominated by a single industry the working female populace, aside from teachers and nurses, either engaged in sexual commerce or in outside jobs such as cooking or washing that replicated their household tasks. In fact, owner of a dance hall, a restaurant, or a small hotel—and Goldfield had women in all these positions—did not represent the height of female aspiration, and women also appeared in a variety of careers far removed from either the sexual or the domestic. The city had at least two practicing woman attorneys, a woman dentist, and two or three woman doctors, one of whom specialized in treating women and children. Williams, though possibly the least scrupulous, was just one of a number of women mining entrepreneurs, including a trained mining engineer. Bessie Miller, another example, not only invested in mining claims but also hiked fifteen miles into the desert in the heat of midsummer to locate some placer claims and returned the same day; she was reported to possess "immense holdings." Others, like the woman who financed a Goldfield office building, invested in fields other than mining. It appears probable that most in this group, like Williams, were widows of mature age no longer concerned with caring for small children or homemaking for a husband.

Although no evidence has been uncovered indicating that Goldfield women worked in the mines, they occasionally turned up in male-dominated occupations ordinarily considered too physically demanding for the "weaker sex." Mrs. S. H. Ferris, for one, was a woman teamster driving her own freighting wagon and team. She met an untimely death while making camp on the Goldfield to Bullfrog run in December 1904. As she drew the loaded gun she kept with her from the wagon, it accidentally discharged into her left breast, killing her instantly. [25]

In the white-collar field, the rapid change that would alter the American clerical force to mostly female by 1920 was well underway in Goldfield, where so many women secretaries worked in the large law firms and brokerage houses that the IWW attempted to organize them as a unit of the One Big Union. The county commissioners, however, resisted the forward thrust of women secretaries with an announcement that male candidates, as bread winners, would receive preference for a courthouse clerical position. This "pure and unadulterated prejudice against women as public employees which savors of a primitive age" prompted an angry protest in the *Goldfield Chronicle* from a woman and provided a rare glimpse of the difficulties faced by many working women in the city: "Does not the honorable chairman know that hundreds of good and well educated women are struggling in Goldfield to support their families? . . . There is a pretty tradition that women should constitute the ornamental part of creation, and men should gladly work to support them and preserve this Utopian condition. . . . But, unfortunately, when it comes to a practical test, men . . . are mostly averse to burdening themselves with the wants of sisters, mothers and daughters, and not infrequently shirking the support of a wife and children. This is in part the fault of this luxurious age, and has driven many an already overworked wife and mother to the wash-tub to piece out an insufficient income—that is insufficient for the calls of the saloon and gaming table and dance hall, not leaving enough for bread and clothes. I do not suppose the honorable board of county commissioners have any sentimental objection to a woman at the wash-tub, it is only at clerical positions and other easy jobs that men should have the first chance." [26]

It should nonetheless be noted that this tug of war over the courthouse position was the only instance that has yet emerged in which prejudice barred the door to the working woman. More often, Goldfielders applauded women like Bessie Miller for their pluck when they moved into predominantly male fields. If the fundamental question on whether the frontier proved as liberating for women as for men is posed in Goldfield, the answer appears essentially affirmative. This may have been partially due to the survival on the frontier of the old colonial attitude accepting women in a broad variety of occupations because their "proper" role had not yet been narrowly defined, combined with the new occupational trends of the late nineteenth century. In Goldfield, both these old and new tendencies flowed together with liberating results. The city contained many homemakers for whom the move into this remote desert region in search of better fortune was a pioneering endeavor shared with a husband; the rise of the woman clerical force and the early inroads of the woman professional were part of a trend generally shared throughout the nation; but the multifarious activities of the women mining entrepreneurs, beginning with Williams, clearly suggest that some women independently took advantage of Goldfield's new economic opportunities in the same manner as men. [27]

There are certain indications that Goldfield women had a tough-fibered streak that differentiated them from the submissive hand-wringing model of Victorian womanhood that still prevailed in much of the country. When Mrs. Archibald, the hefty proprietress of the Imperial Restaurant, received a report that the chef had used a crass epithet toward one of her waitresses, she seized the horse whip kept in a corner of the dining room for such emergencies and gave the cook a striping around the back and the legs. Five men arose to assist her, but as the offender retreated out the back door with the whip snapping around him, they quickly saw that Mrs. Archibald had no need of assistance. "It won't do for any man to insult one of my women here," she declared with finality, and no one present in the Imperial was inclined to dispute her.

Other instances abound. May Phenix, wife of one of the earliest settlers, shot an attorney involved in a property dispute with her husband, George, while that same husband cowered in the background urging her on. Sometimes, instead of protecting a timid husband, Goldfield matrons battled with each other. One such cat fight erupted when Mrs. Phoebe Jones objected to Mrs. Nancy Harris's habit of sweeping the dirt from her back lot onto the Jones property. Combat with brooms and vigorous hair pulling ensued, and soon "enormous quantities" of hair flew around the premises. According to the *Goldfield News*, "Mrs. Jones came in with a left hook to Mrs. Harris' pompadour, Mrs. Harris retaliating with an upper-cut to Mrs. Jones' rat" before police arrived to stop the battle. In justice court the next day, spectators erupted into unrestrained hilarity when "about ten pounds" of raven tresses were introduced into evidence to show the amount of damage done to the Jones coiffure by Harris. [28]

Such evidence would not have been possible had not long luxuriant locks, worn in bouffant upsweeps and supplemented with hairpieces, been the style for women just after the turn of the century. Comparably fashionable clothing also prevailed in Goldfield, even though the rigors of the frontier situation might suggest more utilitarian garb. Merrill advised women embarking for the new camp to wear heavy shoes, a cool dress of "good serviceable material" without a white collar or cuffs, and for protection against the blistering sun, a "wide-rimmed, high-peaked sombrero." Like women everywhere, Goldfield women generally disregarded such sensible advice, to the occasional mystification of proponents of practicality in feminine attire. One miner reportedly described his wife's elaborate new Easter bonnet to his cronies in the following familiar terms: "It resembled very much a roof garden, only the electric lights were missing. The framework was a sort of Fink truss, with a pitch of about 60 degrees. . . . There were a few drifts and crosscuts around the outskirts, but they looked more like assessment work to me than actual development, and I thought probably the workers had gotten disgusted and quit work after running along a couple of months. Looked as though one part of it might have been a good placer, though, and I am sure if it had been panned one could have gotten a color." [29]

Such, then, was the population of Goldfield: rising to a peak abrupt as Columbia Mountain's in the boom years of 1906–07 and afterward sloping downward in similarly rapid decline, racially almost homogeneous, ethnically predominantly native American and north European, with a preponderance of adventurous young men bound by shared experiences at earlier mining booms in Colorado and the Yukon, and a set of equally enterprising and adventurous women. When the men who evoked so rapturous a description from Elinor Glyn met the women Goldfield observers firmly believed were the choicest crop of beauties collected anywhere, the results could be more easily predicted than the outcome of any prospect hole in the mining district.

VII

From the Pretty
Little Cottage to Boot Hill

LOVE AND DEATH

"She knew her charms. She knew Goldfield was a mecca for the rich and adventurous. To hunt, you go where the game is. . . . And she would know that once she'd found her man she'd nail him. Women are the realists of this world. They get what they go after." Emmett L. Arnold, Gold-Camp Drifter 1906–1910.

⏤⏤⏤⏤◆•◆⏤⏤⏤⏤

She was a stunning brunette in her early twenties, petite, curvaceous, and tastefully dressed in a tailored gray suit, and her proposition was decidedly unusual. Would Emmett Arnold, then a young messenger boy in Goldfield, act as her dinner escort that evening? Anyone they met would be told that their families were long-time friends in San Francisco. Arnold readily assented.

All eyes were riveted on the lady as they entered one of Goldfield's poshest restaurants. "Maybe she was beautiful," Arnold later reflected. "Maybe her regal calm gave the impression of beauty. Or maybe the compelling attraction was her poise, her carriage, and what shone from her serene face and level gray-green eyes." Presently the restaurant manager, also purporting to be an old friend of the lady's family in San Francisco, brought a wealthy mining entrepreneur over to their table to be introduced. As this scene was repeated several times over the next few weeks, Arnold inferred that the restaurant manager had a business relationship with the lady, probably ten dollars a head for each eligible man he introduced. Arnold's own role was to "lend respectability to her presence at a place where unescorted females were labeled." For this he received five dollars a date, a fine dinner, and as much champagne as he could imbibe while the lady made sparkling conversation with her new acquaintances.

She told Arnold nothing about herself, but he managed to piece her story together from an occasional clue dropped in unguarded moments. Despite her gentile and regal air, she was a poor girl from a "grubby small town" in the Bay Area. He guessed that she had staked her entire legacy, perhaps the sale of the family home after the death of her parents, on the Goldfield gamble. He also inferred that her bankroll had run low by the time she met a mining engineer in his thirties with lucrative interests in Goldfield and Tonopah, as well as Alaska. Whenever Arnold saw the couple around town together, the lady appeared to fully reciprocate the engineer's obvious adoration. When she presently boarded the train to travel north with her admirer, Arnold was certain she did so as his wife, and inwardly he wished her well. "I trust that she found the happiness a straight-shooting courageous gambler deserves."[1]

Newspaper stories suggest that this was by no means an unusual Goldfield romance. In fact, at a short remove from an age when many young women on the farming frontier felt compelled to marry the first suitor who presented himself, Goldfield women exercised striking independence in seeking out and choosing their husbands. The *Goldfield Chronicle* noted: "They get too independent with so many desert millionaires fawning at their feet. They play with the matrimonial candidates like a kitten plays with a mouse. They often get totally imperious and tell the Bills and Jacks of this golden burg to get out and augment their reputation before talking matrimony to them."[2] Goldfield abounded with "grass widows," a term which in those days signified a woman whose husband had disappeared by mutual consent; one of these frankly admitted to a newspaper reporter that the grass widow's object in coming to Goldfield was "to look for husbands and get married of course." Husband hunting seems to have been tolerantly regarded. It was, after all, an age when homemaking was regarded as the normal feminine role and matrimony as the suitable culmination of romance. And if the grass widows clearly preferred husbands of means, mercenary motives needed little justification among a mining camp's host of fortune seekers.

Whatever their aims, Goldfield's stylish and beautiful women drew wide admiration as they glided along the board sidewalks "radiant in all the colors of the rainbow like living symphonies in silk and lace." More unmarried couples may have been living together than our image of early twentieth century morals leads us to suppose—Sewall Thomas recalled that many rich Goldfielders "acquired wives with or without benefit of clergy." But it was generally believed that matrimonial quests met with more uniform success than other forms of prospecting in the district. The *Chronicle* stated it plainly: "There are no compulsory old maids in Goldfield."[3]

Those who attempted to order a Goldfield spouse by mail—and city officials frequently received such letters from both sexes—probably fared less well. A young (at least, so she said) New York widow wrote to Sheriff William Ingalls requesting him to "please try and get me a nice respectable man who would appreciate a good wife and companion. Of course he must have a little money. . . ." The sheriff declined this mission on the ground that he had more experience in hunting for runaway husbands than in matchmaking. Another young woman of Pony, Montana, describing herself as a 150 pound brunette "of Yankee decent," attempted to requisition a husband in as cut and dried a fashion as if she were placing an order through the Sears catalogue. In a letter to the city clerk, she set forth the specifics for her desired mate: "Height medium or a little over, dark brown or black hair, large blue eyes, weight 168–180 pounds, able to give me a good home and a good position; must have a profession of some sort. . . . Be sure and not have the gent under 25 or over 40; want him to have a good education. . . ."[4]

An eligible bachelor in Goldfield answering this description was more likely to return to his former hometown and marry the girl he left behind him than to enter into correspondence with the lady in Pony, Montana. The newspapers frequently reported these weddings, but sometimes a suitor postponed his return too long. One Goldfield mine owner journeyed back to the childhood sweetheart from whom he had parted in Minnesota six years earlier and literally dangled before her eyes a necklace made of gold nuggets from his mine—all to no avail. She had irrevocably given her heart to another. Sometimes the girl a Goldfielder left behind him was not one to stay behind. On the streets of Goldfield, Esmeralda County Assemblyman Tom Tighe was surprised to encounter Mary Kardona, a clairvoyant he had known several months earlier in the Alaskan. A story book denouement swiftly followed their encounter in the street: "The old love being instantly rekindled, arrangements were made for the wedding ceremony." The new Mrs. Tighe needed no psychic powers to predict the kind of shivaree that awaited them from the Nevada legislature.

For those like Assemblyman Tighe who found brides in Goldfield, an elopement was much in vogue. "They would have had my consent," the father of one runaway bride ruefully observed, "but I suppose they wanted to mix a little romance in their wedding." The impulsive madcap flavor of a sudden wedding was indeed regarded as irresistibly romantic. The union of Ruth Ward, described in the *Goldfield News* as a "bud of sunny Tennessee," and Horace Fuller, an attorney and a fellow Southerner, provided a case in point. The pair met for the first time at a dinner party at the home of friends. When the host jocularly asked Ward why she hadn't married, the blushing girl responded that no one had asked her. Fuller at once rose to this gambit and proposed. A hack was ordered forthwith, and the wedding party rousted the justice of the peace out of his bed at midnight to grunt "rather sudden" at the young couple, while beaming at them in the best traditions of such scenes. The Fullers then took up residence in what the press invariably described as a "pretty little cottage," where one hopes they did not live to repent at leisure.[5]

Not every romance ended in a pretty little cottage, as Frank Crampton's reminiscence of the girl he loved and lost in the Goldfield tenderloin memorably attests. Scion of a wealthy New York family, Crampton had traveled west in search of adventure and set up an assay office in Goldfield in the late summer of 1906. Soon he became deeply involved with a prostitute plying her trade in one of the tiny wooden cribs "on the line." She refused to tell him anything about herself, but the lovers apparently found a great many other things to discuss. Though Crampton well knew that after his departure she would pull up the shade and stand waiting in the window for the next customer to saunter down the line, something about her manner and her composure made him feel as though he was visiting in her home, and for a time the rough realities around them could be forgotten. Before long Crampton was spending a part of every evening with the girl and paying more than double the price for her time. The weeks slipped past, but eventually an evening arrived when he hurried down the line to find another soiled dove in her crib. His girl, the girl with no name, had vanished without warning or explanation.

When Crampton was stricken during the pneumonia epidemic that winter, his friends brought him to Oakland, California, to recuperate. Gradually he grew strong enough to make reluctant appearances at the social entertainments held by one of his aunts. Amidst the stodgy formality of one of these affairs, he was astonished to meet a beautifully garbed society matron and mother of three children last seen against the crude board walls of a mining camp crib – "the girl from Goldfield." Crampton's aunt responded to his subsequent inquiries with a stream of invective. This terrible woman had deserted her husband when he was accused of embezzlement, then returned as soon as his accounts were put in order.

Crampton of course kept his own counsel as to just how those accounts were set right, but he engineered two waltzes with the lady at his aunt's New Year's Eve ball, the last being the midnight dance when 1906 turned into 1907: "Then it came time for the old and new year dance. . . . I held her tighter, and she rested her arm on my shoulder a little heavier. Our hands held each other's more firmly and once in a while there was pressure from one to the other. Nothing more. There was no way to say what I had wanted to say, or what I had in my mind to ask. As we danced the old year ended and the new year came; the past was gone." After recovering from his illness, Crampton permanently left Goldfield because the camp would "bring back memories that I preferred to forget."[6] Some romances that began in the tenderloin lasted longer than Crampton's. Rumor had it that several prominent stockbrokers married women from the red light district, but in the city renowned for its dizzying transformations, newly crowned queens of society with dubious antecedents could rely on Goldfielders to mind their own business.

For those couples whose love affairs progressed to the altar, blissful domestic tranquility did not invariably ensue. Although relatively few battered women were willing to bring charges, public prosecutors acknowledged that "the beating of women is altogether too common in Goldfield" and announced their determination to put a stop to these incidents. To this end, they activated an old 1877 state statute providing that husbands convicted of assault and battery against their wives would spend thirty days chained to a post on a public street wearing a placard that read "woman beater." The press reported that two of the offenders convicted upon these charges were "scathingly excoriated" by the courtroom spectators and the prosecuting attorney, who declared: "The wife beater is the most despicable and despised creature that infests the face of the earth, a contemptible ignominious coward who has not the courage to face a man but to gratify his lust for bestial cruelty picks a woman, and of all others his own wife, upon whom to vent his diabolical instinct." [7]

Sometimes domestic violence escalated to shooting and even death. One fourteen-year-old boy shot and wounded his father in a desperate effort to stop him from beating his mother (lawmen arrested the father but not the teenager). The only woman to actually die at her husband's hands was a middle-aged housewife named Tillie Sheridan who tried to arouse her bartender spouse from his drunken slumbers in time for work. Enraged by her persistence, Jack Sheridan leapt from his bed with a threat to "stick your head in the stove and keep it there" and advanced menacingly upon her; she smashed a coal shovel over his head and attempted to flee. Unfortunately, the screen door at the back of the house was locked, and Tillie Sheridan's struggle with the latch delayed her escape just long enough for her husband to plunge a breadknife into her back, piercing her heart and killing her almost instantly. [8]

Just once did a woman turn upon her husband with lethal effect, and on that occasion, the cause was not abusive behavior but anger over a love grown cold. When Webb Parkison, a brilliant young stockbroker of "dash and judgment" who had amassed a fortune from nothing inside the span of two years while still in his twenties, and the tall dark Spanish-looking dancer who called herself Bonita (though she was actually the convent-educated daughter of a prominent rural Wisconsin family of German extraction) embarked upon a love affair, even Parkison's disapproving friends could not have foreseen that the end would come in a blaze of bullets.

In the beginning, many men envied Parkison. The variety theaters in the tenderloin that featured Bonita's sensational performances were always thronged with customers eager to watch her "gay sways and fetching costumes" and to shower the beautiful, sinuous, and voluptuous dancer with silver. Though several prominent Goldfielders fell in love with her, the only one whose passion she returned was Parkison, dark haired, handsome, and clean-shaven, with a high forehead, a long straight nose, and rather cold eyes. Whether the couple actually married remains doubtful, but Bonita, though "jealous of her profession," abandoned dancing to live with Parkison. He entered the brokerage business in San Francisco, dividing his time between Goldfield and the Bay Area. The couple set up housekeeping in Oakland, where Parkison's beautiful and cultivated wife became an ornament to local society and a baby boy was born to them. Then the idyll ended. Parkison's fortunes, with those of many other brokers, blew away in the 1907 stock market crash and the baby died at five months, breaking his mother's heart.

Returning with Parkison to Goldfield, Bonita began investigating rumors concerning the suicide of a young woman whose name had been linked to her husband's and attempting to persuade the newspapers to publish a photo of her with her baby in which she would be publicly acknowledged as Parkison's wife. Her husband, for his part, brazenly disported himself with a succession of new inamoratas, whom he brought to their apartments in Bonita's presence; the neighbors often overheard loud quarrels through the walls.

Newspapermen who came in contact with Bonita during this period of increasing desperation formed opposite impressions of her character. The *Goldfield Tribune* viewed her as a "harpy," a "consort of inferior station," a "succubus," and a "crouching tigress" who had inveigled Parkison into marriage and was bleeding him to desperation with her "extortionate demands" for money; the editor of the *News* (while also regrettably refusing to publish her photograph) saw the former toast of the tenderloin more sympathetically as a victim of unrequited love, a tragic madonna of "modest and refined" demeanor, now black-garbed, with sorrowful dark brown eyes above prominent cheekbones in a thin and ravaged face. Whatever Parkison's own assessment of Bonita's state of mind, it led him to empty the cartridges from his revolver before leaving it on the dresser.

The *Tribune* thought he seriously underestimated Bonita: "His wife had not lived the rough and tumble existence of the west to be cheated in this childish manner." In the course of the day, Bonita purchased cartridges and reloaded the gun. She wrote in a private letter to a friend in Berkeley: "The two terrible crisis—the loss of my darling son, God bless him, and the unfaithfulness of my husband—have wrecked my future life. . . . I have almost lost my senses. . . . Webb knows how I am suffering, but his heart has turned to stone, and he has forgotten all that I have been to him and done for him." She sent her regards to the "ladies of the club."

That evening Parkison, loosely quoting Shakespeare, had just typed to a business associate who wondered if he was still active in mining finance the ironic line "I know that you have decided that I am dead, but such is not the case not even sleeping. . . ." before stepping into the apartment behind his office to be instantly killed by a rain of bullets from Bonita. He died with a smile on his face, perhaps a trace of the mocking assumption that the revolver aimed at him by his wife was still unloaded. The last bullet Bonita saved for herself, but although she rejected all medical assistance and firmly expressed her desire to die, she lingered on for two agonizing days of internal hemorrhaging. The steely stays of her whalebone corset had slightly deflected the bullet she aimed at her own heart from its intended course.[9]

When marital discord erupted, the more civilized solution was divorce. The frequency of divorce had been steadily rising throughout the nation to the point that by 1906 one in every twelve marriages ended in divorce and divorces were increasing three times as fast as the American population. While Illinois led the nation in the total number of divorces granted during the previous twenty years, divorce had long been more common on the mining frontier than "back East." Nevada, with South Dakota as her closest rival, had started moving to the fore as the mecca for easy divorce, and what was later to become known locally as the "divorce business" was already well established in Reno. However, an occasional divorce seeker from out of state opted for Goldfield over the metropolis to the north. One J. W. Stoneburner, for example, who had thrice tried and failed to divorce his wife in two other states over a period of eleven years, arrived, with dogged persistence, to renew his quest in Goldfield.

Despite continued resistance from Stoneburner's wife, it is probable that he at last achieved the success that so long eluded him; among the outcomes of Goldfield divorce suits reported in the press, only one was denied. Apparently the prejudices of the court had considerable influence upon the results, and plaintiffs understandably preferred District Judge Peter Somers' "divorce mill" to the less tolerant scrutiny of Judge Theron Stevens. Of those divorce suits in which marriage dates were mentioned, two-thirds of the marriages had collapsed within eight years of the wedding, the largest number in the fourth through sixth years of marriage. Still, the duration of a blighted marriage sometimes ranged from two weeks to over twenty years, and the time frames indicated that shedding a spouse who had decamped was not always regarded as a matter of the utmost urgency. Henry Gallini, for instance, waited nineteen years before seeking a divorce from the wife who had deserted him after a month of marriage.[10]

Though such novel grounds for divorce as "incompatibility" were beginning to be heard in Reno, nearly three-quarters of the women divorce seekers in Goldfield based their complaints upon desertion, nonsupport, or a combination of the two, a pattern roughly in line with the nation as a whole, where desertion was the largest single complaint in divorce actions. A similar proportion of Goldfield's male divorce seekers charged their wives with desertion. It appears that nonsupport for wives was a matter of deliberate rejection rather than a harsh offshoot of poverty.

In part, the prevalence of desertion and nonsupport reflected the language of the divorce statutes and the judgments of attorneys on which complaints would be favorably received by local judges, but other factors also played a part. Some of these involved frontier realities: separation from wives who had not accompanied their husbands to Goldfield or husbands who drifted on to pursue a new will-o'-the-wisp no doubt contributed to the marital breakdowns; the mobile boom camp atmosphere fostered easy abandonment of family obligations; and the "flight from commitment" was a phenomenon by no means confined to the late twentieth century. But in all likelihood, a substantial portion of the complaints of desertion sprang from the disinclination of many couples to air their private affairs in public. It may be significant that although infidelity sometimes figured in Goldfield divorce suits as a justification for abusive behavior, and infidelity was then the second leading cause in American divorce suits brought by men, complaints of infidelity as the principal grounds for a Goldfield divorce case were extremely rare.

After desertion and nonsupport, cruelty loomed large in Goldfield divorce suits. Women brought three-quarters of sixty Goldfield divorce suits listed in the press, and of those in which the grounds appeared, a little less than a quarter were based upon cruelty, often in the form of drunkenness and physical violence. Men based an equal proportion of their divorce suits on cruelty. The behavior specified by these male divorce seekers often involved "vilification," "unbearable temper," "opprobrious language," "constant quarreling," and the like, but sometimes they complained of wives who threw crockery or otherwise threatened their lives. Billy Sherwin testified that his wife, Minerva, had prodded him with table forks and pitchforks, making his life "thoroughly miserable" (he received his divorce). John Wickerstroh, who, in Goldfield's impulsive fashion, had instantly married a girl named Mollie Yell to whom he "took a fancy" at a dance, declared his intention of seeking legal release from the "long nightmare" that had entangled him ever since. Soon after Wickerstroh built a home in Los Angeles with the small fortune he had made in Goldfield, his new mother-in-law "moved in and camped." Before long the tyrannous old lady was voicing her objections to everything Wickerstroh did, even forcing him to give up smoking. The final straw came when his bride and mother-in-law began waking him up in the morning by rapping him so forcefully over the head with a heavy sugar bowl that they nicked the bowl. Offering the chipped crockery as evidence of the cruel indignities he had suffered, Wickerstroh brought suit for divorce. [11]

Though most Goldfield divorce seekers preferred the neutral generalities of a desertion complaint to entertaining the public with stories of pitchforks and sugar bowls, a few divorces involving notable Goldfielders were scandalous enough to set tongues clucking even in the most tolerant of cities. Indeed divorce seems to have been fairly common among the Goldfield elite, and it was a safe assumption that the more prominent the parties, the more scandalous would be their divorce. January Jones, an important mine promoter whose entrepreneurial activities had been widely covered in the press during the camp's early years, was sued for divorce by his wife of three years, Lucile, on the ground that he had taken "the daughter of the vine to spouse." According to Lucile Jones, January had embarked upon a fifteen-month drinking spree and even during brief lapses of sobriety, during which he reverted to making money, had failed to provide for her support (divorce granted). [12]

Several divorces also occurred among the original pioneers present when the camp was organized. May Phenix, the formidable lady who had once fired a gun at her husband's enemies while he lurked behind her, eventually sued him for a divorce. Diamondfield Jack Davis, despite the image he had long cultivated for himself as a wealthy mine owner, faced a divorce suit from his wife, Minnie, who claimed that not only had he deserted her but also he had failed to provide her with the necessities of life and forced her to depend upon the charity of friends. And Harry Stimler made headlines with the titillating allegations of his divorce action against his wife, Queen. Stimler's charges that his slender fair-haired wife had been amusing herself with other men at dances, late suppers, and saloon wine rooms were soon splashed across local newspapers. Moreover, Stimler claimed that when he protested against his wife's "undue conduct" she threatened his life and reached for a revolver.

Conduct even more undue emerged in the divorce action brought by Nellie Johns against her husband, Robert, prominent attorney, mining investor, and another of the founding fathers of Goldfield. According to Nellie, her husband's cruelties commenced soon after their marriage in 1895 when she was eighteen and he was thirty-three; in a fruitless attempt to force a confession of infidelities from her lips, he had suspended her from a small boat over the waters of a deep lake. Life with Johns had not improved over the ensuing fourteen years. Her husband had physically attacked her invalid mother. Nellie and her mother (who evidently slept together) had been awakened at night by Johns standing over them with a long knife and advising them to say their prayers. Beyond expressing doubt that his wife sincerely loved him, Johns had little to say for himself and did not attempt to deny that while under the influence of liquor and drugs he had been "grossly indiscrete." So far as is known, the Johns case was the only Goldfield divorce action in which the influence of drugs became an issue. [13]

While drugs did not figure in the divorce suit that George Wingfield's first consort, May, brought against him in Tonopah, her complaint contained plenty of other juicy and scandalous tidbits. Wingfield was vindicated on every count. The court declared that he had not pistolwhipped May, beaten her with chairs and fists, kicked her, threatened her life at gunpoint, raped her, infected her with syphillis, informed her that he would buy any lawyer who took her case, nor announced that the judge would not dare to rule against him. Above all, back in the lean winter of 1902–03, when Wingfield still ran his game in the smoky haze of the Tonopah Club, he had never married the woman many believed was a lady of the line. Whatever the truth of May Wingfield's allegations, the case was to cast a longer shadow than the divorces of most prominent Goldfielders. Wingfield's fury over the scandalous personal charges made against him is generally believed to have played a large role in his protracted feud with May's attorney, future United States senator Patrick McCarran.[14] That feud was to long delay the ambitious McCarran's rise in politics until 1932, when the financial and political empire that Wingfield was building at last began to crumble.

The human casualties left behind by gold rushes on the mining frontier have not been fully computed. The wild excitement, inflated expectations, and careless bravado long celebrated in western lore were mirrored in the epidemic diseases, foreshortened lives, and violence that constituted the boomtown way of death. Reckless pursuit of wealth infected people in every walk of life. Businessmen refused to endanger their chance for wealth by acknowledging the existence of health problems in the camp. Miners disregarded the needs of their families to join the frenzy of speculation at the stock exchange. Gorgeously gowned grass widows, ignoring the garbage at their feet, paraded the city in search of rich husbands. All these, and legions more, showed indifference to building a safe and permanent community—and the unlucky ones paid the ultimate price.

When the so-called black plague struck, the dangers inherent in a gold rush could no longer be ignored, and some on their way to the new boom turned back, fearful to set foot in a city where death stalked the streets. A survivor of the epidemic in Tonopah described its symptoms as follows: "The mysterious death was like the bugaboos of a child's darkness—we couldn't see it nor say what it was.

"Perhaps your friend or bedfellow would look, startled, over his shoulder, and there grinning and leering was that devilish thing. . . . Then your friend's head would ache and his side would get painful and his lungs would get creaky and his heart rusty, and in a few hours he would gurgle in your face and die.

"Then his corpse would turn black and spotted . . . and you would have to bury it hurriedly. And perhaps you would be the next."[15]

Despite the alarm aroused by its inexorable spread, the mysterious malady was less exotic than these panicky descriptions made it appear. In fact, the same disease had ravaged Nevada mining camps for years and ranked as the nation's second leading killer at the turn of the century—influenza/pneumonia. The local press, fearing stories in outside newspapers might dampen prosperity, airily dismissed the epidemics. "Those who died would have died anywhere had they led the same lives they did in Goldfield," declared the *Tonopah Bonanza*, emphasizing the role played by alcoholism and exposure during cold weather. In a similar vein, the *Goldfield Tribune* mocked "stories of human beings piled up like cordwood in the streets." Erroneously believing that thousands had died, Goldfielders themselves placed little credence in this journalistic whistling in the dark. As Frank Crampton, one of the fortunate survivors of the 1906–07 epidemic, observed, it was "a humdinger and a lot of hard rock stiffs, and stiffs, went over the hill to whatever reward they had coming to them."[16]

Although pneumonia is a contagious disease spread by a variety of microorganisms, the causative agent is widely present in healthy persons. Not until such predisposing factors as alcoholism, exposure, or most commonly, another disease—such as influenza—weaken their resistance does pneumonia develop. Thus, living conditions in boomtown Goldfield undoubtedly fueled the epidemics. Influenza could spread among the crowds thrown in close contact in streets, saloons, and communal dwellings. In a tent or a drafty shack, shivering in the strong winds of a cold snowy winter, unable to light a fire in the midst of a fuel shortage, a gold rusher with influenza could readily contract pneumonia. Rich and poor alike shared such hardships because even the affluent could purchase few amenities in a boom camp when desperate men were stealing telephone poles for firewood.

The results of the boom camp way of life showed in great seasonal waves of epidemic disease. One pneumonia outbreak occurred in April and May 1905, and two others during the winters of 1904–05 and 1906–07, when exposure and cold weather undoubtedly played a role. Although there were no bodies stacked like cordwood in the streets and the black plague was less catastrophic than the subsequent 1918 influenza epidemic, pneumonia caused 80 percent of Goldfield's deaths in the worst epidemic month, November 1906, when the boom crested.

During the entire period from late 1904 to early 1909 for which records have been preserved, pneumonia accounted for a third of all deaths, by far the largest single cause. But, as the boom abated, so did the epidemics. In 1908 pneumonia was responsible for less than 10 percent of annual mortality. In 1910 officials reported only one pneumonia death in all of Esmeralda County. Improved living conditions for a decreasing population and the probable development of immunity to the current strain of the influenza virus may both have contributed to this result. Given the prominence of pneumonia in national mortality, the most startling observation to be made about Goldfield may not have been the initial presence of pneumonia there, but its eventual disappearance.

When the epidemics still ravaged the city, Goldfield's medical services dealt as best they could with the crush of patients. In 1905 a new county hospital replaced the tent that initially served as a "pest house." By late 1907, the WFM and the Catholic sisters had built two more hospitals. The city directory of the same year listed forty physicians, which meant a ratio of one doctor to each 375–450 residents, but the quality of medical care may nonetheless have been rather poor. In advance of an effective state licensing system, the training and competence of these physicians probably varied almost as widely as their counterparts in the days of '49. Moreover, even the best physicians lacked an effective treatment for pneumonia before the age of antibiotics. Dr. Simeon Lee, secretary of the Nevada State Board of Health, observed: "In the majority of cases, our best efforts result disastrously." No doubt recognizing the impotence of medical science, patients often turned to home remedies. For instance, Anne Ellis attributed her husband's recovery to keeping him "well plastered in onions."[17]

In a population heavily weighted with young men unlikely to contract the chronic diseases common to old age, infectious diseases predictably became the main killers, accounting for half of Goldfield's mortality. It is worth noting that this was the same proportion of death from infectious disease as in gold rush Sacramento, but while Sacramento's main killers were diarrheal disease, especially cholera, and unspecified fevers (probably yellow fever and malaria), respiratory disease was the leading cause of death in Goldfield. In contrast to the forty-niners, no one died of smallpox in Goldfield, where Dr. Lee found quarantined patients contentedly sunning themselves on the woodpile beside the set of tents serving as a pest house.

Tuberculosis, the leading killer in the nation at that time, was rare in the camp and the incidence of diseases predominantly associated with old age, such as cancer and cardio-and cerebrovascular illnesses, was far lower than in more stable communities. (Among today's much older American population, more than 80 percent of mortality is attributable to chronic disease.) The youthfulness of the population may explain the strikingly low incidence of chronic disease in Goldfield, but other factors also played a part. People suffering from chronic maladies may have avoided the rigors of the Goldfield adventure. Many of those who became ill at the camp probably returned to the families left behind in their home communities, sought better medical care in the Bay Area, or departed for a restorative sojourn at the California seashore.

Overall, adult women comprised a small part of Goldfield mortality (77 of 779) deaths, though as the population profile altered women's deaths rose slightly. As expected, women were more rarely victims of accident or homicide, but they showed a proportion of death from cardiovascular and cerebrovascular disease that nearly doubled the figure for men, and they were more than seven times more likely to die from cancer. Housewives were the largest occupational group and accounted for all the maternal mortalities and almost half the suicides. While pneumonia reaped more lives than any other single cause among women, as among all adult groups, the proportion that succumbed to respiratory disease was less than half the figure for men, perhaps because women remained so small a segment of the population during the pneumonia epidemics.

While the epidemics affected them less, the evidence indicates that mining camp life took an unusually harsh physical and psychological toll on women. The median age of death for Goldfield females was only twenty-five, compared to forty-one for men. This ran counter to national trends: in 1910 median age at death for American females reached almost forty-five, nearly three years above the figure for males.

Why did Goldfield women succumb at such an early age, fully twenty years younger than other American women? No doubt part of the answer lies in the age composition of the female population, but we should also consider the connections some researchers have drawn between health and the ability to predict and determine outcomes that enables individuals to cope with stress. While the enormous pressure entailed in gambling everything on Goldfield must have affected the health of both sexes, wives had the least control over events. Not only were they tied to the chaotic vicissitudes of a mining boom economy but also they depended upon sometimes irresponsible husbands. Domestic violence, the prominence of desertion and nonsupport in Goldfield divorce suits, and numerous homicidal fracases between husbands and "home wreckers" all hint at the erosion of families under gold rush conditions.

In place of the wealth of their fantasies, boomtown wives often found themselves more impoverished than ever. Anne Ellis, having purchased a large veil to wear in the new automobile that she anticipated her husband, Herbert, would buy when Goldfield made them wealthy, soon found herself in desperate circumstances. Though Herbert made good wages as a miner, high prices consumed all his earnings. Anne's various odd jobs from cook to seamstress did little to help. In short order, the couple lost their entire savings at the mining stock exchange: "Each day we studied the stock reports and each day we were disappointed. I was frantic to make money, and rebellious at so many around us getting rich. . . ." Far from buying themselves an automobile, the Ellises eventually realized their "white bread" days were behind them. Though many women like Anne Ellis came as eager partners in the Goldfield adventure, they often lacked a realistic conception of the difficulties ahead. The intense stress crushing these women showed in a percentage of suicide more than three times larger than the figure for men, a pattern also found in the earlier trans-Sierra mining camps, especially among prostitutes.[18]

The terrible psychological burden imposed by prostitution is unmistakably reflected in the fact that a third of the prostitutes in Goldfield's death records committed suicide, typically around the age of twenty-one, suggesting that the high level of suicide found among prostitutes from the Comstock to the Colorado mining camps underwent little change by the close of the frontier. Emmett Arnold observed, "The hectic, unnatural, often brutish life was hell on many of the girls who were not born to it." Many dance hall girls went into "crying jags" as the nights waned toward morning: "Their grievances covered a lot of ground. Pimp beat her up or snitched the bankroll to buy a new suit, but instead took a new gal on a binge. Maybe her lover boy was keeping her broke on a system to beat the wheel, a system, which, of course, never worked. Or trouble about a small son whom Aunt Susie back in Iowa was keeping. . . . Oh, there were lots of reasons."[19]

Suicide in the tenderloin (Police Gazette)

Sometimes the crying jags worsened into suicidal dejection. In one pathetic instance, a young prostitute from Texas who went by the name of Ray Raymond sank into despair over her lover's disappearance and shot herself in the head with a pistol; her body was laid to rest in the sandy earth of the Goldfield cemetery because her father refused to have his errant daughter returned to Texas for burial. In the tent cabins of the pioneer housewife, as well as the cribs of the tenderloin, what was then regarded as the "female inclination to morbidity" could take hold. All too often a housewife might end her life by quietly swallowing a lump of opium. It may be significant that no women working outside the home, other than prostitutes, took their own lives, raising the possibility that even menial jobs gave mining camp women a sense of self-esteem and mastery over their futures that acted as a powerful antidote to depression.

Like women, children under eighteen comprised an initially small sector of mortality that increased as Goldfield developed into a more normal community. In 1905 officials recorded only a handful of perinatal mortalities (stillbirths, and so forth), infant fatalities, and childhood deaths. By 1908 the figure had expanded to 27 percent of the year's roster, and in August children accounted for 69 percent of that month's dead. While influenza/pneumonia typically attacks children at a higher rate than adults but less often with fatal results, Goldfield children occasionally succumbed during the epidemics, or came perilously close. The parents of John Koontz told him that when he was an infant only a few months old suffering from pneumonia during the 1906–07 "black plague," the family physician had pronounced him dead. All the same, his mother refused to accept the verdict. By massaging the tiny chest and performing other ministrations after the doctor had left their tent, Ada Koontz saved her baby's life. Young John was at a highly vulnerable age, since perinatal fatalities and deaths of infants twelve months old or less accounted for nearly half of childhood mortality. In 1908 perinatal and infant mortality emerged ahead of respiratory disease as the leading cause of death in Goldfield, a reality considerably at odds with the myth that "they died with their boots on."

Predictably, infectious disease was the predominant killer of older children. Though meningitis claimed many victims, the worst single scourge for older children was diphtheria, which pioneer belief regarded as so inevitable a childhood calamity that children were sometimes deliberately exposed to it when considered healthy enough to survive. Nearly a third of the children over the age of one in the courthouse records died from diphtheria. Like many other Goldfield mothers, Anne Ellis was prostrated with grief after losing a young daughter to this terrible disease. Years later, on stormy nights when Ellis worried for her children, the thought that little Joy was not yet safe at home would still flash through her mind. [20]

In several respects, the elderly showed a mortality pattern similar to the young adult population. As with younger adults, respiratory disease was the largest single cause of death in the older group, and by a much larger proportion. This could possibly indicate that previous epidemics had conferred no significant immunity against the current strain of the influenza virus. The elderly group did, however, account for two-thirds of Goldfield's few cancer deaths and half of the deaths resulting from sunstroke or exposure to cold, suggesting more vulnerability to weather extremes than younger people. Other accidental deaths were somewhat lower among the elderly, and the percentage of suicides and homicide victims attained less than half the level among young adults. The oddest cause of death appearing in the courthouse records occurred among the elderly, the demise of a fifty-five-year-old man as a result of "eating library paste." (Whether this was a case of starvation or a bizarre craving remains a mystery.) The oldest mortality listed in Goldfield was that of a one hundred-year-old teamster, evidently not yet retired.

Previous work on other mining camps engenders the expectation that Goldfield's records should show a high rate of occupational disease among miners. Since the introduction of machine drilling in 1870, hard rock miners ingesting the sharp dust particles created by the drills had started to develop phthisis, or "miners' consumption." Research in one Colorado mining district after the turn of the century found phthisis wholly or partially responsible for nearly one-third of the deaths among miners and attributed more than half their fatalities to respiratory disease. Rates of lung disease among miners were three times those of the general adult population. [21]

Yet the Goldfield records do not suggest serious occupational disease on the Colorado model. Forty percent of mortality among Goldfield's miners was due to respiratory disease (primarily pneumonia), but this figure was 10 percent below the proportion of deaths from respiratory disease in a professional and white collar occupational group consisting of lawyers, stock brokers, and book keepers, among others. Moreover, the question of whether the term pneumonia might have masked chronic respiratory diseases with an occupational relationship to mining can be answered by looking at the changes over time. Chronic occupational maladies would not have shown the marked seasonal pattern noted in the influenza/pneumonia epidemics, nor would they have disappeared as the boom abated, even though mining continued to employ a large proportion of the work force. The scarcity of phthisis in the courthouse records makes it equally difficult to argue that occupational disease contributed substantially to miners' fatalities. Only nine deaths from tuberculosis (miners' consumption included) occurred among miners, or about 4 percent of their mortality, less than the proportion of tuberculosis among housewives or among the general population of the state. Lung cancer was virtually unknown.

Some caveats must be borne in mind. Labor historian Mark Wyman has suggested that many phthisis deaths were missing from mining camp statistics because the stricken miners left work and moved away. Also, in an era when life expectancy lingered below age fifty, many miners did not survive long enough to develop occupational diseases before being felled by the infectious diseases that were the primary causes of death. Nonetheless, their survival seems to have compared favorably with other occupational groups. Median age at death for miners was forty-five, which was almost the same as carpenters and teamsters, higher than the figure for professionals and white collar workers (thirty-seven), and much above the median for laborers (only thirty-two). In fact, miners' median age at death was substantially exceeded only by prospectors (median fifty-two), apparently the hardiest occupational group in the camp. [22]

Despite this relative longevity, no other prospector encompassed so many lifetimes as Hamilton Washington ("Saint") Gray. Prior to his residence in Goldfield, Gray had kept a saloon and desert emporium farther south, where he advertised "secondhand coffins" and purveyed fine wines and "repeater" mules, trained to kick off the packs of their purchasers and return to Gray for resale. When newspapers reported that Gray had died while visiting his Death Valley mining claims, the aged prospector announced that he had actually died and been reincarnated many times. Moreover, he was prolonging his present incarnation by an "elixir of life" he had discovered while traveling in Peru, though he acknowledged that the substance was a little hard on his stomach. With or without Peruvian elixir, the prospectors' mode of work probably contributed to their higher median age at death. For instance, it is possible that long periods spent in isolation in the desert spared them from many infectious diseases that might have shortened their lives if they had continuously resided in town.

Miners in Goldfield apparently died no younger than other occupational groups, prospectors excepted, but they differed significantly from the general population in the category of accidental death. Nevada did not tabulate statistics on mining injuries until after the office of Inspector of Mines was created in 1909, and even then, officials did not correlate injuries with the number of men employed. Nonetheless, in 1906, when the *Goldfield News* reported 1,400 unionized miners in Goldfield and estimated an additional 600 at work in the district, some conception of the extent of death in the mines can be developed. Eight fatal mining accidents, all individual episodes involving one or two people, occurred that year, giving Goldfield miners an occupational accident rate of at least 4.0 per 1,000, and perhaps as much as 5.7, compared to 3.0 per 1,000 for American railroaders and 1.5 for loggers. Even by the standards of the period, this was a serious rate of occupational fatality, substantially exceeding the rates for hard rock miners in Idaho, Colorado, and Montana (the figure for today's miners has happily plummeted to 30.1 per 100,000). [23]

Goldfield's high accidental death rate may have had a good deal to do with the character of mining in the district, where the leasing system had long prevailed. In their haste to obtain maximum profits within a limited period, leasers sometimes neglected to construct proper timbering and lapsed into other careless practices, with fatal results. On a passage through the Hayes-Monnette workings, reporter William McClure Gotwaldt noted "pitfalls beneath" and dangers overhead: "one must trust to cool-headedness, well shoddedness and the strength of the occasional rope wherewith to scale dizzy heights or swing across bottomless pits. He must cling to cribs, stulls and projecting rocks, candle in mouth. He must have confidence in God. . . ." [24] Yet the miners who coped with these perils on a daily basis apparently did not often fall into the "bottomless pits." Hoist accidents and cave-ins occurred more often, despite the absence of geological difficulties of the kind that made mining so hazardous in locales like Butte and the Comstock.

The heavy toll in the mines raised Goldfield's accidental deaths to 10 percent of total mortality, a substantially higher figure than in more stable communities. Other causes of accidental death dwindled to minor perils by comparison. Although guns were widely, albeit illegally, carried in Goldfield, gun-related accidents accounted for relatively few deaths. In one predictable case, a man was handling a revolver he wrongly supposed to be unloaded; in another, less predictable, a deputy sheriff, armed to the teeth and mounted upon a "very fractious" horse, dropped one of his three guns, fatally shooting a lovely young woman as she walked past in the street. A contributing factor in her demise was, of course, that essential means of transportation and ancient menace to human life, the horse. Accidents involving bolting horses caused an occasional fatality, as well as numerous injuries. That auto accidents, one day to loom so large in America's mortality, had as yet claimed no lives in Goldfield was apparently a matter of sheer good luck. For the time being, railroads remained the main source of transportation-related fatalities.

Although the worst effects of harsh weather appeared when cold winters tightened the grip of the epidemics, some deaths directly attributed to cold and exposure occurred, most in the early years. Heat stroke, or any variant of this diagnosis, was not a term used in the courthouse records, even in the case of a man in his fifties whose unwise decision to walk across the desert in the torrid heat of July brought about his death; it is thus strongly possible that the records conceal additional deaths due to heat stress under other causes such as heart disease. Death from malnutrition, by contrast, was noted but almost unknown, despite the shortage of both food and fuel in the winter of 1906–07. Food supplies seem to have been sufficient, even in the camp's first year, to preclude such gold rush era health problems as scurvy. In this respect, at least, the last boom camp benefited from the progress of Western settlement and transportation.

Succumbing to food poisoning from "ancient fowls and embalmed beef" was a stronger likelihood than malnutrition. The *Goldfield Chronicle* noted: "Meat is sold and served daily which is unfit for anything but carrion."[25] Cases of food poisoning became so frequent during the late summer and early autumn of 1907 that the *Chronicle* called for a popular boycott to discourage butchers from selling spoiled meat. Other causes for concern were the omnipresent flies, in combination with garbage, including dead animals, which Goldfielders often unloaded in the streets or on the outskirts of the city. Fortunately, food poisoning was not invariably fatal, and the number of deaths from food poisoning and gastritis or gastroenteritis of unspecified origin did not soar too high. Children and the elderly showed the most vulnerability.

A more serious killer, also closely related to poor sanitary conditions, was typhoid, the cause of nearly a third of Goldfield's deaths within the nonrespiratory communicable disease category. In view of the camp's primitive water and sanitation systems, doctors had feared an even larger death toll. Privies with dangerously shallow vaults remained in use in much of the city after Goldfield acquired sewers in late 1906, but the county commissioners compelled householders in the downtown area to connect with the new system, a measure that probably saved many lives. The majority of typhoid deaths clustered in 1904–06 before the sewer system was completed. In conformity with the usual pattern of this disease, typhoid victims tended to be young adults (median age twenty-eight). Like pneumonia, the disease was minimal in 1908 and had virtually disappeared in 1910, suggesting that its presence had been another offshoot of boomtown conditions.

Casual disregard of sanitary matters was not the only element effecting mortality in a boomtown replete with saloons, bordellos, and opium dens, or "hop joints," as they were then called. Still, despite the presence of a busy tenderloin district, only a small number of syphilitic deaths, all men, occurred (of course, the same official gallantry that declined to designate any woman as a prostitute in the death records may have veiled a few feminine cases). As in the California gold rush, venereal disease was present but evidently not a serious health problem. Goldfield did, however, have a health problem that had burgeoned since the days of the forty-niners — drug addiction. Lawmen arrested numerous "slaves of the poppy pill" in a raid on the opium dens of Hop Fiends' Gulch. One of the addicts, crazed by the sight of the confiscated opium, seized one of the precious cans, clasped it to his chest, and raced desperately out of the courtroom pursued by the judge, who succeeded in recapturing him a block from the courthouse.

Despite the difficulties caused by these prisoners, lawmen showed compassion to the "miseries of Hades" suffered by the addicts as a result of enforced withdrawal while they languished in jail. The sheriff permitted them to chew yen-shee (ashes of opium) and did not object to the morphine supplied by a compliant doctor. Yet even addiction was evidently not lethal. No deaths were attributed to unintentional drug overdoses, though morphine and opium were used in several suicides. The only unintentional drug-related death was a housewife's overdose of "headache powders." Heavy drinking in the saloons proved more dangerous to the gold rushers than the exotic dissipations of the opium den. Alcoholism was either the sole cause or a leading factor in more than 5 percent of the deaths in Goldfield, the greater part of them concentrated in the boom years when travelers often commented on the drinking habits of the populace. "Booze is cheap and flows like water," reported one shocked visitor in 1907. However, alcohol-related deaths dropped to a low level during 1908, when the camp was waning. [26]

Boomtowns were also expected to exceed the norm in violent death, and Goldfield fulfilled these expectations. Homicide victims occupied 4 percent of Goldfield's death list, a proportion eleven times greater than the nation as a whole. In the worst years, these homicide rates lie within the range found by historian Roger McGrath in the earlier trans-Sierra mining camps, Aurora and Bodie. As McGrath observes, such levels far outstripped not only America's nineteenth-century Eastern cities, but also modern homicide rates. [27]

Although Orin Merrill was struck by the optimism of Goldfielders facing frequent reversals of fortune, Goldfield suicides far surpassed the norm in more stable communities. Over the entire period, suicide accounted for almost 3 percent of Goldfield's mortality, a small figure in comparison to the major causes of death but still much greater than in gold rush Sacramento or in the rest of the nation. Suicide, like homicide, plunged to a negligible level in 1906, the peak year of the boom, and afterward rose once more to reach a high level (4.5 percent of mortality) in 1908 when the camp's decline was well underway. This general tendency may signify that as opportunity contracted and competition over increasingly scarce economic resources grew more intense, violent death in both forms rose substantially.

In general, Goldfield's high proportion of suicide conformed with the social trends researchers have uncovered in communities outside the mining frontier. High population mobility, rapid alterations in status, weak control by the group over its members, an absence of lasting social relationships, the reversals of an economic decline—all these elements elevate suicide rates, and all were abundantly present in Goldfield. Newspaper reports on suicides recounted a variety of causes: gambling losses, financial reversals in mining, ill health, and "turning in repulsion from the life of sin she had been leading." The number of single or widowed suicides of both sexes barely exceeded married persons, suggesting that the affection and support of a family exerted little deterrent effect. Over 35 percent of the suicides were young people in their twenties and only four individuals were over fifty, which contradicts the general rule that suicide increases with advancing age and indicates that the typical suicide was not the veteran of many mining booms who had finally "played out his string." In fact, the typical suicide was more likely to be one of the women comprising nearly a third of those who took their own lives but less than 10 percent of mortality. In mode of death, suicides turned to morphine, opium, or poison (usually cyanide) almost as commonly as the gunshot. [28]

For the suicide, as for many of Goldfield's dead, final repose came in the graveled earth of the cemetery west of town beside the clifflike wall of the Malapai Mesa. Nearly 30 percent were returned to their home communities. The refusal by so many to bury their dead in Goldfield revealed the scant connection many residents felt with the camp. The absence in the Goldfield cemetery of elaborate monuments of the kind that grace the cemeteries of such mining towns as Bodie and Virginia City bears out this view. Goldfield, with its simple markers, seems more akin to a potter's field, rarely envisaged as the place where a loved one's grave would be revisited year after year and a family would finally rest together over time. Few monuments from Goldfield's boom days endure. Following the establishment of the present cemetery in late 1905, at least 444 Goldfielders were buried there from 1906 through early 1909, but only thirty-four markers from this period with identifiable names remain. The best known monument in the cemetery, the tombstone carved with the name Joy, is actually a replica of an original eroded to illegibility. Too poor to afford a marker for the daughter she had lost to diphtheria, Anne Ellis stole a white stone step from the schoolhouse by night, laboriously lugged it home in a child's wagon, and chiseled her little girl's name upon it with a nail.

Possibly the most striking memorials stand not in the graveyard but in the pages of *Miners' Magazine* where Goldfield's Socialist revolutionaries saw a bitter ideological lesson in every death among their union "brothers." "Again a worker's life has been sacrificed to the God of greed. . . ." read a 1907 letter written in the wake of another fatal accident in the mines. "Goldfield Miners' Union No. 220, Western Federation of Miners . . . enters a protest against a continuance of such an order of society that makes it possible for the master class to be able to sacrifice the lives of its workers without being held responsible for the same."[29]

Both love and death in Goldfield obliquely mirrored mining camp life. Romance was often impulsive and swiftly accelerated through the slow stages of normal courtship, and while men hunted gold, the boldest adventuresses of the day hunted wealthy husbands, not infrequently with greater success. Yet not all Goldfield romances ended in blissful tranquillity. Domestic violence and divorce split many homes. Just as love had a dark underside of human suffering, so, too, did the fabulously rich mines, the convivial saloons, and the bordellos of the "half world." There was a fine pioneer bravado in joining the stampede across the desert to pitch a tent in a raw new camp with none of the restrictive encumbrances of an established city. There was a heady exhiliration in slipping a revolver inside your pocket and elbowing up to the bar in a saloon crowded with fortune hunters full of great expectations. But with the excitement came very real risks. Influenza and other infectious diseases spread along with the yarns of bonanza in those convivial saloons and crowded streets. Pneumonia, the dreaded "black plague," swept in with the winter winds that howled through the flimsy tents. Spoiled provisions carried the peril of food poisoning; indifference to sanitary regulations turned typhoid from danger to reality; the comforting weight of a revolver in the pocket multiplied the chance of a deadly fracas; careless unconcern with safety in the mines, where timber was worth more than human life, brought a high rate of fatal accidents.

Despair also awaited the gold rushers when their hopes of vast fortunes dwindled into the harsh reality of poverty. Already elevated suicide and homicide figures soared as the boom abated, bringing Goldfield a proportion of violent death far in excess of the national norm. For reasons not fully explained, the social costs of a gold rush fell disproportionately on its women, who contributed much more than their share to the roster of suicides and died tragically younger than other American women. Some suggestions also emerge that the human casualties of a mining boom had climbed since the California gold rush, despite the progress of settlement during the last half century in the West. At least in the years for which records exist, epidemic disease claimed a smaller proportion of the dead in gold rush Sacramento than in Goldfield, and Sacramento's figures on violent deaths are strikingly lower. Perhaps the last great mining boom of the Western frontier was also the one that commanded the highest price in human lives. Buried beneath the rounded board markers among the tumbleweeds and scattered joshua trees in the graveyard overlooking the city were many Goldfielders who had planned to stay just long enough to make their fortunes.

VIII

In Search of Pleasurable Excitements

ENTERTAINMENT

"People today just don't know what fun is! The parades and the dances we had! And everyone went, the grandparents, the mothers, the kids, and the babies. We'd dance all night till 10:00 or 11:00 on a Sunday morning." Catherine McKenna.

It commanded the attention of Goldfielders in the same way as Columbia Mountain jutting forth on the landscape. It seemed to dwarf the discovery of gold in the Mohawk, the stock market crash, the downfall of the radical unions, and all other momentous events in the annals of the camp. Any old Goldfielder, asked for his recollections, would almost certainly speak of it first, as the penultimate happening of his years in the last great Western boomtown. New arrivals reckoned the time of their coming as "just before" or "soon after" it took place. Those who had left the city journeyed back, even all the way across the continent, so as not to miss it. Those who had never before set foot in Goldfield flocked in by every arriving train to witness the great spectacle. It was the lightweight championship boxing match between Joe Gans, the black champion from Baltimore known as "the Old Master," and Oscar "Battling" Nelson, known as "the Durable Dane" or "the Bat."

By securing a title match in a camp only three years old and far smaller than the large cities where most major bouts took place, the promoters had scored a coup. But just then, in the wake of the Hayes-Monnette discovery, nothing seemed beyond Goldfield's reach. The man primarily responsible was one of the proprietors of the Northern Saloon, Tex Rickard, a tall hatchet faced Texan with twinkling eyes and an infectious grin, who generally sported a gold headed cane, a cigar, and a pale snap brim fedora. After learning that Nelson was receptive to a fight in Goldfield, Rickard decided to bid for a championship. Gans showed himself willing, provided the purse could be raised to thirty thousand dollars, and the fight was on.

It promised to be an exciting match. Gans, former welterweight champion and current lightweight champion, was then thirty-two. During fifteen years of professional boxing, he had lost only 6 of 145 bouts. Nonetheless, he had barely squeaked through in his last title defense, and he suffered from undiagnosed tuberculosis. Battling Nelson, then eight years younger than the Old Master, had been fighting professionally since he was fourteen, after emigrating from Denmark to Illinois as a child. Boxing fans admired his ability to withstand terrible punishment in the ring, and one of his fights, in which he and his opponent had been floored forty-nine times, held the all time record for knockdowns. By any standard, he was a formidable challenger.

Rickard scheduled the fight for September 3, and Goldfield hastily began to erect an arena, which somewhat inauspiciously bordered on the graveyard. By mid-August both fighters were training in Goldfield. The *News* remarked that "little else is talked of and in the excitement of the moment even the Mohawk is forgotten," or more precisely, combined with the great event by means of numerous publicity photos of the fighters taken at the mine workings. During the week before the match, newspapermen, photographers, and spectators began pouring into a city ill-equipped to accommodate them. As many pullman sleeping cars as the Tonopah and Goldfield Railroad could secure were rolled onto newly built sidetracks to serve as temporary hotels. When the throngs outstripped the railroad cars, many slept inside the arena. Frank Crampton, who had trouble finding a space for his bedroll among the other "hard rock stiffs" already encamped on the ground, recalled: "Places to shack up were almost nonexistent, for everything was occupied that had a roof or was reserved for incoming fight fans. Tents had been thrown up wherever there was space for them, but there still was not enough shack room. . . ." Betting soared to ever higher levels, with Gans the favorite. George Graham Rice alone claimed to have wagered $45,000 for Gans, including the purse money Gans authorized the broker to stake upon his own victory, against $32,500 put up by the fans of Nelson.[1]

By the time the crowd filled the arena, gate receipts reached $70,000, a record for the period. No one could deny that the spectators received full value for their money. The forty-two-round fight was a marathon of endurance lasting nearly three hours, a record for a modern championship. In Crampton's words: "No fight that I have seen since has equaled it in any way. Gans was a boxer and Nelson a bruiser. It was a fight from start to finish, and not once did either man let up trying to knock the other out . . . Nelson must have known he was licked from the beginning. He never was a clean fighter, and he poured it on that day."[2]

Most in the crowd shared Crampton's sympathy for Gans, whom they saw as "a gentleman as well as a pugilist." Despite a serious sprain to his right hand suffered in the sixteenth round, Gans came close to knocking out Nelson in the twentieth, but the younger fighter rallied. After the thirtieth, both men were clearly tiring, and foul warnings fell thick and fast upon Nelson. Despite his injury, Gans managed to endure, and even to dominate his opponent, for the remainder of the contest. It finally ended, as the skies were darkening, when Nelson drove a hard punch into Gans's groin, Gans sank to the floor in pain, and the referee declared him the winner, disqualifying Nelson. Spectators booed the Bat as he left the ring.

Several days later the young attorney George Springmeyer, riding on the train from Goldfield with Nelson, was shocked to see that the fighter's head appeared to have swollen to twice its normal size and the bruised flesh had cracked and turned violent hues of green, yellow, and purple, graphic evidence of the battering he had endured in the ring. In later years, when he became as well known for the array of diamonds twinkling on his red woolen shirt as for his endurance and his arrogance, Nelson's recollections of the epic contest in Goldfield proved no less discolored than his face, and he began to find fault with every aspect of it excepting his own performance. He insisted that he had been "beaten by jobbery" over a fair half-scissors hook to the champion's liver, and despite a photo of himself grinning toothily between stacks of twenty-dollar gold pieces, he claimed that the size of the purse had been a mere publicity yarn. "You hear an awful lot about those big-hearted miners in Nevada," he sourly wrote. "Well, the majority of them you would have to chloroform or hit with a mallet to loosen up on any of that alleged gold dust, a bootfull of which every man is supposed to be carrying around with him."[3] Two years later Nelson was to win the title from the aging and ailing Gans, only to lose it to a newer champion, Al Wolgast, in 1910.

Though the hope that more title bouts would be fought in Goldfield in the years to come proved as phantasmagoric as other predictions on the camp's glorious future, boxing remained the king of sports in Goldfield. The athletic clubs arranged numerous pugilistic contests between local fighters. When the hubbub (and the betting) among Goldfield's many boxing fans over a title match grew intense, the stockbroker with his own direct wire to San Francisco who invited his friends to his office to hear the results as fast as they became available was regarded as the best possible host. For those without a broker's connections, the Mohawk Saloon installed a direct wire to report returns, and an expectant crowd thronged the saloon "almost to suffocation."[4]

Goldfielders pursued a variety of other sports with scarcely less avidity than they devoted to boxing. Wrestling was conducted in the same marathon manner as the Gans-Nelson fight, with one bout between champion Victor Ajax and a challenger stretching on for nearly three hours of sweating, grunting, and straining. Ajax, who reputedly came to central Nevada as the chef of a traveling circus that went broke, owned the Ajax Saloon and dance hall in the tenderloin district. There, in his Parisienne Cafe, he reportedly purveyed the best food in the city, far outdoing the expensive restaurants in respectable locations. Hoping to prod him to the mat, prospective champions would post their pictures, lettered with challenges to Ajax, all over the city. To such a "defi," Ajax was apt to reply that he felt "about tired of being repeatedly challenged by every wrestler who happens to travel this way" and unless the purse increased to levels worthy of his efforts, he intended to "take no notice" of the upstart.[5]

When Ajax refused the bait, Goldfield offered other sports. Both parents and sports fans followed high school football with intense interest, and play was sometimes interrupted when an excited crowd dashed out into the field at critical moments. After a game, the teams were treated to a banquet at one of the city's best hotels. The camp's baseball team also competed against other cities in state league play. Broom ball, a form of hockey played on roller-skates, drew large crowds when teams from local businesses—perhaps the stock exchange versus the Palace Saloon—played at the rollerskating rink built to accommodate eight hundred skaters. In the camp's new bowling alley, Goldfield's doctors so shamefully trounced the lawyers that the latter found themselves at a loss for words—at least, temporarily.

Occasionally the refreshments at a sporting event sounded as interesting as the athletic contests. So many people signalled plans to attend the bull's head breakfast and barbeque sponsored by the Goldfield Athletic Club at the base of the Malapai that club members had to scramble for enough bull's heads to serve more than two thousand. While some interest focussed on the tug of war teams, the major event of the day was a mountain-climbing contest. Long in advance of the date, Goldfielders could see the defending Canadian champion and his several challengers crawling like spiders up the rock-rimmed crest of the long mesa in hope of finding a fast and easy route to the prize money.[6]

Unsurprisingly, in a camp where gun culture so thoroughly permeated the atmosphere, trap shooting was a popular sport, and marksmen organized at least two gun clubs. When the marksmen celebrated Thanksgiving by convening a shoot, Goldfielders who observed the holiday in more tradi-tional ways found themselves compelled to carve their turkeys amidst a chorus of popping guns. Some local marksmen preferred to pursue their avocation in solo style. Diamondfield Jack Davis, who reveled in his own reputation as a gunman, was often seen speeding over the desert in his auto as he picked off jack rabbits with a pistol. So quickly did this inno-vation in target practice gain popularity that the newspapers soon began calling it "quite a fad."[7]

The new autos themselves were the central feature of other sporting events. The auto club would lay out a twelve-mile race course on the white shimmering hard-packed sands of a nearby playa, a striped tent would be erected for refreshments, and Tex Rickard's big Thomas flyer would roar forth to race against other contenders, perhaps a French Durac, a Pope Toledo, or a Pierce Arrow, with the Thomas usually the winner. Smaller cars and another recent innovation, motorcycles, zipped past in other races, and the day might end, perhaps a little nostalgically, with the most venerable pioneer amusement—a horse race.

Of course, Goldfield never so far outgrew frontier traditions that horse racing ceased to be a high point on the Fourth of July and other special celebrations such as Railroad Day, and a "Derby Day" still drew thousands of spectators. On one such occasion, the *Goldfield Tribune* observed, "Everybody who owns a horse, or had enough money to hire a horse, or who could borrow a horse, was out on a horse yesterday at the Goldfield derby." The race was run right down Main Street, with spectators overflowing the board sidewalks and many seated on the roof of the courthouse, while bookmakers clustered in the lobby of the Casey Hotel. Fittingly, in a camp long viewed by the mining world as a dark horse, the winner, by just a neck, was a dark horse named Dollie Gray which covered the quarter-mile track in twenty-two seconds. For awhile, another venerable sport, cockfighting, held under the auspices of local Hispanics who groomed the feathered champions, became a regular event. [8]

Inspired by the stockbroker George von Polenz, who brought a European flavor to the local sporting scene, Goldfielders also organized a hunt club. On a fine crisp November day, anyone who had spent a night draped over the bar in a saloon might well have supposed that bourbon still addled his wits when he glimpsed a host of pink-jacketed huntsmen, their mounts bounding gracefully over the sagebrush, in pursuit of a fox. Fortunately, no one attempted to force the skulking local coyote into this unfamiliar role, and a rider with a fox tail pinned to his jacket played the part of the quarry—at least, up to a point. The hunt club, however, marked the high point of gentrification in local sports. Despite his best efforts, von Polenz never succeeded in getting Goldfielders started on polo.

More traditional mining camp amusements brought Goldfielders into the streets at every hour of the day and night. "No matter whether the visitor arrives at noon or midnight, he will see the same number of people passing up and down the street in aimless fashion, thronging the saloons and seemingly busied with one occupation, time killing." The mines were the reason that Goldfield was a true twenty-four hour city half a century before Howard Hughes decided to headquarter his business enterprises in Las Vegas because it was the only place he knew where he could go out to buy a sandwich at any hour. Men worked in Goldfield's mines in three eight-hour shifts during every twenty-four hour period, and activity throughout the city generally followed the twenty-four-hour-a-day pattern set by the mines. Especially in winter, few found much appeal in spending their leisure hours in a cold and comfortless tent cabin. In consequence, miners coming off work paused only long enough for a wash and a change before sallying forth to sample the city's high life. The *Goldfield Review* declared that most Goldfielders spent their time "in search of pleasurable excitements." [9]

Some found their pleasurable excitements in the raucous dance halls of the tenderloin district, the most famous of which was Jake's, noted for its maple wood dance floor, as well as its girls and the woman entertainer who sang "coon songs." Proprietor Jake Goodfriend faced considerable competition from other dance halls like Ragtime Kelly's, the People's Dance Hall, the Orpheum, which advertised "All New Faces," and the hurdy-gurdy houses that sometimes spilled over the well-understood boundaries of the district. These dance halls differed little in their essentials—a long bar, a style of decor that Sewall Thomas called a "tawdry, artificial show of Oriental splendor," a crowded dance floor, uproarious with laughter, shrill chatter, the scraping of fiddles, and the tinkling of pianos plunking out waltzes and two steps, and girls, the principal attraction in woman-starved Goldfield. According to Emmett Arnold, the girls wore low-necked dresses with skirts above the knees and "painted themselves like totem poles." Many were veterans of the Klondike with names like Eskimo Sal, Klondike Kitty, Porcupine Nellie, Swivel Bottom Sue, and others shading off into obscenity. Some took the names of prizefighters; Battling Nelson, Jimmie Britt, or Fighting Bill. Not infrequently they lived up to those names in wrestling, scratching, public cat fights in which the combatants ripped off each other's clothes. A tour of Goldfield high life might proceed from the cheap glamour of the dance halls to the bordellos or the cribs, each with a name plaque and a small bay window where the "soiled dove" displayed herself to prospective customers. [10]

The area southwest of the Goldfield jail known as Hop Fiends' Gulch offered even more disreputable diversions. After Chinese laborers brought opium with them to the American West, the opium den took its place as a staple mining camp institution. During the seventies the practice began to spread outside the Chinese ghettos, first among the gamblers and prostitutes of the white underworld in California and Nevada, and later more widely. Sensational press reports on the ruination of innocent girls by sinister Orientals and the dissipations of the "idle rich" in search of exotic thrills soon led to state legislation aimed at both den proprietors and addicts. Sporadically these penalties were even enforced. Yet the opium den persisted until the close of the frontier, little changed in appearance since the days when Dan De Quille crossed its portals in Virginia City: "At first we can see nothing save a small lamp suspended from the center of the ceiling. This lamp burns with a dull red light that illuminates nothing. . . . gradually our eyes adapt themselves to the dim light. . . .

"We now observe that two sides of the den are fitted up with bunks, one above the other, like the berths on shipboard. A cadaverous opium-smoker is seen in nearly every bunk. . . . Before him is a small alcohol lamp burning with a blue flame which gives out but little light—only enough to cast a sickly glare upon the corpselike face of the smoker as he holds his pipe in the flame and by a long draft inhales and swallows the smoke of the loved drug. These fellows are silent as dead men. . . . The peculiar sweetish-bitter odor of the burning opium fills and saturates the whole place—one can almost taste it." [11]

Despite the similarity in essentials, Goldfield's opium dens differed in two respects from the establishments of De Quille's day. Since Goldfield excluded the Chinese, white men with such sobriquets as "Frenchy" and "Goodwin, alias Blackie, King of the Hop Fiends" operated the dens in place of the "gaunt, wild-eyed Mongolians" observed by De Quille. Customers might include such occasional users as a party of young mining engineers out for a night on the town. Constable Claude Inman later estimated that Goldfield's addicts numbered "something about" 380, besides "literally thousands" of these occasional users who would drift over to the hop joints after an evening of gambling in the saloons.

In addition to their white ownership and patronage, Goldfield's opium dens differed from the establishments on the Comstock in the substances they purveyed. Not only did they provide a setting for communal opium smoking, as in the past, but also they served as virtual drug emporiums offering cocaine and morphine to customers, some of whom had become addicted to morphine after receiving it as a medical treatment. Public awareness that cocaine posed no less danger than the "Mongolian curse" had developed tardily. The nineteenth century was, after all, the era when no less a personage than Mark Twain seriously considered entering global trade in this "vegetable product of miraculous powers" (cocaine)—only an early twist of fate prevented America's greatest writer from instead becoming its first drug lord. As late as the 1890s, some saloons in the Colorado mining camps where many miners had worked prior to coming to Goldfield sold shots of cocaine-laced bourbon as an antidote to fatigue. For some time the concoction was openly sold under such suggestive names as "Bright Eye."[12]

Opium dens in crude barrel hovels and dugouts in the hillside sloping upward from the Brewery Avenue wash had operated since Goldfield's earliest days, and their existence was obviously no secret, judging from the piles and drifts of empty opium cans, morphine vials, and cocaine packets surrounding them. If Inman's recollections can be trusted, some of these dens were commodious enough to house sixty bunks. Despite the role of the den as a kind of "vagabonds' inn" for a knavish clientele, drug-related crime was almost unknown in Goldfield, and the presence of such establishments seems to have been usually tolerated—so much so that a stranger in a saloon would ask the way to the nearest hop joint and receive directions from a deputy sheriff. From time to time, a lawman energetically declared his intention to rid the town of "vagabonds, saloon sleepers, and rounders" and commenced his program with a sweep against the "hop layouts." It sometimes took a short while before the gulch reverted to business as usual.

In the largest of these raids in February, 1907, Constable Inman and his deputies seized two thousand dollars worth of drugs, along with pipes, glass lamps for cooking opium, delicate scales for weighing the drug, and antique Oriental trays. It was considered one of the largest hauls ever

Goldfield lawmen pose with opium pipes and other paraphernalia confiscated in a 1907 raid on "Hop Fiends' Gulch" (Larson Collection, Nevada State Museum)

made in the West. When lawmen rousted the dazed "slaves of the poppy pill" from their bunks, one grandly protested that he had just purchased the Mohawk Mine and could not possibly spare the time to go to jail just then because he was presently expecting a visit from the Shah of Persia. Another offered Inman a huge bribe. The chief constable soon realized that "it would not be policy to publicize" the names of many of those netted in the raid because they were the "important people of the town, men and women." He sent the wife of one prominent Goldfielder home in a push cart. Other influential detainees were quietly "weeded out."[13]

Despite the popularity of drugs among the elite, the days of the frontier opium dens were numbered. The ban on imports and the stiff penalties imposed by federal legislation in 1909 caused the price of opium to skyrocket. Over the following two decades, most addicts reluctantly switched to cheaper and ultimately deadlier drugs, primarily morphine and heroin. When Goldfield slid into decline, the opium dens of palmier days went out of business. Time would show that the last of the boomtowns marked the swan song of the frontier opium den, one day to emerge anew in far more dangerous form as the crack house.

While the patronage of the opium dens remained relatively small, the saloons were every man's amusement, a pastime for most and a passion for some, the informal clubs where business deals were closed at the bar and men congregated in search of good fellowship. As *Goldfield Gossip* observed, a Goldfielder was "possessed of such a feverish restlessness to see what is doing and take part in it that he can rarely settle down quietly at home."[14] Indeed Goldfield men found themselves under intense social pressure to be "good fellows," which meant "being away from home, up late nights, hanging around saloons or clubs, and drinking and gambling." Not only was this nightly round of activity expensive, but also it eroded families because wives were left stranded at home. Moreover, the custom often proved more addictive than the substances purveyed in Hop Fiends' Gulch because many men who had tasted the freedom and commotion of mining camp nights could never return to the more conventional routines of family life.

Another strain conjoined with the urge to join one's friends in congenial surroundings, hear the latest rumors on new bonanzas in the mines, gyrations in the stock market, and big deals in the making, and share the excitement. Those who had staked their lives and fortunes on a gold rush were gamblers almost by definition. According to W. P. De Wolf: "In a mining camp, the gambling instinct is an inherent trait of the population, having its inception probably in the spirit of adventure which permeates the residents. . . . Life is always more or less of a gamble to these hardy nomads, and the zest of the game is just as keen to them in the seventieth milestone as in the twentieth." Emmett Arnold recalled that Goldfielders would bet on anything, "where the next fly would light, whether the next female passerby would be blonde or brunette, who could spit a stream of tobacco juice farthest and straightest—Arkansawyers barred—and a jillion other screwball bets."[15] In consequence, the saloons that also featured gambling exerted an attraction even more powerful than conviviality over many Goldfielders.

The earliest saloons offered more congeniality than creature comforts. Before the new district had been organized a month, it boasted three saloons, all primitive facilities. W. S. ("Ole") Elliott's Combination Saloon was literally a combination—a saloon and a blacksmith shop. Lacking funds to pay a bartender, Elliott allowed the customers to help themselves and make change from a cigar box behind the bar when he was absent. However, his newspaper advertisements of the "Combination Cellar" showed the usual mining camp tendency to emphasize the positive: "The most complete stock in Goldfield of the best brands of liquors. 'Draw your drink straight from the barrel.'"[16]

The drinking emporiums erected in later days illustrated the undeniable advance of civilization in Goldfield since the early tent saloons. Inside, behind the typical long mahogany bar with a footrail but no stools, saloon decor often featured a large oil painting of a voluptuous and scantily clad woman—or perhaps an even more bovine buffalo. A few tables and chairs might be positioned near the door, and a small loft for musicians sometimes occupied part of the space. Some saloons included a short-order counter where customers could sit on stools and eat chops and other quick meals; many provided the bountiful free lunch typical of the period, bread, salami,

cheeses, and pickles. Because respectable women never crossed the portals of a saloon in that day and age, most saloons also had private "wine
rooms" where women could be entertained. Anne Ellis thought her visit
to one of these wine rooms a "very tame affair" not worth repeating—the
real fun was audibly in progress inside the main saloon. Beer and bourbon being the most popular drinks, bar orders were usually "give me a
shot" or "give me a boilermaker." Though many Goldfielders regarded
"wining" on champagne as an integral part of a grand spree, anyone who
asked for a mixed drink risked being greeted with ridicule or disdain. To
call for an absinthe frappe was to mark yourself at once with the ignominious brand of the tenderfoot. [17]

Not all saloons offered gambling. For instance, the call of the croupier,
"seven, by heaven," never sounded in Carl Fuetsch's California Beer Hall,
located near the mines and catering primarily to miners stopping in for
a few drinks on the way home from work. But many other establishments
resounded with the rattle of dice and the whirr of the roulette wheel. Sewall
Thomas saw "crowds, three deep" around the wheels, "scrambling to get
bets down." The house provided "liberal potations" and free cigars to players
to incite ever more reckless "plunging." Craps and roulette were great favorites,
and blackjack, poker, faro, panguingui, keno, and chuck-a-luck were also
offered, but Goldfielders showed little interest in a relatively recent innovation, the slot machine. De Wolf noted that old timers favored faro—understandably, since the odds were so favorable to players that faro is rarely seen
in casinos today. Though throngs of gamblers jostled noisily around the
other games, silence usually ruled at the faro table. "No loud talk or boisterous
laughter is ever interspersed with the stringing of a bet or the coppering
of a card, for . . . most of those gathered around the table have burned
the midnight oil in an attempt to figure out a system. . . ." [18]

The tenderfoot, on the other hand, was invariably attracted to roulette,
"the primary grade in a novice's gambling career, from whence he passes
along in successive stages until he matriculates in the faro or collegiate
degree and becomes a full-fledged member of the fraternity." After matric-
ulation, attempts by these novices to imitate the silent reserve and unshake-
able aplomb of the veteran players clustered around the faro bank were
often the "subject of quiet jest" between the experienced players and
the dealers and house "lookouts" (armed guards deputized as lawmen and
generally stationed near the faro tables), with whom the veterans enjoyed
a long and "intimate" acquaintance. The garb of the tenderfoot, as well
as his demeanor, provided amusement to the regulars. The press described
one of these unmistakable young gentlemen as resplendently arrayed
in a new Stetson, a plaid suit, French patent leather shoes, a Mexican
carved leather belt, a nugget chain, a turquoise matrix pin, and a large
diamond ring. No one was surprised to see him "drop his wad" at the
craps table. [19]

Gamblers in a Goldfield saloon, 1905 (Nevada Historical Society)

As night waned toward morning, the loungers fell asleep at the saloon tables or stretched out in the music loft, and celebrants wove their way homeward, "making wide detours over a straight road, walking around pebbles, and falling over shadows." When one of these sotted revelers resoundingly collided with a streetside cabin, the owner and a passing stranger decided to take him home. They helped him into the cabin they thought was his, though he had apparently lost the key, and quietly put him to bed, supposing that the feminine apparel lying about the room belonged to his wife. Only several days later did the good samaritans learn that they had tucked the boozer into the bed of a widow who was entirely unacquainted with him.

Meanwhile, preparations for the day to come were underway in the saloons. Bartenders cut ice, while others weighed the dice and tested them for balance, checked the roulette wheels for hidden wires, and examined new packs of cards looking for a marked deck that had been cleverly resealed. Soon customers would be thronging inside to begin the day's activities with the traditional "bracer" at the bar. As the day wore on, the professional gamblers trailed inside to resume their customary posts—Beefsteak Mike, Alabam, Fifteen Two, Short-Bit Kid, Right-Change Sam, Billy the Wheel, Society Red, Cyclone, Stud-Poker Frank, Sure-Shot Dave, Dusty Rhodes, Crap-A-Jack, Charlie Rockinghorse, and all the rest. De Wolf considered these professionals "in a class by themselves" with characteristics "as distinctive and as easily discernible as those which mark the clergy": "They have their own code of honor and many of its ramifications contain the essence of integrity and square dealing. A gambler's word given to another member of the fraternity is as good as his bond, and once broken he is ever a proscribed man. . . . As a rule they pay their bills promptly and without a kick, and they are liberal contributors to all public and charitable causes. They are keen judges of human nature and seldom make a mistake in sizing up a man. Their friendship once given is rarely revoked and is sometimes more lasting than that in which the ties of consanguinity enter. As a class they have a quick wit and humor. . . ."[20]

A new Arizona statute prohibiting gambling gave rise to an exodus from that state which substantially swelled the ranks of Goldfield's professional gamblers in late 1907. Or, as "A. M., Jr." more poetically described the situation:

'They're packin' up the cards and dice,' says Arizona Red.
'They'll come in handy 'cross the line,' the faro dealer said.
'But here the boys won't have no use for all their tools and traps.
It's 'gin the statute to deal bank or make a pass at craps.
An' the sports have all got Arizony coppered on their maps.
So it's me away for Goldfield in the morning.'

'Well, certain poker ain't cut out,' says Arizona Red.
'As sure as threes will beat two pair,' the faro dealer said.
'Then what the devil can we do?' says Arizona Red.
'Go play old maid with Charley's aunt,' the faro dealer said,
'You're up agin the real thing now; the old time games is done.
And for your hard-earned money you'll never get a run.
You'll have to take to solitaire and such like games, my son.
So your uncle hikes for Goldfield in the mornin.'[21]

Although the saloons posted limits (such as twenty-five dollars for roulette) on the sums a player might risk when "bucking the tiger," the signs were widely ignored. In practice, a high roller could "stack his chips to the ceiling" if he chose. Yet the sums reported in games the press considered newsworthy seem fairly modest by modern standards, even when multiplied into today's dollars. In these newspaper stories, large losses hovered around $2,500 and the largest wins under $5,000.

According to the *Goldfield Tribune*, the record marathon for roulette occurred on an April night in 1907 when two Eastern high rollers played the wheel for seventeen hours straight with twenty-dollar gold pieces. While the game was in progress, they swilled champagne, the owner urged them to "go it as high as you want, boys," and an awestruck crowd clustered around the table. Their fortunes seesawed up and down, reaching over four thousand dollars at one point and dwindling only to rise anew. At last they virtually covered the wheel with twenty-dollar gold pieces. Noticing that number twenty-three remained empty, a drunken tramp shuffled out of the crowd and plunked his dime on the spot muttering, "Mussn't leave it out, y'know. Me old fren'. . . ." The little ivory ball skipped around to perversely land on twenty-three. This inauspicious omen marked a turning point in the game, plunging the high rollers into an "ill mood" and a series of steadily mounting losses, multiplied by their foolhardy efforts to change their luck by doubling and trebling their bets. The big winner, as usual, was the house.[22]

Perhaps much larger sums occasionally changed hands at gaming. Denver attorney Orrin Hilton claimed that he had seen an old prospector sell his half interest in a mine for seventy thousand dollars, lose it all at roulette in a single night, and set off into the hills again the next morning on a loaned burro. Thomas Rickard heard of individuals that won as much as thirty thousand dollars or lost fifty thousand dollars. The actual records may well have been set in private poker games. Saloon owners Ole Elliott and Kid Highley were said to be "inveterate poker players" whose games in the back room ran on for days on end. Moreover, gambling appears to have been a favored indulgence among the Goldfield elite. Wingfield, after all, had commenced his central Nevada career as a professional gambler. Myers' heavy gambling was almost legendary. George Graham Rice cheerfully admitted that at one point in his Goldfield career he squandered everything he had made in his advertising business at faro and left on the stagecoach as penniless as when he arrived (he later returned to temporarily recoup his fortunes). And Charlie Taylor, who may have gambled away his most valuable mines to Wingfield, unquestionably had a weakness for testing new systems to beat the wheel at roulette—with predictably disastrous results. "He was the coldest gambler I ever saw, and I've seen a lot of them," the proprietor of the Elks Club in Tonopah told Carl Glasscock. "He never batted an eye or fluttered a hair on a $5,000 bet, win or lose."[23]

Goldfielders agreed that a man stood a better chance of quitting winners at the wheel than he did if he had risked his money on Goldfield's greatest gamble—the mining stock exchange. When the Nevada legislature began to consider outlawing gambling in 1909, Ole Elliott declared that they would be better advised to crack down on dishonest stockbrokers. In his opinion, if the proprietor of a gaming establishment permitted comparable chicanery, "everybody connected with it would be breaking rocks" at the state prison. Thomas Rickard, among others, expressed similar views: "I venture to say that to bet on the red or the black is more sane than to buy shares on a margin and, upon the whole, the player at the roulette table gets a better show than the speculator on the stock exchange. Certainly, the game is far less crooked. . . ." Nonetheless, the anti-gambling bill passed the legislature, apparently as a palliative to reformers who agreed, in return, to avoid the far more sensitive issue of Prohibition. In the autumn of 1910, dealers draped the roulette wheels in black crepe, and Arizona Red, Crap-a-Jack, and all the rest lost the last bastion of legalized gambling in the nation. Or, to be more precise, they were forced to pursue their old activities underground in back rooms and private clubs over the next twenty years, as the law gradually dissolved in a welter of exceptions, legalistic obfuscations, and indifferent enforcement. This ended decisively in 1931 when the legislature ceased to dally with reform and reinstituted legalized gambling in Nevada. [24]

The institution most indispensable to mining camp life, the saloon, had arrived soon after the pioneers organized the new Goldfield district in October 1903. Nearly two years were to pass before the earliest tent churches, with rippling canvas walls, made a belated appearance in 1905. In the late spring of 1904, the first visiting missionaries held services in a law office and a private home. Soon a group of women, in keeping with their general reputation as civilizers of the frontier, began organizing a Ladies Aid Society to raise money for a building where religious meetings could take place. They succeeded in this endeavor, and the new hall apparently welcomed all faiths. Goldfield's Jews, although never numerous enough to erect a temple at the camp, were invited to celebrate Yom Kippur and Rosh Hashanah at the hall. The hall also served as an all-purpose recreation center for dances, concerts, and boxing matches by night, and as the camp's justice court on week days.

While Goldfield fell far short of the common mining camp boast that churches actually outnumbered the saloons, the town could take pride in the new churches erected by several devout congregations; Catholics, Presbyterians, Episcopalians, Methodist Episcopalians, and Christian Scientists, as well as a Salvation Army hall. By 1907 Goldfield's black community could also worship in their own church, the Goldfield Union Mission, while their children attended Sunday school. Yet the new church bells had scarcely sounded before congregations dwindled with the camp's precipitate decline, and ministers departed to heed "the call" from other parts, leaving empty pulpits behind them. The Christian Scientists probably never progressed beyond a temporary structure. The Catholics moved in 1907 from their original modest church to a new one so large and ambitious that the basement alone could seat more than one thousand people, only to languish without sufficient funds to complete the church. In the end, forced to abandon the lofty superstructure conceived in more affluent times, they settled for roofing over the foundation.[25]

In the same way that the grand, if unfinished, outlines of the Sacred Heart Church dominated religious architecture, its priest, Father James Dermody, dominated the ecclesiastical scene. Beloved by Goldfielders of all faiths or none at all, this great Irish giant of a man enjoyed trading jokes with those he called the "haythens" in the Montezuma Club of an evening. George Springmeyer later recalled that his own atheism posed no barrier to his friendship with the jovial churchman because Dermody "never tried to talk me into being a Catholic and I never tried to talk him out of being one." Not the least of Father Dermody's virtues lay in his position as a one-man charitable institution incapable of restricting his benevolences to his own congregation. Anne Ellis, ailing from a recent miscarriage, was eking out an impoverished existence during the miners' strike when Father Dermody came to call at Christmas time. Brushing aside her tearful protest that she was not a Catholic, he told her "That makes no difference if I can do anything" and laid a ten-dollar gold piece on the table. "I shall never forget him for this," Ellis later wrote.

Those who attended Father Dermody's sermons found them attuned to the human failings of a gold rush congregation. The Irish priest may well have been the unnamed divine whom Frank Crampton heard denounce the sin of stealing to his flock when the mine owners enlisted the churches in their intensive campaign to halt highgrading. "The sermon was punctuated with vivid descriptions of torments in hell—fire, brimstone, and boiling oil—as penalties for breaching the Commandment, 'Thou shall not steal.'" This fearful diatribe obviously made so deep an impression on those around him that Crampton began to wonder if highgrading might really be finished at last. However, a "sigh of unrestrained relief" rose from the congregation when the sermon ended with a definite suggestion of absolution, "But gold belongs to him wot finds it first." That sounded a lot like Father Dermody.

On other occasions the good father exhorted his flock to eschew the sins of gambling and drinking. He would then add in the heavy Irish brogue that resounded from the farthest corners of the church, "But if you *must* drink, go down to Mike's place." In 1913, on the occasion of his forty-fourth birthday and his twentieth year of priesthood, parishioners and friends presented Father Dermody with a solid gold chalice, which they likened to his heart; the priest, for his part, warmly reciprocated the affection that

Goldfielders in all walks of life felt for him. He had first come to Goldfield when the camp was nothing more than a collection of tents in 1904. He was to remain until 1917, when the former boomtown was fast shrinking to the point at which most of the population of the city could easily fit inside the great empty walls of the Sacred Heart Church. [26]

Another Goldfield social institution that assumed the attributes of a church to its most zealous members was union hall. As Wallace Stegner has noted, the IWW in that era was a "militant church," which commanded "all the enthusiasm, idealism, rebelliousness, devotion, and selfless zeal of thousands." [27] Whatever a man's degree of commitment to the union cause, the large barnlike structure where the combined WFM/IWW held their Tuesday night meetings served a variety of social functions extending well beyond union business. It was home to the homeless, where bindlestiffs could bed down for the night, soup kitchen for the hungry during strikes, host to religious services for congregations that shivered in poorly heated churches in the dead of winter, club and gathering place for working men, and scene of the regular Saturday night dances and grand New Year's Eve balls that were one of the principal pleasures of camp life—that is, until George Wingfield smashed the union in late 1907.

While few organizations came close to providing so much for so many as did the WFM/IWW in its heyday, Goldfielders could attach themselves to a great variety of social groupings. As a social organization, volunteer firemen played a smaller role than in earlier mining camps. Nonetheless, the major lodges and fraternal orders of the period were present in force, and long after more ephemeral clubs had disappeared from the scene the Elks Club continued to host dances well remembered by many Goldfielders. People would travel fifty miles or more to attend one of these Goldfield dances, and everyone was welcome, from the aged Jett Canyon rancher and his wife, who danced every set with a whirlwind energy that few could match, through the tots who stared wide-eyed at the dancers, to the ladies of the line, who slipped unobtrusively inside a little before dawn. Even then, time still remained for many a turn around the floor, since Saturday night dances often lasted well into Sunday morning.

Although efforts to launch a University Men's Club evidently met with little success, other organizations flourished. They ranged from a Junior Literary Club, through the Malapai Club and the Pirates of Cruiserine (both evidently mixed societies of men and women), the press club, the Nevada Club, a veterans' organization, which included both the last survivors of the Civil War and the young veterans of the Spanish-American War, a mandolin club, and The Altruists, a club for devotees of Esperanto. Clubs might sponsor parties, sleigh rides, or musical evenings, but by far the most popular club activity was a dance, sometimes an affair in which participants found a boisterous amusement in reversing the rough masculine image of the camp. A dance held by the Malapai

Club to which men came garbed as women was described in lush detail by newsmen obviously enjoying the change from chronicling the "gorgeous habilaments" of society women. Various stockbrokers or prominent gentlemen "donned fish net over black cheviot," or perhaps "puttees under black lingerie," looked "very chic and fetching in a frock of mousseline de soie with trousers," wore "a gorgeous gown of challis, a la directoire, with garnitures of high grade," and one attired himself in a simple but becoming frock of black broadcloth "which intensified the brilliancy of his luminous eyes."[28] Unfortunately the newspaper failed to mention whether the ladies looked similarly fetching in men's clothing.

In addition to the imaginative entertainments of the Malapai Club, women enjoyed themselves at card clubs, guilds connected with the churches, the Tuesday Afternoon Club, the Bedonia Club, and the Gold-field Women's Club, formed in 1909 for the purpose of "providing requisite forms of profitable and harmless amusement and recreation . . . without sacrifice of time required for domestic and social duties." Though membership was restricted to Goldfield residents of "recognized social position," which had an elitist ring, the ladies of the club may have harbored a broader sense of sisterhood than their bylaws declared.[29] When the ill-fated Bonita Parkison died at last, with the name of the husband she had slain upon her lips, the Women's Club decided to ignore her flamboyant days as a dancer in the tenderloin and offered to attend to her burial.

While the Women's Club may have denoted the high-water mark of feminine social aspiration in Goldfield, the most famous men's organization by any standard was the Montezuma Club. Organized in a small adobe house in early 1905, the Montezuma quickly ascended to the level of such elegant mining camp institutions as Virginia City's Washoe Club. Later the same year membership expanded from a handful to over one hundred, and the club moved to new quarters, regarded as "quite in keeping with the wealth and importance of the Goldfield mining district," on the second floor above the Palace Saloon. The club's decor, by far the most luxurious in Goldfield up to that time, aroused admiring commentary in the press. The ceiling was embossed aluminum, with a chased pattern of flowers and trailing vines; the walls, covered in terra cotta paper; the floor, of matched, polished, and dove-tailed eastern oak; the furnishings, also of oak in a dark ebony finish, with leather and heavy satin upholstery. These sumptuous couches, said the *News*, "will lull the restive gold seeker into dreams of untold wealth; or, perchance, grant forgetfulness for the moment to the spirit beneath the weight of disappointment. . . ."[30]

When not lost in the aforementioned reveries, the club's denizens pursued a variety of amusements, including billiards, pool, and pleasant luncheons. Drinking, swapping stories, and discussing mining deals, probably topped the list of pastimes, but the more sportive and inebriated members had been known to play leapfrog, and the club hosted many smokers, ladies' evenings, and musical entertainments. A typical musical program included selections by an Italian pianist, a baritone soloist, an exhibition by a professional whistler who had copyrighted the songs of over fifty birds, and "coon songs" by a vaudevillian. The audience at these events often displayed as much variety as the program, with some men in evening dress, others straight from the mines in corduroys and top boots, and prominent guests from all over the world.

"Conceived in enthusiasm and born in luxury" as it was, in the pungent phrase of the *Tribune*, the Montezuma Club overreached itself in much the same way as the ambitious new churches. Scarcely had the club undertaken to build a three-story clubhouse of its own to accommodate a roster swollen to 750 members during the boom days than the monopolization of the mining industry under Wingfield, the stock market crash of 1907, and the camp's swift decline left the organization with a diminished and considerably impoverished membership. Perhaps, as the *Tribune* also implied, the politicization of the Montezuma Club by Wingfield as part of his 1907 campaign to suppress the radical unions also contributed to the club's demise as a social organization. Although the spacious new club belatedly opened, after many fits and starts, in 1908, not much time elapsed before the Elks took over the building, complete with a cornerstone containing mementos dear to the hearts of the Montezuma Club crowd—an ivory pool ball from the Northern Saloon and a replica of the gold tooth that glittered in the enticing smiles of "Gold Tooth Bess," a popular cyprian in the tenderloin.[31]

If entertainment at the clubs should pall, Goldfielders also amused themselves at a plethora of private parties. These progressed from a social tea in the early days of the camp, at which the hostess, having only three chairs, seated her guests on wood boxes and coal oil cans, to the plush events of the boom years, when guests might enter a veritable bower of carnations and asparagus fern, all imported at great expense from California. The pleasure that greenery-starved Goldfielders derived from flowers, combined with the desire to display one's new wealth to the maximum degree, ensured that the hostess who wished to make a statement would feature elaborate floral decorations. Sewall Thomas recalled, "Social leaders proclaimed themselves, and contests for supremacy were fierce and without mercy."

Descriptions of Goldfield social events make clear that mining camp hostesses devoted a great deal of time and thought to every detail. For instance, at a party celebrating the engagement of Tom Lockhart's daughter, Myra, to a young army officer, guests passed through a replica of the sagebrush desert not far outside to seat themselves beneath the flags at a table made to simulate a rock wall with military campfires on each side, while musicians played military airs in the background. Now that the last great Indian scare in the region, some fifteen years past, was rapidly fading from memory, Indian themes grew popular at the "swellest social functions." Hostesses rechristened the card games "scalps," war whoops announced each new round of games, and winners received Indian baskets and souvenirs, not purchased from the indigenous Shoshone but imported from San Francisco. A February week's activities on the Goldfield social calendar might include two whist parties, a "valentine German," a Nevada Club dance, a euchre party, a tennis party, and ladies evening at the Montezuma Club. [32]

Sometimes social activities ranged farther afield. George Springmeyer often joined a group of young men and women for a moonlight horseback ride to a grove of joshua trees ten or fifteen miles from the city. Winter brought sleigh riding. Picnics on the cool heights of Stonewall Mountain south of Goldfield offered a popular summer pastime, as did a day of swimming in the reservoir at Alkali Springs, a pleasant twelve or thirteen mile ride from the city. Closer to home, private parties could, and did, rent Goldfield's Turkish baths for a secluded evening of dipping and paddling by the light of Oriental lamps, lounging in the reception room furnished in the Turkish style, or repairing for other pleasures to the private "rest apartments." Picnickers enjoyed gathering near a campfire for a moonlight feast on the Malapai Mesa. When Halley's comet swung close to the earth in the spring of 1910, Goldfielders turned out en masse to view the celestial spectacular, and bonfires of sagebrush and joshua trees burned throughout the night on the Malapai. However, cloudy skies prevented the comet from fulfilling expectations. "Shame on you, you cheap fourth-rate barnstormer," the *Tribune* scolded Halley's. "Pass on and hide your diminished head for the next seventy-five years, or longer if you like, and take your etherial satellites and wardrobe with you." [33] Goldfielders had better things to do than spend the night straining their eyes for a glimpse of a cloudy smudge in the sky.

These included gourmet meals at the city's finer restaurants. Historian Joseph Conlin has cogently argued that gourmet dining thrived on the mining frontier because the hard rock miners were epicureans always ready to blow their paychecks on a luxurious meal. A stable of race horses, a mansion on Nob Hill, or a European tour might be beyond the miner's reach—at least, until he too struck bonanza. But he saw himself as a potential nabob, able to afford an elegant meal in the same restaurants patronized by the elite.

This outlook, conditioned by the miners' visions of future wealth, had prevailed for more than half a century, and the last boomtown strayed outside the boundaries of frontier foodways only in limited respects. Understandably, in the baking heat of summer, the new ice cream parlors enjoyed a certain vogue. Lacking a Chinese community, Goldfield also lacked the Chinese restaurants so popular in other Western cities; at the same time, though the area had no Spanish cultural background and no sizeable Hispanic population, the Mexican food that Conlin found had failed to win acceptance in other mining towns was strongly represented in a Goldfield cafe offering tamales and "Spanish beans" and two popular chili parlors (Goldfielders, incidentally, preferred to eat their chili with noodles). They were also noted for their deeply held conviction that the only steak worth eating was a T-bone, no matter how high the price.

Otherwise Goldfield remained within the traditions of the mining camp gourmand. Even the delicatessans featured offerings likely to appeal to the most discriminating palate—stuffed mangoes, for example. Oysters, long prized as the ultimate dining luxury despite the logistical difficulties of transportation across the deserts before spoilage set in, often appeared on the sumptuous sounding restaurant menus. Diners at the Casey Hotel on an ordinary day would enter a room decorated with hand-painted china plates and sit down at linen-covered tables graced with cut glass wine decanters to a meal of gargantuan proportions for $1.50, including wine. It would commence with raw oysters (of course), and progress through the soup (clam chowder or consomme), the fish course (tenderloin of sole or broiled bass), salad, entrees (fricassee of veal or braised beef tongue in piquante sauce), banana fritters, roasts (prime rib, pork loin, or turkey), vegetables, desserts (cakes, cookies, or pineapple ice cream), and finally cheeses, nuts, coffee, and claret. A Thanksgiving menu might add a few extra flourishes, such as lobster newburg and sweetbread patties "ala financier" followed by punch ala Amontillado or Marasguisio glace to clear the palate before the turkey arrived, and fresh crab mayonnaise as a salad— but not many. Breakfasts were similarly substantial. Those who took the special seventy-five cent breakfast at the Goldfield Hotel grill were offered not only the usual hotcakes, biscuits, eggs, fried mush, and citrus fruits, but also strawberries or raspberries in cream, boiled salt mackerel, steak, mutton, pork chops, and fried calves liver.[34]

Aside from Victor Ajax's La Parisienne, the most renowned restaurant in the city was probably the Palm Grill, a two-story affair able to accommodate two hundred guests in private dining rooms and elegantly appointed main dining halls on both levels. Carl Glasscock later recalled the strange juxtaposition between this refined restaurant and the crudities of journeying to Goldfield on a stormy night in an open stage while large numbers of coyotes prowled and howled on the outskirts of the city: "half an hour later we were in the Palm Grill, washed and warmed, with Julius Goldsmith's violin displacing the mournful howls of the coyotes, and quail on toast before us on fine china laid upon immaculate linen."[35]

Although Goldfield dining at its best could be very good indeed, much of the food purveyed in the city was probably ghastly. The frequency of food poisoning, the boycott against the sale of spoiled meat, and the swill barrel chicken scandal at one of the butcher shops all bear graphic testimony to this. The suspicion arises that dishes like the "East Indian Chicken Currie" advertised by a local restaurant may well have been inspired by the need to conceal the questionable condition of the poultry in a preparation spicy enough to make smoke curl out of the customers' ears. Moreover, some diners reacted less rapturously than Glasscock to the culinary offerings of local restaurants. "There is a strange, dry, choking passion of rage that sweeps over a man at intervals after he has lived in one of these desert towns for a year, and fed in their restaurants," Parmeter Kent observed. The sight of yet another "galaxy of oddly colored varieties of flesh and vegetables in their thick, white oval dishes" brought on these attacks, causing the customer to rise in his seat and grind out through his teeth "some two or three sincere, crisp, crackling profanities." C. A. Walters, an early visitor to Goldfield, no doubt agreed. He thought that the "strenuous life" he had anticipated on his desert adventure began in the restaurant which served him a chicken dinner of bare bones without "even a suspicion of breast or thigh." In response to his protests, the waiter brought some rubber necks "all curled up into rings." Walters mournfully concluded that "a forty year old rooster will always cause pain."[36]

Some might differ over the merits of Goldfield's restaurant cuisine, but few would deny that they paid the top dollar for their meals by the standards of the period. Upon being presented with the bill for a T-bone steak smothered in onions, one diner studied the document with obvious displeasure and loudly inquired, "Is this a quit-claim deed to the house?" As laughter and murmurs of approval from other patrons rippled through the restaurant and the proprietor hastened forward, the customer declared in lordly fashion that he had decided against buying the establishment.

An evening's entertainment that commenced with dinner, either delectable or horrendous, often continued with a theatrical performance offering a similar range of possibilities. From an early date, amateur theatricals enjoyed considerable popularity. Anne Ellis admired the exquisitely embroidered costumes and the hand-painted Chinese lanterns used as programs in a performance of "The Mikado" staged by local talent. The Volunteer Firemen's band gave Sunday afternoon concerts for awhile. Members of the group also exhibited their talents in an occasional vaudeville show, in which one fireman "sent the audience into ecstasies with a mild and subdued rendition of the hula-hula dance." Other skits featured such items of local humor as a dance imitation of Constable Inman chasing a horse thief. The show closed with a fascinating novelty for 1907, a home movie of the firemen careening madly down the street on the new fire engine's first run.[37]

When the camp was in its heyday, Goldfielders could choose from various theatrical offerings. The Hippodrome was the largest and best known theater, but the Ross-Holley Theater, where touring theatrical companies often settled in for prolonged runs, offered close competition. The Lyric, not to be outdone, strove to stimulate attendance by giving away a diamond ring (no doubt with a microscopic stone) every Saturday night.

No details are recorded on the Electric Theater or the Areata, known as "the house of seven doors," which may have offered bawdy entertainments in the vicinity of the tenderloin. The Lyric illustrated the transitional nature of the times. First the theater began showing the new motion pictures during intermissions to enliven the "tiresome waits" between acts. Gradually movies absorbed a larger part of every program until the Lyric metamorphosed into a motion picture theater, and the Musical Arcade also entered the field. While some of the films, such as "How Glue Is Made," sounded a good deal less riveting than a volunteer fireman's hula, the film depicting the Japanese at war during a period of tension with that country reportedly aroused the audience to a patriotic frenzy.

Before the movies took over, well-known theatrical stars played the city. Nat Goodwin's financial involvement with mine promoter George Graham Rice gave him an extra incentive to appear at the Hippodrome in "A Gilded Fool," "The Genius," and other plays. Lew Dockstader, the noted minstrel, also came to Goldfield, and though Anne Ellis could not afford to attend his performance, she managed to get close enough when he paraded through the streets to touch his white satin coat. A typical vaudeville program offered comedy sketches, singing and dancing artists, "an eccentric comedian," an acrobat doing stunts on the Roman rings, "a funny tramp act," and an "Electric Spectacular." Special effects like the electric spectacular elicited as much admiration as the stars. For instance, during a 1909 performance of "The Jolly Widow" at the Hippodrome, a "splendid electrical effect" that mimicked glow worms flitting above the heads of performers charmed the audiences, as did a blacksmith number in which the company hammered vigorously at anvils, sending showers of sparks across the darkened stage.

Even when little else could be found to praise, newspaper headlines like "Whirlwind Dance Covers a Mile" applauded the amount of energy expended on Goldfield stages. The *News* informed statistically minded readers that during a recent performance at the Hippodrome the Pendleton sisters had kicked their heels above their heads a total of 229 times and raced madly across the stage 50 times. Judging from the photos, even these exertions failed to reduce the chorines from a rotund and chunky state that newsmen feebly commended as "attractive." In a mining camp with such a dearth of women, that was evidently good enough, for Anne Ellis recalled that some of the perfomers in these traveling companies married miners and stayed on in Goldfield.

In general, theatrical taste seems to have been less cultivated and sophisticated than on the Comstock. "The Three Musketeers" came as close to classic fare as the local theater afforded, and Goldfielders showed a marked preference for light comedy, vaudeville, and minstrel shows. Possibly there were good reasons for this. The *News* reported that at a musical recital given by Anna Colburn-Plummer, "Nothing showed the real skill and training of the artist more than the 'Monotone,' a single note conception, which in itself was difficult enough to render but made doubly difficult by the idiosyncracies of the piano, which was woefully out of tune and given to flatting." The press suggested that this recital occupied the pinnacle as the most "artistic evening" in the history of the camp. [38] At the same time, the "Monotone" may have provided about as much high culture as Goldfield could tolerate.

At the opposite end of the cultural spectrum from the "Monotone," "Flying Merriman" hung by his toes as he walked upside down through loops suspended from the ceiling of the Lyric Theater in a display of trapeze virtuosity that the *Chronicle* called a "first class act," a hypnotist known as Willard the Great endeavored to mesmerize his audiences, and circuses promised, among many other things, "the smallest brute actors," "ice bears," "100 imperial amazing acts," a "congress of beautiful women in physical culture exploits of perfect equilibrium—artistic posing and thrilling, hazardous gymnastic exercises," and a performance from which "all vulgarities and ancient impoliteness" had been eliminated, which raises considerable curiosity over past uncensored performances. Cozad's Dog, Pony, Monkey, and Goat Circus, evidently the first to play Goldfield, featured not only riding goats and acrobatic monkeys in its 1905 performances but also dramas and comedies in which the press declared "the animal actors do everything that human performers accomplish." [39] One hopes that this was not an oblique comment upon the Goldfield theater.

No one enjoyed the circuses more than Goldfield's children, and as an added attraction, they received free rides on the Cozad company's three hundred Shetland ponies. But even when the circus was not in town, children had plenty of amusements. The wild burros—always pronounced "bore-uhs"—that scavenged the garbage dump could readily be enticed with hay, captured, ridden (albeit with some display of recalcitrance by the burros), and kept as pets, that is, until one's parents laid down the law about a braying burro in the yard. Said John Koontz: "We didn't have any saddles. We'd just put a strap or a rope around their belly and hang on bareback, and away we'd go, buckin' and snortin,' like a deer. After they'd buck a little while, they'd straighten out, and you'd go all day on 'em. You'd just wear yourself out riding burros all over the desert." [40]

In addition to swimming, picnicking, rollerskating, sledding, fighting, and other pastimes common to children throughout the country, Goldfield youngsters took advantage of the desert whirlwinds that danced through town. They would make a tiny parachute from a handkerchief, or best of all, an old piece of silk, tie its four corners, balance it with a rock, and race after a whirlwind to stand in the middle and watch the parachute fly several hundred feet in the air. The boy whose parachute soared the highest was the winner.

Children who made games from whirlwinds could also turn a flood into an occasion for a wild ride more thrilling than a turn on a Ferris wheel. When the 1913 flood swept through the city, bearing floating shacks and desperately paddling horses, cows, and chickens, John Koontz and one of his brothers stole wash tubs from their mother. They waited until the flood "a-ragin' down" from the Malapai reached a point behind their house. Then they jumped in their tubs and rode the flood waters "halfway to the other end of town." Only after a harsh scolding from their mother did the boys realize how easily they could have drowned. [41]

Youngsters also delighted in practical jokes. After they nailed the bellrope to the timber, the officer in charge of ringing curfew was obliged to laboriously climb the tower and work the clapper with his hands. On Halloween night, a great deal of adolescent sweat and toil went into raising a buckboard to perch atop the spire of the Sacred Heart Church. Adults derived enormous pleasure from practical jokes as well, though no one knew exactly who was responsible for rounding up a herd of burros and enclosing them in the yard of a newly married couple to disrupt the wedding night with raucous braying. The favorite practical joke, almost a venerable tradition for hazing tenderfoot arrivals in the fabled West, was the fake gunfight. When tenderfoot visitors streamed into Goldfield for the Gans-Nelson fight, Frank Crampton noted that plenty of "wild west stunts were pulled." Throughout the city he saw: "Holdups, robberies, six-gun fights, men sprawled around dead or in the last agony, with ruptured bags of catsup giving the final touch of realism. It was good entertainment, and a wonderful show, but as far from anything out of real life as could possibly happen." [42]

Famous women visitors made perfect targets for these stunts. When the well-known actress Grace George remarked that she had seen everything except a gunfight while performing in Goldfield and Tonopah, the denouement could be readily predicted. As the actress and her touring company departed by train, a man on board whipped out his revolver and threatened to blast a fleeing claim jumper through the heart. Evidently the act was convincing, as Grace George fled to take refuge behind a seat and the railway car resounded with screams and pleas for mercy from her companions. [43]

Fraudulent gunfights may well have been the only entertainments lacking at Goldfield's grand holiday celebrations. At Thanksgiving the newsboys were treated to rides in autos and a feast at the Casey Hotel. The Christmas season, in addition to its spiritual significance, brought a heightened round of parties and dances. Huge bunches of red peppers decorated store windows, children received handsome gifts from the Elks Club ("You can see by this how free money was," noted Anne Ellis), and in 1907 the Mohawk Saloon hosted a free Christmas dinner for 1,400. At Easter banks of lilies decorated the churches, the camp's always fashionable women outdid themselves in finery, and so many worshippers flocked to the old Catholic church that 400 had to be turned away at the door. To celebrate the arrival of the railroad in 1905, Goldfielders thronged streets decorated with flags, streamers, and rows of fir trees to see sights that ranged from a bullfight to the ceremonial driving of the golden spike. [44]

But the grandest celebration of them all, the one that made all previous festivities seem like preliminary rounds and all subsequent holidays appear anticlimactic, was the Fourth of July celebration in 1907. On that day the old pioneer belief that the nation's birthday was the high point on the calendar and the festive mood combined with the wealth, the high hopes, and the burgeoning population of the camp in a holiday to remember. It began with a mighty blast at dawn, a series of dynamite shots fired from the peak of Columbia Mountain alternating with an equal number of earth-shaking booms from the Malapai.

It continued with a parade, the grand marshal in the lead, flanked by rafts of urchins on burros. Carriages, autos, bands, and floats followed, as did marchers, rank on rank. There were schoolchildren dressed as Uncle Sam, the Goddess of Liberty, and Columbia. Others wore ribbons representing each of the mines. Firemen in blue uniforms carried their axes, the Order of Redmen wore Indian costumes and war paint, and the Elks bore flags and white parasols. Small boys darted among the spectators exploding dynamite canes, torpedos, and other firecrackers. Crowds massed on sidewalks, balconies, and rooftops. Some spectators even perched on telephone and power poles. At one point, the crush grew so heavy that a balcony stairway began to buckle beneath the weight of the onlookers, but many strong arms propped the stairs aloft until everyone scrambled to safety.

Patriotic oratory, sporting events, and contests occupied the afternoon. Laughing contestants spilled all over the track in the wheelbarrow race. There were races for boys, men, perspiring fat men, girls, women discreetly raising their long skirts, and oldsters, who, according to the *Tribune*, used to "run down jackrabbits for a pastime." There was a ballgame between the Original Order of Abbreviated Runts (no player over five foot-six, official yell to consist of three grunts and a hogshead), garbed in straw hats and overalls and the Ancient Order of Elongated Giraffes (no player under five-foot-ten), who wore mother hubbards and sunbonnets.

These light-hearted games contrasted with the thunderous drama of the drilling contests, in which miners hammered their drills into a block of granite for glory and prize money. Historians have pointed out that the advent of electric drilling in the mines had already transformed hand drilling from a necessary skill to an anachronism. Nonetheless, the crowds found it a stirring sight to watch the brawny contestants, many of them former partners or old rivals, pound the steel at a rate reaching a hundred strokes a minute in the single-jack contest. In the double-jack, partners alternated positions every minute or so, one holding the drill while the other swung the long-handled hammer. The winners drove their spike 41.5 inches into the rock in fifteen minutes.

Of course, the day could hardly pass without a hitch or two. The lady who won the egg race ecstatically hugged the egg to her bosom with unfortunate results for her brown silk gown. A rising wind cooled the crowds but prevented the balloon ascension. The horse race was cancelled when one of the onlookers was shot in a scuffle. Teams of firemen competing to demonstrate their speed in working the hose succeeded in breaking a coupling and thoroughly drenching the spectators and themselves as the hose writhed about like a mammoth serpent on the rampage—altogether too realistic a demonstration.

The celebration culminated that night in a costume parade, with prizes awarded for such categories as best fancy decorated burro and rider, best clown, most elaborately dressed woman, best hobo, best fairy, best patriotic couple, best "colored dude," and many others. Local seamstresses had been busy sewing costumes for weeks, and many Goldfielders sent away to San Francisco for their finery. Women dressed themselves as men, men as women, and both as animals: the elephant, the giraffe proficient in social graces, and the Lohengrin swan especially pleased the onlookers.

Finally came an "All Fools Carnival," with a grand cakewalk and more prizes for the best fancy dances. As the town "slipped its leash," in the *Tribune's* words, normally sedate stockbrokers donned milkmaids' caps and ran around blowing horns. Later, amidst singing, blaring horns, and showers of confetti, the hobos, fairies, swans, clowns, and all the rest cavorted with each other until dawn flushed the skies and the revels finally came to an end. [45]

The "pleasurable excitements" of mining camp nights did much to assuage the loneliness of gold rushers torn loose from their families, their friends, and their familiar haunts. Yet many succumbed to homesickness all the same. Writing in the bumpkin mode of James Whitcomb Riley, an amateur poet named Jack Merriman mused upon a common Goldfield malady:

> Listen, pardner, and I'll tell you
> What all your ailment is;
> You have got the homesick fever.
> Yep, the 'blues' has done the biz . . .
> when old night comes a creepin'
> 'Crost the malapai's brad back;
> And with it you go a sneakin'
> By your lonely to your shack. [46]

The poet looked forward to the day when he would "drink a toast to Goldfield, in the old home, way back east."

Some, crushed by the loneliness and strangeness of the place, would quickly turn back. A few would stay on through the declining years as Goldfield evolved into a close-knit small town not very different from an extended family. Many more would leave as the boom abated, taking with them lasting friendships and associations. Whatever their disparities of background and temperament, the common experience of having been together in the last great gold rush set them forever apart from other men like the veterans of a great war. These were the pioneers who had ventured forth to "see the elephant" for themselves, and most would afterward remember those few frenzied years as the time of their lives.

IX

Scalping Boards and Legal Lollipop

BUSINESS AND THE PROFESSIONS

"Permit me to give you a piece of advice. . . . let others do the mining. The whole tendency—in fact an unceasing pressure—in a booming mining camp, is to get your dollars away from you . . . and put them into mining, and a more stupendous folly could not be imagined," J. B. Knoblock to James O'Brien, 1904

———————————————•·•·•—————

When the gold rushers round about Columbia Mountain assembled in the October sunshine in 1903 to organize Goldfield, twenty-six of thirty-six called themselves miners or prospectors, though some were novices still in the process of learning these occupations. Other callings were sparsely represented by a single physician, lawyer, or merchant. Never again during the boom years that lay ahead would so large a proportion of Goldfield's populace be physically engaged in mining. At the peak in 1906, miners probably comprised less than 15 percent of the Goldfield population, compared to between 53 and 80 percent of the male contingent in the earlier California gold towns. Yet all the fortunes being made in Goldfield in a broad spectrum of enterprises depended on the mines, which had transformed an uninhabited region of desert into a booming metropolis within just a few years. Gold was the "magic wand" that accomplished this wondrous change, and from the broker in his luxurious mahogany-trimmed offices to the popcorn vendor in the street, Goldfield abounded with entrepreneurs who had abandoned the well-rutted routines and predictable prospects of ordinary life in the hope that the cornucopia pouring from the mines would similarly transform their own fortunes.[1]

For a time, the opportunities seemed boundless. Even the deputy government surveyors who carried the chains to measure the early mining claims came to Nevada "poor as church mice" and emerged as tycoons. Soon they owned lucrative pieces of multiple Goldfield mining companies, used their positions as presumed neutral experts to foist their silent partners upon investors, and learned to promote and manipulate their mining stocks as cleverly as the slickest brokers at the exchange—all in defiance of federal regulations against the ownership of mining claims by employees in the land department. Not only were these abuses widespread, they were blatant. As one former deputy surveyor told a team of federal investigating agents, the surveyors "don't attempt to excuse" their illegal activities because "they are all making money at it." Despite the howls of defrauded investors, the surveyors faced no greater penalties than the loss of their government positions—not a serious blow to men whose only surveying by then consisted in gazing idly at the passing scenery from the windows of their private railroad cars.[2]

The Nevada state controller's reports on Esmeralda County clearly suggest that the government surveyors were not the only Goldfielders whose fortunes had multiplied. In 1903 Esmeralda ranked as one of the poorer counties in a severely depressed state. By contrast, in 1907 the value of Esmeralda County real estate had increased nearly twelve times over due to the Goldfield boom, and state property taxes from the county showed a comparable advance. Total state and county tax revenues from Esmeralda far exceeded those of any other Nevada County. Although Reno (situated in Washoe County) had been the leading population center before the gold rush and would presently reclaim that distinction, total tax revenues from Washoe county lagged 40 percent behind Esmeralda in 1907. This brief but spectacular dominance in the state financial picture would undoubtedly have been even more one-sided if Goldfield mining companies had not routinely manipulated their books to reduce tax levies—when they did not altogether ignore their bullion taxes.[3]

As in so many other camps, the first business to open its doors in Goldfield was a saloon, soon to be joined by many others. In 1905 the press reported that Goldfield had sixty saloons, about one for every 142 people if populations estimates for that year were roughly correct. The 1907 Goldfield directory listed fifty-one saloons, probably the largest and most respectable, but a survey of the smaller and more disreputable establishments would undoubtedly have boosted the total much higher. By late 1908 liquor licenses indicate that ninety saloons and small bars remained in business, or about one for every 132 people. While this may have sounded shocking in small-town America, it seems moderate by frontier standards. Leadville, for instance, may have had as many as one saloon for every eighty residents in 1880; Deadwood boasted one for every sixty residents in the same year; and three weeks after the 1907 stampede began, Rawhide weighed in with one saloon for every twenty-five inhabitants. Such figures were not entirely a reflection of the conviviality and the notorious drinking habits of the gold rushers. All these camps contained disproportionate numbers of men, the primary patrons of saloons. Consequently, the number of saloons per capita would naturally be higher than in communities with more women and children.

Even after the decline had unmistakably commenced, the state issued far more liquor licenses in Esmeralda than in any other Nevada county, and gaming fees closely followed the bullion taxes from the mines in the revenue totals in the Esmeralda County treasurer's reports. Collectively, these saloons did a business second only to mining and stocks in the Goldfield economy. In one month in 1907, the Northern announced $30,500 net winnings from the gaming tables and $15,000 in bar receipts. Returns had reportedly soared even higher at the height of the boom. In 1908 the daily payroll at the Mohawk Saloon still averaged between five and six hundred dollars, a figure far beyond the daily payroll at any mine in the golden horseshoe except Goldfield Con and the Rogers Syndicate. If the other four corner saloons did as much business as the Mohawk, the monthly payroll at these four saloons alone would have been around sixty-six thousand dollars—almost as much as the monthly payroll at Goldfield Con at a time when construction workers at the new mill boosted the company's employment figures. In keeping with the position of the saloons as highly profitable businesses, the owners organized both the Northern and the Mohawk as joint stock corporations. Goldfielders joked that henceforth when a customer ordered a dandified drink like a pousse cafe, the bartender had better stifle his natural response ("G'wan— you'll take it straight if you want a drink") because the elbows on the bar might belong to a stockholder.[4]

Despite the reputation for dishonesty that frontier gaming has enjoyed (and, quite possibly, deserved in camps like Tombstone), observers of the saloon scene unanimously affirm that Goldfield gaming was fundamentally honest. Many a dealer grew adept at palming an extra silver dollar into his pocket as he reached for his handkerchief; many a gambler sanded the edges of certain cards, or carefully drilled holes in two corners of a die, leaving one cavity empty and loading the other with mercury; and confessed counterfeiter and Goldfield gambler Jack Russell no doubt was not alone in possessing a brass device fitting inside his sleeve and connecting by cords and springs to the calf of his leg, so that a leg movement would slide the cards down his sleeve into his hand. But the house did not rig the games. As Emmett Arnold put it: "Gambling being big business, its paraphernalia had to be kept above suspicion. Any evidence of crooked games would kill the play. . . . the big house percentage lay in human nature. When the average person gets ahead of the game he inclines to play conservatively and to pinch at least a part of his winnings. But when the same person loses, he inclines to increase the bets and plunge to retrieve his losses. Therefore . . . he wins less on a winning streak than he loses on a losing streak."

W. P. De Wolf was of the same opinion, pointing out that saloon operators, in their wisdom, anticipated that sooner or later they would rake in the gambler's money without tipping the odds (a point which today's casino entrepreneurs seem to have grasped as well). Thus, they did not begrudge the gambler his occasional winnings, "for they know full well that it is but a question of time, and a short time at that, until he will gravitate back to the table and 'dump' his roll."[5]

With so large a volume of business, saloon operators needed to ensure the safety of the till. Thomas Rickard recalled that in the casino of the Goldfield Hotel a guard with a sawed-off shotgun stationed behind a screen kept watch over the roulette table. However, the sawed-off shotgun probably inspired less respect among customers than did the bouncer in the California Beer Hall—a huge Saint Bernard dog. When revelry degenerated into fisticuffs in the beer hall, the dog would pad over to the combatants at a word from proprietor Carl Fuetsch and emit a terrifying growl that brought every brawl to an instantaneous halt.[6]

These were palmy days for saloonkeepers. The wife of Carl Fuetsch could travel to Austria to visit her parents. Ole Elliott, who had commenced his working life stuffing sausages and gone on to make a sizeable stake in the Alaskan gold rush, could wager princely sums in the never-ending poker game in the back room. And "Shanghai Larry" Sullivan, a large dark man with the voice of a bellowing bull, could provide the capital that made him president of the brokerage company masterminded by George Graham Rice simply by reaching into a leather sack of gold coins garnered in his saloon. Shanghai Larry may have earned his sobriquet as proprietor of a cheap Seattle boarding house for sailors who sometimes awoke the morning after a binge to find themselves far out at sea, but in Goldfield he became an influential man whose opinions carried weight. Decades earlier Mark Twain had noted the lofty social position of saloonkeepers on the Comstock: "Youthful ambition hardly aspired so much to the honors of the law, or the Army and Navy, as to the dignity of proprietorship in a saloon." Rice made similar observations in Goldfield: "Owners of the gambling places now stood as much for financial solidity in Goldfield as did savings-bank directors in the East."[7]

Indeed the saloons often functioned as banks, since many Goldfielders rightly believed their savings more secure in the safe of a saloon. The affluent saloonkeepers also grubstaked prospectors and served as bail bondsmen. When a bank panic sent hordes of depositors milling anxiously around the teller's window to withdraw their money, a saloon keeper might deign to save one of these weaker financial institutions. Tex Rickard was said to have preserved the John S. Cook bank from bankruptcy during a panic by taking the money brought to the Northern Saloon by bank customers for safekeeping out the back door to the bank to be paid out anew. As Phillip Earl tells the story: "The bank closed with its reputation intact, and a reverse operation was carried out in the middle of the night so the men could collect from Rickard and redeposit their funds in the bank the next morning."[8]

Even when the golden age of leasing waned, mining companies (455 of them) far outnumbered any other form of enterprise in the 1907 Goldfield city directory, the only such compilation made during the boom years.

Aside from these two great staples of the local economy—mines and saloons—Goldfielders strove for the "almighty dollar" in a plethora of other enterprises, even including two interior decorators, who anticipated that those who lately sat bathless on empty barrels would soon be agonizing over the most fashionable styles in draperies and mission furniture. Perhaps her decorator was the one who inspired a Goldfield society woman to install ceilings of plaster icicles in her home to create an impression of coolness in the summer heat.

The interior decorators were not alone in their efforts to civilize the camp. Three architects hung out their shingles on the assumption that the building boom would not only continue but would involve more elaborate under-takings than a miner whacking up a new cabin for the winter on a Satur-day afternoon. Similar assumptions drove the fifty-five real estate firms listed in the directory—an extraordinary number for a town with a population that probably never exceeded eighteen thousand. These realtors handily outnumbered Goldfield's physicians (forty). The ratio of morticians (ten) to physicians was a good deal higher than in many modern communities, perhaps a grim reflection of the toll taken by the pneumonia epidemics. Unlike the morticians, relatively few nurses were listed (fifteen, all women), a number almost exactly paralleling the fourteen dentists. Entrepreneurial women also appeared as the proprietors of several stores and restaurants and were even more strongly represented among the lodging houses. In addi-tion to the inevitable milliners (eight), stitching busily to keep Goldfield's grass widows crowned with the latest in peach basket hats, all but one of the ten public stenographers listed were women. Presumably a substantial force of private stenographers assisted in dispatching the business of ninety-two lawyers and 162 brokerage firms. Even if the demand for stenographers outran the supply, Parmeter Kent declared that Goldfield set high standards for them: "If you make a mistake in your notes we throw the furniture about; if you misspell our words we throw you out of the window."[9]

Given Goldfield's reputation as the mecca of heavy drinking, none would have been surprised to see that the saloons greatly outnumbered the restaurants (twenty-seven). Of course, with the generous free lunches they offered, saloons partially usurped the function of restaurants. For several years Goldfield had its own brewery, where customers congregated in the German beer garden outside and snakes, attracted by the warmth, con-gregated in the boiler room. Early in the morning prostitutes and their companions would throw sand at the brewmaster's bedroom window, urging him to get out of bed and bring forth the beer. Nonetheless, more discri-minating customers found Goldfield beer an unappetizing concoction adversely affected by water that tasted like spoiled whitewash, and in 1908 the brewery closed for good. In addition to the restaurants and the food purveyed in saloons, six bakeries, a like number of confectioners, and two ice cream parlors also provided culinary treats.[10]

Other Goldfield businesses included: a brick factory with three large kilns producing bricks for the Goldfield Hotel and other construction projects; an ice plant; a breeder of angora cats, capitalizing upon the latest craze among Goldfield society women willing to pay up to seventy-five dollars for a kitten; a florist, who used to sell thousands of potted plants and cut flowers before he could even unpack them at Easter time; a greenhouse, where the attempt to provide the city with fresh produce, unspoiled by the long hot journey across the desert, evidently wilted along with the seedlings; and a massage parlor, a term probably devoid of the hidden meanings it has acquired in the late twentieth century because Goldfield bordellos were licensed and legal enterprises.

A good deal about the relative importance of the luxurious and the utilitarian in the mind of a gold rusher can be deduced from the fact that the camp had five jewelers but only one plumber, who turns up belatedly in the 1908 reports on business licensees. Even allowing for the dearth of indoor plumbing in much of the city, he probably had a longer waiting list than the interior decorators. As Kent feelingly observed to plumbers considering a move to Goldfield: "We are glad to see you. There is work for you. In accordance with your usual scale you get a house and lot for working a day; an automobile for finishing any job; and a share of the Mohawk mine if you remain with us all winter. Come, and be of good cheer, for the earth is yours."[11]

In 1904 an early entrepreneur named A.C. Campbell made two trips from Reno to Goldfield with wagon caravans of merchandise. While Campbell's cargo was not mentioned, it probably ran to staple food items and other necessities. A mere three years later, when goods could easily (albeit expensively) be shipped to Goldfield by railroad, luxuries abounded. Although 1907 was in many ways a lean Christmas that followed hard on the heels of the destruction of the miners' union, a shopping tour in the pages of the *Chronicle* provided a glimpse of the variety and extent of merchandise available. Among many other establishments, John Holley's store offered "gloves, petticoats, veils, garters, shawls, doilies, table covers, and everything to delight the heart feminine." For the heart masculine, Harry Coffee, who somewhat enigmatically advertised himself as "your bosom friend," and other haberdashers sold "Crusader" dress shoes, rubber coats, and silk underwear and handkerchiefs, in addition to suspenders, Stetsons, and other regulation items.

Farther down the street, the Palm Studio displayed photos, "which are always acceptable as presents . . . and of the greatest interest to friends elsewhere." It may be parenthetically noted that the Palm Studio's photographer, Per Larson, was probably as close as Goldfield came to a resident artist. No young adventurer sketched the denizens of the camp as John Borthwick had done during the California gold rush. Nor did a traveling journalist and illustrator indelibly record his impressions of Goldfield

In the Palm Studio, Swedish-born photographer Per Larson's wares dangled from the ceiling and stood stacked on every available surface. During the Goldfield phase of his career, Larson took at least 1,000 photos, some of which have fortunately survived (Larson Collection, Nevada State Museum)

as J. Ross Browne had done on the Comstock. Even the principal newspaper illustrator, Boyd Moore of the *Goldfield Chronicle*, showed only minor talent in comparison to his savage but brilliant contemporary, Arthur Buel of the *Tonopah Sun*.

After mailing Larson's photos of local scenes to distant friends, the holiday shopper might pause at the Bank Cafe for goods "of a liquid order," perhaps a sustaining draft of the proprietor's famous Denver punch or a bottle of the 1854 vintage cognac purchased especially for the season. At the Lord-Cochran jewelry store, the *Chronicle*'s reporter waxed almost lyrical over the "dazzling gems," gold cigarette and match cases, gold cigar cutters, gold-mounted hour glasses, Chinese jade, ladies' combs mounted with gold and gems, watches (up to $450 each), lorgnettes, diamond and sapphire crescents, gold and silver belts, silver brandy flasks, and local nugget jewelry, including hatpins made of blue ore from Bullfrog. Though not mentioned in the Christmas shopping tour, alluring "kimonas" were much in demand in the tenderloin, and the stores always kept a plentiful supply of silk, lace, and crepe de chine kimonos and luxurious lingerie in stock for this free-spending clientele. Lena Hammond, a young sales girl in the Max Meyer and Company department store, slipped on a particularly tempting pink silk kimono with lace on the bosom and admired herself in the mirror only to be sharply reprimanded by an older clerk, "You take that off! That's for floozies!"[12]

Goldfield's furriers displayed more luxury goods, chinchilla, ermine, sealskin, mink, sable, fox, black lynx, astrachan, and Persian lamb, including many fur "sets" for children. However, gifts for children such as "fancy toys" were scarcely mentioned in the holiday bazaar, perhaps reflecting the continued predominance of young single adults in the camp. The confectioner, at least, had children in mind when he placed a giant candy cane in his window, amidst the handmade candy baskets and other temptations, and promised to award it to the child who came closest to guessing its weight.

While the merchants enjoyed considerable success, they seem to have loomed less large in the social and political life of the camp than mine promoters, lawyers, and saloon keepers. This, of course, was not true of the newspaper editors, who not only presided over prosperous businesses but wielded enormous influence. In addition to the usual functions of the early twentieth-century urban newspaper—focussing public attention on local problems, keeping a diffuse population informed on public events, and articulating community opinion—mining camp newspapers had a further role. The successful development of a town on the mining frontier depended upon the promotional activities of a local newspaper geared to distant investors and potential residents, as well as local readers. Mining camp editors well understood this necessity. Goldfield newspapers could—and did—soft pedal political corruption and the ravages of the black plague, along with other unpleasant subjects, but never did they falter in their primary function of promoting the camp.

In its heyday, the Goldfield Press Club boasted over seventy members, variously employed at several newspapers. None of these ascended to subsequent fame as did Mark Twain from the Comstock, nor did their reportage sparkle with the humor of earlier Nevada journalists like Dan De Quille and Sam Davis. But the best reporters, men like W. P. De Wolf and William McClure Gotwaldt, continued to write in the fine tradition of frontier journalism. Some of these reporters had migrated westward pursuing a wide variety of vocations, of which journalism was only the most recent. Joseph Donohue, born in Ireland, schooled in Massachusetts, real estate salesman in Kansas, police magistrate in Cripple Creek, and finally mining editor of the *Tribune* was probably typical.

The fledgling camp's first newspaper was the *Goldfield News*, an eight page weekly, which published its premiere issue on April 29, 1904 on an old hand press welded together by an ingenious blacksmith from an assortment of scrap metal. Goldfield's residents had reportedly subscribed five hundred dollars to launch editor and publisher James O'Brien, a recent arrival from Denver, and his partner R. E. L. Windle in the business of publicizing the camp. The first issue of the *News*, promising "All That's New and True in the Greatest Gold Camp Ever Known," was so eagerly received that O'Brien cursed himself for cranking out only 1,500 copies on his rickety press and hastily bought back as many as he could at twenty-five cents each to be resold for a dollar. During the next two years, O'Brien's newspaper prospered to the point that the manager of the *Denver Mining Record* wrote him with a shade of envy: "Understand you have made so much money that it will take the rest of your days to count it. Hope this is true." In January 1906, O'Brien sold the paper to Charles Sprague, who more strongly infused it with his own Democratic viewpoint and added an evening daily edition in February 1909. [13]

By that time several other Goldfield newspapers had come and gone. The *Goldfield Vigilant*, *Nevada Mining Bulletin*, and *Joshua Palm* vanished almost as fast as they appeared. *Goldfield Gossip*, edited by the witty Parmeter Kent and making no pretense at comprehensive coverage or objective reporting, lasted a little over a year. It succumbed in January 1908, sometime after Kent was obliged to make the embarrassing admission that he had behaved like an "amazing ass, unable to take care of a dollar." Yes, Parmeter Kent and Sidney Flower, former editor of a Chicago magazine called *New Thought*, were one and the same. Yes, in the persona of Flower he had used the magazine to promote stock in a hodge-podge of disastrous commercial enterprises from hair tonics, nicotine-free cigars, and milk diets to gold mines. And yes, he had lost these funds at the race track, postal authorities had closed down *New Thought* for mail fraud, and Sidney Flower had borrowed enough money to head for the new mecca for men of promotional talents, Goldfield, where he metamorphosed into Parmeter Kent. Apparently the "amazing ass" had not yet been entirely laid to rest. In 1909 a federal grand jury indicted him for promoting stock through the pages of *Goldfield Gossip* and pocketing both the investors money and the stocks. Considering that Flower/Kent's past career had so admirably prepared him for the conduct of business in Goldfield, *Goldfield Gossip* should have lasted a good deal longer. [14]

In February 1905 the first daily, the *Goldfield Sun*, made its debut. It was edited by the virulently anti-IWW Lindley Branson, who also published the *Tonopah Sun*. Bitter conflict with the union, compelled Branson to suspend publication in August 1906 and retreat to Tonopah, where he continued to excoriate Goldfield's union radicals through the pages of the *Tonopah Sun*. To refute the "misrepresentations and slanders of our capitalist press," Goldfield's radical Socialists attempted in the summer of 1907 to launch a newspaper of their own, *Nevada Workman*, but the venture foundered in less than six months.

By contrast, the former *Goldfield Sun* prospered. Sold to J. M. Burnell and John Martin, it reappeared as the *Goldfield Tribune*, a publication destined to rise over several contenders as the ultimate winner in the newspaper field. At its peak, the *Tribune* had over five thousand subscribers, in addition to news wagon sales, and also did a big business in job printing for mining firms anxious to hasten their newsletters to investors and willing to pay large bonuses. In those flush times, the demand for printing in Goldfield so far exceeded the capacity of its newspaper plants that one hundred thousand dollars worth of job printing was farmed out each month to firms in Reno and Carson City. Even news wagon dealers and newsboys floated high on the tide of prosperity. Their voices could be heard bawling above the cacophony of street sounds: "Get your home paper! Papers from everywhere! New York, Chicawgo, St. Louie, Den–ver, Salt Lake, Los Angeles, Frisco, and the Gold–field papers."[15]

A second daily, the *Goldfield Chronicle*, published by Horace Dunn, entered the field at the height of the boom in November 1906. In early 1908 the *Chronicle* acquired the *Goldfield Review*, a weekly which had been appearing since 1904, and continued it as a weekly edition of the *Chronicle*. Despite this consolidation, Goldfield still had more newspapers, with three weeklies and two dailies, than her dwindling population could support. Why the *Chronicle* was to be the loser in the ensuing contest with the *Tribune* had little to do with the lively and entertaining quality of the newspaper's reportage and a great deal to do with the political enmities aroused by its muckraking and its independent stance.

In the autumn of 1907, the *Chronicle* committed what was probably a fatal error by inspiring and covering a grand jury investigation into official graft, a subject which the other newspapers tactfully avoided. Under heavy pressure, editor Dunn refused to reveal his confidential sources in court. Angry officials threatened to put the *Chronicle* out of business, while the newspaper issued defiant blasts against the "pathetic" incompetence of county officials. As a result, the *Chronicle* lost the contracts for county printing which might have helped to tide the enterprise over when subscribers and job printing orders dwindled. Dunn bitterly declared: "Had the *Chronicle* so desired it could have ambled up to the democratic trough and been fed so long as it were humble; it could have wallowed, even." While continuing to relentlessly expose scandals in powerful quarters, the newspaper fell into debt, and the John S. Cook bank acquired its obligations. By 1909 the *Chronicle* was floundering desperately. Dunn cut the newspaper's price to five cents (half the cost of the *Tribune*) and also sharply lowered subscription rates. But newsdealers refused to sell the paper for reduced commissions, a union decision allegedly engineered by the *Tribune*. In February 1909 the bank foreclosed, and the crusading *Chronicle* ceased to exist.[16]

The *News*, which sought to benefit from the *Chronicle's* demise by commencing daily editions, was next to succumb. Unlike many other Goldfield reporters, Charles Sprague, the editor since 1906, was an educated man who had studied journalism at Princeton. Born in Ohio in 1865, he had edited three newspapers in Colorado, where he became a prominent politician in the state legislature. When he moved on to Goldfield in 1905, Sprague brought his political ambitions as well as his journalistic gifts. At first his prospects seemed promising, but after his financial backers, Loftus and Davis, withdrew in the wake of the stock market crash, he inherited a large debt for the extravagantly expensive *News* building. By the time he ran for congress in 1910, he had incurred the malevolent enmity of George Wingfield, who made it a high priority to defeat Sprague and destroy his newspaper. As usual, Wingfield succeeded in his aims. Sprague lost the election and was forced to sell the *News* to the *Tribune* in March 1911. Unlike so many of his fellow gold rushers, Sprague did not decamp in the face of defeat. He served the county in the state senate, and through the declining years, he continued to reside in Goldfield, where the civic-minded qualities he had long displayed as a newspaperman made him a strong asset to the community. [17]

The *Tribune* emerged the apparent winner of the newspaper wars. Yet, in a sense, the *Tribune* lost as well. The *Chronicle* and the *News* had at least gone down with their flags flying and their independence intact. The *Tribune* survived financially but at a price the other two dailies refused to pay. Wells Drury, in his account of Nevada journalism, blamed its downfall upon the "machinations" of two stockholders who maneuvered the *Tribune* into acquiring the defunct *Goldfield Review* plant, and with it a crushing burden of debt: "This sounded the death knell of the *Tribune* as an independent newspaper, for it was only a short time before it was numbered with the satellites of interests that found it necessary to have an organ to shape the course of public affairs." [18] In short, the *Tribune* became an anomaly—a notably conservative and Republican newspaper serving a community of predominantly Democratic and Socialist voters.

While Goldfield may have lacked artists and novelists, she had no dearth of visionaries. Those visions that did not emerge in fantastical mining and business schemes sometimes took the form of new inventions, for the camp abounded with incipient Edisons. Some devised improvements for the mines, including a safety device for the crossheads to prevent mining accidents and a new method of timbering that required less wood than the commonly used square sets developed on the Comstock. George Truax, a practical inventor, sought to resolve the problem of the omnipresent fly with a screen sectioned so that flies (which only walk upward) would be tricked into making an exit. Evidently the sectioned fly screen found less favor than an earlier Truax invention, an ore car which became standard equipment in the mines. Another inventor, drawing his inspiration from the surrounding scenery, concocted a plan for making building blocks from sagebrush.

At the dawn of the motor age, Goldfield inventors looked both forward and backward. Before the new carriage brake designed by an ingenious Goldfielder could sweep the transportation field, carriages slid into obsolescence. Inventor Charles Chrisman, with a better sense of future trends, developed the Chrisman "Desert Flyer," a sixty horsepower auto with no gears. On a demonstration run, the "Desert Flyer" bounded over the rough seventy-mile road from Goldfield to Rhyolite in two and a half hours, which was considered remarkably good time. Saloonkeeper Ole Elliott and other capitalists organized a company to produce Chrisman's auto, but apparently the venture met with no success. [19]

Schemes even more imaginative than desert flyers and sagebrush adobe were nonetheless afoot. Several Goldfielders had turned their talents to airships, and the *News* quipped that Wilbur Wright had telegraphed to reserve a place among the charter members of the Goldfield Aero Club. A. E. Beller, a railroad man, contrived a dirigible with cigar-shaped gas reservoirs and an aluminum passenger compartment fastened underneath by encircling bands. J. R. Froberg, a forty-five-year old mining engineer, had been at work on his version of the airship at odd moments for seventeen years. He had been known to predict aerial warships and aerial travel between major American cities—ravings that caused his wife and friends to exchange pitying glances. Froberg, whom even his nearest and dearest tended to dismiss as a mad visionary, had difficulty persuading investors to finance a prototype, but one of the desert inventors may have succeeded. People reported seeing an airship making secret test flights through the night skies near Rhyolite. With a large headlight beaming rays afore and a small twinkling stern light, the apparition appeared to travel at twenty to forty miles per hour on a level course about half a mile above ground. [20]

Due to Goldfield's unique position at the end of the frontier and the start of the twentieth century, these harbingers of future air travel were curiously juxtaposed with the oldest form of transportation—the horse, and all the forms of knavery and enterprise surrounding him. While the mysterious airship sailed tranquilly through the night skies, horse traders dickered in the dusty streets below, just as they had in the earliest pioneer settlements. A local doctor who purchased a shining black horse that "scintillated and irradiated and was altogether lovely" from one of these plausible charlatans observed a disconcerting change in the animal. As the days passed by, its shining black coat dimmed to a muddy gray and finally a scruffy white. The new owner declared that he only wished the former owner had sold him the black polish along with the horse. [21]

Many in the hoarse, shouting, coatless, uncollared crowd of brokers massed around the caller inside the Goldfield stock exchange were in fact a short step removed from the horse trader in the street. Stock trading in Goldfield had commenced in the winter of 1904–05 with informal nightly sessions in the Northern Saloon where brokers gathered to trade thirty or forty thousand shares. The Goldfield Mining Stock Exchange opened in a basement in October 1905 with single daily sessions at 1:30 P.M., later moving to a commodious flat-roofed stone building with large plate glass windows. Morning and evening sessions soon became the norm and a second exchange, the Goldfield Stock and Exchange Board, opened its doors in 1906. Goldfield women, from the laundress in gingham to the society woman in diamonds and silks, sandwiched in the crowd or seated on chairs in the "ladies' corner," shared in the feverish excitement. Sometimes the yelling literally rattled the windows. If the electric power failed, the brokers would continue by candlelight rather than cease trading. In periods of particular euphoria, they reverted to the practices of early days and convened informal sessions of "curb trading" outside the exchange during off hours, a sea of hats in the street. After mining stocks crashed in 1907 and the market shriveled, the two exchanges combined into one.

Between 1860 and 1930, some two hundred stock exchanges specializing in mining and oil securities were organized in the United States, the earliest in San Francisco. The first mining town stock exchange opened in Virginia City in 1863, soon followed by exchanges in other Nevada mining camps. Throughout the latter nineteenth century, the fundamentals of "stock devilment" in the market and widespread gambling in mining stocks among all sectors of the local populace remained unchanged. Comstock historian Grant Smith considered the great mining discovery a "boon to the thousands who found in it opportunity for persistent and useful work" and "also a bane to the thousands who converted it into an instrument for trickery and passionate gaming."[22] Developments in Goldfield would further extend the accuracy of his assessment.

In the Goldfield era, the Los Angeles, Salt Lake, Chicago, and New York exchanges played some role, but San Francisco remained the sun around which the Goldfield exchanges orbited. San Francisco "made the market" on Goldfield mining stocks in the morning, and if San Francisco decided to drop a stock from the board, the death knell sounded. When Goldfielders wined and dined a visiting delegation of three hundred San Francisco stockbrokers at a banquet and a grand ball in as lavish a fashion as the crudities of the camp in 1905 allowed, they did so because they were acutely aware of the importance of this group to Goldfield finance. The San Franciscans were impressed. Indeed so much impressed by the "excitement and revelry" accompanying their arrival, as well as the mines on display, that a number of them decided to abandon the "prosaic curb" in the Bay City and stay in Goldfield. Though the new camp drew brokers from exchanges throughout the nation, former San Franciscans, sometimes operating branch offices of San Francisco firms, or more loosely linked to old associates there, became a major force at the original Goldfield exchange, while Coloradans formed the nucleus of the new exchange.

At the peak, 370 mining stocks were listed, the membership of both Goldfield exchanges included three hundred brokers, many of them new-comers to the profession, and a seat cost $2,400 (compared to $10,000 on the San Francisco exchange). Evidently commercial activity still provided a swift avenue upward for the foreign born in mining camps, much as it had in Grass Valley and Nevada City half a century earlier. The press commented on the polyglot origins, as well as the "restless energy" and "perpetual chance taking" of the "struggling howling mass" in the exchange: "There are found the bright and quick thinking Jews, the sturdy and slow going Germans, the restless and lucky Irish, who have acquired for themselves at least a temporary prosperity—temporary, because, in many cases this maelstrom of trading compels hitherto lucky operators and traders to disgorge their winnings to help onward the star of ascendency of some new Richmond in the field. Here are also found the cast off relics of the Big Exchange, broken in spirit and in pocket, who . . . watch at the gates for a fortune which will never come."[23]

The most successful among the brokerage fraternity built offices elegantly furnished with overstuffed leather chairs and mahogany desks and wall trimmings, the better to impress their clients. Donald Mackenzie's offices, the largest, contained space for forty clerks, as well as mailing and stock rooms where the work force labored to "float" seven major mining prop-erties. Other brokerage offices ranged downward from this enviable peak to family mail order firms where a man designated himself as "General Manager," his wife and daughter as "Clerk and Typist," and his son as "Mine Superintendent." Unfortunately, much of Goldfield mine promotion was sheer surface display because many of those purveying mining stocks were laughably ignorant of mining. George Graham Rice later acknowledged that his partner, Shanghai Larry Sullivan, knew no more about mining than "an ostrich knows about ocean tides." Unaware that the mining term "winze" denotes a shaft dug from the lower levels of a mine, Shanghai Larry once boasted in his booming voice to a group of potential investors in the L. M. Sullivan Trust Company, "Right now I've got a whole carload of winzes coming in to rush development work on half a dozen properties."[24]

Shanghai Larry was by no means unique. Henry Miles, an old Gold-fielder, described the steps by which newcomers to the camp who had never been underground or done any work connected with mining trans-formed themselves into "mining men." The first step was to get an option on a claim, however remote from the mineral-bearing zone, and a member-ship in the Montezuma Club where potential investors from the East con-gregated: "Then get a Khaki coat and trousers; a miner's candlestick; a broad-brimmed hat; high-lace boots. Next liberally sprinkle candle grease on coat; pants; hat, and boots; stick the candlestick in one boot leg. It was essential to memorize some mining terms: e.g. 'winze'; 'cross-cut'; 'locus of the vein' . . . 'foot wall' . . . 'shattered dioxide'; 'gangue'; etc. The foregoing being done then lounge in the Montezuma Club or the 'Northern'; endeavor to contact a well-to-do 'tenderfoot.' . . . Often . . . substantial business, and professional men, in the East, could be induced to invest, and keep on investing for years on ground that never produced a ton of ore."[25]

Some regarded ignorance of mining as a positive asset for promoters, perhaps because it gave freer rein to their imaginations. "A man does not have to be a miner to make money under right conditions in a mining camp. Oftentimes the less he knows about such things the more fortunate it is for him," observed the respected mine promoter J. P. Loftus, of Sandstorm fame, to James O'Brien.[26] Together with the candid reminiscences of George Graham Rice, Loftus's private letters to the young newspaper editor, with whom he was involved in mine promotion schemes, offer startling insights on the methods of two highly successful mining entrepreneurs.

The potential for profit was enormous, and true stories abounded of men who entered the camp with nothing but pocket change and later strutted through the streets as millionaires. Rice was one of these. According to historian Richard Lilliard, Rice (born Jacob Herzig) had "stolen, gambled, forged, swindled, and tipped at race tracks since boyhood when his first victim was his father." Having done time in the New York State Reform School and the state prison, Rice left what he always termed "my youthful Past" behind and arrived in Goldfield in the winter of 1904–05 flat broke with fifteen dollars of borrowed money. Though he managed to persuade a newspaper to hire him, his boundless ignorance of mining got him fired in less than a week. Undaunted, Rice started an advertising agency which placed advertising copy for Goldfield brokerage firms in newspapers throughout the nation and blossomed into a huge success.

Soon Rice announced his own brokerage firm, the L. M. Sullivan Trust Company, capitalized with the gold coins from Shanghai Larry Sullivan's leather sack. Like most Goldfield brokerage firms, Rice's company dealt in stocks for clients at the exchange and also promoted its own "flotations." Following the common practice of placing a governor, a United States senator, or some other prominent personage on the directorate to lend respectability to the enterprise, Rice induced Nevada's governor, "Honest John" Sparks, to assume the presidency of several of these mining companies. Though the mining companies produced no ore of any value, profits rolled in all the same. After Rice ran display ads in the big city newspapers, stock in one of his new mining companies was oversubscribed inside two weeks, bringing him one hundred thousand dollars in profits. As fast as Rice could announce a new mining company, investors gobbled up the stock. Sometimes Rice was forced to cancel his ads because his offerings were oversubscribed before the copy reached the newspapers. Before the decline in Goldfield mining stocks, the absence of genuine value in Rice's mining properties, and the enmity of George Wingfield combined to bring his house of cards tumbling down, Rice's energetic promotion had parlayed a few poor mining claims into a multimillion dollar business.[27]

Why were American investors so gullible? Rice's answer was: "The stock offerings undoubtedly *struck a popular chord.* Tens of thousands of people . . . whose incomes were not sufficient to permit them to indulge in stock-market speculation in rails and industrials, found in cheap mining stocks the thing they were looking for—an opportunity . . . to give full play to their gambling, or speculative, instinct." Another broker opined that investors accepted the dark-horse odds of mining stock speculation in hopes of making huge gains. Yet much of the advertising for Goldfield mining stocks aimed for the innocent "sucker," not the sophisticated investor aware of the risks and able to afford them. One mine promoter observed of his stock sales to investors in upstate New York: "I know they are fresh, and not overloaded with mining stocks and have not had everything hawked at them furthermore I know that a large percent of them are now susceptible. . . ."[28]

A host of mendacious advertisements and prospectuses in editorial guise cleverly attempted to relieve working people of the life savings set aside for old age by arguing that investment in mining had ceased to be speculative. Indeed they claimed that mining had turned into a "regular business undertaking, as certain of success as either banking or manufacturing, and the profits are immensely greater." The Nelly Bly Mining Company (never a producer) promised investors that their money would be "safer than in a bank," while bringing returns of several hundred percent. With no moral compunctions, these promoters preyed upon the fears that plagued many people in an era that predated social security: "One of the problems of the present day that is confronting both men and women is how to provide a competence for old age. A man may toil for years on a farm, in an office, in a workshop or factory, and find himself unprovided for against the certain coming of infirmities. . . . As a man or woman passes the years of middle life, his or her services become less valuable to employers, and the time will come when it will be difficult for them to find employment. How, then, can a wage-earner use his savings to make them . . . bring him an income?" Where else but in mining stocks, and what is more, the promoters of the Nellie Bly obligingly allowed the "toiler . . . with no brighter prospects than to drudge day by day" to sink his money into their stocks on the installment plan.[29]

In Goldfield and throughout the nation, working people responded eagerly to these seductive arguments. Anne Ellis and her miner husband invested and lost their entire savings in mining stocks, as did the owners of the busy bakery where she worked for awhile, along with countless other residents of the camp. American investors may have lost as much as $150,000,000 when Goldfield mining stocks crashed, and a comparable amount on the unlisted stocks vended by the "wild cats." As Rice observed, Goldfield became "the graveyard of a million blighted hopes."[30]

The rules set forth by the American Mining Congress for the protection of investors reveal both the unconscionable scheming of the "lemon peddlers" and the regrettable fact that investors who followed every rule could still wind up with nothing but a drawer full of handsome stock certificates. If the investor ascertained, as the Mining Congress suggested, that a legally incorporated mining company held clear title, without debts or encumbrances, to a well-located property, this might protect him from wild cats who never owned a foot of ground. But not from Rice, whose flotations were legitimately purchased and organized. Or from Loftus, who urged O'Brien to acquire properties indiscriminately: "Go right ahead and use the pool money, use your own money, or any other money that you may pick up honestly or dishonestly, even to the extent of acquiring it by holding up men in the streets, for the purpose of acquiring mining interests anywhere and everywhere. . . ." Loftus knew that the value of the claims hardly mattered because "the stocks would sell regardless."[31]

The Mining Congress recommended inquiring about development work done on the property. Again, no protection. Some promoters, like Loftus, preferred to limit development to one or two assessment holes "in soft places." He advised O'Brien: "Do not do a single thing that you do not have to. For instance, should you at any point open anything that looks good, I would suggest that you do not attempt to sink ten feet on it. Get some fellow . . . and give him a lease . . . and thus get the development work done for nothing." But Rice, who believed in laying out expenditures to multiply returns, stirred up a veritable whirlwind of development work on his properties without ever producing pay ore.[32]

Then was the mine's past production the critical question for investors? Production gave no clear guidance either, because producing mines often played out early (like the Sandstorm) and those which had never produced might suddenly strike bonanza (like the fabulous Mohawk). If the investor demanded to be shown an engineer's report on the mine, this too provided no certitude. Companies often presented reports from engineers who viewed their mines favorably and sometimes held a hidden financial stake in them. Even honest engineers could be addled by the enthusiasm surrounding them and submit "elastic" reports that exaggerated proven ore reserves. In short, even a company that met all the Mining Congress's criteria could still be a disastrous investment.

Other methods of selecting mining stocks proved no better. Many investors relied heavily on newspaper reportage. But newspaper mining editors long trained to avoid the cardinal sin of "knocking the camp" routinely turned in favorable reports. Furthermore, they often lacked time for careful analysis, and even when they had not received gifts of stock from a mining company to sweeten their opinions, they often succumbed to the excitement surrounding a promising discovery—a recurrent phenomenon in the Western mining camps since Comstock days. Nor did the presence of famous names on a mining company directorate provide investors with any guarantee. Senator Nixon and George Wingfield, though their association with the Mohawk gave their names a golden luster, appeared as officers of numerous worthless mining companies useful only for purposes of stock promotion. John Cook, Goldfield's most prominent banker, lent his name to the notorious Union Securities swindle, while Governor Sparks assumed the presidency of several Rice flotations. Famous mines offered no better security to the investor than famous names. The best of mines, like Goldfield Con, might still make very poor investments when their owners had overcapitalized them at levels far beyond their real value. If steel king Charles Schwab could be so badly buncoed on his mining investments that he characterized Nevada as a den of thieves, less worldly investors scarcely stood a chance. [33]

A number of practices at the exchanges multiplied the opportunities for profit among the unscrupulous. In 1906 the *News* urged the exchange to make an organized effort to protect the public by exposing hundreds of fraudulent Goldfield flotations then in progress, an evil that the listing committees empowered to investigate all mining companies with stocks quoted by the exchange had failed to correct. Needless to say, because its membership profited hugely from questionable stocks, whether listed or not, the exchange looked the other way. Though the San Francisco earthquake and fire destroyed remarkably few of the records on stocks in San Francisco brokerage offices, overissues of stock and forged stock certificates remained a persistent problem that occasional attempts at stock registry never solved.

Then as now, "sharpers" hammered stock up and down for profit, often using rumors to exploit the public mood of the moment. Loftus candidly noted: "When the craze is on locally, any old thing will bring good money." The *Tribune* further explained: "Goldfield is essentially mercurial. . . . At times optimistic, the people are the next moment plunged into the depths of despair by a flickering breeze and they rush to the other extreme. This knowledge has helped the speculators who toy with the savings of their patrons with a callousness to all moral susceptibility." The *Tribune* also charged that labor negotiations had been needlessly prolonged because both sides used the vicissitudes at the bargaining table to play the stock market: "The stock exchanges are the root of the evil. . . . the common people are between two millstones which grind and grind until the last cent of money has been extracted from the poor deluded fools who imagine that they can make a fortune in a day without possessing any knowledge of the inside workings of the cabal that has the market in its clutches." [34]

The list of knavish practices by this "cabal" went on and on. Exploiting the differences in stock prices between widely separated exchanges like San Francisco and New York had long been a favorite ploy. Now, so long as two separate exchanges operated within Goldfield, brokers could profitably milk the minor differences between the two for profit. By late 1908, the exchanges had combined into a single "scalping board," and those brokers who had survived the great stock crash a year earlier acted in concert on "wash sales" (that is, matched orders) so blatant that the *Chronicle* thought them "evident to the merest tyro at the game." First, investors were induced to purchase a certain stock by glowing reports of new bonanzas planted in the newspapers. Then, through "preconcerted plans," the brokers would break the price within a few minutes with wash sales and "shake the sucker down."[35]

In the end, many in the brokerage fraternity reaped what they had sowed. With the dawning of the day of reckoning, sharpers who had bought stocks on margin and speculated unsuccessfully on the market with clients' funds went broke as swiftly as they had risen in the heady days of 1906 while the market soared. Though actual developments in the Goldfield mines and shared trends in the national financial markets affected this rollercoaster process, so too did the machinations of George Wingfield. The heavy loans made to margin traders through the Cook bank in which Wingfield was heavily interested undoubtedly stoked the fires of speculation at the same time that they stimulated investment in Goldfield Con; the dominance of Goldfield Con, as some had foreseen, choked off the diversity on which a local mining stock exchange depended; and Wingfield's practice of destroying rivals who had incurred his ill will, most notably Rice and the once great house of Mackenzie, accelerated the decline of the Goldfield traders.

Those brokers who came out winners had probably followed the general Wingfield modus operandi—selling high and diversifying. But few of those who for a time had played and won at the grand gamble of Goldfield mining had the self-control to walk away. It was often said among Goldfielders that all the money they had raked in "went back into the ground" in fruitless searches for new bonanzas and purchases of worthless mining stock. Many brokers no doubt bore their losses lightly, like the inveterate gamblers they were, and moved on to greener pastures. Rice, for one, promoted more mines from Reno. He later went on to New York, more shady promotions, a conviction for mail fraud, and the publication of his memoirs, aptly entitled *My Adventures with Your Money.*[36]

But not all showed themselves so resilient as Rice after financial disaster struck. Major William Stanton, an old Civil War veteran and former chief of the Salt Lake City fire department, more lately executive of the Goldfield Business Men's and Mine Owners Association and a major player at the stock exchange, fired a bullet into his own mouth. Another suicide was Thomas Niblock, whose brokerage house had raked in hundreds of thousands of dollars in the heady days of 1906. Despite his youth, Niblock's success had appeared no more than his due, for he had seemed destined for great things, almost from the cradle. Born Thomas Prooban to a distinguished family in Ireland, he had entered politics soon after graduating from Dublin University. According to the *Chronicle*, his eloquence marked him at once as a "man of unusual gifts." After he took a seat in parliament, his constituents idolized him, and his future as a statesman of renown seemed assured. But he became enamored of the wrong woman and eloped to roam the continent with her, throwing his political prospects to the winds. In time his passion cooled. After finally leaving the lady, he read a newspaper report of her death in a French railroad crash with a male companion erroneously identified as himself and taken home to Ireland by his family for burial. The young man decided to let the error stand and changed his name from Prooban to Niblock. He resolved to make a fortune in America that would compensate his family for his misdeed on that future day when he would return to Ireland in triumph.

After Niblock left the New York stock exchange to join the Goldfield rush, the dream of the prodigal son's return as a financial scion seemed on the verge of realization. But his huge winnings on the rising tide of mining stock speculation later evaporated when the market collapsed. A move to the newer camp of Rawhide failed to change his luck. By the time he ended his own life in early 1909, he was penniless. Goldfielders remembered only his reckless Irish charm and ignored his reversal of fortune. Everyone in Rawhide turned out for his burial in the desert cemetery where he lies yet, a long way from his other grave in the misty verdure of Ireland. [37]

Not far behind the stockbrokers in the fanciful realms of speculation were Goldfield's bankers, a wholly different breed from the staid and cautious gentlemen who gave banking the reputation for conservatism and financial solidity that it enjoyed in many American cities of the period. Of Goldfield's five banks, all but one founded in the 1904–05 period, three collapsed within five years, bringing financial ruin to their depositors. The reason in every case lay in the bankers' financial manipulations. In advance of legislation regulating banks and providing federal deposit insurance, no restrictions hampered Goldfield bankers from treating the depositors' funds in a manner that recalled buccaneers on the Spanish Main leaping aboard a captured treasure ship.

Goldfield's most successful bank was the John S. Cook and Company, which opened its doors in January 1905 in a wooden shack adjoining the Palace Saloon. Later that year the bank moved to statelier quarters in the "Nixon block," a three-story stone structure with striped awnings shading its large windows. Those fittings that signalled success to the business community were soon in place, mahogany desks and trimmings and overstuffed leather chairs, in addition to a steel ceiling to foil bank robbers descending from above and a much admired novelty, a rubber-tiled floor. Considerable assets lay stashed in the vaults beneath that floor, for the bank had fueled the stock boom with its practice of easy lending to purchasers of stock in Goldfield Con at the same time that it enriched Wingfield and Nixon, principal shareholders in both the bank and the mining company. In the spring of 1907, the bank reported deposits well in excess of six million dollars. If estimates that deposits in all Goldfield banks had reached ten million dollars are correct, the town's per capita deposits of $555 more than doubled the level found by historian Watson Parker in Deadwood in 1904 and exceeded the national average almost seven times over. [38]

When the speculators went broke, the Cook bank held a host of bad loans, but it still stood while other banks failed. Perhaps one of its most important assets was the influence of Senator Nixon, an experienced banker who had no intention of ruining his political career with a bank failure. In 1909 Wingfield took over the Cook bank, acquiring Nixon's bank holdings at the same time that he purchased Nixon's share of Goldfield Con. When he subsequently acquired Cook's interest as well, Wingfield became sole owner of the bank, as he also was of so much else in Goldfield by that time. The only other viable bank in town, the First National, founded in 1908 by Lucien Patrick and others, including Wingfield's rival, Tom Lockhart, proved unable to compete with the well-entrenched Cook bank for the rapidly diminishing business of a mining camp in decline and gave up the ghost in 1913. [39]

Along with other peaks jutting forth on the landscape of memory like the Gans-Nelson boxing match, old Goldfielders are likely to reminisce about the bank runs that accompanied the October 1907 financial panic. First, a rumor licked through the streets like wildfire: all the banks were in serious trouble. George Springmeyer, the young attorney, heard it and rushed to the Nye and Ormsby County bank with his friends to withdraw the capital of the mining company they had organized. An anxious crowd milled around inside the bank. Slowly the young men worked their way forward to the teller's cage. After a glance at Springmeyer's short, slight form, his clean-shaven boyish face, and his candid blue eyes, the cashier derisively responded,

"What's the matter, kid? Are you scared? You take all that money and someone will rob you."

The prospect of robbery frightened them a good deal less than the imminent demise of the Nye and Ormsby County. Laden with eight thousand dollars in gold, the young men toiled home to the dirt-floored stone hut they shared. There they stood guard over the gold coins night and day and narrowly missed shooting each other by mistake. [40]

Other depositors fared less well in their dealings with the Nye and Ormsby County, part of a chain initially organized by Nixon and his associates and later sold when Nixon shifted his focus to the Cook bank. The Goldfield Nye and Ormsby bank progressed from the corner in a grocery store where business had been carried on in the summer of 1904 to new quarters in a stone building adjoining the Palace Saloon, but the bank was never to occupy the expensive new building constructed for it, nor to fully reimburse its depositors. In 1909 it permanently collapsed. A subsequent grand jury report on the bank's affairs scathingly condemned its directors for their large borrowings while the bank tottered and "their apparent utter disregard for the interest of the depositors."[41]

Similar attitudes came to light in the collapse of the camp's first bank, the State Bank and Trust, also the Goldfield branch of a Nevada chain. Like the other banks, the State Bank and Trust progressed from humble beginnings in the front portion of Ole Elliott's saloon in the summer of 1904 to a fine stone building conveying a false impression of financial solidity within. After the October run on the Goldfield banks, the State Bank and Trust never reopened, blaming the bad loans made on mining stocks at four to one margins. In fact, the banking chain's financial affairs were a good deal more complicated and also included a welter of fictitious dividends, questionable loans to the doomed L. M. Sullivan company, among others, and inflated construction costs. Initially the bank's president, Thomas Rickey, promised to repay the depositors dollar for dollar, and many believed him. After all, "Honest Tom" Rickey, the aged pioneer cattleman, with far-flung interests in mining, irrigation projects, land holdings, and the Nevada-California Power Company serving Goldfield, was reputedly the richest man in the state. One of those who did not believe him was Donald Mackenzie, the bank's largest depositor. A battle of the sharks ensued, in which Rickey and Mackenzie at first cooperated at the expense of other depositors in an elaborate paper shuffle with the bank's principal asset, its stock in the Keane Wonder Mine in Death Valley. Then, as the *Chronicle* phrased it, Rickey walked "away with the swag." Mackenzie at least managed to salvage more from the bank than did the other depositors. [42]

Although none of Goldfield's "bank wreckers" received their just desserts in court, one of them met his end in a blaze of gunfire. The most short-lived institution, the Goldfield Bank and Trust Company, closed its doors in May 1905, just six months after opening in a temporary tin and corrugated iron building in 1904. Rumors that only 80¢ remained of the $80,000 deposited in the bank's vaults proved apocryphal. The actual sum was $21.05. The bank's president, its principal director, and its cashier had prudently skipped town but were subsequently arrested. Acquitted in court but far from vindicated, the former bank director, Francis Burton, continued to flourish unabashed, making Mina his new base of operations. Indeed Burton was a man not easily abashed, even when a delegation of residents met him upon his arrival in a new mining camp and compelled him to take the next stage out of town. A Colorado attorney of unusual persuasive powers, Burton had shammed injuries incurred in a train wreck in order to secure heavy damages from the railroad company. When the fraud was exposed, Burton went to prison in Massachusetts, but this only took the wind from his sails temporarily. He persuaded the warden to entrust him with fifteen thousand dollars for mining investments. Upon his arrival in Goldfield, he used this capital to organize the Goldfield Bank and Trust, among several other schemes.

After J. Holman Buck labeled him a "shyster lawyer, ex-Goldfield bank wrecker, Lida mining fakir" in the pages of the *Rawhide Rustler*, Burton threatened the editor's life. Buck began carrying a short-barrelled shotgun. When he saw Burton approaching him on Mina's main thoroughfare, Buck called on him three times to put up his hands. Instead Burton drew a revolver from his pocket. Buck fired first, riddling his body with buckshot and killing him instantly. The district attorney declared that he would refrain from wasting the taxpayers' money on a trial because no Esmeralda County jury would convict Buck—a measure of the "bank wrecker's" general unpopularity. [43]

It may be noted in passing that despite the rampant crime in Goldfield, no one robbed a Goldfield bank during the boom years. Moreover, one of the fire-proof safes lived up to its manufacturer's claims by surviving the conflagration of 1923. The real dangers to depositors' funds came not from fires, nor floods, nor masked bandits, but from the unprincipled activities of the bankers themselves, both shysters like Burton and respected financial titans like Rickey.

While local physicians must have done yeoman service during the pneumonia epidemics and other health crises, no detailed information on them has yet come to light. When a Goldfielder committed suicide by drowning himself in the water tank, one of the camp's first doctors declared that he could revive the unfortunate but demanded his fee in advance. Outraged Goldfielders buried the suicide and literally kicked the medico out of camp. Other doctors soon took his place, but their interest in ministering to the sick often proved short-lived. Like Goldfielders in all walks of life, physicians seem to have readily abandoned their professions for careers as mining entrepreneurs. For instance, Dr. D. W. Robinson, failing to prosper in the practice of medicine in Denver, arrived in Goldfield with no more than pocket change and soon made a fortune in mining. Other mine promoters with medical backgrounds included Frances Williams, the woman doctor who had specialized in electricity cures, and Dr. Whitewolf, both among the earliest arrivals in Goldfield. [44]

Lawyers, true to form, had a good deal more to say about themselves than physicians. They had flocked to the camp at an early date, well knowing that rich mines would inevitably lead to endless litigation, from the loaned horse lawsuit that plagued Charlie Taylor to the legal clubs used by Wingfield to destroy Donald Mackenzie. Mining litigation appears less pervasive in Goldfield than on the Comstock, where lawsuits were regarded as the great lode's "principle industry" in the early years and Smith found over 350 such cases clogging court calendars. But those lawyers who alit in Goldfield and edged up to the long bar at the Northern in search of what they called "legal sugarplums and lollipop" generally received their reward—often in the form of mining stocks, which they later bequeathed to their descendants in mouldering bundles.

One of these pioneer attorneys described the conditions of his practice in 1905: "A fellow who takes one of the boom camps however, must be full of home [sic] and carry his library and possessions in a suit case and trunk. He must be full of motherwit and able to adjust himself to any condition that may arise. He may be called on to draft an important conveyance on a poker table without blank forms, typewriter or scarcely legal-cap paper, but if he picks the right place, gets acquainted with the boys, has enough money to support himself for three or four months and 'rustles' (taking lots of contingent fees in the shape of interests or stock in corporations) he ought to succeed if he sticks to it."[45]

Court appearances in those early days sometimes showed a certain lack of formality. When both a gentleman accused of disturbing the peace and his attorney appeared in Judge Ed Collins's justice court in a drunken condition, the proceedings ended with the defendant expressing his outrage against being remanded to jail by pitching a lamp at the judge's head. As late as 1909, two aged legal warhorses grew so enraged at each other over a mining case that one called his opponent a "cur" and received a punch in the jaw that sent him reeling over the tables.

Violence in the courtroom was nonetheless exceptional, and it would be erroneous to envisage Goldfield justice as a rowdy affair in which legal ignoramuses dispensed decrees in the idiosyncratic manner of Judge Roy Bean and his "law west of the Pecos." The two district judges appointed for Goldfield in 1908—Theron Stevens and Peter Somers—would have lent distinction to any courtroom. Somers had served as United States congressman from Milwaukee, his former home; Stevens had presided on the bench in Colorado, former residence of many of Goldfield's better lawyers. Proceedings in their courtrooms were as correct and formal as any in the land, indeed so much so that an attorney who appeared in court without his jacket on a roasting hot day, when dogs lolled panting in the street, was sternly reprimanded for not being "entirely clothed." While the prejudices of Goldfield district judges may sometimes have skewed court proceedings, no one questioned their integrity—a welcome change from the scandalous days of the territorial judiciary. Unfortunately, the same standards did not always prevail at the justice court level.[46]

Though rowdyism rarely erupted in Goldfield courts and judges maintained high standards, a grand theatricality prevailed among the members of the bar. Goldfielders clearly saw a juicy trial as the theater of the real, and they crowded in to watch in such numbers that the courtroom sometimes overflowed and spectators stood on the window sills peering inside. They were rarely disappointed. Witnesses performed pantomimes of events they had observed. Models of the scene of a crime were built and brought into court for visual reconstructions. And many members of the bar cultivated an emotional style designed to reduce juries to tears. [47]

The Goldfield bar included older attorneys at the zenith of their careers, men like the witty and eloquent "Lighthorse Harry" Morehouse, a hawk-nosed, clean-shaven, silver-haired Confederate veteran and former California legislator, Orrin Hilton, a Colorado attorney with long experience in doing battle for the radical unions, and Robert Hubbard. At the same time, Goldfield courts produced some of the future stars of the Nevada legal profession, John Sanders, a Nevada Supreme Court justice to be, Springmeyer, a future United States attorney, and Springmeyer's roommate, future Nevada attorney general Jack Diskin, among them.

The heavy crush of litigation provided these young attorneys with ample opportunity to practice. Springmeyer recalled court sessions that lasted until eleven at night. Afterward he would continue at his desk in the district attorney's office until past midnight, then tumble out of bed at 5:30 to open his law books once more. In retrospect, Springmeyer believed that it was his rigorous Goldfield training, more than his legal education at Stanford and Harvard, that made a lawyer of him, though like most other gold rushers, he left the camp no richer than he came. No honest lawyer ever grew rich on the salary of an assistant district attorney, and those mining stocks he accepted in lieu of payment in private practice were mainly useful for decorative purposes.

But the experience of being part of the last great boom could scarcely be tallied in an accountant's ledger. Indeed many seasoned gold rushers saw the sudden gains and disastrous reversals of mining camp businesses as a normal part of their way of life. So long as they made enough to elbow up to the bar with the boys of an evening, and stand for the drinks now and then, they were, at heart, content. It was the pursuit of El Dorado that mattered, not actually reaching the golden shore. In fact, not a few may have subliminally feared losing the old way of life to success. Why else did they gamble away their long-sought fortunes so fast?

W. G. Searles, a veteran of the California gold rush, gave voice to a point of view still widely shared in the last boomtown. Upon his arrival, Searles declared with enthusiasm that Goldfield reminded him of San Francisco in the days when he had first stepped off the trading ship that carried him around Cape Horn: "It almost makes me think I had sloughed off about forty years and gone back." During the ensuing years, he had known "dull times and good times" as he hastened to mining excitements from Tombstone to Siberia, but he had always known how he wanted to live: "When we had money we always spent it, and when we were broke we worried along as best we could until we got some more. I fell in love with the life, and I want to live and die . . . in a mining camp." [48]

X

Getting Ours

HIGHGRADING AND OTHER CRIMES

"Stand on the corner and note . . . that desperate class of men with hard faces bearing that look which tells of days, aye many years spent in jail, men who will do anything from stealing ore to holding up a bank or a lonely wayfarer, who would rather commit a desperate crime than not," Tonopah Bonanza, 1904.

His was the image of crime that has been associated with Gold-field in the public mind ever since the boom days—the miner lurching forth from his shift with up to sixty pounds of highgrade ore concealed in his lunch bucket, his long pockets, his inner shirt, and his double-crowned hat. Some reportedly bought jobs in the bonanza mines where their wages could be multiplied by highgrading. According to Anne Ellis, miners commonly kept roasting pans on their stoves to heat the stolen ore and force out the golden blisters. Often they took it to be processed in the shop of an assayer discreet enough to ask no embarrassing questions, provided he received his 50 percent commission.

In 1907 Constable Inman and his deputies raided one of these establishments. It was an unpretentious frame structure, modestly set back from the road and nestled amidst barrels of tailings concealed under piles of old clothes. No signs solicited business, and the dark entrance at the rear of the building could be handily reached from the mines. Only an unusually tall stovepipe rising from the assay furnace distinguished it from hundreds of other shacks. By night the shop came to life. The proprietor, stripped to his undershirt, busied himself at his electric crusher, his furnace, and his cyanide tanks. Security arrangements foreshadowed the speak-easies of the Prohibition era. Windows were boarded up on the lower portions and heavily curtained above. If visitors gave the correct signal on the electric bell, the proprietor pulled the rope raising his latch. Otherwise he scruti-nized them through a peephole in the door—that is, until the night when the diminutive but determined chief constable threatened to kick in the door and recovered six thousand dollars worth of gold.[1]

After highgrading miners and their partners in crime at the assaying offices had filched their share, gold ore managed to disappear at virtually every stage of production. The president of the Great Western Mining

Company found to his dismay that a rail shipment of fifty tons of rich gold ore mysteriously shrank by fourteen tons before reaching the smelter in Salt Lake City. Apparently intending to later reclaim their loot, thieves mixed highgrade with the waste ore at the Little Florence—a pleasant five-thousand-dollar surprise for the subsequent purchaser of the mine's waste dump. And gold concentrates had been known to disappear into little scoop-shaped devices attached to the tables by employees in the Goldfield Con mill. These larcenies, large and small, not only enriched the thieves but also the saloon owners and merchants, as stolen largesse rippled out through the community in ever-widening circles. Large numbers of miners firmly believed that "God put the gold in the rock and it belongs to the man who digs it out," which seemed compatible with the socialist ideology that many espoused. Highgrading was seen as a legitimate perquisite, almost a natural right. The practice became so widely accepted that, as the news-papers noted, it ceased to be a "term of accusation" and gained clever and fashionable connotations as an insiders' game. An entire section of the city became humorously known as "Highgraders' Heights."[2]

The notable exception in this atmosphere of tolerance was George Wingfield. He saw highgrading not only as theft that siphoned profitable ore from his mines but also as a personal affront that interfered with his control of the work force. During the leasing era, leasing companies primar-ily interested in extracting as much ore as possible inside a limited time period with a contented work force had turned a blind eye to highgrading. But after Wingfield's rise to dominance with the formation of Goldfield Con in late 1906, a multi-pronged crackdown on highgrading commenced. At the mine owners behest, the Nevada legislature enacted tough new laws against highgrading. In place of the customary presumption of innocence till proven guilty, the new laws compelled suspected highgraders to prove themselves innocent, and mine owners gained the right to examine the assayers' books. When this proved ineffective, Wingfield sued for a federal injunction to prevent assayers from purchasing ore without his permission. An intense struggle with the union over change rooms, in which the mine owners hoped to curtail highgrading by obliging the miners to change from their work clothes under observation, was resolved the Wingfield way by the destruction of the union. Lawmen received large rewards for intensi-fying enforcement—40 percent of all highgrade he recovered went to Con-stable Inman and 10 percent to his deputies. In a single year, Inman reclaimed one hundred thousand dollars worth of highgrade, including a four-inch-thick sheet of gold concealed by Yugoslavian miners in a trunk of "gaudy" clothes. Bearing in mind that the salary of the Nevada governor in that year was less than five thousand dollars, we can see that the chief con-stable had considerable incentive to kick in an assayer's door.[3]

Yet, despite Inman's energetic participation in the anti-highgrading drive, Wingfield believed that lawmen were generally corrupt and reposed little confidence in them. Among the deputies and guards with criminal records recruited to fight the union, there may well have been some basis for this belief. But the more fundamental reason lay in the position of lawmen and district attorneys as elected officials, necessarily responsive to community attitudes and conditioned by legal safeguards and customary law enforcement practices. In short, even when Wingfield pointedly reminded them in the midst of a highgrading case that they owed half their salaries to the county's largest taxpayer (himself), they lacked the necessary single-minded devotion to the interests of Goldfield Con. As a result, Goldfield Con's attorneys and detectives, led by hard-boiled security chief Clarence Sage, increasingly usurped the functions of elected officials. This was clearly shown in the 1910 Mike Smith case when Sage seized one of the principal figures. A Goldfield Con attorney then questioned the man and extended offers of immunity to elicit a confession, apparently without the presence, or even the knowledge, of the district attorney. On other occasions, when Goldfield Con detectives failed to find ore on the persons of suspected highgraders, they searched the miners' homes. According to Sewall Thomas, "a little arson party was organized" to burn down an assayer's plant. Detectives twice shot and killed highgrading suspects, and they kidnapped an alleged middleman known as the "Anheuser Kid" in Butte, Montana, at gunpoint. One of Nevada's state Supreme Court justices had good reason, in a dissenting opinion, to remind those engaged in the pursuit of highgraders that legal safeguards intended to protect the innocent ought not be cast aside.[4]

By and large, the massive drive against highgrading produced few convictions. Suspected highgraders jumped bond, escaped from jail, or agreed to return the ore and leave town. Charges against many of them failed to hold up in court—scarcely a surprise, in view of the questionable methods used by Sage and his detectives. When a case went to trial, highgrading miners could be charged with nothing more serious than petty larceny, and all the detectives and engineers that mining companies placed on the witness stand could rarely prove where an assayer had obtained his ore. Among the seven Goldfield highgrading convictions mentioned in the press over the years 1904–10, only two were assayers and one a miner, whose claim to have discovered five dollars worth of ore on an outhouse shelf gained little credence. Of at least twenty-nine highgraders arrested in the 1907 crackdown, only five were convicted.

As these cases suggest, the common claim that no Goldfield jury would convict in a highgrading case was an exaggeration, but a large segment of community opinion defiantly supported highgrading, and acquittals and hung juries sometimes resulted in the face of the most damning evidence. This broad support for highgrading, in a community where highgraders were even found among the social and business elite, was coupled with antipathy to the highhanded methods of Goldfield Con and the iron-fisted Sage. For this reason, prosecutors in the second trial of assayer Mike Smith exercised the utmost care in jury selection. Prospective jurors were asked whether they harbored "any feeling" against Goldfield Con, doubted the honesty of Sage, had heard criticism of the company store, and so forth. The attorneys nearly exhausted the entire venire of jurymen to find twelve who passed these tests, and several of those selected were from small towns and mining camps far from Goldfield. In the final analysis, change rooms, union busting, arrests, new laws, and all the other weapons in the Wingfield arsenal never succeeded in controlling highgrading. Old timers relate that to the very end miners secreted highgrade in unused portions of the mines, later removed it by other entrances to the subterranean honeycomb of tunnels, and sold it through a fence known as "Dirty-faced Jack" in the mining camp of Manhattan some distance to the north. [5]

How much ore was lost to the Goldfield mine owners through highgrading will never be definitively known, though some guesses run very high. Historian Guy Rocha finds the charge that ore equivalent to about 18 percent of total production was highgraded during 1906 alone "excessive" and incompatible with mint statistics. While the actual figure may well have been substantial, it was undoubtedly dwarfed by the sums lost in stock swindles. In truth, highgrading was but one aspect of the grand bacchanal of larceny in Goldfield, a point clearly noted by observers at the time that has often been lost sight of since then. Thomas Rickard believed that rich ore subverted the integrity of everyone involved, miners, leasers, mining companies, railroads, and smelters: "There was not much to choose between them all; it was a case of catch as catch can, with the odds in favor of the one who first placed his hands on the ore—the miner himself." Highgraders testifying in the Mike Smith case put it even more succinctly: "As long as George Wingfield and the company are getting theirs, we might as well get ours." [6]

While none of the sheriff's books on Goldfield larcenies survive, it is evident that a host of the criminally inclined in every walk of life were busily engaged in "getting ours." Indeed the great rush to Goldfield had revolutionized Esmeralda County crime rates. At the close of 1903 the district attorney reported: "no criminal business has been transacted in this county. I am sorry to state that things do not look so favorable for the ensuing year. . . ." His apprehensions that the somnolent but peaceful state in which Esmeralda County had long languished was destined soon to pass would prove well founded. The 1905 report listed over a thousand crimes in Goldfield alone, many of them of a serious character. Robbery, theft, and burglary apparently peaked in the autumn of 1907, when at least one such crime was reported every day. In fact, a lawman declared that at Lothrop's store alone, forty burglaries had been attempted within the span of six months. Recurrent reports surfaced on criminal gangs operating in Goldfield, and the press perceived a crime wave in progress, perhaps rightly so, since such crimes had been minimal on the trans-Sierra frontier a generation earlier. These crimes were sometimes as callous as any of the present day. After an accident in the mines, thieves riffled the clothes of a dying miner for his life savings. [7]

Well-founded distrust of banks, which led many to keep large sums of money and valuable jewelry at home or on their persons, no doubt fostered theft and mugging, and the guns many Goldfielders carried plainly exerted no deterrent effect. The robbers could be choosy at times. When two masked men with guns relieved one Goldfielder of his money in his cabin, they took $340 in gold and cast aside the silver. Criminals sometimes made their entries by ingenious means. The occupant of a hotel room awoke in the night to see his valuables disappearing through the transom, hooked on the handle of an umbrella. The flimsiness of many Goldfield dwellings made burglary easy, and more than one Goldfielder awoke thinking that a packrat had scrambled under the canvas flap of his tent, only to find a human packrat racing off with his trousers. Occasionally a criminal encountered more than he bargained for. One Goldfielder threw an iron casting he was carrying in his pocket for use on a headframe and felled the "footpad" who tried to mug him. Another, anticipating the litigious mood of the late twentieth century, instituted a law suit for heavy damages against the burglar who filched his suit of clothes and thus prevented him from attending lodge meetings and other social events.

Aside from a holdup at the railroad depot, no train or stage robberies occurred in Goldfield's immediate vicinity, perhaps because no robbers were foolish enough to tangle with the formidable old frontiersman Jack Longstreet, who rode shotgun guard on the stage from Tonopah. As in Aurora and Bodie, no one attempted a bank robbery. But the large amounts of cash at the saloon gaming tables offered an irresistible temptation. In the dregs of the night, between 3:00 A.M. and dawn, masked men would burst through the swinging doors of a saloon and make off with the bankroll. During one of these episodes at the Mohawk, saloon patrons appeared so blase that the robbers had to race about shouting "hey, hey!" to get their attention and line them up against the lunch counter. On none of these occasions did the lookout stationed with a shotgun beside the roulette table succeed in foiling a robbery (his function seems to have been largely ceremonial), nor did anyone resist the masked men, nor was anyone hurt. [8]

No object was safe from Goldfield's thieves. They stole everything, from the fanciest hat in the millinery store to the long rope belonging to the fire department and the American flag. They furnished their stolen tents with stolen stoves and bedsteads, curled their toes in stolen rugs, and warmed themselves at fires of stolen wood, while smoking stolen cigars, swigging stolen liquors, and munching on stolen hams, chickens, and candy. Unfazed by the bindlestiffs who slept in Union Hall, they blasted open the safe, muffling the explosion with blankets, and also the post office safe. Nor was any object too large for their endeavors. The owners of the Old Kentuck Mine were disconcerted to observe the disappearance of their hoisting machinery, sold by a fast-talking swindler to an unsuspecting mining investor. They fortunately recovered their hoist at the railroad depot. Jennie Enright, the woman prospector known as the "Desert Amazon," also thought big, in contrast to Goldfield's other larcenous ladies, who picked pockets or engaged in shoplifting. She became one of the few women in the camp to face criminal prosecution when she was charged with stealing two entire houses. Burglars with more modest aspirations and a thirst for culture purloined a violin and the works of Shakespeare. When a prospector near Goldfield was even robbed of his Bible, it is to be hoped that the thieves absorbed some moral benefit from perusing it.

With the first autos, the first auto thefts made a predictable appearance. Joyriders, one day to loom large in the annals of crime, stole two autos belonging to wealthy stockbrokers and careened madly over the desert until the autos gave out. While this larcenous innovation was making its appearance, the venerable pioneer crime of horse thievery lingered on. In the most exciting of these episodes, Constable Inman trailed Tom Argentos, a notorious horse thief, toward an outlaw hideout at Steniker's ranch on the fringes of Death Valley. After Argentos unwisely allowed his stolen horse to drink too deeply at one of the springs along the way, his pace slowed. Inman and his companion, riding so hard that they covered a thirty-five mile stretch in three and a half hours, managed to close the distance. Soon Inman spotted Argentos ahead in Grapevine Wash. The constable cut over the ridges to station himself behind a boulder on the trail. When Argentos reached the spot, Inman ordered him to throw up his hands. Argentos spurred his horse and attempted to reach for his six-shooter, but Inman warned him, "The next time you lower your hands you will be a dead Greek in hell." On the way back, Argentos offered Inman a five thousand dollar bribe, which the constable rejected as "too cheap." [9] Unfortunately, the slippery Argentos would soon be out on bail to commit a murder.

Although Argentos was a very dangerous man, he preferred to pose as a legitimate financier. Other Goldfielders gloried in bad reputations and cultivated lethal images as professional gunmen. Not infrequently the gap between the image and the reality was broad enough to drive a stagecoach through. Sewall Thomas recalled: "The bad men themselves mostly were fakes. . . . They were swaggerers; one part head and ten parts mouth, with a happy faculty for being absent from scenes of real strife. Some of them had the courage to shoot men from behind; preferable targets were men when asleep." [10]

The prime example in this genre was Diamondfield Jack Davis, who appears under another name in a thinly disguised portrait in Thomas' memoirs. A man of medium height with dark mustachios "grown long enough to chew on when angry," Davis wore black broadcloth and a black sateen shirt and sported a "mean-looking bowie knife, exhibiting it at frequent intervals as a slicer for his chewing tobacco." At that time Davis was serving as bodyguard to George Wingfield, as well as promoting mines in the Diamondfield district near Goldfield. Attorney George Springmeyer often saw Davis stride with his two bodyguards into a restaurant for supper, seat himself at a table facing the door, and ostentatiously place his guns beside his plate.

During the union troubles, Davis capitalized on the opportunity to enhance his image, freely offering advice, speeding into town with his auto stacked high with guns for the deputies engaged by the mine operators, and firing fearlessly into an empty alley where phantom assailants were said to lurk. Yet Thomas notes that "at every occasion when he could put his advice to some good use he was away somewhere else and doing something else." At the crisis point, he selflessly offered to stand guard at the most strategic post of all, behind the thick stone walls on the third floor of the Nixon building. If the truth were known, Diamondfield Jack had never killed a man, though largely as a result of his own boasting he had been wrongfully convicted of killing two Mormon sheepherders in Idaho and reprieved in the nick of time when the real killers confessed. But Davis had no interest in letting the truth be known when it conflicted with the gunman image he was trying to cultivate. Instead he preferred to go about displaying the rope nearly used at his hanging. Perhaps Wingfield himself had no great faith in Diamondfield Jack's proficiency as a bodyguard, or he would not have found it necessary to arm himself with several guns at once, creating the storybook picture of the wild West that charmed Eastern financier Bernard Baruch.[11]

Since Davis, despite his best efforts, was "ten parts mouth," in the apt phrase of Thomas, did Goldfield have any larger than life figures corresponding to the Western gunfighters and lawmen of legend? To find such a man, one would need to travel northeast to the Kawich range, where Jack Longstreet lived in the mountain fastnesses with his Indian wife and his notched Colt .44. Inside the boundaries of Goldfield, the most obvious candidates were Constable Claude Inman and Virgil Earp. Inman was easily Goldfield's most energetic lawman, and the only one who made serious attempts to combat concealed weapons and drug abuse. His Goldfield adventures were colorful enough to inspire a screenplay and an occasional article many years later. But Inman's efforts to change Goldfield had little effect, and he fell considerably short of the legendary lawmen. Similarly, those who encountered the elderly Virgil Earp evidently harbored no suspicions that they were in the presence of a legend. Long after the bloody events in Tombstone, Earp arrived in the camp in 1904, worked uneventfully as a guard in one of the saloons, and "made his final camp," as the newspaper obituaries phrased it, about a year later following a bout of pneumonia. The retrospective fame of the Earps seems to have followed the relatively recent elevation of the gunfight at the OK Corral to the realm of mythology, and Goldfielders paid little attention to Virgil Earp. [12]

The lawman who aroused greater interest in his own day was William Foley, and if the exaggerations and tall tales that circulated over the incident in which he beat Frank Smith to death with his shotgun in 1907 are any indication, Foley might in time have metamorphosed into a legend — given the right biographer. Though no photos have been located, he was evidently a handsome man, engaged to marry Maude Raymer, a tall statuesque blond regarded as one of the most beautiful women in Goldfield. They made so striking a couple that whenever they went out together they attracted all eyes. Unfortunately, Foley's career was cut short only eight months after the encounter with Smith when he died under circumstances fully as mysterious as his fellow Arizonan John Ringo. Foley quarreled with his sweetheart, and though she did not return to her estranged husband in San Francisco, she left Goldfield for the East. Foley remarked to a friend, "It don't much matter what happens to me now. If a man stuck a gun in my ribs, I'd tell him to shoot." [13]

His mood was obviously reckless and despairing when, according to the *Chronicle*, he set off in pursuit of "two members of a gang of desperate crooks whom he had reason to suspect were planning a robbery near Goldfield." He followed them all the way to Hazen, a small hamlet more than two hundred miles northwest of Goldfield, and there he died. Various accounts mentioned poison, heart disease, or a blow on the head. Constable Inman, for whom Foley was then working as a deputy, suspected suicide and eulogized him as "a splendid officer, always loyal to his friends."

Yet suicide in the midst of pursuing a criminal gang struck a discordant note that other friends found unconvincing. "Sombody got Bill Foley," one of them wrote from Hazen. "He had a drink or two with a bunch up here, and I think somebody put something in his glass. They found him dead in bed. . . . it looks now as if somebody had done for him." Perhaps they had. Years later Inman delivered his last word on the subject: Foley was no suicide. He had been poisoned. The mystery of the deputy's death has never been definitively resolved. [14]

If fame has failed to canonize any of Goldfield's lawmen, the camp's bad men fell equally short of earlier legends like Billy the Kid and the Comstock's Sam Brown — even when we allow for the fact that the claims made for them have often been grossly exaggerated. Unconfirmed rumor had it that Jesse Vortrees had killed men in Arizona and Oregon. But in Goldfield Jesse's most serious crime was working the "badger game" upon prospective lovers of his luscious and tempting wife, Annie May.

While the badger game made its victims feel thoroughly foolish, men of the ilk of Jesse Vortrees posed less danger to the pocketbook and ran greater risk of punishment for their misdeeds than did the stockbrokers. The *Chronicle* candidly admitted, "So many swindles have been perpetrated that investors have become timid."[15] Large numbers of these wild cats and "mining buzzards" had glimpsed the camp briefly or not at all before settling down to business in New York, Chicago, and other Eastern cities. A few of the most infamous landed in jail, chiefly as a result of federal action against mail fraud by crooked operators purveying Goldfield mining stocks in other states, but as a rule, state authorities both east and west did not vigorously prosecute the anti-wild-catting laws, despite the indignant fulminations of swindled stockholders. Nor could more energetic enforcement have saved investors from themselves because the greater—and probably the more dangerous—part of the mine promotion business was entirely legal.

Even when financial legerdemain crossed the fine line between sharp practice and crime, indecipherable bookkeeping could muddy the evidence, when the books had not been entirely destroyed, and "mining sharks" could slip out of one state just a jump ahead of the police to set up business in another. Occasionally, they exited the country altogether. For instance, Michael O'Farrell, office manager and advertising man for one of the leading Goldfield brokerage firms, described in the press as "a young man with the voice and demeanor to inspire the confidence of any ordinary businessman," took a fast ship to the Orient with thirty thousand dollars in stolen mining securities in his suitcase. Another factor working against the prosecution of crimes in the realm of finance was the high social status of the perpetrators. After the State Bank and Trust went into receivership, Thomas Rickey, the "millionaire bank wrecker," charged by the press with committing the "greatest crime of the generation" against Nevadans, was indicted in Carson City for embezzlement. He equably opined that his lawyers would delay the case until "a long time after I am dead." In this, as in all his calculations, Rickey proved correct. The struggle to disentangle the bank's affairs became the subject of a legislative investigation and dragged on into the 1920s without reaching a satisfactory conclusion.[16]

The case of Henry Weber, one of the few members of the financial elite to face criminal charges, provided another case in point. Born in Wisconsin, Weber was a dark, handsome, and convincing young man, despite his strangely hostile gaze. Though broke when he rode the rails into Nevada, he was soon living high on the hog through the Atlanta, Great Bend Annex, and other mining companies he organized in Goldfield and surrounding camps with the assistance of his brother, Arthur. Some of Henry Weber's obvious affluence may have been due to misuse of other people's money. An irate investor accused him of diverting to his personal use ten thousand dollars paid to him for treasury stock in one of his mining companies instead of expending it upon development of the mines. Though the prosecution was hampered by the fact that Weber burned the ledger in which these financial transactions had been recorded, he was nonetheless prosecuted for embezzlement. During this unpleasant ordeal, so rare for a Goldfield financier, the sheriff allowed Weber to stay in a courthouse anteroom to spare him the rigors endured by lesser folk in jail. After a jury promptly pronounced him guilty and he was sentenced to seven years in the penitentiary, the judge let him out on bail, citing his pulmonary condition and his proclivity for nervous breakdowns.

When Weber won his appeal on a technicality, the district attorney tactfully forebore from subjecting him to further unpleasantness and dismissed the charges. Drawing the obvious moral from this experience, Weber had already resumed his old tricks. The *Chronicle* accused him of concealing a strike in one of his mines for purposes of financial manipulation. Bearing in mind that one highgrader served six months for stealing five dollars worth of ore and others, who had stolen nothing, spent several years in the state penitentiary for merely exhibiting an intention to do so, one can only conclude that the camp's often remarked leniency to highgraders was far exceeded by the carte blanche accorded to white-collar crime. [17] In the Calumet mining stock scandal—a typical affair involving phoney reports of a great strike and money obtained from an investor under false pretenses—one of the principal figures took a shot at another and a near riot erupted in court, possibly because everyone concerned well knew they had little chance of obtaining legal redress.

Men who passed bad checks, or "uttered false paper," in the parlance of the times, were almost as unlikely to land behind bars as stockbrokers. Although the press complained in 1907 that "phoney check players" had multiplied, juries continued to treat them tolerantly. So much so that after another acquittal in a "flagrant case" the judge criticized the jury and the district attorney angrily declared that he interpreted the verdict as "a direct command . . . not to spend any more of the county's money in these fruitless prosecutions." [18]

Those individuals who landed in the Goldfield jail showed a definite disinclination to stay there—understandably so, since inside the jail's thick stone walls up to ten prisoners, including women, were sometimes confined in a single small narrow cell seething with vermin, while odoriferous fumes from the pile of manure outside an adjoining livery stable wafted through the tiny barred windows. Working on the chain gang that graded and maintained Goldfield's streets held little more appeal than festering in a cell. Moreover, prisoners no doubt considered it the last straw when the county commissioners decreed that they would no longer be served whiskey, lest they regard jail as "a comfortable winter quarters." As a result, so many prisoners escaped through the jail roof that lawmen finally had to line it with steel. [19]

Although financial misdeeds of all varieties blossomed luxuriantly in Goldfield, some crimes rarely appeared on the sheriff's roster. A few arsonists, such as the woman activated by jealous rage and the man who hoped to collect insurance, put the city at risk. Sexual crimes were an even greater rarity, as had also been true on the trans-Sierra frontier. The main incident was a case of indecent exposure, in which a man who may have tired of awaiting his turn for several weeks at the Goldfield baths stripped off his clothes and persuaded a friend to hose him down in the street. Finding no relevant statute on the books, lawmen forebore from arresting him. The only case of attempted rape that has yet come to light, ably defended by George Springmeyer, resulted in an acquittal. According to the *Chronicle*, the evidence was "slight," and "conflicting statements stood out in particular." Another sexual crime involving the theft of two cows and "undo advances" made by the thief to the little daughter of his neighbor apparently failed to reach the trial stage. Yet one suspects that the deputies who fed on the tenderloin may often have coerced sexual favors from prostitutes. [20]

During the boom years, two major scandals erupted over graft in the tenderloin by Goldfield officials. The first, in 1905, marked an attempt by several unusually plucky prostitutes to impeach the justice of the peace, the district attorney, and a law officer for extorting illegal fees from them. The second, in the autumn of 1907, resulted in investigations by the county commissioners and the grand jury and the prosecution of a deputy, who probably served as the scapegoat for many who had abused their official positions. The scandal was evidently sparked when "Shorty" Burns, who operated a hop joint in the gulch under police protection, mistakenly tendered bribes to two honest officials.

The ensuing testimony revealed a good deal about the way lawmen had been living off the denizens of the red-light district, primarily those whose race or ethnicity made them especially vulnerable. The Frenchmen who operated the Three Musketeers Restaurant in the district were obliged to pay or remain confined in jail on vagrancy charges. A mining man carrying a large sum of money was arrested for saloon fisticuffs; when deputies returned his belongings, more than half his money had disappeared. Sixteen black men arrested in a raid on a bordello paid up to secure their release without arraignment. Pansy Burr, a black prostitute, paid $250 to a deputy to gain her release from jail. Sheriff Ingalls, while insisting that he was "perfectly satisfied" with most of his deputies, acknowledged that the "men who police the tenderloin are subjected to a world of temptation." [21]

In fact, the relationship between lawmen and the "lower districts" extended beyond temptation and shaded into public policy. When the numbers of lawmen recruited during the union crisis outstripped the county's ability to pay their salaries, the constable was officially directed by the county commissioners to pay them from a "corrupt fund" collected in the tenderloin. Even after the commissioners discontinued this system of meeting the payroll, rumor had it that collection of the "corrupt fund" continued for purposes of private enrichment. When Constable Inman revoked the commissions of his horde of unneeded deputies and Sheriff Ingalls demanded at year's end that his deputies post bond, swear to collect no more illegal payments, and turn all fees over to his office, it was clear that lawmen had continued to abuse their power.[22]

The effect of the 1907 influx of deputies upon Goldfield crime rates was evidently mixed. During the spring lockout, civil suits shrank and felonies and petty crimes such as vagrancy and drunkenness dwindled. The jail stood empty for days at a time. Justice of the Peace Isaac Solomon called the period the "quietest" in the history of Goldfield, even though the hardships of a work force reduced to the soup kitchen gave crime an economic incentive lacking in ordinary times. Intense police vigilance may have had something to do with this, but other factors were also at work. With the miners who stood idle in the streets likely to notice any untoward incident, "guardianship" reached the maximum level. Moreover, the news that the old free-spending Goldfield was temporarily down and out may have produced an exodus of criminals and deterred others from making the camp their destination.[23]

By September this halcyon situation had passed, and officers announced a crackdown against two hundred "resident" criminals. The *Chronicle* sarcastically responded: "Why bother the criminals? Haven't they any right whatever? It seems that they should enjoy some immunity from molestation by reason of their thorough and extensive organization. . . . The officers of Goldfield have acquiesced in their presence here for some time past. . . ."[24] Indeed they may have done more than acquiesce. No small part of the crime wave may have been traceable to the former deputies themselves, many of them ex-convicts recruited for the toughness and lack of scruple they would bring to the struggle with the unions, and later turned loose upon the community. They would also assume a place in the annals of Goldfield homicide.

XI

Hang Me If You Will

HOMICIDE

"I came 7,000 miles to kill this man. Hang me if you will," Jack Hines, 1907.

In 1905 the *Goldfield Review* censured Goldfielders for the practice of giving "vent to their exuberance by discharging weapons in the streets, roads, or in whatever place the fancy suits them." No doubt these nightly fusillades, coupled with numerous assaults with intent to kill that happily fell short of the intention, produced Goldfield's retrospective reputation as a scene of rampant homicide. Helen Croft, for instance, has claimed "there was a killing almost every night." Goldfielders such as Justice of the Peace William Bell would have ridiculed this suggestion and, indeed, regarded Goldfield as a model of nonviolence compared to earlier bonanza camps such as Bodie. This was ascribed to the better class of people Goldfield had attracted, the increasingly scientific nature of mining, and the advance of civilization in the form of electric lights, telephones, and other "comfortable necessaries."[1]

The truth on violence in Goldfield lay somewhere between these views. Goldfield homicide did remain below the Bodie figures, now well documented by historian Roger McGrath. Moreover, the absolute number of Goldfield homicides appears low (31 from 1904 through 1909). But Goldfields volatile population was also small for much of this period, with the result that Goldfield homicide rates usually exceeded the levels in modern American cities and sometimes entered the range noted by McGrath in the trans-Sierra camps. The Goldfield rates must be viewed with caution because McGrath's method of calculation depends on population figures and in the absence of census material Goldfield's population figures are only estimates. Nonetheless, in the interest of comparing the relative level of violence in boom camps, some tentative figures may be proposed. Using a mathematical formula to calculate homicide rates per 100,000 persons for comparison with modern FBI figures, McGrath found a homicide rate of 116 in Bodie and 64 in Aurora, a camp of the early 1860's. Goldfield's rates apparently ranged from a possible high of 79 in 1907 to a low of 20 in 1906.

This suggests that while killings had notably declined from the apex reached a generation earlier in Bodie, a strikingly high rate of homicide continued all the way to the close of the mining frontier. Moreover, the later camps showed higher homicide rates than the early one, Aurora. Considered as a percentage of total mortality, Goldfield homicide far surpassed the national figures of its own day and those of gold rush Sacramento half a century earlier. On a yearly basis, Goldfield homicide showed an interesting pattern over time. It plunged to the lowest level relative to the population in 1906, the peak year of the excitement, then rebounded in 1907 when the boom began to wane.[2] It seems clear that the abundant economic opportunities and the climate of optimism in 1906 de-escalated dangerous quarrels and acted as powerful antidotes to the forces that usually increase mining camp homicide. In that banner year, Goldfielders simply had too much to live for.

When the character of the camp changed, so too did the nature of the quarrels that aroused Goldfielders to a killing rage. In the early years, the usual cause was the drunken saloon quarrel, which had precipitated so many mining camp homicides from Virginia City to Bodie. Myron Angel observed many years earlier in *The History of Nevada*: "The expectation of gaining sudden wealth . . . fires the hearts of a restless class. . . . Defeat of expectation begets a reckless disposition. . . . The greater proportion of homicides result from reckless bravado. Persons meet in saloons, bagnios, and gambling places with deadly weapons upon their persons; they drink, gamble, dispute when half intoxicated, banter each other, and at last draw out their weapons and for fancied causes alone slay each other."[3]

The early affray in the streets of Goldfield between W. J. Dixon, a miner, and Albert Moore was cast in this venerable frontier mold. Dixon and Moore had formerly been the best of friends, but when the two met on a July afternoon in 1905 in the Cabinet Saloon, Dixon's behavior grew increasingly obstreperous during several hours of heavy drinking. "Joking words and badinage" with Moore deteriorated into an "exchange of acrimonious remarks." Dixon struck Moore, who drew his gun and warned his one-time friend to desist. Dixon went home to get his revolver, instantly aiming it at Moore when the two met on Main Street a few minutes later. Moore grappled with him for the weapon, and several wild shots were fired. Unable to wrest away Dixon's gun, Moore broke free and opened fire, hitting Dixon three times. In his dying statement, Dixon exonerated Moore of all blame and urged lawmen to free his former friend. Dixon was not the only victim who attempted to shield his killer when he recognized, too late, the triviality of their dispute. As Michael Kieran, a miner, lay mortally wounded after a 1906 "shooting scrape," he refused to identify his killer, insisting that the fault was his own.[4]

Yet the times were changing. Killings connected with highgrading and other forms of robbery were virtually unknown in the camp's early days, but as Goldfield declined, robbery-related killings reached 15.6 percent of homicides, almost the same proportion found in Chicago today. Moreover, by 1909 three-quarters of Goldfield's homicides were crimes of passion, a type of killing rarely seen in Bodie and far outnumbered by gambling disputes and drunken quarrels in early Nevada.[5] As economic rewards constricted and hopes dwindled in Goldfield, personal relationships began to assume increasing importance.

Sometimes a jealous husband drilled the "home wrecker" who had seduced his wife; on the other hand, the virtuous wife who rejected the "unwelcome attentions" of a would-be lover might provoke a rage of frustration that culminated in murder. So it was when Ernest Priest, a miner, became infatuated with the wife of his neighbor, Mayo Taylor. Mrs. Taylor, the "innocent cause of the tragedy," was a respected and educated young woman, slender, olive-skinned, and noted by newspaper reporters for her "unusually prepossessing appearance." When she rejected Priest's advances, he attempted to kidnap her at gunpoint, feigned suicide in order to arouse sympathy, spread obscene stories about her, and threatened her husband.

Following several months of these persecutions, the two men finally confronted each other in the street near their homes. After a few insulting remarks about Mrs. Taylor, Priest began firing, striking Taylor in the abdomen with his first shot. Though mortally wounded, Taylor emptied his revolver at his assailant and managed to inflict a comparable wound before Priest took cover behind a rock pile, where he continued to fire. Oblivious to the whining bullets, Mrs. Taylor attempted to race to the side of her stricken husband.

Rumor had it that as the two men lay dying in St. Mary's Hospital, each became consumed with an ambition to outlive the other and would inquire at intervals whether the enemy was yet dead. Threats to kill Priest from the grief-stricken Mrs. Taylor so alarmed the good sisters at the hospital that they requested a police guard for the patient. Priest's demise soon rendered guards unnecessary, but unconsciousness deprived Taylor of the satisfaction of knowing that he had succeeded in outliving his assailant.[6] As in other Goldfield crimes of passion, the lady for whom they fought was not one of the Klondike Kitties of the tenderloin but a virtuous wife— perhaps especially prized for reasons of scarcity. Only once did a quarrel over a prostitute figure, even remotely, in a Goldfield homicide, but two faithful wives were felled by the bullets of rejected lovers—a change for the worse since Bodie, where McGrath noted that respectable women had nothing to fear. Fortunately, both women recovered.

While crimes of passion were far from uncommon in Goldfield, another variety of murder was notable by its absence. Goldfielders slew each other for many reasons in a plethora of individual quarrels, but rarely could the violence be linked to a basic and extended conflict between factions engaged in a power struggle on the order of the economically based Johnson

County War, the Lincoln County War, or the famous rivalry between the Earps and the Clantons. Yet a power struggle as intense as any of these had riven Goldfield. The camp contained two strong factions, the mine owners and the radical unions. Both espoused ideologies so unalterably opposed that no compromise was possible and the victory of one could only mean total defeat for the other.

Despite the high stakes on all sides, this combustible situation produced little violence. The only exceptions were the killing of restauranteur John Silva by union organizer Morrie Preston and, possibly, the deaths of two highgraders in traps planned by Goldfield Con security chief Clarence Sage. Even these incidents do not readily fit the mold of a factional power struggle. Convincing evidence has established that the Preston-Silva killing was the unintentional result of a picketing dispute, and the highgrader killings may also have contained an element of self-defense. In view of the remarkably bloodless record of the conflict between the arrayed forces of the mine owners and the radical unions, it was ironic that alleged "domestic violence and unlawful combinations and conspiracies" in Goldfield were to be advanced as the justification for bringing in federal troops to break the union.[7]

The experience of the twentieth century has regrettably disproven the theory that the advance of civilization in the form of telephones and electric lights would produce a decrease in homicide. Nonetheless, Goldfield's killings did subside as the camp evolved into a stable small town not unlike other Western communities. For instance, legal authority Lawrence Friedman has noted a sharp decline in homicide when Oakland "settled down" during the early 1870s. Demography may have contributed to this change. Homicide generally rises in a population with more than the usual component of young men in the "violence-prone" years before age thirty-five, as the maturation of America's post-World War II baby boom illustrated in the late sixties, and gold rush populations contained a disproportionate share of young men. Moreover, many of these were rootless men, without emotional attachments to individual or community, on the loose in a raw new mining camp that lacked legal and social controls, and the worst of them were obvious sociopaths. Regrettably, a gold rush magnetized the social misfits most likely to commit violent acts.[8]

Two other forces pressed in the same direction. Gold rush values extolled masculine bravado and condoned any killing remotely related to self-defense. An equally significant element in escalating petty quarrels to homicides was the widespread presence of guns, the weapon used in over 80 percent of the killings in Goldfield (a higher figure than the proportion of homicides committed with guns in the 1980s). Deputized officers of the law and a few individuals receiving permits from the county commissioners were the only persons authorized to carry guns in Goldfield. The law forbade concealed weapons, guns, swords, and slingshots included, but the law was only sporadically enforced. Soon after taking office in 1907, Constable Inman announced one of these intermittent crackdowns, "I am now going after the man who carries the gun—the artillery man—and I will get them if I have to shoot every such character in town."[9] Not long afterward, when lawmen made a drive to confiscate guns in March–April 1907 during the lockout against the WFM/IWW, the accumulating stack of weapons quickly outstripped available storage space. In the Northern Saloon alone, lawmen confiscated three wheelbarrows full of guns.

More often law officers preferred to overlook the guns bristling from the pockets of Goldfielders. For instance, when Patrick Casey spilled some cartridges on the floor in a saloon, a deputy standing nearby inquired whether he had a gun. Casey denied it, and the deputy did not further pursue the matter. This was an unfortunate omission, since Casey went on to shoot two unarmed women, killing one of them.

Guns became a kind of vicious circle. The more Goldfielders packed guns, the more did other Goldfielders feel compelled to procure them in self-defense, but rarely did they succeed in firing a shot before the enemy mowed them down, even when they had reason to expect trouble. The fate of radical union leader Vincent St. John vividly illustrated this point. Both St. John and a more conservative union rival, Paddy Mullaney, had for some time been packing guns in "anticipation of a mortal struggle." Nevertheless, when the showdown finally arrived as the two men stood arguing in front of the Palm Grill, St. John never managed to get off a shot before Mullaney's bullets struck him in the arm and wrist, crippling him for life. St. John's experience was by no means unusual. The *Goldfield News* observed that the Goldfielder who packed a gun for protection against a holdup "will generally stop a bullet" if he tries to use his weapon. The editorial continued: "If he gets into an altercation, either when sober or intoxicated, if the other fellow knows he has a gun, he is liable to get shot. With some men, the possession of a gun gives a false courage that leads them to look for trouble. They generally find it."[10]

As the *News* clearly recognized, not only did guns give little protection to ordinary people without the lightning reflexes of the legendary gunfighters, but also the assumption that an opponent carried a gun escalated the level of violence—take the night when Deputy Constable William Foley made a fateful move to hitch up his pants. Foley and Frank Smith, a blacksmith and a former deputy, had been drinking in the Palace Saloon. Smith departed around three in the morning, followed a few minutes later by Foley. When Foley reached down to adjust his trousers, Smith misinterpreted the gesture as a move to draw and unlimbered his own gun. Foley, who was in fact unarmed, dodged back into the saloon and secured a sawed-off double-barrelled shotgun. He then accosted Smith and told him to throw up his hands. Smith instead fired, missing Foley at close range. For a well-known "rough" who frequently threatened to "do a little killing" and had actually slain a man in Tonopah three years earlier, Smith seems to have been a notably poor shot. Foley fared no better with his firearm. Though he squeezed the trigger, the shotgun refused to fire. After Smith sent another bullet wide of the mark, Foley beat him to death with the butt of the shotgun.[11]

In addition to the misreading of innocent gestures, the assumption that opponents were "heeled" and dangerous escalated violence in a more fundamental way. Historian Richard Maxwell Brown has rightly pointed out that in America the legal concept that a threatened individual has "no duty to retreat" gained a broad acceptance it never acquired in British legal practice and may well have contributed to American homicide rates far in excess of the British. As the Nevada Supreme Court phrased the issue in its ruling on a Goldfield case, a threatened individual "need not flee for safety but has the right to stand his ground and slay his adversary."[12] When Goldfielders disagreed, the omnipresent fear that an antagonist was armed gave a powerful incentive to shoot first, a gun in the pocket offered a ready opportunity to act on these apprehensions, and "no duty to retreat" provided a firm legal justification for doing so. In the early days, this doctrine of self-defense even extended to a kind of pre-emptive strike. If someone had threatened you, even if no immediate face-to-face confrontation developed, he might have a gun that would enable him to carry out his threat at any time. Therefore, you were considered justified in ambushing him.

Goldfield's first killing was a case in point. When the camp was no more than a haphazard collection of tents, Howard "Doc" Sharp and Curtis "Kid" Kendall, both miners, quarreled over an option on Sharp's mining claims. The atmosphere between them grew more poisonous over the ensuing months. Sharp avoided the Kid whenever he could, but in a settlement as small as Goldfield, some contact was inevitable. Kendall's older brother Zeb, a widely respected central Nevada pioneer, warned the Kid to give the reticent and surly Sharp a wide berth. Like much good advice from older brothers, Zeb's exhortations had no visible effect. Whenever the Kid was on a drinking jag, a not infrequent occurrence, he would threaten Sharp and pick quarrels. Each time they came to blows Sharp, a big rawboned, fair-haired man, six feet tall and weighing close to two hundred pounds, gave the Kid a good licking.

The crisis arrived in April 1904 when the Kid, accompanied by two friends, went hunting for Sharp at his tent. Although Sharp hid out in the gully, the incident apparently convinced him that the Kid had to be stopped once and for all. When morning came and the Kid sauntered forth to breakfast, Sharp began firing at him, mortally wounding the unarmed youth as he fled, stumbling, across the street. As soon as he heard the news, Zeb Kendall whipped his team for thirty miles to reach

Goldfield while his brother still clung to life. The young man died with Zeb weeping at his bedside. Sharp, meanwhile, made no effort to resist arrest. Despite the fact that Curtis Kendall had been shot while fleeing, Goldfielders expressed general satisfaction when the grand jury accepted Sharp's plea of self-defense against the Kid's previous threats and refused to indict him. Zeb Kendall, however, was outraged, believing that Sharp should at least have stood trial for his "premeditated, malicious, brutal and cowardly" murder. "I think a man should be punished for taking the life of another when he can avoid it," he declared in a public letter to the citizens of Goldfield. [13]

As it happened, the Kid was unarmed when Sharp shot him down, but anyone so handy in a fist fight as Sharp would probably have regarded him as no great threat without the ubiquitous presence of guns. The contrast between Goldfield and Dawson sharply highlights the role of guns in escalating the level of violence. Only a few years separated the two gold rushes. Indeed many of the same sourdoughs who thronged the streets of Dawson later headed down to Goldfield, but Dawson remained free of major crime during the boom year of 1898. In his history of the Klondike, Pierre Berton attributes this remarkable circumstance to the rigorous policies of the Canadian Mounties, who confiscated all side arms in the camp. Berton notes, "If there had been a Dan McGrew in Dawson, and a Malemute Saloon . . . there could never have been a shooting because a Mountie would have been on the spot to confiscate the guns before the duel began." The denizens of Dawson knew that threats without guns to back them up could rarely excuse a killing, "The old American stall of self-defense just doesn't go." [14]

The lower levels of violence in the early gold rush towns, Sacramento in the 1850s and Aurora in the early 1860s, as compared to Bodie in the 1880s and Goldfield twenty years later, may be equally instructive. Historian Foster-Harris has rightly observed that the day of the gunfighter did not really dawn until after the Civil War, when accurate reliable firearms became widely available. Prior to that time, taking on an opponent with knives or bare fists demanded far more nerve and skill than blasting away at him from a safe distance with an "equalizer." [15] Thus, the change in weaponry in towns that otherwise resembled each other in their culture and the composition and characteristics of their populations may well have contributed to the less violent records of the early settlements.

Had most of those who strode the streets of Goldfield bristling with equalizers been better shots, the homicide rates would no doubt have burgeoned even higher. Goldfield homicides totalled four in 1905, but the district attorney's report listed sixteen additional assaults with intent to kill and thirty-seven of a less serious character. Ineptitude often made the difference, as on the January morning in 1907 when Charles Clark shot up the Mohawk Saloon. After Clark and his companion got into a drunken fight over the relative merits of various brands of Turkish cigarettes,

Edward Sites, the Mohawk's large and muscular guard, threw the cursing pair bodily from the saloon. A few moments later, Clark staggered back through the swinging doors. Telling Sites to "stand back" and be killed, Clark lunged forward brandishing his gun and firing. Sites, a man of remarkable cool, stood without moving a muscle at his post at the far end of the room while gamblers, girls, and other denizens of the Mohawk dived under the faro table and behind the bar. The first shot missed Sites by about six inches, the rest by even more, and Clark exhausted his ammunition without even grazing his target. The only casualty of the whole affair was a prostitute in one of the upstairs rooms who received a slight wound in the foot when one of Clark's wild bullets rocketed through the saloon ceiling.[16]

Perhaps Sites well knew the odds were with him when he stood his ground and staked his life on Clark's abysmal marksmanship. It will also be recalled that though Taylor and Priest had emptied their revolvers at each other in the duel over Priest's "unwanted attentions" to Taylor's wife, each had hit his target only once. Similarly, Smith, despite his reputation as a dangerous character, had twice missed Foley at close range. Sewall Thomas sarcastically noted: "Nevada shooting was just plain rotten, but about on a par with most Western shooting."[17] While some Goldfield killers had vicious tempers, it appears that none of those on whom sufficient information can be garnered had more than one previous homicide to their discredit. In fact, many seem to have been fairly ordinary men and women caught up in a gun-toting culture's climate of violence.

An examination of Goldfield's killers reveals a number of interesting patterns, some running counter to the prevailing wisdom. Killers ranged in age from the twenty-one-year-old Albert Jackman, a gambler from the Indian Territory, to the sixty-year-old Edward Hughes, a miner who shot the lover of his estranged wife. But the majority of killers (54 percent) belonged to the "violence-prone years" before age thirty-five. Overall, the median age for killers (thirty-one) was nearly ten years below the median age for victims (forty). Where national origins are concerned, the foreign born accounted for 21 percent of killers, about 7 percent less than victims. The 21 percent figure mirrored the proportion of the foreign born in Esmeralda County as a whole in 1910, suggesting that insufficiently assimilated immigrants had not pushed Goldfield's level of violence upward. Rather the immigrants probably became acculturated to the American mode of violence surrounding them.

Among the American born, not a single killer or victim was a Nevada native, suggesting that local traditions had little bearing upon the crime patterns found in Goldfield. None of Goldfield's killers traced their origins to the deep South, and only two came from the border states. The notable absence of Southerners from the roster of Goldfield killers showed that the diaspora of former Confederates, schooled by guerrilla groups such

as Quantrill's raiders or cut loose from their moorings by the severe disrup-
tions of the Civil War that swelled the ranks of the Western outlaws for
years, had long since run its course. Instead the largest single group of
those who committed homicides in the last boomtown (43 percent) had
been born in the upper Midwest and the old Northwest territories—even
though such phrases as "Wisconsin, cradle of killers" may not be the ones
normally associated with this group of states.

Though miners and mining men predictably appeared in force, the occupations of Goldfield's killers and victims revealed some equally surprising
twists. While it has sometimes been suggested that violent crime in the
mining camps was largely confined to the denizens of the so-called lower
districts, few killers or victims seem to have been professionals in the saloon-
dance hall world. The truth was that in Goldfield housewives loomed larger
in the statistics than those individuals with ruffled shirts and names like
"Billy the Wheel" who presided at the roulette wheels. Class in a mining
camp can not always be readily pinpointed, but homicide seems to have
been primarily a working-class phenomenon. Only about 17 percent of
the killers' occupations placed them above that level, while middle and
upper class victims formed a little over a quarter of the total.

A sizeable group of Goldfield's killers of known origins, fully a quarter
of the total, were lawmen and former lawmen, sometimes involved in those
incidents that would today be termed "police violence." Lawmen shot and
killed highgraders on two separate occasions, one of them an operation
of entrapment in which Goldfield lawmen cooperated with Goldfield Con
security forces commissioned as state detectives under the overall direction of Goldfield Con security chief Clarence Sage. The lawmen claimed
that they only reacted defensively against threats from the highgraders,
but use of excessive force can not be ruled out. The unarmed highgrader
who survived the entrapment shooting stated that he did not know if
his companion attempted to use his gun "but it seemed to me that the
officers commenced shooting immediately."[18] In the other incident, state
detective C.O. ("Curly") Lovell, a veteran of the Alaska gold rush who
had served as a deputy during the lockout against the union in the spring
of 1907, blasted away with a short-barrelled shotgun at an unarmed
highgrader holding a drill that he evidently mistook for a weapon in the
darkness. It may be suggestive that the main roles in both killings were
played by detectives under Sage. Despite the protestations of the officers,
the suspicion arises that Sage's men may have been under orders to shoot
first and ask questions later in order to make an example of the highgraders
who continually frustrated George Wingfield's best efforts at control.

If these were his orders, Lovell would no doubt have executed them
with relish. Evidence from a variety of sources documents the fact that
the deputies and the Goldfield Con security forces included the hard-
est cases in Goldfield, an old pattern on the mining frontier. Constable

Inman later recounted how he collected his deputies by making a sweep through the Smoky Valley and the badlands in search of men who would be certain to have a "quietening effect" on their opponents. Inman admitted: "Many of the men I got were outlaws and bad men that were being hunted." But Governor John Sparks had authorized him to promise his deputies immunity from arrest. The newly deputized desperadoes included "Three Fingered Thompson," still a crack shot despite the loss of part of his right hand, "Swedish Mick," a quiet operator so good at disguises that "his friends could hardly tell him at times," and The Duke, a handsome, brilliant, and educated foreigner with a dark complexion. Inman thought "The Duke" was "about the best shot that I ever saw." For obvious reasons, these men preferred to be known only by their nicknames. [19]

Historian Laura White cites evidence that during the labor troubles in the spring of 1907 the Goldfield Business Men's and Mine Owners Association recruited numerous ex-convicts, many with long records as "thugs" or holdup men, to oppose the union . This group included such notables as Thomas Bliss, alias "Gunplay Maxwell," a member of the Wild Bunch, later to be gunned down while planning payroll robberies from Utah coal companies. Jesse Vortrees, the alleged Arizona killer and an old chum of George Wingfield's, Ernest Priest, and Frank Smith also sported deputy's badges. So did George Gibson (almost certainly a psychopath), who killed a young mining engineer during a brawl in the tenderloin, afterward remarking to bystanders shocked by the shooting, "I don't care a damn." At the apex of the Goldfield Con security system stood Clarence Sage, a clean-shaven man with a loose lipped scowl and an arrogant stare, well remembered by old Goldfielders as a "hard one." Sage had worked as a Thiel agency detective before becoming Goldfield Con security chief. In his leisure hours, he had been known to use his shotgun to beat in the head of an opponent during a brawl in the red-light district. [20]

The effect on Goldfield homicide of the deputies and mining company guards hired during the union crisis and later let go may have been analogous to the postwar upsurges in homicide that generally occur when veterans trained to use violence and act upon their aggressive impulses are loosed upon the community. It is suggestive that a recent sharp increase in homicide in Mexico City was ascribed to large numbers of unemployed policemen fired from their jobs in a government cutback. In the late nineteenth and early twentieth centuries, the role of former deputies and guards may account for some of the otherwise puzzling differences in the level of violence in various Western localities. Historian Robert Dykstra identified lawmen with violent inclinations as the largest single group of killers in the Kansas cattle towns, and McGrath found that they also played a substantial role in Bodie. [21] The arrival of a host of guards and deputies on the scene probably contributed to the large 1907 surge in Goldfield homicide, a little noticed side effect of industrial conflict.

Indeed, if unsolved killings are omitted from the total, lawmen and former deputies committed one-third of Goldfield's homicides in the 1907–09 period that followed their recruitment. It is no surprise that the sheriff soon found it necessary to require bonds of his deputies in an effort to keep them "clear of trouble."[22] In an age when better training and education have resulted in the "professionalization" of the police, it is easy to forget that at the turn of the century the police were instead criminalized, and many individuals readily crossed back and forth across the blurred line between law breakers and law enforcers.

How much this first hand knowledge of criminal behavior gained on the wrong side of the law may have contributed to the effectiveness of Goldfield lawmen is difficult to assess. But by and large, their performance was efficient, their task was simple because killers usually turned themselves in or submitted to arrest without incident, and the assumption that boomtown society in its early stages remained too crude for "law and order" was absolutely false in so far as the arrest and detention of violent criminals was concerned. This may well have been a change from earlier camps; in Treasure Hill, a Nevada silver camp of the late 1860s, most killers reportedly escaped.[23] In Goldfield, by contrast, none of the killers awaiting trial made a getaway, and only 19 percent of Goldfield's homicides remained unsolved—a proportion much smaller than in modern America. Often the unsolved slayings appeared related to robbery, a man found shot in his cabin and bereft of his valuables or a corpse, his face mutilated to conceal his identity, discovered on a desert road outside the city.

In the great majority of cases, however, the identity of the killer was never in doubt. The issues over which titanic battles would later be fought in court devolved not upon "who done it" but was he justified? Had the killer drunk enough to successfully plead "alcoholic insanity?" Or, perhaps, did the victim possess a weapon which would permit the killer to plead self-defense? Just once did a Goldfield crime unravel into a saga of clue and pursuit, regarded by local newspaper reporters as a detective story come to life, and on that occasion, relatives of the deceased journeyed into Death Valley in the deadly heat of midsummer to pursue the investigation while the sheriff took his ease in Goldfield.

This episode illustrated that amateur involvement in law enforcement on an individual basis still had a place at the close of the frontier, but factional tampering with the legal process by lynch mobs and vigilante movements never strung a killer from a Goldfield lamp post, though several near misses occurred. After assayer Sherman Parker was fatally shot in an argument, grief over the loss of a man especially esteemed by many old friends among the Goldfield mining fraternity resulted in a disorganized rush to lynch his assailant. Lacking leadership, the impulse soon collapsed, though the sense of loss remained and hundreds wept openly at Parker's funeral.[24]

Lynching became a more serious threat when union radicals Morrie Preston and Joseph Smith were jailed prior to their indictment for the Silva shooting, and the city seethed with sensational rumors of impending union violence. An aspiring vigilante movement took shape with the formation of a "Committee of Public Safety" controlled by George Wingfield and the mine owners. Soon a lynch party dispatched by the committee and led by Diamondfield Jack Davis prowled the streets of the city with a coil of greased rope in readiness, planning to lynch Preston, Smith, and other union leaders. Meanwhile, the rabble-rousing *Tonopah Sun* fueled the fires of vigilantism, declaring in a front page cartoon, "When a few of these anarchists stretch rope, then and not until then can we boast of our Western blood." The *Sun* also considered shooting union men "like the dogs they are" an acceptable solution. But District Attorney Henry Swallow had wisely spirited the prisoners away to Hawthorne, still the Esmeralda County seat, and shortly afterward moved them once more from the "rickety old county bastile" to the solid fortress of the state prison at Carson City. Since successful lynchings generally depend upon the acquiescence of lawmen, these prudent precautions proved effective. [25]

It was no mere coincidence that the threat of vigilantism against Preston and Smith erupted not at the trial stage but after the verdict of the coroner's jury, which accepted Preston's plea of self-defense and refused to fix responsibility for the crime. This, as the men with the coil of greased rope no doubt understood, was the stage at which Goldfield killers most often eluded punishment. More than one-third of those who committed homicides claimed self-defense and were never indicted—a substantially larger figure than the unsolved fatalities.

Prosecutorial discretion, long the source of much of the elasticity in the American judicial system, was candidly admitted in Goldfield. Prosecutors might press a case when the coroner's jury found no fault with the party responsible. At the same time, even when the coroner's inquest failed to reach a conclusion of justifiable homicide, the prosecutor might refuse to proceed with the case because he thought the killer too popular to be convicted—one reason for the record of successful homicide prosecutions by his office. Killers in certain categories could rest assured of lenient treatment. No one ever questioned police violence, even though one of the corpses proved to be a respected businessman and member of the social elite. On the contrary, police violence elicited praise. After the death of Frank Smith, one admirer sent Deputy Foley a five-dollar check for "killing a hobo."

The district attorney's decision not to indict Paddy Mullaney for assault, following the shooting in which he seriously wounded Vincent St. John and two innocent bystanders, suggested that those who attacked union radicals could also count upon prosecutorial indulgence. Moreover, members of racial minorities who killed within their own communities were generally considered outside the bailiwick of the Goldfield legal system. The old concept that the taxpayers would refuse to finance a coroner's inquest over an Indian killed by another Indian still prevailed in central Nevada for much of this period (a practice also approved by the Indians, who usually preferred to settle matters according to their own customs). By the same token, W. J. Burnell, who mortally wounded another black during a fight in a Goldfield saloon, received a fine, but the district attorney never prosecuted him for homicide.[26] However, let a member of a racial minority slay a white man, whatever the reason, and he was as good as dead. An Indian named George Williams, tried in Goldfield for a homicide committed elsewhere in Esmeralda County, provided a case in point.

Perhaps the most interesting aspect of this practice of freeing killers prior to the trial was the change that occurred over time. In 1904, the year when Goldfield's first homicides took place, both killers were released without standing trial. Several gained their freedom in the same way in 1905–06, but by 1908–09, only lawmen won release through the coroner's inquest. Since the particulars of early crimes such as the Sharp-Kendall ambush appear as inexcusable as some of the latter day shootings, it was Goldfield's tolerance for violence that had changed.

Though leniency at the coroner's inquest prevailed in Goldfield's early years, severity characterized the trial stage throughout. Trials generally followed speedily on the heels of crimes—perhaps too speedily. Supporters of Preston and Smith believed that trying them "on a rush order" less than two months after the Silva shooting while public excitement still ran high had strongly influenced their conviction. Yet Goldfield juries seem to have been compassionate, often wrangling for hours over a defendant's degree of guilt. Their sympathy toward criminals as members of the same human family, perhaps a surviving trace of the old sense of brotherhood in the mining camps, starkly contrasted with late nineteenth-century Oakland, where the criminal was regarded almost as an evil being from another world. Even in the most egregious crimes, Goldfielders took the death penalty very seriously, and no popular outrage emerged when two local killers won their appeals to the Nevada Supreme Court.

Astonishingly, only one of the nine Goldfielders tried for murder won an acquittal, a marked change in practice from earlier mining towns. Angel noted that in Virginia City "adequate punishment is meted but to few" because repeated postponements and sympathetic jurors permitted many to escape justice. Similarly, McGrath took note of numerous acquittals in Bodie, often through the legal wizardry of Patrick Reddy, the one-armed lawyer who "never lost a case." Though a successful supreme court appeal and two hung juries enabled George Gibson to elude punishment for the murder of engineer Charles Maunsell, no Goldfield criminal lawyer won laurels comparable to Reddy's.[27]

Given the strong likelihood of conviction, combined with the widespread reliance on plea bargaining that had already altered the American criminal justice system in the late nineteenth century, Goldfield's killers had strong incentives to plead guilty. All the same, only one did so. Spike Hogan had brutally killed James Flynn in the street outside a Goldfield saloon after Flynn, in the euphoria that followed a big win at the gaming tables, spread his largesse among numerous patrons of the saloon but gave none to Hogan. Despite the nastiness of his crime, Hogan received only a five-year sentence for manslaughter. Aside from this exceptional plea bargain, Goldfield killers, like the rest of the populace, behaved like gamblers and staked their lives on the chance that the time-tested pleas of self-defense or acute alcoholic insanity would win them an acquittal against all odds. [28]

Sometimes, it is true, they did achieve a lighter sentence than the circumstances of the case would seem to warrant. Nonetheless, three Goldfield killers faced the death sentence following convictions of first-degree murder. Since one committed suicide in prison and another won a second trial on appeal and then received a lighter sentence, only one of Goldfield's thirty-one killers actually went to the electric chair, a huge burly unemployed watchman known as "Pegleg" Casey, because injuries received in railroad work had left him limping like a mining camp Quasimodo. When the neat young Irish wife of his neighbor spurned his advances, Pegleg's ardor soured into a deadly grudge. It would end in a fusillade of bullets that killed a neighboring housewife and left the luckless object of his affections crippled for life. Casey's last resort plea of "acute alcoholic insanity" failed to save him, and he received the death penalty. The severity of the sentence should not, however, be interpreted to mean that Goldfield always dealt harshly with the killers of unarmed women. After stabbing his wife with the bread knife as she fled, Jack Sheridan was only convicted of manslaughter. The varying outcomes at Goldfield's murder trials depended heavily on the degree of sympathy—or opprobrium—that the prisoner in the docket evoked from the community. [29]

Never was this more evident than in the sole acquittal on the roster of Goldfield's murders, the trial of Jack Hines for slaying a Polish nobleman, Count Constantin Podhorski. Events leading to the trial had started more than a year earlier in Nome, in the wake of the Alaskan gold rush, when Edith and Jack Hines became acquainted with Podhorski. The young couple were in modest circumstances; Podhorski, by contrast, was an imperious, handsome, and mustachioed aristocrat who came to America to represent the financial interests of the Czar's inner circle. Then in his forties, the count had an eye for the ladies, and his marked attentions to Edith Hines, a blue-eyed, statuesque beauty of twenty-one with golden-brown hair, married just three years, became a matter of comment in Nome.

Evidently these attentions were not unwelcome. When the count left Alaska to pursue business in Seattle, Edith Hines boarded the same boat.

She said she sought a respite from the rigors of the "dreary frozen north" and intended to visit her family, promising to return to Nome before winter set in. Yet weeks and months passed by, and still she lingered in Seattle. After her eventual return, the couple began to travel erratically. Hines sold his Alaskan mining interests and left his job as a salesman for a liquor company. The couple visited friends in Washington, Oregon, and Idaho, where Hines wandered distractedly in the wilds. They journeyed to New York and then, in March 1907, to Goldfield, where the drama that began in Nome was about to end.

Soon after their arrival, Edith and Jack Hines alit from a hack in front of the Sunset Cafe at the hour of the evening meal. Count Podhorski sat at a table inside dining with a companion. Edith stepped over to the table, greeted them, and requested a few moments of private conversation with Podhorski. The count's companion moved aside. Immediately, Jack Hines entered the cafe and opened fire from ten feet away. The count slumped to the floor, riddled with bullets. The smoking gun in hand, Hines then turned to the assembled bystanders and recklessly declared, "I came 7,000 miles to kill this man. Hang me if you will." It was a remark his attorneys would have considerable difficulty in explaining away.

By the time Jack Hines' trial for murder commenced the following autumn, all eyes in the community were focussed on the young couple. Newspaper reporters described Hines as a man who had "fought in the wastes and wilderness and to whom written laws would of necessity mean less than to the man bred in town. . . . Full blooded, with heavy lidded eyes and expanded nostrils, he is seen at a glance to be a man of impulse and passion."

But reporters reserved their most rhapsodic flights of prose for Edith Hines: "Her face was that of a frightened child, and yet its drawn lines showed the agony of the Dolorosa. There is a haunting sense of the ruthlessness, of the relentlessness of fate . . . the girlish naivette suddenly stamped with the imprint of world-old suffering." Was she a naive young bride, seduced by a worldly European aristocrat or the "willing victim" painted by the prosecutors? All Goldfield waited on the answer. [30]

Though the plethora of jurors eliminated because they acknowledged prejudice in favor of Hines augured well for the defense, District Attorney Henry Swallow and his assistants fought a mettlesome battle. Their first move nearly crippled the defense. They confined their presentation to prima facie evidence on the shooting alone in an attempt to forestall defense testimony on what was becoming known in Goldfield as "the justification." Without this central saga of seduction and revenge, the defense would surely crumble. Only after much legal maneuvering did the presiding judge permit Edith Hines to relate how the count, following a theater party with mutual friends in Seattle, had plied her with wine at a late-night supper and then waited in her hotel room to make love to her while she was too

Edith Hines at her husband's murder trial in 1907. Goldfielders crowded the courtroom for a glimpse of the face that charmed a Polish count and launched an odyssey of revenge (Boyd Moore drawing in the Goldfield Chronicle, *Nevada State Historical Society)*

intoxicated to resist. Intimidated by the count's threats, she then went traveling with him to Vancouver. After her reunion with her husband, she admitted the count had ravished her.

Her husband reacted violently, tearing at her face with his hands. Edith declared that his distracted state of mind accounted for their journeys of the ensuing months. Only after they arrived in Goldfield did she finally tell him the details of her intimacy with the count. In consequence, when he unexpectedly saw the count in the cafe, a sudden rage swept over him, and he shot the seducer. Despite the discrepancies in her story, the state declined to cross examine the witness.

Reporters avidly described the emotional reaction to Edith Hines' recital. Her husband "listened and wept as a child." Later, he "reached out his arms convulsively toward her and then sank back into his chair, his face hidden in his hands." Her mother also hid her face. A woman in the court-room sobbed uncontrollably. Other spectators averted their eyes from Edith Hines' look of "frightened appeal." (Indeed such scenes were far from unusual at the turn of the century. In an age we wrongly associate with strong silent men and stiff upper lips, Goldfield courtrooms were often awash with the tears of weeping defendants, relatives, spectators, and even histrionic attorneys.)

If any doubted the defense contention that "the inscrutable decree of an avenging fate" had cast Podhorski in Hines' path by chance, the defense attorneys had more ammunition in store. They attempted to shore up the Hines story with expert testimony on temporary insanity by two psychiatric experts, or "alienists," as they were then known, one with an impressive sounding German name. Pleas of "temporary insanity" by jealous husbands who shot "home wreckers" had grown so commonplace in American courts during the late nineteenth century that the *Tribune* scornfully termed Hines' new line of defense "frayed out." Nor was expert testimony on psychology an unusual occurrence elsewhere in the nation. Alienists and other psychiatric experts had long been contradicting each other and thoroughly confusing the laymen in murder trials, perhaps the most famous of which was the trial of Charles Guiteau for the assassination of President James Garfield in 1881. In Goldfield, however, alienists were a distinct novelty. Ordinarily the defendant in a murder case related in detail the prodigious amounts of liquor consumed in a drinking bout and relied upon the testimony of local doctors to bolster his plea of acute alcoholic insanity (as did Pegleg Casey).[31]

Under the guidance of the alienists, Goldfield began to explore the un-familiar territory of psychology. Questioned by the defense attorneys, Dr. George von Waedelstedt explained that Hines' constant desire for revenge had so enlarged his brain cells that as soon as he saw Podhorski he became an "irresponsible creature." During the months elapsing between Hines' first intimation of the "dread secret" and his confrontation with the count, his mania became "organically" fixed. The point was critical for the defense because most of the outraged husbands exonerated in American courts had reacted violently when first learning of a wife's infidelity, not five months later. The attorney inquired whether a chronic case could be cured. Dr. von Waedelstedt declared, "It can, just like removing a splinter from the hand." The prosecution, laboring under budgetary restrictions that prevented them from hiring their own experts, had to content themselves with hypothetical questions to the defense's alienists.

If the psychological testimony had confused the jurors, both sides endeavored to set them straight during closing arguments. The prosecution ridiculed the opposition's flipflops from one line of defense to another: "His counsel have brought forth almost every defense, consistent and inconsistent, excepting alibi, and I suppose they didn't happen to think of that." They also attempted to dispel the romantic mists enveloping Hines' crime. Edith Hines' intoxication, suggested the district attorney, was just "an ordinary drunk, and the result in her apartment was but a logical and natural sequence." She had then willingly gone traveling to Vancouver with the count. In closing, District Attorney Swallow found little to admire in Hines' attempts to use his wife's seduction to save his skin: "Any man who will allow his poor shivering wife to come into court and tell the story of her degradation is not worth the rope to swing his withered soul into eternity. We ask for a verdict of guilty as charged."

The defense, however, portrayed Hines as a heroic defender of family values against the "lecherous foreigner." Even those accustomed to florid speech in the courtroom commented upon their purple oratory, and Judge Frank Langan privately termed them the biggest "hay-makers" he had ever seen in court. Attorney Cochran declaimed to the jury: "The eyes of the civilized world are upon you. There is a host of good women looking to you with uplifted hands and crying out, 'Gentlemen, gentlemen! Are you going to put the foul destroyer of a home upon a pedestal, or are you going to place the laurel on the brow of the man who slew him. . . .' Plant the banner of virtue on the highest peak in this state, so that the whole world can see it."

After a mere hour and a half in conclave, the jury agreed to plant the banner and Hines was acquitted. He flung his arms around his wife and "planted a whopper on her lips," embraced Cochran, and received congratulations from the judge, his Alaskan friends, and hundreds of well-wishers surging into the courtroom. As soon as the news spread through town, the streets and the saloons became scenes of general rejoicing. [32]

How had Hines, a new arrival with no ties to the community, won the sole acquittal in the annals of Goldfield's early homicide trials? Any who concluded that the favorable outcome signified open season on "home-wreckers" soon discovered his mistake, as did Edward Hughes. After Hughes slew his estranged wife's lover in 1908, under circumstances in which the victim had no more chance to defend himself than did Count Podhorski, Hughes was not only convicted, but convicted of first-degree murder. He committed suicide in his jail cell while awaiting execution.

Hines' Alaskan friends in the Arctic Brotherhood evidently believed that their influence had turned the tide. It is true that allegations of intimidation also surfaced in the only other Goldfield homicide trial in which a killer eluded conviction, the George Gibson affair. The two hung juries that enabled Gibson to walk free after the murder of engineer Charles Maunsell may have been influenced by Gibson's known friendship with George Wingfield and the campaign of intimidation by Diamondfield Jack Davis, who menacingly told the chief witness for the prosecution that he had a "notion to stamp your head in the ground." Yet the obvious sympathy that Hines elicited from Goldfielders suggests no need for intimidation.

Then had the alienists, with their unfamiliar psychological jargon, succeeded in reversing the usual tendency of juries to convict? It seems unlikely. Though the jurors refused to disclose their deliberations, they had undoubtedly noted the improbabilities in the defense story, including Edith's lapse into senselessness while the count ravished her, and above all, the chance encounter in the Sunset Cafe. The *Chronicle's* assessment no doubt sounded more convincing: "It is the old, old, sad story of man's depravity and woman's frailty—a poor husband with a pretty and pleasure seeking wife, and a rich, suave, distinguished gallant, willing and anxious to supply the husband's deficiencies."[33] In all likelihood, Goldfielders thought Hines had spoken the simple truth when he said, "I came 7,000 miles to kill this man," and they sympathized with him.

The Hines trial remained exceptional. As the boom waned, Goldfield's increasingly harsh attitude toward homicide reflected an important shift in community values. George Gibson, who had once escaped justice after a wanton murder, was sent to state prison by deputy district attorney George Springmeyer in 1910 for an assault upon a deputy sheriff whom he had not even wounded.[34] Goldfield had become a very different place than in the days when the grand jury refused to indict Doc Sharp for shooting Kid Kendall in the back. At last Zeb Kendall's grief stricken words, "I think a man should be punished for taking the life of another when he can avoid it," had become the community standard.

XII

The Power to Rule or Ruin

POLITICS

"Get an axe . . . look up around you and use your axe at the system that makes slaves of you, makes you old before you are young . . . your mind atrophied with the monotonous daily grind of toil. Unite, brothers, under the banner of Industrial Unionism. . . ." Harry Jardine, Socialist congressional candidate from Goldfield.

"I hope you break the backs of everyone of those suckers down there," instructions from George Wingfield's Reno office to his subordinates at Goldfield Con.

Long after large-scale mining ceased and Goldfield shrank to a shell of its former self, the city was to cast a long shadow over Nevada politics. The central Nevada mining boom had triggered a long-lasting partisan realignment in state politics and produced the new elite that would later dominate the state. Moreover, Goldfield nourished the two major dissident political movements of twentieth-century Nevada, the Progressives and the Socialists. The streets of Goldfield became the arena where the ultimate ideological battle between capitalism and Socialism was waged. And the final solution imposed.

Against this backdrop of high stakes and large ambitions, local government in Goldfield remained crude and elementary throughout the boom years. In the manner of miners ever since the California gold rush, Goldfielders had organized and christened their district in the autumn of 1903, with the election of a recorder for their mining claims as the primary order of business. Aside from setting wages and hours at the top of the union scale, they apparently made no attempt to regulate camp life in other spheres. Most governmental authority remained in the hands of the three county commissioners in Hawthorne, the Esmeralda County seat, some 135 miles distant. [1]

As the camp's population swelled into the thousands, government by a body far removed from local needs became increasingly untenable. After an explosive meeting at which Goldfielders demanded "home rule" and lambasted the commission's neglect, the commissioners authorized the election of a town council for Goldfield. The council would act upon much-needed improvements and other local matters, subject to the subsequent approval of the commission. While this stop-gap measure fell short of home rule, Goldfielders accepted it in the belief that the problem would be solved when the city incorporated at the next session of the legislature in 1907. In view of the general mining camp tendency to award political offices to professionals and merchants, the membership of the five-person council elected in the summer of 1905 included some surprises. Ole Elliott garnered the most votes, a testament to the influential position of saloon-keepers, and several other candidates were outdistanced by a Socialist waiter named Joseph William Smith—later to be known far beyond the boundaries of Goldfield as one of the defendants in the infamous Preston-Smith murder trial.[2]

Local government ground along under this two-tiered system, while services lagged and the emoluments of local officials soared, until the next legislative session convened in 1907. Then Goldfielders of all political persuasions, spearheaded by the Chamber of Commerce, united for one supreme objective—moving the Esmeralda County seat from Hawthorne to Goldfield and ending the expense and inconvenience of traveling to Hawthorne to transact their legal business. Although the commission had thwarted a 1906 attempt by Goldfield to hold a special election on the county seat issue, changes when the population center of a county shifted had ample precedent. Hawthorne itself had won the county seat from the old mining camp of Aurora, and in 1905 nearby Tonopah had wrested the prize away from Belmont, the old Nye County seat. Thus, Goldfielders had every reason to anticipate success. But, just to make certain, they threw their money around in royal style.

Following what the *Tribune* termed a "monster mass meeting" at the new stock exchange, a special train bedecked with streamers and loaded with boosters from business and organized labor departed for Carson City to lobby the legislature. To sustain themselves during the journey, the delegation imbibed forty cases of rye whiskey and sixty of champagne, with double these amounts on hand for the siege at the capitol. Carson treated the visitors to a grand ball, and the Goldfielders lavishly reciprocated. "They spent money like water and kept a local bank on the jump all day and night," related the *Tribune*. "Such a flow of champagne and jingling of twenty-dollar gold pieces has never been seen here in years." Lest the merry-making be too abruptly curtailed, the legislators delayed a few days before making Goldfield the new county seat without a dissenting vote. Goldfielders topped off the festivities by shooting up the town.[3]

On the way back to Goldfield, the special train paused in Reno for another round of banqueting and champagne. A Goldfield booster named Millard later recalled: "About us were gathered a swarm of children, including newsboys and street gamins of every degree of filthiness. Some of us boosters started a cry of 'Throw 'em the coin.' Rolls of wads that make the wads of ordinary Wall Street financiers blush green for very shame, flashed in the air. Coin was drawn from the pocket . . . including gold pieces of various denominations. Greenbacks and coin were hurled promiscuously into the crowd. Such a scrambling I never saw." Shortly afterward Governor Sparks and a large party of legislators and their wives arrived in Goldfield to be wined and dined at a reception in the Montezuma Club and a dance at Union Hall, to which the entire city was invited. The reception committee announced: "Everybody will be allowed to go to bed when he pleases but until daylight shall appear, it will not be deemed the thing to do."[4] The legislative party, less accustomed to all-night celebrations than Goldfielders, no doubt retired first.

After the county commissioners took up the reins of local government in Goldfield, superseding the town board, the drive to incorporate lost momentum. Though the Chamber of Commerce and the *Chronicle*, among others, continued to press for incorporation, several factors undercut the effort. Many apparently believed that incorporation would mean an expensive duplicate set of officials in a city already noted for wasteful spending. Officeholders predictably showed little disposition to share their power and perquisites with a new set of rivals. Moreover, in a camp with such a mobile population, the legal requirement to secure the signatures of a majority of the tax-paying voters in the last election posed a considerable hurdle to those circulating petitions for incorporation. Finally, while none would have openly admitted it, doubts over the permanence of Goldfield had started to surface. The declining market in mining stocks and the bitter lockout against the unions in the spring of 1907 were eroding the old optimism. By summer the *News* gave voice to the once unspeakable thought that Goldfield's duration was "purely problematical." Many camp residents with no intention of making Goldfield their permanent home showed little interest in incorporation, and the mercantile middle-class sector represented by the Chamber of Commerce proved too weak to prevail. As a result, the town that was, for awhile, the largest city in Nevada never incorporated. This did not prevent Goldfield from making a farcical and unsuccessful attempt to snatch the state capital from Carson City in 1909.[5]

The *News* praised the quality of government provided by the commissioners on the ground that Goldfield "practically has no government at all and still is the best governed city of its size and business importance throughout the land." Few would dispute that Goldfield had almost "no government at all," but not everyone saw it as an asset. The *Chronicle* constantly blasted the commissioners' extravagance and incompetence—at least, until the demise of the newspaper permanently silenced its criticisms.[6] In fairness it should be borne in mind that the need for a courthouse and several schools in a new and populous settlement where none had previously existed compelled the commissioners to embark upon an expensive building program primarily funded by bond issues; decline then set in before the new infrastructure had been paid for. Yet the building program failed to explain the disappearance of the bountiful revenues from taxes and licenses pouring into county coffers (an audit revealed that two hundred thousand dollars had mysteriously evaporated through embezzlement or misappropriation, never to be recovered). It appears that the *Chronicle*'s scathing editorials on the commissioners' "power to rule or ruin" and the looming bankruptcy of the richest county in the state had some foundation in fact. In 1908 rebellious citizens, believing themselves "taxed to the limit of human endurance," demanded a tax reduction to levels commensurate with other Nevada counties. As the camp's decline accelerated, auction sales of Goldfield property for delinquent taxes proliferated. Early in 1909 the county that had squandered its funds in such profligate fashion began negotiating a bank loan to meet its bills. [7]

Even before this day of reckoning arrived, the commissioners generally starved essential services or attempted to have them performed without payment. Teachers and firemen worked without pay for periods as long as five months at a time. Streets were graded and cleared by a chain gang of prisoners from the local jail, a practice strongly opposed by Constable Inman, whose enlightened views often set him at odds with the commissioners. Graft became an integral part of the system when the county commissioners reportedly authorized the constable to secure salaries for a new force of deputies by covertly assessing the inhabitants of the tenderloin, an old system that had moved westward from the Eastern cities, where it probably originated, to gold rush California and later to Kansas. [8]

The concept of poverty as a public responsibility was alien to the commissioners, as to most local officials at the turn of the century. Esmeralda's commissioners personally scrutinized every bill presented to the county with Scrooge-like intensity. They compelled patients suspected of malingering at the county hospital to take the "paupers' oath" before granting them assistance. Providing a destitute individual with a railroad ticket out of the county was the only other form of public assistance they undertook (also the system in Aspen during the silver boom). While the call by the *News* for a charity organization to provide systematic assistance to Goldfield's poor produced no results, private acts of charity relieved the misery of some. For instance, a piece of embroidery might be raffled to assist a "lady in unfortunate circumstances," or the Ladies Aid Society might hold a benefit to "alleviate the sufferings of the unfortunate." The fraternal lodges gave some aid to their destitute members, and the benevolences of churchmen like Father Dermody also did much to assist Goldfield's poor. Nonetheless, even before the blacklisting of union men by the mine owners multiplied the privation, poverty assumed alarming proportions in the very camp known for easy money and big spending. In the early autumn of 1907, the *News* noted the presence of hundreds of unemployed men, stranded in Goldfield with their families and too impoverished to leave town. [9]

Vagrancy was seen as a problem in law enforcement rather than an off-shoot of poverty, and the sheriff periodically arrested "hoboes" and offered them a choice of jail and work on the chain gang or departure from Goldfield. Yet it appears that many of these men were really the "working poor." Nearly all those arrested in a sweep against "vags" camping out in Rocky Canyon during the summer of 1907 could prove that they held jobs. [10]

If town ordinances provide a reliable clue to the concerns of Goldfield officials, the danger of fire overshadowed all else. The bulk of the ordinances passed by the Goldfield town council are devoted to outlawing fire hazards in minute detail, including home barbeques, firecrackers, and sales of gasoline within the town limits. Though Goldfield's vulnerability to fire obviously worried the city fathers, they showed complete indifference to that complex of pastimes under the broad umbrella of "vice." Unlike the California mining towns analyzed by historian Ralph Mann, Goldfield experienced no moral reform drives against the sinners in bordellos and saloons—possibly a sign of the pallid influence of churches, especially the Protestants who often spearheaded moral crusades. Demography may also have contributed to this tolerant attitude. The large ratio of men to women has been called the "single most important factor" behind the flourishing tenderloin district on the Comstock. In an era when other communities less replete with adventurous young men were busily enacting laws to regulate morality, and even Deadwood banned gambling in the famous "badlands," Goldfield harked back to the wide-open traditions of the old frontier. With the exception of a vague prohibition against drunkenness, no ordinance attempted to regulate drinking, gambling, drugs, or the conduct of business on Sundays.

Segregating prostitution was apparently Goldfield's only real concern in the moral realm. While prostitution was never forbidden, ordinances barred women other than employees from saloons, and the commission confined dance halls and bordellos to an area officially designated the "Red Light district," a solution which, as in the California gold towns of the 1850s, catered to the miners while insulating the residences of the middle class from brothels. Goldfield officials actually closed a few establishments that violated these rules, including The Idler, a notorious "refreshment and amusement resort" where worthy matrons allegedly fell into sin and ladies of doubtful virtue prowled about in search of a mining camp Midas. [11]

Although the county commissioners appeared in theory to share power with other elected officials, most notably the district attorney, the sheriff, and the town constable, they had ways of influencing these office holders. The commission used their appointment powers freely, as when they made the brother-in-law of one of the commissioners an assistant district attorney and later justice of the peace despite his doubtful qualifications. When a vacancy failed to occur through the death or departure of an officeholder, the commission sometimes created one by raising the amount of bond an official was required to post to an impossible level. By this means, they deprived Socialist District Attorney J.E. Davidson of his office in 1906, appointing in his place a conservative Republican, John Douglas, who was more to their liking. The commission instantly reduced the district attorney's bond to a minimal level, and Douglas occupied the office until the voters rejected him at the next election. After District Attorney Augustus Tilden, elected in 1908, and his deputy George Springmeyer undertook a number of sensitive prosecutions, including a graft case and bullion tax suits against several large mining companies, the commissioners attempted to eject him from office by the same method. Tilden, however, had more resources at his disposal than Davidson. After a desperate scramble for backers, he succeeded in raising most of the extraordinary sum demanded of him and holding on to his post. Besides these maneuvers with the bond of other officials, the commission's financial powers proved useful when a host of deputy sheriffs were reportedly hired in 1908 to work for the re-election of the local triumverate—the commission, the sheriff, and the district attorney. [12]

Of these offices, the combined position of sheriff and tax assessor was seen as the political plum, probably because it entailed such lush financial rewards through the so-called fee system prescribed by state law. Under this mode of governance, the sheriff augmented his annual salary with fees for all taxes and licenses he collected. Other local officials received similar fees. The district attorney, for instance, collected fees for felony convictions extending upward to one hundred dollars for a successful first-degree murder prosecution. The office of district recorder initially occupied by Claude Smith was reputedly one of the most lucrative, with fees that swelled the occupant's remuneration to one thousand dollars a month (exceeding the president's salary, when multiplied into today's dollars). Goldfield justices of the peace also received fees, which may have stimulated the volume of legal business they processed. Justice Isaac Solomon, for one, was called to explain to the county commissioners how he had managed to hear thirty-one cases in a single day. [13]

The press strongly decried this "vicious and obsolete" form of government: "Office holders fatten at the expense of the taxpayers, and accumulate fortunes through encouraging litigation. If an official is worth his hire he should receive a suitable stipend that will abundantly reward him for his services. . . . A peace officer can graft through meretricious arrests by raiding disorderly houses at his pleasure. The justice, constables, and district attorney come in for their share of the plunder, and an endless chain is established, with the helpless taxpayer wearing the collar that compels him to pay an exorbitant levy for the conduct of his business." [14] Considering that a good deal of money, along with power and prestige, was at stake, it is scarcely surprising that lawmen once fought for their piece of the turf with drawn guns and arrested each other. When the sheriff and the constable finally arrived at detente in the summer of 1907, the diplomatic

WHEN RENT DAY COMES 'ROUND

SHERIFF INGALLS IS PART OWNER IN BUILDINGS RENTED AS "CRIBS."

During the 1908 political campaign, the Goldfield Chronicle *charged that Sheriff William Ingalls was a landlord in the tenderloin district (Nevada Historical Society)*

ramifications of the resulting peace treaty recalled a settlement between nations at war.

If fees, legitimate cuts from the stolen ore recovered from highgraders, and graft from the "corrupt fund" regularly collected in the tenderloin provided a sheriff with insufficient remuneration, the standards of the day posed no barriers to private business ventures in the saloon-dance hall world. William Ingalls, a lean, stooped, elderly man with a drooping white mustache had held the office of Esmeralda County sheriff in Hawthorne long before the Goldfield rush began and kept it for most of the decade, not the only instance in which an old timer managed to hold onto office because thousands of newcomers were too passive and disorganized to wrest it from him. Throughout these years, Sheriff Ingalls remained a part owner of the Palace Saloon, where he maintained his offices. Political enemies charged that he was also the landlord from whom many cyprians in the red-light district rented their cribs. While newspaper cartoonists satirized him in the tattered velvet and ermine robes of high office, no one publicly suggested that the solid gold badge, encrusted with diamonds, rubies, and sapphires, that Ingalls' deputies presented to him in 1907 might have connotations disquieting to the advocates of good government.[15]

How easily Goldfield's minimal government of lawmen and county commissioners could be elbowed aside was memorably demonstrated in the spring of 1907 when the camp gained a new de facto government. Popular hysteria in the wake of the shooting of restauranteur John Silva by union organizer Morrie Preston in a picketing dispute on March 10 led to the formation of the Goldfield Business Men's and Mine Owners Association at a meeting in the Montezuma Club. For Wingfield, the shooting proved providential. Public fears that violence by the radical unions was an immediate threat enabled him to unite the individualistic mine owners and leasers behind his supreme objective—destruction of the radical unions. Indeed the Association ledger clearly announced "but one purpose," denying employment to all members of the IWW.

"The vigilante has traditionally rationalized his action by convincing himself that he lives in a state of anarchy . . . since the authorities are unwilling or unable to protect him from predators," observes author William Burrows in *Vigilante*, "so he is really trying to preserve the essence of law and order until he is relieved of that burden by effective lawmen and judges." Since similar rationalizations were voiced in Goldfield, a question should be raised at this point: did the Silva shooting signify a breakdown in law enforcement that demanded a vigilante response? First, no one could seriously suggest that the incident was one in a series of union crimes that the Goldfield legal system had failed to punish. Despite their violent reputations, the radical unions had conducted themselves with remarkable restraint in Goldfield. Secondly, Preston was unlikely to elude punishment. He had turned himself in to legal authorities and remained in custody pending his probable indictment and trial. In fact, the Goldfield law enforcement system had scarcely failed, having not as yet had much opportunity to proceed. Vigilantism in Goldfield arose not as a response to any real deficiency in law enforcement but rather from the misperception of an isolated crime as a major public threat.[16]

To accomplish its stated purpose of destroying the union, the Association proceeded to usurp the functions of local officials. It employed a special prosecutor, John Douglas, who largely took over the Preston-Smith case from the district attorney. Douglas's use of false witnesses paid by Wingfield and his vituperative tirade against the two union men as cold-blooded "assassins" undoubtedly influenced their conviction. While the case against a list of radical union leaders for their part in the "assassination plot" eventually crumbled, the indictments provided a useful weapon to drive leading radicals who might have resisted the destruction of the union out of town.

The Goldfield Business Men's and Mine Owners Association also levied assessments upon its members and apparently employed detectives working under cover inside the unions. It foisted thirty-five special deputies of its own, commanded by Goldfield Con security chief Clarence Sage and his lieutenant Curly Lovell upon local lawmen. Association records also reveal expenditures for large numbers of rifles destined for its supporters. During the prolonged lockout against the union in March and April 1907, the Association ruled the city.

Unanimity nonetheless proved elusive in a community of frontier businessmen accustomed to following their own pursuits as the spirit moved them. Saloonkeepers refused to join the Association, and stockbrokers rejected Senator Nixon's plea to close the exchanges for the duration of the lockout. All the same, the Association achieved Wingfield's main objectives. After more than a month of soup kitchens and standing idle in the streets, the union men who had dreamed of making Goldfield a workers' paradise knuckled under to most of the mine owners' demands. This victory was completed the following December when the mine owners eradicated the unions under cover of federal troops and Association representatives paraded the Preston-Smith case before federal investigators as one of the principal justifications for action against union violence. [17]

Having served its purpose, the Goldfield Business Men's and Mine Owners Association faded from the scene. As Richard Maxwell Brown rightly notes, "Vigilante movements were characteristically in the control of the frontier elite and represented the elite's social values and preferences." Although the elite assumed their accustomed role in Goldfield, their concerns had broadened from horse thieves and criminals to include labor leaders and political radicals, and their methods had grown more sophisticated than the San Franciscans of the 1850s, the Missouri Bald Knobbers, and other frontier vigilante groups. By engineering the conviction of Preston and Smith, they succeeded in turning a run-of-the-mill self-defense shooting that would otherwise have attracted little notice in a mining camp into a public relations coup against the unions with statewide repercussions. No such effect could possibly have been achieved by "taking the law into their own hands" through the crude methods of earlier vigilantes. [18]

From the perspective of almost a century, the triumph of capitalist values by means of modernized vigilante tactics may seem a foregone conclusion. Yet it is important to bear in mind that in the first decade of the twentieth century the Socialist challenge from political outsiders appeared strong and real. The American Socialist party founded by Eugene Debs in 1901 garnered only a small percentage of votes, but its potential alarmed mainstream politicians from President Theodore Roosevelt to the state capitols. In Nevada politicians had great cause for alarm because in a state so scantily populated a small number of votes could easily alter the electoral results. In the 1906 election, no state candidate polled as many as nine thousand votes and no winning margin exceeded four thousand. Moreover, the Socialist vote was rising in every election, nurtured by the organizers in the avowedly Socialist WFM.

The same fragile electoral equation that alarmed the ruling elite quick-ened the hopes of Goldfield's Socialist dreamers, men like Vincent St. John, Harry Jardine, and Joseph Smith. Of these, St. John, a slight, clean-shaven, gray-eyed young miner and union organizer of thirty, with a calm face and demeanor and a heart seething with fury, was already a well-known figure to American radicals. Born in Kentucky in 1876 of Dutch-Irish parentage, St. John had lived in four different states with his unsettled family before he went to work in the mines at nineteen. His participation in the armed resistance during a miners' strike in Cripple Creek in 1901 gained him a lasting reputation for violence and his successful union organizing in Idaho's Coeur d'Alene marked him as a doubly dangerous man to the mining corporations. By the time he arrived in Goldfield in the autumn of 1906, he had emerged as one of the most radical leaders in the anarcho-syndicalist IWW, a missionary dedicated to emancipating the entire working class by organizing them in a single union. Or, as he put it, "an organization which asks no quarter and will give none; whose battle cry is 'an injury to one is an injury to all'; an organization which recognizes no division among workers. . . ."[19] Wingfield's spies inside the union reported that he saw Nevada as an isolated state where the radicals could gain control. His ultimate agenda was no secret: first, the organiza-tion of the working class in "One Big Union"; next, a series of strikes, culminating in a general strike; then the union's assumption of control over the means of production; and finally, the workers' commonwealth.

St. John later remembered the winter of 1906–07 as a kind of golden age in which these visions seemed on the verge of realization through the city-wide union of the combined WFM and IWW. For a brief time, the union's word was law and the employers came humbly to Union Hall in-stead of the other way around. The influence of Goldfield's radicals crested at the "Bloody Sunday" parade held on January 20, 1907, to commemorate the St. Petersburg massacre of Russian revolutionaries and to support union leaders then awaiting trial in Idaho. On union orders, Goldfield's mines, restaurants, and saloons closed for the parade, and thousands marched while thousands more watched from the board sidewalks.

That night an overflow crowd massed in Union Hall under a red banner inscribed to the union leaders: "If they pack the jury to hang our men, we will pack hell full with them." St. John, who rose to a standing ova-tion, was the star orator of the evening. He spoke of the "coming revolu-tion" and promised the audience that if the union leaders were executed "we will sweep the capitalist class out of the life of this nation and then out of the whole world." The meeting concluded with rousing resolutions

Union leader Vincent St. John, the "Saint" to his followers, during the Preston-Smith trial in 1907 (Arthur Buel drawing in the Tonopah Sun)

dedicated to the Russian revolutionaries. "We have no enemy but the capitalist class! Our country is the world! Our flag is the banner that is dyed red with the martyrs' blood of our class! Down with capitalism! Long live the International working class republic!"[20]

From that point onward, however, St. John's influence in Goldfield steadily waned. Though his followers idolized him, many miners did not share his radical views, and his conservative opponents within the union detested him almost as much as did his corporate enemies. Perhaps his persuasive powers, his infinite patience, and his charismatic personality prolonged the spring lockout, but in the end, "the Saint" could not dissuade the membership from caving in before George Wingfield's "compromise be damned" policy. Over the ensuing months, St. John's radical positions went down to defeat time after time in union meetings. Nonetheless, his mere presence may have harmed the union by fueling public fears of the radicals and alienating potential supporters. Even before Mullaney's crippling bullets put an end to St. John's Goldfield career and federal troops moved in at the mine owners' behest, the golden age of union radicalism had passed. [21]

In keeping with his syndicalist ideology, St. John had acted on the belief that union organization was the means to political power. Other Goldfield radicals combined union organization with conventional politics and sought public offices. Harry Jardine, a miner and union organizer and an old friend of St. John, with a similar background in Colorado and the Coeur d'Alene, contended for Nevada's single statewide congressional seat on the Socialist ticket in 1906. Though the Democratic candidate easily defeated him, Jardine made a notable showing that appeared to demonstrate the incipient dangers of Socialism to the traditional parties. While he won only 1,251 votes (8.8 percent of the congressional vote), 30 percent of his votes came from Esmeralda County. This suggested both his local popularity among those who knew him best and the future possibilities of a mining camp dominated by the radical unions as a Socialist power base. Within Esmeralda County, Jardine garnered 20 percent of the congressional vote, placing him only 7 percent behind the Republican candidate.

Jardine's flamboyant radicalism made his showing particularly alarming to the proponents of politics as usual. Unlike Grant Miller, the Reno attorney whose mainstream appeal later made him the most popular Socialist to contend for national office in Nevada, Jardine may well have been the most extreme candidate ever to take the field in the state. On the pages of *Miners' Magazine*, the official publication of the WFM, he authored many a burning manifesto which lambasted union conservatism as a "shallow-brained painted woman, whose thoughts do not rise above her hips," aimed a few shots at "conventional respectability that boweth down to platitudes, phrases, and perfumed wind: fell in love with the fleshpots of Egypt," and preached the gospel of the One Big Union. "Get an axe . . ." he advised, "and use your axe at the system that makes slaves of you. . . ."[22]

None could doubt that a vote for this Socialist firebrand was a vote for revolution. It may have been no coincidence that Jardine, along with St. John and Joseph Smith, was among the union leaders indicted for

conspiracy in the wake of the Silva shooting. A year after his congressional campaign, Jardine agreed to leave Goldfield in exchange for the
dismissal of these charges.

In retrospect, the only successes achieved by Goldfield Socialists occurred
in the early years when the radical unions formed a large component of
the local electorate and the opposition had not yet mobilized. In 1904,
while Goldfield was still a tent camp, the Socialists fielded a full county
ticket, electing J.E. Davidson as district attorney and James Russell as constable. A nasty struggle to retain these positions ensued. Within four
months of taking office, both Davidson and Russell, together with the
non-Socialist justice of the peace, were threatened with removal in a graft
scandal. Winning their petition to the Nevada Supreme Court, they
succeeded in keeping their offices, but the county commissioners subsequently ousted Davidson by raising his bond to a level that a Socialist,
lacking wealthy supporters, could not meet, and Constable Russell's unsuccessful suit against the commissioners for full payment of his fees dragged
on for years.[23]

The principal remaining achievement for Goldfield Socialism was the
election of a dark-haired British immigrant in his mid-thirties with brown
eyes and a bushy handlebar mustache named Joseph William Smith to
the town board in 1905 (the absence of party labels makes it difficult to
determine whether some other candidates may also have been Socialists).
In gaining this office, Smith, a waiter and union organizer, had outdistanced
the expected winner, a well-known local attorney, as well as a pioneer mining entrepreneur and other notables. Smith's domineering methods in
advancing the union cause and his strong rhetoric made him anathema
in some quarters—quite possibly the reason that he was tried and convicted along with Preston, although he had nothing to do with the Silva
shooting. At the same time, Smith seems to have been a simple and compassionate man who lived his egalitarian faith, sharing his own family's
meager portion with impoverished neighbors and providing free meals to
the hungry at the small restaurants he occasionally operated. These qualities
accounted for his failure as a businessman, but they also probably had
much to do with his popularity in the community.[24]

Collusion between the major parties may have forestalled other Socialist
successes. For instance, the Republicans endorsed Democratic candidate
William Ingalls for the important and lucrative office of sheriff in 1906,
no doubt because they feared that fielding a candidate of their own might
split the major party vote and turn the Socialists' 43 percent into a victory. As this suggests, the Socialist candidates did not compete upon a
level field.

Despite the obstacles, Socialism was still on the upswing in the state as a
whole: Nevada Socialists would elect a state senator and two assembly-
men, as well as a number of local officials, and Grant Miller, United States

senatorial candidate, would win nearly 30 percent of the vote in 1916. Perhaps more important, many of the reform issues championed by the Socialists, in such areas as labor conditions and woman suffrage, would be co-opted by the major parties and enacted into law. Yet these successes signified a rejection of Goldfield's revolutionary brand of Socialism for a more moderate variety with broader popular appeal. The downfall of the Goldfield Socialists was evident in the election statistics. In 1906 Esmeralda County had contributed a quarter of the state Socialist gubernatorial vote. In 1910 the figure had dropped to 11 percent—and this at a time when the Socialist proportion of the vote was rising and the number of voters in Esmeralda County had climbed, despite the precipitate decline in population. The destruction of the unions and the diaspora of radicals from the city had done its work. Despite all the *sturm und drang* of "Bloody Sunday," revolution had failed at the polls, just as it failed in Union Hall. [25]

As the dream of radical Socialism evaporated, the Democrats emerged as the big winners in Goldfield politics. Goldfield voters were no "yellow dog Democrats," who, in Texas parlance, would even vote for a yellow dog if he had the right party label. Rather they showed enough independence at the polls to split their tickets for popular candidates of either party, throw the rascals out of office on occasion, and rebuff an unappealing Democratic presidential candidate. Thus, Goldfield, along with most of the West, rejected Democratic presidential candidate Alton Parker in 1904 in favor of Theodore Roosevelt. In 1908 they ousted the incumbent Democratic sheriff and district attorney in favor of Republicans at the same time that they gave a resounding victory to Democratic presidential candidate William Jennings Bryan. Indeed so overwhelming was the sevenfold increase in the Esmeralda County Democratic vote over the previous presidential election that Bryan awarded Major Minnemascot, the Democratic mule, to Goldfield. Much ceremony, as well as much humor from Republicans, accompanied the arrival of the big black gleaming mule at the train station. Democrats boasted that Minnemascot would live up to his role by bucking any Republican voter who climbed upon his back into fragments. No Republicans volunteered to put the matter to a test. [26]

The symbolic gift of Minnemascot was entirely appropriate because the new Democratic voters in Goldfield and other localities undergoing rapid population growth were realigning Nevada politics. After Nevada became a state in 1864, the Republicans predominated, and the Central (later Southern) Pacific railroad political machine soon came to rule from behind the scenes. During the nineties, the Silver party coalesced around the locally popular free silver issue and swept Nevada elections. While the nineties have sometimes been mistaken for a realigning era in Nevada politics, the Silverites remained under the control of the old party elite, principally Southern Pacific boss Charles "Black" Wallace, and after 1896, the Nevada electoral system began reverting to the pre-Silver party norm. This process was reversed when the influx of Democratic voters to Goldfield and other booming counties produced a lasting realignment in 1908. The state's total presidential vote more than doubled in the span of just four years, labor in the mining camps responded strongly to Democratic appeals, and Nevada became one of the Democratic islands in a nation where the Republicans were the normal majority party. The old Republican realm of nineteenth-century Nevada gave way to a competitive state system, tilted in the Democratic direction, that was to endure for decades. In this fundamental political change, Goldfield played a substantial part. [27]

Though the Republicans failed to regain their majority status, Goldfield politicians invigorated the state Republican party and infused it with the new spirit of Progressivism. Elsewhere in Nevada the new reform movement then sweeping the nation failed to take root. In Goldfield, however, factional fighting in the local party presaged the emergence of Republican reformers as early as 1908. Augustus Tilden's successful race for district attorney in that year showed that reform could win a popular following. Tilden, then nearing forty, was a self-taught lawyer and a man of liberal sympathies. He had fought boss Abe Ruef within the San Francisco Republican party and, after moving to Nevada in 1904, had defended the WFM against the mine owners in a major injunction suit. Voters evidently approved his sizzling condemnation of incumbent district attorney Henry Swallow for failing to take prompt action against banker Thomas Rickey after the failure of the State Bank and Trust, and labor displeasure with the Preston-Smith prosecution may also have contributed to Tilden's electoral victory.

Once in office, the Tilden administration lived up to its reform promise. Tilden's chief deputy, George Springmeyer, was primarily responsible for the Rawhide graft case, in which local officials stood trial for defrauding the county through fictitious billings, and for the criminal indictment of Pittsburgh Silver Peak mining corporation officials for failing to pay their bullion tax. The county commissioners tried and failed to oust this inconvenient reformer from office by the same maneuver that had ended the public career of Socialist district attorney Davidson. [28]

As Nevada's first direct primary approached in 1910, Progressivism broke forth from Goldfield to the arena of state politics under the leadership of two Goldfield attorneys, "Lighthorse Harry" Morehouse and Springmeyer, who had decided to make a second bid for the attorney general's office. Despite his credentials as a former California legislator opposed to the Southern Pacific machine, Morehouse, a Southern-born ex-Confederate soldier wounded in the Battle of Mobile Bay, scarcely fit the Progressive prototype. Nor did Springmeyer. In the movement historians have seen as "a veritable Protestant religious crusade," he was an atheist; among reform leaders whom historians have contended were typically drawn from old Yankee stock, he was the son of German immigrant ranchers. Nonetheless, Springmeyer was the man who would lead the Nevada Progressives until they ceased to exist as a distinct political movement in 1916. Because the Southern Pacific and the regular Republican organization were obviously campaigning for his opponent, Tonopah attorney Hugh Brown, Springmeyer set out alone to canvas the cow camps and mining towns, armed only with a set of posters proclaiming him "The Unspiked Rail in the Path of Railroad Domination."

Late in August "Lighthorse Harry" entered the fray. He was the moving spirit behind the large meeting held in Goldfield to form a Lincoln-Roosevelt League to back the Nevada insurgent in the same way that California's league of the same name supported Hiram Johnson in his drive for power outside the regular party organization. Although the new league endorsed various Progressive reforms, notably the direct primary, recall, and popular election of United States senators, the overriding preoccupation of its members was the Southern Pacific, an acute issue in the party long controlled by the railroad. The league's declared purpose was "to overthrow this evil power in the Republican party."[29] The demand for a strong elective public service commission to regulate the railroad would become a central feature of Springmeyer's campaign.

Springmeyer won the primary, but reports of foul play by the Republican regulars began to appear. A legion of Southern Pacific employees received two-weeks furlough to work for the ticket, and from his Reno mansion on the bluff high above the Truckee River, Senator Nixon conveyed a final message to Springmeyer, "We've turned loose a river of gold against you." Springmeyer lost by sixty-five votes, badly hurt by losses in Reno, the long-standing stronghold of the machine and major population center of the traditionally Republican northwestern region, where a Republican candidate needed to draw a sizeable proportion of his vote. Future senator Key Pittman's election day post-mortem on the "extensive bribery" by Nixon and the Southern Pacific machine could be as well applied to the Progressive insurgency.[30] Democratic newspaper cartoonists, who depicted Nixon and Wingfield distributing coins from the "corruption sack," had reached the same conclusion.

Another unsuccessful electoral contest ensued before the insurgents finally re-entered the Republican fold. The strengths and weaknesses of the movement were, for better or worse, very much Springmeyer's own. Nevada Progressivism reflected his disinterest in organizational work, his scanty financial resources, and his lack of skill in combating machine tactics, but it also mirrored his passionate idealism and his courage in fighting impossible odds. Beneath the bronze portrait of Theodore Roosevelt that always hung in Springmeyer's law office, a motto was engraved, "Aggressive fighting for the right is the noblest sport the world affords."[31]

Though neither the Socialists nor the Progressives would have acknowledged common features, both the early twentieth-century Nevada reform movements nurtured in Goldfield shared similar corporate enemies – the mining companies and the Southern Pacific. Both elevated leaders with similar strengths – impassioned and uncompromising idealists whose rhetoric outdistanced their practical political savvy. Both movements saw their leaders defeated at the polls, yet witnessed the eventual triumph of many of their ideas. The fact that both drew a large measure of their strength from Goldfield may have been far from accidental. Though in theory the old northwest region around the Comstock, more middle class and Protestant than Goldfield, should have provided the most favorable social conditions for Progressivism, Goldfield proved to be the catalyst. Perhaps Goldfield's newness, her disorganized leadership, and her weak and rudimentary political institutions allowed new movements to swiftly rise during the early years as they could not have done in the counties rigorously controlled by the old guard. Moreover, while new Nevada towns abounded in this period of rapid population growth, the glamour of Goldfield and the substantial population base it offered as a political springboard attracted talented and ambitious men – almost a process of natural selection. These men, seizing the opportunities at hand, would bring the national political reform movements of the day into Nevada. Corporation politics would continue to reign supreme, successfully repulsing both the Socialist and Progressive assaults, but after another decade passed, the new leadership emerging from central Nevada would end the long domination of the old elite clustered around the Comstock.

As Goldfield increasingly resembled a company town, Wingfield exerted political control through the staff and the security detectives at Goldfield Con and various compliant local officials. Among the latter, the principal "man to see," as hopeful job seekers put it, was Deputy Sheriff John Donnelley (later to become Nevada's director of Prohibition when the Wingfield machine was at the apex of its power during the 1920s). From his Reno office, Wingfield commanded his men on the spot in Goldfield: "I hope you break the backs of everyone of those suckers down there." Security chief Sage vetted the suitability of political candidates and investigated alleged "adgitators" on the Goldfield Con work force. The general manager of Goldfield Con dutifully reported to his superiors: "I have endeavored to carry out fully the suggestions of yourself and Mr. Wingfield. I have started cautiously to see how our employees will line up on a question of law and order regardless of candidates. I hope to know soon how they stand and if they don't stand right we shall have to get rid of the bad ones."[32] The electoral defeat of the few "dynamiters" (that is, Socialists, in the lingo used at Goldfield Con) who still dared to contend on the local ballot in 1910 demonstrated the effectiveness of these activities.

In public Wingfield modestly acknowledged that he expected to be "somewhat of a factor" in the 1910 election, in which he made the defeat of Democratic candidate Charles Sprague, the editor of the *Goldfield News*, a top priority. To this end, Wingfield made vigorous use of his increasing influence over the Nevada press through loans and other favors. During this period, his behind-the-scenes political manipulations meshed with the old Southern Pacific railroad machine led by his former partner, Senator Nixon. Long an agent of the railroad, Nixon had lately inherited the powers of the earlier railroad bosses, Black Wallace and H.M. Yerington. This transitional situation abruptly changed when Nixon died in office in 1912. Citing his desire to remain in Nevada and attend to his business interests, Wingfield declined the senatorial appointment offered him by his old protege, the compliant Republican governor, Tasker Oddie. Some suggested that he feared the relentless exposure of political campaigns. Not only would his political and financial manipulations come under scrutiny, but also there was the scandal involving his former common-law wife, May. An embittered Diamondfield Jack Davis observed: "Had he [Wingfield] tried to take his seat in the Senate I would have fought him off the cross. He showed good judgment in laying down."[33]

In the years after Nixon's death, the venerable Southern Pacific machine, buckling under the assault of the California Progressives, gave way to the new bipartisan political machine headed by Wingfield, for Wingfield's decision not to follow the usual route of the mining millionaire to the senate did not signify indifference to politics, only a distaste for broad responsibility and public scrutiny. He preferred pulling the strings to secure his business empire, reward his friends, and punish his enemies. Not infrequently he relied upon a generous favor that compromised before his quarry realized that a Wingfield favor could never be repaid like an ordinary debt. These subtle and oblique methods have sometimes concealed his machine's existence from scholarly scrutiny. Wingfield might give oral instructions, leaving no trace. He might issue no explicit orders at all. As he himself later said of his two right-hand men: "I do not know that I gave them any instructions. They knew what I wanted."[34] After Goldfield's eclipse, the machine reached the zenith of its power in the 1920s when numerous Wingfield associates from the boom days assumed political office.

Goldfield reformers had furnished the ideological sustenance of early twentieth-century state politics. Later the new elite spawned by the central Nevada mining boom assumed political leadership under Wingfield's aegis. When Wingfield died in 1959, John Sanford, an astute political observer, wrote in the *Reno Evening Gazette*: "For more than 50 years George Wingfield was a mighty power in Nevada and for a greater part of that half century his rule was absolute. . . . Any criticism of the Wingfield machine's methods and operations, any rebellions against its rule, were quickly and mercilessly put down."[35] Never again, in the years since his death, has one man wielded so much power in Nevada.

EPILOGUE

The End of the Last Gold Rush

"There never has been and probably never will be a second Goldfield," Alva Myers, 1936

———————————————◆•◆•◆———————————————

Inside seven years, the great boom had ended. No longer did throngs of fortune hunters wedge themselves inside the saloons like bees in a hive, nor did the stock exchange resound with the din of clamoring speculators, nor did gorgeously gowned grass widows parade the sidewalks in search of Mr. Goldbar, nor did the red visionaries of the IWW conjure up the workers' paradise to come before the crowds at Union Hall. All the grand ambitions that brought them together in Goldfield had vanished into the blue air like the mirages of lakes in sylvan parks that trembled over the sands of the Clayton Playa. Gold was still pouring out of Goldfield at such a pace that the superintendent of the government assay office at the former Carson City mint found himself literally up to his elbows in tons of bullion and forced to strip off his coat, roll up his sleeves, and work with his men, even as he barred the door to further shipments. But the bonanza spirit had drained away.

Sewall Thomas noticed an unmistakable "difference in morale," visible in the way people walked and greeted one another. They even spat differently. Crowds thinned, brokers' offices posted "For Rent" signs, stores advertised bankrupt sales, saloons began to close, one after another, signs lay where they fell, tin cans, empty bottles, and other uncollected trash littered the streets, and the Montezuma Club was "transformed from a roaring place of joy unconfined to a gloomy retreat where one might contemplate suicide and find it attractive." Dance halls were torn down for lumber. Sand and tumbleweeds blew inside the broken windows of once fine houses, and "birds nested in living rooms not so long ago the glittering scenes of social triumphs." Those who remained were a "chastened people." Former society women gave up "the evening gown for the bungalow apron," while "potential statesmen blew up like punctured balloons."[1]

No more did the crowds of former days swirl around a horse-drawn wagon, banners flying, packed with specimen ore, parading through the streets from a mine in search of investors. The new craze was the South American placers. Goldfielders began studying Spanish, and many headed in the same direction as Diamondfield Jack Davis, who announced that he was setting forth with an armada of men and mules to seek a new

El Dorado in eastern Brazil. The Goldfield that remained was a more tran-
quil place, in which the visionary hopes of palmier days had withered into
small things. Opportunity, for those who stayed on, meant digging up
the ground around the cabin of a dead prospector to see if he had buried
his gold in a jar or sifting through the sand and mud swept down in a
flood from the Malapai for one of the tiny leather purses, worn on the
garter, in which a lady of the line had kept her pay. By 1911 Goldfield
had diminished to a small and quiet mining town. In 1916, with production rapidly falling, Goldfield Con reverted to the leasing system. Russell
Elliott has discerned a certain symmetry in this: leasers had opened the
mines in the early days; now they would blast the final tunnels in the
golden horseshoe. Large-scale mining ceased in 1919 when the Goldfield
Con mill closed its doors. Although some leasing and small operations
continued, the town's population sharply diminished.

A few desert rats hung on hoping for a new bonanza. These hopes no
longer flourished in the posh mahogany-paneled brokers' offices of the
boom days but in the shacks of a batch of eccentric prospectors.
"Chickenhawk Mulligan," for one, could be found at his Goldfield cabin,
when he was not working at his mine in Montezuma seven or eight miles
away or scavenging the streets for additions to his tin foil collection. "Thirty-
seven years, eight months, ten days, sixteen hours, fourteen minutes and
I'll have a ton of this," he would mutter. "Then I'll have control of the
market." His real name was Charles Chambers; his nickname, Chickenhawk
Mulligan, derived from his habit of shooting hawks for mulligan stew when
he grew hungry out in the hills. The youngsters who stopped by the old
gentleman's cabin to smoke his cigarettes and persuade him to help them
with their mathematics believed that Chickenhawk was an educated man
from the East—some said a former Harvard mathematics professor. His
true origins may have been more humble. Court records show that when
he arrived in Goldfield during the boom he had been mining for twenty-
five years. But he certainly knew mathematics and he wrote wonderful
epic poetry on the mining men he remembered. Regrettably, none of this
has been preserved.

Other sometime prospectors and odd characters around town included
Montezuma Pete, Scotty the Pig, Poker Bob, Pickhandle Pete, Coyote Bill
(who trapped coyotes and sold their pelts for a living), and Johnny-Behind-
the-Rock, a Death Valley prospector so named because he was too small
to be seen when he stood behind a rock. One of these bearded old prospectors continued to mine even after he went blind by following a string
for a mile and a half from his boarding house to his mine. Though no
longer able to see gold ore, he claimed he could recognize it by the taste.
Silkhat Harry, another notable character, was nicknamed for the headgear
he sported on the Fourth of July, the grand occasion for which he also
took his annual bath. For part of the day—sometimes the better part—

the old prospectors would collect on the cement bench outside the Goldfield Hotel and talk mining in an assemblage known as "the spit and argue club." The principal event in the annals of its gatherings occurred in the 1930s when Will Rogers happened to pass through town and took all the gaffers on the bench to breakfast in the Goldfield Hotel.[2]

By then, the raucous boomtown that once spread from the Malapai to Columbia Mountain must have sounded like another tall tale in the mouths of these old men. In 1923 the conflagration so narrowly averted in 1905 with prompt action and liberal dousings of beer at last arrived, and the liquor that once saved Goldfield became her undoing when Prohibition ruled the land. The fire apparently started with an explosion in a bootlegger's still in the early morning of July 6. By the time firemen arrived, the blaze had spread from the bootlegger's house to a neighboring garage. Fanned by a brisk southeast wind, it soon licked through an entire block in the heart of town. The mounting flames could be seen thirty miles away from the Tonopah Hills. The fire chief's attempt to create a firebreak by dynamiting buildings fizzled when the buildings remained intact, and firemen fled before the intense heat of the advancing wall of fire, abandoning their equipment. Thereafter nothing remained to be done but help the scurrying Goldfielders to save their lives and as many of their belongings as possible. Horns honked steadily as autos and trucks piled with household furniture moved through the streets. A motley army of people, toting as much as they could carry, hastened alongside. The *Tonopah Times* recounted the ensuing spectacle: "Streets and avenues were congested with livid streams of fire that seemed to consume everything in their path. . . . Shacks and massive stone buildings crumbled as though of wax."

By the time the fire had burned itself out that afternoon, twenty-five square blocks—about half of the city—including some two hundred buildings in the downtown and northern residential districts had burned, leaving 150 families homeless. When young John Koontz arrived home at dusk, riding a horse from Tonopah, he stared in disbelief at the blackened smoking ground before him, punctuated by the gaping walls of burned buildings: "I didn't recognize the town. . . . to me, it was just desolation personified."[3]

A few landmarks still stood—the Goldfield Hotel, the courthouse, the old bottlehouse, the small red brick Tex Rickard residence, with its leaded glass window in lapis lazuli blues and its white picket fence, and at the point where the highway turns sharply south toward Las Vegas, the nine-room Charles Sprague stone house, once noted for its "unique" interior and exterior features and the city's first residential hot water heating system. But Goldfield never rebuilt. Among the 150 families left homeless by the fire, many gave up and accepted the half price tickets out of town charitably offered by the railroad.[4] In speaking of the years that followed the fire, people tend to preface their remarks with the phrase "after Goldfield died."

All the same, depopulation and fire did not result in the return into dust that has been the fate of so many Nevada mining camps. No one tore down the old hotel to cart away its mellow-hued bricks to enhance the suburban residences of distant cities as in Aurora. No one has bulldozed the earth for souvenirs as in Rawhide. The entry for Goldfield in the ghost town guidebook does not read "foundations only," often the signal that a well-trained archeologist will be needed to identify the site.

On the other hand, Goldfield has not risen from the ashes into a second life as a tourist mecca like Virginia City, Deadwood, and Tombstone. From time to time grandiose plans are announced: the Goldfield Hotel will be remodeled and modernized and day trips will introduce sojourning tourists to the unspoiled charms of the surrounding desert—unspoiled, that is, outside the confines of the nearby federal bombing and gunnery range. At least once, reconstruction actually commenced. But it has never been completed, and unless the golden touch of movie fame that transformed a rather mundane shooting in Tombstone's OK Corral into a legend attracting over a half million tourists a year lights upon Goldfield, these plans will probably continue to evaporate. No tourist paces the ground with reverential awe to stand upon the spot where Jack Hines said, "I came 7,000 miles to kill this man. Hang me if you will." No local entrepreneurs have as yet supplied boot hill with false and entertaining grave markers as in Tombstone. No antique dealers and fashioners of handmade jewelry and macrame have arrived in force as in Bisbee. No tour buses line the parking lots as on the Comstock. In fact, Goldfield has not yet developed the need for parking lots.

Instead the city survives in an intermediate position between "foundations only" and the tourist playgrounds. Her position as the Esmeralda County seat and a stop on the main highway between Reno and Las Vegas pumps enough blood into her veins to keep her alive. Occasionally, mining reawakens. For quite some time, the most notable mining activity was conducted by Goldfield Deep Mines, an operation in keeping with Goldfield's less admirable traditions. "Deep Mines," at least, was no misnomer—the mines sank deeper and deeper, reaching more deeply still into the stockholders' pockets for assessments, without locating a new bonanza.

More recently, as Nevada has emerged at the forefront of American gold-mining, surface operations have been attempted. Modern gold mining methods involve heavy earth-moving equipment processing tons of ground for a thimble sized amount of gold—a far cry from the old hunt for the highgrade that larcenous miners carried out in their double-crowned hats from dark underground tunnels. For several months the conical heaps of tailings in celadon greens and sulphurous yellows that had come to seem a benign and rather lovely part of the landscape where they had reposed for so many years were hauled into a mound nearly half a mile long and chemically leached for the last traces of gold. Then operations abruptly halted. Goldfield survives intact because the new mining yielded too little profit to proceed with the massive rearrangements of the land that have elsewhere decapitated an entire mountain and left old mining towns like Rhyolite, Tuscarora, and Gold Hill poised on the brink of advancing pits. The new conveyor belts stand idle as the old headframes abandoned so long ago. For the moment, the sunlit peace of the desert has returned.

On the surface, the last great gold rush of the mining frontier closely resembled the excitements that preceded it—the same horde of adventurous young men, the same crude and hastily erected buildings, packed saloons, and dusty streets thronged with burros and freight wagons (albeit interrupted by the occasional automobile). Like earlier rushes from California to the Klondike, Goldfield went through the same stages of rapid boom, industrialization, and decline, perhaps accelerated by the ready availability of capital and transportation at the close of the frontier. The camp also passed through similar political phases, from the democratic open meeting that organized the district, through the influx of the politically apathetic intent on getting rich and getting out, and the ultimate affirmation of traditional values and forms. In Goldfield, that meant capitalism and machine politics.[5]

At the same time, Goldfield enjoyed none of the features that elsewhere extended the lives of mining towns, such as the discoveries of late bonanzas, the presence of large low-grade deposits that could be profitably mined for decades, or the introduction of new technologies. Nor did Goldfield possess a vigorous merchant class or a favorable geographic proximity to large population centers, agricultural regions, or future ski runs that would facilitate her conversion into a supply center or tourist playground when mining ceased. Still, measured against the past ambitions of mining centers that once aspired to remain hubs of commerce and industry, an expensive ski resort like Aspen and the empty stone ruins at Treasure Hill may only signify different forms of decline. As historian Duane Smith has noted, the mining frontier failed to develop into a "permanent urban civilization."[6]

Despite the comparable rites of passage through which she evolved, Goldfield was not entirely interchangeable with earlier mining booms. In so far as can be determined from fragmentary evidence, the proportion of actual miners was probably smaller than in earlier booms, the position of women more liberated and less secure, the casualties in suicide and epidemic disease higher, the mania in mining stock speculation unsurpassed, and the general tone of camp life rougher and more rapacious, with the typical mining town ambition to build a permanent community for families easily swamped in the atmosphere Emmett Arnold called "hell-roaring Goldfield." Though the process of elevating new political and economic leadership had been characteristic of many mining camps, the last boomtown differed in nurturing not just powerful individuals but movements. Goldfield differed as well in the kind of man it elevated. George Wingfield shared the humble origins of many of his mining camp predecessors and like them became what Richard Peterson has termed a "flexible frontier capitalist" with diverse interests,[7] succeeding on a scale beyond the schemes of such rogues as George Graham Rice and Parmeter Kent. Yet unlike the bonanza kings with backgrounds in commerce or the mining world, Wingfield was a former gambler (possibly excellent preparation for his later activities in the stock market), and he developed shady connections very different from a William Clark or a Marcus Daly. His early consolidation of mining in the golden horseshoe would enable him to imprint his personal economic goals and leadership style on Goldfield, and later the state, in a way that no mining tycoon in the towns with more diverse leadership ever accomplished.

On the broader national canvas, Goldfield lacked the impact of the most influential mining booms. The California gold rush gave enormous impetus to the settlement of the West, stimulating transportation, agriculture, other mining excitements, and the rise of cities like San Francisco that rivalled their Eastern counterparts. The influence of Goldfield was more limited, primarily affecting the Great Basin region, but on a smaller scale, it stimulated regional development in much the same directions as the California gold rush.[8]

More recently, the longstanding conception of the positive role played by mining booms in Western development—indeed development itself—has fallen under critical scrutiny. In the words of Wallace Stegner, "every boom and bust leaves the West physically a little poorer, a little worse damaged."[9] Yet it is necessary to bear in mind that a pristine desert where the deer and the antelope play has not been a likely alternative for the Goldfield region. Were it not for the thin human residue of communities and transportation routes cast up by the central Nevada mining boom, this corner of the world might well have been incorporated into an expanded federal bombing and gunnery range, its earth poisoned by atomic bomb tests. Or it might have become a repository for highly radioactive nuclear wastes, at present the probable fate of Yucca Mountain some distance south of Goldfield. As the concept of the Nevada desert as national wastebasket and artillery range increasingly holds sway, the environmental consequences of mining dwindle into insignificance.

From the perspective of almost a century, what difference has it made to Nevada that a Shoshone prospector named Tom Fisherman found gold near Rabbit Spring? In the economic realm, Goldfield, together with Tonopah, Ely, and a host of lesser camps, played a vital part in the great boom that reversed almost twenty years of depression and decline in Nevada and doubled the state's population within the span of ten years. Yet actual bullion production from the mines formed a smaller component of the economic boom than is commonly realized. Estimates indicate that losses suffered by investors in mining stocks during the 1907 crash exceeded the entire production of the Goldfield district for the half century following Fisherman's discovery by at least one-third. [10] From this it can be readily inferred that the value of transactions in mining stocks during the grand bacchanal of speculation surpassed mining production many times over. Moreover, the saloons—forerunners of the casinos of the present day—conducted so large a volume of business that their payrolls ran a close second to the mines.

Today these relative positions have been reversed. After minimal interruption by Prohibition and anti-gambling laws, tourism based on legalized casino gambling emerged as the foundation of the state's economy. Though Nevada now produces more gold than any other state in the nation, mining runs far behind. They did not know it, but the Goldfielders who swarmed inside the Northern to try their luck against Fifteen Two, Society Red, and other sporting gents were seeing the economic future. It was not down in the mine tunnels. Instead it surrounded them in the smoke-layered air and clicking roulette wheels of the Goldfield saloons.

In the political realm, it would be difficult to overestimate the importance of the central Nevada mining boom in which Goldfield had played so large a part. New voters realigned Nevada's once Republican politics in the Democratic direction, and central Nevada served as the spawning ground for the new state political elite. Despite the indifference many gold rushers felt concerning politics in a community where they did not plan to remain, Goldfield nurtured the two major dissident movements of twentieth-century state politics, Socialism and Progressivism, both destined to fail in their drives against corporate domination. Goldfield became the scene of the decisive battle between Nevada capitalism and the new egalitarian radicals flying the red flag, and the final solution imposed by the master of Goldfield Con has endured ever since. While a number of Socialist reforms intended to better the workplace and democratize the political process entered the mainstream, collectivism lay discarded with the waste rock in the mine dumps mounded in hillocks throughout the golden horseshoe. Individual economic advantage, the passion for profit that historian Patricia Limerick calls the "core of the Western adventure," [11] has remained Nevada's ruling ethos.

In part, the victory of this mining camp ideology of untrammeled individualism resulted from Nevada's extreme poverty and the weakness of strong competing ecomomic interests. Demography also contributed to the outcome. The predominance of rootless unmarried men in Nevada's population and the general impotence of organized religion, as historian Jerome Edwards has rightly pointed out, had much to do with the values that carried the day. [12] There were Nevadans, like the immigrant German ranchers walking with shovels on their shoulders beside the Carson Valley ditches, who intended to stay and raise their families, to make the land a better place, and to build for the future. Community spirit was not a phrase that lost all meaning between the Sierras and the Utah border. But the communities harboring philosophies different from the gold rush ethos proved too weak to prevail.

In many ways, present-day Nevada represents the triumph of the mining camp ideology that Goldfield did so much to strengthen. Along with its fine free adventurism, that ideology involved the primacy of the individual over the community and materialism over moral values. It meant bursting free from the restraints of small-town America into a world without social controls where drinking, gambling, and prostitution had free rein. It meant a "let's take the money and run" attitude espoused by a highly mobile population with little regard for the future of communities from which they expected to vamoose in short order. The dark consequences of this attitude emerged in the impoverishment spread by fraudulent mine promoters, the corruption of local politics, and the death records so closely tied to careless living conditions. Today it is reflected in neglect of the environment and developments undertaken for short term gains with disregard for future consequences. Then as now, mining camp ideology brought high social costs in crime and elevated suicide rates. Both the few remaining natives and the flood of new residents in America's fastest growing state cherish an imperfectly articulated but deeply held belief that may be roughly stated as, "In the West, you're free to do what you please." Let it never be denied that this mythic ideal of the West, with policy consequences both large and small, retains its hold on the popular imagination. [13]

In the years that have passed since the rickety trains swinging into Goldfield held standing room only, the state where mining camp ideology triumphed earliest and in its purest form has ceased to be an anomaly on the American scene. Indeed Nevada stands in danger of becoming a victim of its own success, widely imitated by other states. Nevada has demonstrated that a poverty-stricken state can support itself by gambling—and indeed grow and prosper—that gambling can be run relatively cleanly, probably with no greater infiltration by organized crime than affects the sanitation-carting business in New York, and that conservative religious groups, such as the state's many Mormons, can peacefully coexist with an economy based on vice.

Now, as an economic crunch squeezes them and old values crumble, other states are rapidly following suit. Slot machines whir from the shores of Atlantic City to the heights of Deadwood. The long-renowned morality of the Midwest no longer bars riverboat gambling, horse racing, dog racing, city video lotteries, and many other varieties of gambling. Lotteries proliferate in one state after another. And in California, where card games have long been permitted, an influx of new residents of Asian origin has resulted in enormous annual revenues in certain localities from Asian card games—scarcely the quiet hands of poker in back rooms envisaged by those who resisted banning cards.

Easy divorce, another relic of Nevada's frontier values, may offer a historical lesson. The so-called divorce business that played an important part in Nevada's economy from the twenties through the forties ended when other states eased their divorce laws to a level commensurate with Nevada's. As gambling laws follow a similar course, Nevada's tourist-based economy could meet the same fate, unless Nevada establishes such a firm hold as what Las Vegas television commercials term "the American way to play" that new rivals can not readily break her grip. If they do break it, the end of Nevada's prosperity will also signal the triumph of her philosophy of unfettered individualism over other value systems.

And what of those Goldfielders whose individual strivings had collectively and unwittingly shaped the future order of the region? Al Myers, the "father of Goldfield," who kept the faith in the summer of 1903 when other prospectors abandoned the camp, found himself restless in retirement at his luxurious Long Beach mansion with the golden door-knobs. Evidently mining still ran in his blood. In addition to investing at Wonder, Tuscarora, and other locales, he gained control of the Johnnie Mine near Pahrump and succeeded in putting an enterprise at which several previous owners had failed on a paying basis. He then went on to expend the riches taken from the Johnnie in a fruitless search for new deposits. Though Myers' luck was the result of hard work and vision, he also made his share of mistakes.

His romantic embroglios may have been in this category. In 1910 a minister's daughter sued him for seducing her and making false promises of marriage. As proof of her allegations against the recently divorced mining magnate, she produced bundles of love letters which, according to the press, revealed that "the burning Romeo was but a piffling trifler compared with Myers." The outcome of her lawsuit is not known.

Losses in a 1927 bank failure left Myers financially ruined. Over the ensuing years, whenever word of a new mining excitement broke, he headed into the desert like an old hound with the well-remembered scent in his nose. The promoters of these booms must have heartily dreaded his arrival. Down in the diggings he would go with his pick to investigate and out he would scramble to pan his samples. Then came his verdict—invariably thumbs down. "Save Nevada from such as that," he would say. "A person would have just as much chance to find gold out here in the streets of Las Vegas." On the last of these occasions, reporters asked him if the new Awakening mining district north of Winnemucca would prove to be another Goldfield. Myers told them severely, "There never has been and probably never will be a second Goldfield." He died in a modest southern California bungalow in 1949 at the age of seventy-seven.[14]

Some Goldfielders from the pioneer group that gathered to organize the district in the autumn of 1903 succeeded better at retiring. Harry Ramsey, who had arranged the fateful sale of the Mohawk and other claims to Senator Nixon, left Goldfield for Berkeley at the height of the boom and embarked on a European tour, during which his wife died in Rome. Though he never returned to Goldfield for so much as a visit, the newspapers reported his remarriage not long afterward to "the prettiest girl in California" and his purchase of a valuable ranch in the northern part of the state. Nonetheless, he eventually fell into debt to George Wingfield, like so many other nabobs who had once been the objects of envy and admiration.[15]

Like Ramsey, the first woman in Goldfield, Mrs. George Kernick, retired with her husband to the Bay Area, following a European tour in the best traditions of Eilley Bowers and the Comstock millionaires. For the Kernicks, the European fling must have offered considerable contrast to their previous tour—the grueling journey on foot over many miles during which they prospected their claims in the Goldfield district. The second woman in Goldfield, Dr. Frances Williams, continued to make the camp her base of operations and died there from a heart attack in the midst of a new mining promotion scheme in 1909.[16]

Most Goldfielders left the camp with too little money for elegant retirement in California or a European tour, and many of these moved north to Reno. Henry ("Tex") Hall, another of Goldfield's founding fathers and later a close associate of George Wingfield, surfaced in the 1920s as a bootlegger operating the exclusive Reno Social Club during the Prohibition era. Despite the best efforts of another former Goldfielder, George Springmeyer, then the United States attorney, federal agents never succeeded in cracking Tex Hall's speakeasy. Springmeyer nonetheless managed to oust Nevada Director of Prohibition John Donnelley, a former Goldfield deputy sheriff and another Wingfield comrade, for his flagrant tolerance of bootlegging.[17]

When the flush times ended in Goldfield, some saloon owners once venerated among the premier businessmen of the camp went on to open saloons in other quieter towns (Ole Elliott in Ely and Carl Fuetsch in Tonopah); some, like Kid Highley, went into luxurious retirement. The exception was Tex Rickard. After indifferent success with new saloons in Rawhide and Ely, he parleyed his role in "the battle of the century" between Gans and Nelson into a major career as a boxing promoter. Phillip Earl observes that Rickard "introduced an exciting promotional style to American sports, largely based on wringing every ounce of publicity from the large purses he was able to promise." Long after the last of his Northern saloons had closed, Rickard introduced the million-dollar purse for a title fight and went on to manage New York's Madison Square Garden in the twenties. There, as he watched a huge crowd assemble for some sporting event, he was apt to drawl in his Texas style, "I never seed anything like it." While Tex Rickard's fortunes arched upward, Shanghai Larry Sullivan's tumbled downhill. He evidently held onto none of the gold coins once poured so freely from the leather sack in his saloon to finance George Graham Rice's brokerage company. He ended his life as a janitor in a derelict warehouse on the Seattle waterfront—not far from the spot where he once ran a cheap boarding house for sailors before the Goldfield boom. [18]

In later years, Goldfield law enforcers and desperadoes traveled various paths to obscurity or sensational death, and the blurred line between them often smudged still further. Clarence Sage, former Goldfield Con security chief and enforcer of Wingfield's dictates on highgrading and politics, later slid over to the wrong side of the law. In 1920, in Jerome, Arizona, where he had been working as a mining company guard, he received an eight-year sentence in the state penitentiary for his part in the gang rape of a young woman. Soon he was at large again and back in Nevada, only to end up behind bars once more after killing a man in Silver City. [19] Former Goldfield deputy sheriff George Gibson, an old friend of Sage and Wingfield, managed to beat the rap for the 1907 murder he committed in the tenderloin. But after his attempted murder of a deputy sheriff in 1910, he went to the state prison vowing revenge against the prosecutor who convicted him—Springmeyer. Prison failed to rehabilitate Gibson. Following his release on parole several years later, the lawmen of several cities found him a dangerous troublemaker. Reno police suggested that he leave town. Tonopah police did the same after he pulled a knife in a saloon fight. The Goldfield sheriff took him to the train and handed him a ticket to Tecopa, a mining town across the California border. For the time being Nevada had seen the last of him, but Gibson still nurtured his vow of revenge.

Some time after his return from service in World War I, Springmeyer was walking down the street near the Reno railroad station when several people warned him that Gibson had come gunning for him. Springmeyer never carried a gun, and his reckless courage was a source of bemusement to his friends. Looking across the street, he saw the cat-like features and cold eyes of Gibson watching him. Without a moment's hesitation, Springmeyer walked briskly across the street and said, "I hear you're looking for me. Here I am."

Gibson appeared nonplussed. "I was going to shoot you the first chance I got," he said, "but I see you've got guts, and here you are, so let's forget about it." The two ex-Goldfielders shook hands. [20]

Diamondfield Jack Davis, Wingfield's former bodyguard and a friend of Gibson's, spiraled down into obscurity in his later years. Despite his habit of swaggering about as a wealthy mining entrepreneur, he turned to a chiseler's game that won him little popularity in the waning days of the Goldfield boom. With a surveyor's aid, he determined that many of the Goldfield claims that prospectors had informally paced off fell a few feet short. He would then locate claims on those small wedges, compelling the miners to purchase his holdings in order to continue working their properties. In 1908 he attempted to turn his colorful sobriquet into cash by bringing a lawsuit for defamation of character against the author of a *Saturday Evening Post* story involving an unsavory killer named Diamond Jack—a new kind of sensitivity for the braggart who had gone about town displaying the rope that nearly hanged him for the Idaho murders and encouraged the erroneous popular belief that he was responsible for them. Apparently this lawsuit fared no better than his proposed 1910 invasion of the Brazilian gold fields with an army of men and mules. Subsequent mining ventures failed to enrich him, and he became, in his biographer's words, a "sorry figure," drifting from place to place and cadging money from people who had known him in better days. "Diamond Tooth Lil" (Vienna-born Evelyn Fiala), the dance hall queen who was briefly Davis's inamorata in Goldfield, wrote an unforgettable portrait of the one-time black clad swaggerer in these last years: "He is all in cant hardly breed. . . . He owes me a few dollars, wich I dont care, and he is so mean, uses bad language and he wont give me no decent answer so am glad he is gone there is no way I can find out were he lives, as he talks foolish. You know he must be real old." In fact, Diamondfield Jack was probably seventy-eight when he died in 1949, struck by a taxi after he stepped off the curb of a Las Vegas street. [21]

Thomas Bliss, also known as "Gunplay Maxwell" in the days when he rode with Butch Cassidy's Wild Bunch, came to a swifter and more dramatic end. Like a good many other hard cases, he had arrived in Goldfield early in 1907, probably as a recruit to serve the mine owners during the lockout. He also testified for the prosecution in the Preston-Smith trial. A little over a year later lawmen arrested him for robbing the Rawhide stage of over a thousand dollars in diamonds. But the authorities inexplicably allowed him to leave Goldfield without standing trial; union men thought the reason lay in his knowledge of the dirty tricks used to convict Preston and Smith. Accompanied by one of his wives, Bliss cut a conspicuous figure in the Bay Area that autumn, an array of diamonds glittering on his vest.

Not long afterward he reverted to his former pursuits on the old Wild Bunch territory in Utah. Learning that Bliss planned a series of robberies from the payrolls of Utah coal companies, the companies engaged former Goldfield deputy sheriff Edward Black Johnson to kill him on the first available pretext. A quarrel between Bliss and a railroad detective in the summer of 1909 provided Johnson with the excuse he needed to shoot Bliss down in the streets of Price. Needle marks found on Bliss's arms revealed that he had been addicted to drugs for some time. [22]

The union men that Bliss, Sage, and others of their kind had battled saw the utopian vision of the "Revolution in Our Day and Time" ground into dust. Morrie Preston and Joseph Smith languished in jail for years and became a cause celebre to the radical union movement. As time passed, an increasing number of Nevadans of all political persuasions came to believe that the two union men had been railroaded to jail. Thousands petitioned for Preston and Smith, including half the jurors who convicted them and the trial judge. Two sessions of the Nevada legislature passed resolutions on their behalf, but Governor Tasker Oddie implacably opposed a pardon. After Smith's parole, he moved to California, where he died in 1935, an impoverished and broken man. Following Preston's 1914 parole, he continued his lifelong effort to win a pardon, speaking and writing in union halls in the East and Midwest on the injustice he had suffered. When he died in a Los Angeles industrial accident at the age of forty-two in 1924, he was preparing another pardon application, still convinced that one day "time would discover the facts." [23]

Preston left no children to carry on his cause, but time did discover the facts. After the publication of *The Ignoble Conspiracy: Radicalism on Trial in Nevada* by the author and Guy Rocha in 1986 uncovered new evidence and focused public attention on the case, the descendants of Joseph Smith sought posthumous pardons for both men. On May 12, 1987, in the presence of fourteen Smith family members, including a small and lovely great-granddaughter with Joseph Smith's warm brown eyes, the Nevada Board of Pardons granted Morrie Preston and Joseph Smith the first posthumous pardons in the history of the state. Said Smith family spokesperson Diane Varni, "I can tell my children that justice does prevail." [24] Eighty years had passed since the conviction of Preston and Smith.

Vincent St. John, the most famous of Goldfield's union radicals, became a general organizer for the IWW at the national level and continued to look back on the winter of 1906–07 in Goldfield as a kind of golden age in which the One Big Union had come closest to achieving its goals. Apparently discouraged after some fifteen years on the front lines of the labor wars, he resigned his post in 1915 to prospect in New Mexico. When a panic over disloyalty in war time swept the nation during 1917, St. John was arrested for alleged subversive acts in a general sweep of over one hundred radical union leaders and convicted in a trial he called "mob justice." He died in obscurity in 1929. [25]

Other Goldfield radicals dispersed to untraceable destinies. Former Socialist congressional candidate Harry Jardine, still breathing fire, surfaced briefly in Galveston, and in Globe, then disappeared from view. In a Nevada mining camp far from Goldfield, two men arrested for vagrancy spoke so eloquently of the One Big Union that they nearly succeeded in converting the judge who presided at their trial. Probably the pair were Wobblies in flight after Wingfield smashed the union. But their identities can not be definitely determined because they insisted on giving their names as Andrew Carnegie and John D. Rockefeller.

Though they bore names less renowned than Carnegie and Rockefeller, the Goldfielders who moved north to Reno became the political elite that Wingfield regarded as the "old Goldfield crowd." The "network of personal relationships" linking members of this group, many of whom lived in close proximity to each other on Reno's southwest side, has been caught by Jerome Edwards: "Not all the leaders liked each other, but they had known each other for some time." Nonetheless, Springmeyer and Wingfield reached a parting of the ways over the United States attorney's refusal to desist from prosecuting bootleggers, including several close Wingfield associates. Despite attempted blackmail, death threats, and behind the scenes political maneuvering, Springmeyer completed his term of office unsubdued and intact. He afterward devoted himself to his Reno law practice, his Carson Valley ranch, and his family until his death from a heart attack at the age of eighty-four in 1966. To the end, his memory never wavered, and when he spoke of Goldfield, he made the camp live again before the eyes of his listeners. [26]

By then, Springmeyer was the last survivor of the "old Goldfield crowd." George Wingfield, the biggest winner in the Goldfield sweepstakes, devoted himself to consolidating his business empire after he moved north to Reno in 1908. His investments grew more diverse. He eventually controlled a chain of twelve banks, several hotels, including the Riverside and the Golden in Reno, and various ranches, in addition to Goldfield Con and other mining enterprises. During this period, his marriage to Maude Murdoch gradually collapsed. At a pre-nuptial party, Maude had reputedly told her friends that she cared not a snap of the fingers for her fiance "but he's sure got a heap of money." Wealth for beauty and social position was a time-honored exchange not unfamiliar to the English gentry, but Maude seems to have made the worst of the bargain. Several years later a girl gazing curiously at the rich and much admired Mrs. Wingfield in her box at the races remembered, "She had the saddest face I ever saw." In 1929, after two children and prolonged separation, the marriage ended in a divorce scarcely less scandalous than the May Wingfield affair. A year later Wingfield married Roxy Thoma, a shy Reno beauty almost as reclusive as he. [27]

Clear evidence of the power of the bipartisan political machine controlled by Wingfield surfaced in 1927 when it was discovered that former state officials in collusion with a cashier at one of Wingfield's banks had siphoned off more than five hundred thousand dollars in state funds. As bondsman for these officials and major stockholder in the institution whose cashier had confessed to issuing bogus checks, Wingfield appeared to owe the Nevada taxpayers the entire sum. But he prevailed upon a special session of the state legislature in 1928 to hold him responsible for only 30 percent, a stunning demonstration of his political influence. Wingfield privately considered that the state was lucky to get even this fractional amount, reasoning that he could have liquidated the bank and paid even less.

He may have pursued a similar strategy when his chain of banks collapsed during the Depression in 1932, wiping out the savings of many Nevada depositors. Despite a lengthy FBI investigation, the disappearance of Roy Frisch, an official at one of the Wingfield banks, remains a mystery about which many dark rumors have circulated. The banks never reopened, and in 1935 the former "Napoleon of Nevada Finance" declared bankruptcy, though it was said that he managed to salvage much of his personal fortune.[28]

His political power crumbled with his financial empire. The Roosevelt landslide of 1932 swept his enemy Patrick McCarran into the senate, followed in subsequent elections by other candidates with no ties to the old machine. Yet Wingfield retained a certain influence. Indeed he sometimes took precedence over God Almighty. The bells at Trinity Church near his home were never rung on Sunday mornings lest they disturb his slumbers. Even in the last years before his death at age eighty-three on Christmas evening 1959 after a stroke, Wingfield retained a habit learned as a professional gambler in the days when other poker players in the saloons misread his sly expression: as he was thinking, his hands moved absently and ceaselessly, shuffling silver dollars from stack to stack so that they constantly reformed in even piles.[29]

The acquisitions of the original locators of Goldfield scarcely compared with the Wingfield millions, but Harry Stimler and William Marsh gained a sufficient stake to launch them in the lives of their choosing. The red-haired, freckle-faced Marsh married his childhood sweetheart and used the modest sum received from the sale of the Sandstorm to buy a ranch north of Tonopah at Pine Creek. He irrevocably turned his back on all prospecting and mining investment, one of the few Goldfielders brushed with fortune to succeed in doing so. A few years afterward he lost his ranch when meat prices fell but later recouped his finances sufficiently to buy a new one at Hunts Canyon after World War I. In the twenties and thirties he became a respected local politician, serving Nye County as a commissioner, assemblyman, and state senator. In the legislature, he was mainly noted for his unsuccessful efforts to win approval for a state lottery—like the Goldfield experience, a matter of great odds against winning and large payoffs for the lucky few. When he died at sixty-one in 1938, Tonopah businesses closed their doors and flags hung at half staff as people paid their last respects to a valued member of their little community.[30]

By contrast, Harry Stimler, Marsh's partner in locating the first claims in the Goldfield district, stayed in the mining game for the rest of his life as a successful promoter with offices in Los Angeles and Tonopah. Robert Douglas, son of one of Stimler's early grubstakers, recalled: "It didn't take Stimler very long to see where the money end of it was. It wasn't sitting out there with a pick and shovel." No small degree of Stimler's success flowed from his continuing relationship with Tom Fisherman, the original Indian discoverer of Goldfield. Why Fisherman bore Stimler no ill will for wresting the Goldfield strike from him remains unfathomable, but the Indian afterward brought his discoveries to Stimler. The best of these finds was the site christened Stimler (later known as Nivloc) in the Silver Peak range. Yet, as in Goldfield, where he located his claims outside the golden horseshoe, Stimler failed to break through to the real bonanza and the camp was abandoned because the veins appeared shallow. When further development at greater depths made the site Nevada's largest silver producer in the 1930s, it had long since passed out of Harry Stimler's hands.

In Tonopah, where Stimler returned when the Goldfield boom slackened, the fact that his mother had been Indian did not prevent him from being accepted as one of the local elite, but his own attitude toward his Indian heritage remains ambiguous. Sometimes, to entertain Wall Street investors, he told stories poking fun at the Indian prospectors he depended upon. For instance, he claimed that he had been obliged to buy one-eighth interests in the Gibraltar Mine near Beatty (another Fisherman discovery) from nineteen different Indian miners—nineteen-eighths in all. On other occasions, to attract Eastern investors on his trips to New York, he would turn Indian, shedding the immaculate suits he wore in Tonopah and garbing himself in full regalia as an Indian prospector.

After Stimler's scandalous divorce from Queen in 1908, Tonopah residents had occasion to remark that "Harry went through a lot of women" and "wined and dined at the high end of it." He often drove into Tonopah in a shiny new car with a flashy looking woman clinging to his arm. He could not have guessed that his petite fair-haired first wife would prove to be a kind of good luck charm. Queen later married a tall rawboned man named Charlie Forsythe with a farmer's appearance and a miner's nose for pay ore. After the boom, when most people thought engineers had mapped every ore body in the district, the couple moved to Goldfield, and Queen's second husband uncovered one of the last small bonanzas.

In the late twenties, Stimler's brokerage business apparently shriveled. He closed his offices and moved to Tecopa to operate various mining properties. There, twenty-nine years after he struggled through the sandstorm with Marsh to locate the first Goldfield claims, his life was suddenly cut short at the age of fifty-two. On a midsummer morning in 1931, he was sitting in his car talking to his secretary in front of the Hall general merchandise store in Tecopa when Franklin Hall suddenly erupted from the store, shouted "Now I've got you," and fatally shot Stimler, afterward committing suicide. The cause was apparently a trivial dispute over a borrowed rock crusher, which triggered a killing rage in the mentally unstable storekeeper. [31]

Stimler, Marsh, and other early day pioneers fared better than the Shoshone prospector whose discovery ignited the last great gold rush. Though Tom Fisherman probably gained nothing from his Goldfield strike, Glasscock recounts that he later made enough money from the deposits he uncovered in the Stimler district to open a bank account, hire a half-breed as a private secretary to write his checks, and live high off the hog for a short and glorious time, but this was the exception. From most of his strikes, he received little or nothing, dependent on the uncertain gratitude of men he had made rich.

Most of the time the man who discovered Goldfield, the Stimler district, and a number of other sites possibly including Tonopah made a precarious living by stretching out the grubstakes as far as he could through what sounds a good deal like intentional ambiguities. Over time this turned into a sort of penny ante con game, which he developed into a fine art. According to Glasscock, "when in need of liquor, which was usually, or of grub, which was frequently," Fisherman would show a specimen of high-grade ore that he always carried in his pocket to some affluent newcomer in Tonopah with the innocent question, "What you t'ink 'bout this piece rock?" His cupidity fired by the obvious richness of the ore and the Indian's apparent stupidity, the stranger would press him to tell where he had found his specimen. Fisherman avoided being pinned down on this point, saying only "over there," with a vague gesture toward the boundless reaches of desert behind his ragged shoulder. He would, however, express himself willing to locate a claim in the stranger's name if he were provided with a "little grubstake." When this ploy proved successful and he received his grubstake in cash, Fisherman felt no sense of urgency about locating claims on behalf of these casual patrons. Often he proceeded no farther toward the desert than the next saloon.

On a January morning in 1923, while drunkenly wending his way home from one of these saloons, Fisherman fell eighty-seven feet to his death down the open stope of Tonopah's Silver Top Mine. Although the newspapers and the legislature effusively eulogized Jim Butler, who had also died recently, little notice was taken of Tom Fisherman's passing. Attention should at last be paid. The obscure Indian who died in the Silver Top that winter morning was surely the most gifted prospector Nevada ever produced, perhaps the finest in the West. [32]

Though Fisherman apparently took pride in the discovery of Goldfield, his feelings about it remain unrecorded. For the meaning of the last great gold rush, we must look to the words of those who followed in his footsteps, grand dreamers, some of them, whose hopes transformed the tents and shanties before their eyes into a paradisiacal vision. Goldfield was the moment, forever transfixed in time, when Clarence Eddy, an attorney arriving on a train from the south, saw "a forest of hoisting frames and a fantastic sea of buildings . . . robed in the golden gossamers of sunset" and heard the passengers around him cry out "Goldfield! Goldfield!" [33] Goldfield was in the spirit of the people. Neither the physical city nor the surrounding landscape resounded loudly in memory. Goldfield was the intoxicating excitement in the air, the dense crowds, the boundless prodigality, the spirit of taking a chance. How, after all, could wagering your entire stake on the turn of the wheel seem like much of a risk to those who had cast aside all other prospects and gambled with their lives? Springmeyer said it plainly: Goldfield was the people, the extraordinary gathering of adventurers from every corner of the globe. The young lawyer listened, listened endlessly, to their stories, their lies, their lives—the ones they lived and the ones they only imagined. They were the flesh and substance of the last great boom, and when they moved on, the city of stone and wood still stood unchanged, the mines produced better than ever, but Goldfield was over.

As long as the gold rushers stayed, the city mirrored their brashness and their extravagant hopes. This was the city that made its bid for state capital without bothering to incorporate, the city where con artists of the stamp of George Graham Rice and Parmeter Kent, with long records and fine gifts of gab, converged from far and wide like homing pigeons. Instinctively they knew their ebullient mendacities would flourish in this garden of hopes like the proverbial green bay tree. This was the place where red visionaries who had voyaged so far from the real world that the Socialists seemed cautious and conservative in their company could conjure up the "Revolution in Our Day and Time" before the eyes of the true believers. Perhaps those who passed the hours in opium reveries in the dens up the gulch were the least of the Goldfield dreamers. From the cave dugouts on the hillsides to the mahogany-paneled brokerage offices, people imagined themselves transformed by the magic touch of gold.

Few grew rich, and fewer still held onto their riches, but the experience nonetheless altered them in unforeseen ways. In flimsy tents, battered by the howling winds and winter snows, or thirsting beneath the relentless summer sun, they learned to survive. In pursuits they had never followed before, they found capabilities they had not known they possessed. They worked, with the intensity of youth, and changed from unfinished youths into seasoned professionals in less time than it took the Sandstorm to run from bonanza into borrasca. Like Kipling's travelers "somewheres east of Suez where the best is like the worst,/ Where there aren't no Ten Commandments, an' a man can raise a thirst" many found their upbringing had little relevance east of the Clayton Playa. They cast aside the old moralities and the suffocating dos and don'ts of small town society along with the discarded rigs and empty bottles that littered the roads leading to Goldfield and adopted the free and tolerant ways of a gold rusher. "Perhaps the absence of hypocrisy was Goldfield's big charm," Arnold reflected. "As amoral as a child, the town had danced merrily along, thumbing its high-grade nose at convention and conceding others the same right to waste their lives—if waste it was."[34] In that brief span of time, most of these Goldfielders lived far more than they were destined to do in all the years that stretched before them. Goldfield—that word, spoken low-voiced by an old man remembering, carried a wealth of meaning that only those who had been there could fully understand.

Being there created a bond between them that the most bitter conflicts in the years to come could not entirely sever. Perhaps that bond had much to do with the cohesion of those Wingfield liked to call the "old Goldfield crowd" when the new political elite ascended to leadership. It may also have been the reason why Wingfield and Springmeyer never became enemies, even during the battles that pitted Wingfield and his bootlegger associates against the incorruptible United States attorney. Years later they could meet as old men on the shady streets of Reno, far from the camp in the burning desert beside Columbia Mountain, and say, one to the other, "We're the last of the old Goldfield crowd left alive." Goldfield. In the end, this mattered more than all that came afterward.

They had not realized it then, of course, in what Emmett Arnold called the "spring time" of their lives. Nor did they guess, leaving the camp, that the zenith lay behind them. If the gold rushers thought about the future at all, they thought the feverish crazes of the mining frontier would be reborn again and again, and they would dash on from one to the next like the grizzled old Comstockers who came at last to Goldfield. Arnold and his friends slung their goods into a borrowed spring wagon and headed out across the desert, pointing their team toward Rawhide. "What we did not know," he later wrote, "was that we had seen the last of the great mining boomtowns. There would never be another Goldfield."[35]

Notes

NOTES TO CHAPTER I

1. Myron Angel, ed., *The History of Nevada* (Oakland: Thompson and West, 1881), 401–25, 512–27. On the early history of the area, also see M. B. Aston, "Esmeralda County" and P. E. Keeler, "Nye County," both in *History of Nevada*, ed. Sam P. Davis, II (Los Angeles: Elms Publishing Company, 1913), 847–87, 960–72; and Stanley W. Paher, *Nevada Ghost Towns & Mining Camps* (Berkeley: Howell-North Books, 1970), 309–432.

2. Aston, "Esmeralda," 848–49.

3. George M. Wheeler, *Preliminary Report Concerning Explorations and Surveys Principally in Nevada and Arizona* (Washington, D.C.: Government Printing Office, 1872), 15.

4. Construction of the Carson and Colorado Railroad is described in *The Nevada Adventure: A History*, by James W. Hulse (Reno: University of Nevada Press, 1966), 128–32.

5. Gilman M. Ostrander, *Nevada: The Great Rotten Borough, 1859–1964* (New York: Alfred A. Knopf, 1966), 133.

6. Carl B. Glasscock, *Gold in Them Hills* (New York: Grosset & Dunlap, 1932), 17–33; Russell R. Elliott, *History of Nevada* (Lincoln: University of Nebraska Press, 1973), 210–11.

7. Keeler, "Nye," 965–67; William Caruthers, *Loafing along Death Valley Trails* (Palm Desert, California: Desert Magazine Press, 1951), 47–48. Another version on the Indians' part is related by Curtis Littlebeaver, interview with author, Tonopah, Nevada, May 26, 1990.

8. Zanjani, "Indian Prospectors," *Nevada* 28 (Nov./Dec., 1986), 53–55; the United States decennial census, 1900; and Veltha Fisherman to author, Jan. 19, 1985.

9. Charlotte Stimler Nay, undated oral history tape, Nevada Historical Society, Reno. On Stimler's marriage, see the *Tonopah Bonanza* (*TB*), Nov. 16, 1901.

10. Sources on the discovery of Goldfield include: Aston, "Esmeralda," 860–61; Glasscock, *Gold*, 64–80; Hugh A. Shamberger, *Goldfield* (Carson City: Nevada Historical Press, 1982), 11–14; Elliott, *History*, 211–12; Robert Douglas interview with author, Reno, Nevada, Mar. 30, 1988; Kenneth Eason, telephone interview, May 24, 1990; Harry Stimler's obituary in the *Tonopah Daily Times and Bonanza*, Aug. 18, 1931; and Frank P. ("Shorty") Harris's account in the *Goldfield Daily Tribune* (*GDT*), Apr. 20, 1907. Not unexpectedly, these sources are inconsistent on many details.

NOTES TO CHAPTER II

1. *TB*, Feb. 21, 1903; Shamberger, *Goldfield*, 14–15. In *Deadwood: The Golden Years* (Lincoln: University of Nebraska Press, 1981), 19, 37, Watson Parker gives a clear explanation of unpatented mining claims.

2. Glasscock, *Gold*, 77–80; *Goldfield News 1906–1907 annual issue*, 13.

3. Glasscock, *Gold*, 77–80. The order of Myers' and Taylor's arrivals follows the dates of their claims.

4. Glasscock, *Gold*, 88–89. Also see the *TB*, May 30 and June 6, 1903.

5. The recurrent assertion that Myers was alone at the camp during part of the summer of 1903 apparently refers to Goldfield proper, since the Beauchamp brothers evidently remained in residence about a mile away on the northern fringe of the district; see the reminiscences of Goldfield pioneer O.B. Glover in the *GDT*, Apr. 8, 1907. Also see Aston, "Esmeralda," 862–63 and Glasscock, *Gold*, 91.

6. Glasscock, *Gold*, 94.

7. *Ibid.*, 93, 97–100.

8. Shamberger, *Goldfield*, 23.

9. *loc. cit.* Litigation invariably provides a rich vein of mining camp history, especially see Fox v. Myers, Nevada Supreme Court, *Nevada Reports* (1906), 169–87, and Mechem v. Patrick, reported in the *Goldfield Chronicle* (GC), May 29, 1908.

10. Aston, "Esmeralda," 865–69; Shamberger, *Goldfield*, 17–20.

11. *Goldfield Review* (GR), Oct. 5, 1907.

12. *TB*, Nov. 7, 1903, Jan. 30 and Feb. 27, 1904; Shamberger, *Goldfield*, 24.

13. J. P. Loftus to James F. O'Brien, Feb. 10, Mar.7, and Mar. 21, 1904, James F. O'Brien papers, Nevada Historical Society, Reno.

14. *TB*, Aug. 20, 1904; *Deeds. Esmeralda County 1902–1906*, book Y, Esmeralda county courthouse, Goldfield, 170 and 355; and Shamberger, *Goldfield*, 16.

15. Charles F. Spilman, "Two Men Met under a Joshua Tree," GC, Sept. 14, 1907; Glasscock, *Gold*, 109–15.

16. *Goldfield News* (GN), Sept. 1, 1905 and June 9, 1906.

17. Aston, "Esmeralda," 864–65; *TB*, Jan. 2 and Feb. 20, 1904; *GN*, Apr. 29, 1904; *Walker Lake Bulletin* (WLB), Mar. 11 and Apr. 1, 1904; M.D. Draper, "The Goldfield District, Nevada," *Mining and Scientific Press* 90 (Mar. 11, 1905), 150–51.

18. *Mining and Scientific Press*, 90 (June 17, 1905), 393–95. Goldfield geology is discussed in: J. P. Albers and J. H. Stewart, "Geology and Mineral Deposits of Esmeralda County, Nevada," *Nevada Bureau of Mines and Geology Bulletin 78* (1972), 50, 57, 67–69; Fred Searles, Jr., "A Contribution To the Published Information on the Geology and Ore Deposits of Goldfield, Nevada," *University of Nevada Bulletin*, XLII (Oct., 1948), 3–21; Thomas A. Rickard, "Goldfield, Nevada – III. Geological Notes," *Mining and Scientific Press* 96 (May 30, 1908), 738–42.

19. *Mining and Scientific Press* 91 (July 8, 1905), 22.

20. GR, Nov. 16, 1905.

21. Orin S. Merrill, *"Mysterious Scott" The Monte Cristo of Death Valley and Tracks of a Tenderfoot* (Chicago: Orin S. Merrill, 1906), 15–16.

22. *Mining and Scientific Press* 90 (Mar. 25, 1905), 180.

23. On Myers, see: Glasscock, *Gold*, 77–80; Dane Coolidge, *Death Valley Prospectors* (New York: E. P. Dutton, 1937), 85–87; Shamberger, *Goldfield*, 180; and Zanjani, "Alvah Myers: Fast-living Father of Goldfield," *Nevadan* 28 (Sept. 24, 1989), 16CCC–17CCC.

NOTES TO CHAPTER III

1. Merrill, *Tenderfoot*, 27, 33–34; Zanjani, *The Unspiked Rail: Memoir of a Nevada Rebel* (University of Nevada Press, 1981), 99.

2. Merrill, *Tenderfoot*, 30; Zanjani, *Rail*, 99.

3. Shamberger, *Goldfield*, 173–75, 186, 191, 199.

4. George S. Nixon to John S. Cook, Jan. 7, 18, and 23, and Feb. 5, 1904, George S. Nixon papers, Nevada Historical Society, Reno; *Deeds*, book Y, 232 and book X, 496; Shamberger, *Goldfield*, 179.

5. *TB*, Nov. 12, 1904 and Mar. 11, 1905; *GN*, Oct. 20 and Dec. 1, 1905, Mar. 20 and Dec 23, 1906; Jumbo Mining Co. v. Dist. Court, Nevada Supreme Court, *Nevada Reports* 28 (1904–1905), 253–64; and Ford v. Taylor, U.S. District Court, Nevada District, *Federal Reporter* 137 (1905), 149–51, v. 140 (1906), 356–61.

6. *GN*, Mar. 30, 1906.

7. Glasscock, *Gold*, 38, also see 106; Shamberger, *Goldfield*, 186.

8. Glasscock, *Gold*, 36, 106, *GR*, July 6, 1907, *GC*, June 23, 1908, and *Deeds*, book Y, 178.

9. *Mining and Scientific Press* 93 (Dec. 22, 1906), 730. Also see the *GN*, June 29, 1906; *GR*, July 6, 1907; *GDT*, Feb. 15 and Apr. 12, 1907; *GC*, Jan. 24, 1908; and Elliott, *Nevada*, 213.

10. Rodman W. Paul, *California Gold: The Beginning of Mining in the Far West* (University of Nebraska Press, 1947), esp. 332–33.

11. *GN*, Oct. 20, 1905. On Goldfield leasing, also see Russell R. Elliott, *Nevada's Twentieth-Century Mining Boom: Tonopah, Goldfield, Ely* (Reno: University of Nevada Press, 1966), 16. In *Aspen: The History of a Silver-Mining Town, 1879–1893* (New York: Oxford University Press: 1986), 74–75, Malcolm J. Rohrbough presents a more negative view of the leasing system.

12. *Mining and Scientific Press* 93 (Dec. 22, 1906), 730; *GC*, Mar. 24, 1908.

13. Zanjani, "George Wingfield: The Goldfield Years," *Nevada Historical Society Quarterly* 32 (Summer, 1989), 111–13; on production figures (rounded here to the nearest ten thousand) see the *GR*, Jan. 19, 1907 and *GN*, Mar. 2, 1907. The final figure on Hayes-Monnette production was actually lower than the $5,500,000 to $6,000,000 popularly assigned to it; labor and other costs were rough projections that nonetheless provide some idea of the percentage of profit.

14. *GN*, Dec. 29, 1906.

15. *GN*, Nov. 17, 1906 and Mar. 2, 1907; Shamberger, *Goldfield*, 183–85.

16. *GN*, Nov. 10 and 17, 1906.

17. *GN*, Sept. 22, 1906; also see the May 4 issue.

18. *GN*, Oct. 20 and 27, 1906.

19. Guy L. Rocha, "Radical Labor Struggles in the Tonopah-Goldfield Mining District, 1901–1922," *Nevada Historical Society Quarterly* XX (Spring, 1977), 3–45. Radicalism in the WFM is incisively discussed by Melvyn Dubofsky, "The Origins of Working Class Radicalism, 1890–1905," *Labor History*, 7 (Spring, 1966), 131–54.

20. Sally S. Zanjani and Guy L. Rocha, "A Heart for Any Fate: Vincent St. John in Goldfield," *Nevada Historical Quarterly* XXVII (Summer, 1984), 75–91; and *The Ignoble Conspiracy: Radicalism on Trial in Nevada* by the same authors (University of Nevada Press, 1986), esp. ch. 2.

21. George G. Rice, *My Adventures with Your Money* (New York: Bookfinger, 1974, orig. published 1911), 148–49.

22. Zanjani, "Wingfield," 113; *Deeds*, book Y, 198; *Tonopah Miner* (TM), Aug. 22, 1905. Also see Barbara C. Thornton, "George Wingfield in Nevada from 1896 to 1932" (unpublished master's thesis, University of Nevada, Reno, 1967), 1–14.

23. *TB*, June 6 and 13, 1903; *Deeds*, book Y, 170; Thomas A. Rickard, "Goldfield, Nevada—II," *Mining and Scientific Press* 96 (May 16, 1908), 664.

24. Nixon to Wingfield, July 11, 1904, Nixon papers. Also see Zanjani, "Wingfield," 114–15 and the *TM*, Aug. 22, 1905.

25. Zanjani, "Wingfield," 115; *GDT*, Mar. 7, 1907.

26. *Mining and Scientific Press* 94 (Jan. 5, 1907), 16. Also see Zanjani, "Wingfield," 115–16.

27. See Nixon's speech reported in the *GDT*, Oct. 7, 1910. Interesting details on the purchase of the Combination emerged in the course of Van Riper and Hutchinson v. Botsford (District Court), reported in the Goldfield press during most of January, 1908. Also see *Deeds*, book Z, 320, the Goldfield Consolidated Mines Company report published in the GN, Mar. 3, 1907, and Zanjani, "Wingfield," 115–16.

28. Rice, *Adventures*, 125, 147; GN, Nov. 10, 1906.

29. GN, Nov. 10, 1906.

30. Nixon to Wingfield, July 11, 1904, Nixon papers. Goldfield stock prices can be followed in the daily quotations in the press. Also especially see the GN editorial, Nov. 10, 1906, and Rice, *Adventures*, 123–32, 144–68. On the Sierra Nevada deal, see Grant H. Smith, *The History of the Comstock Lode* (Reno: Mackay School of Mines: University of Nevada Bulletin, Geology and Mining Series, No. 37. 1st revised ed., 1974), 224.

31. Rice, *Adventures*, 129, 148.

32. Zanjani, "Wingfield," 116–17.

NOTES FOR CHAPTER IV

1. Rocha, "Labor," 18; Russell R. Elliott, "Labor Troubles in the Mining Camp at Goldfield, Nevada 1906–1908," *Pacific Historical Review* 19 (Nov., 1950), 378–80.

2. Zanjani and Rocha, *Conspiracy*, 27. Also see 38–45.

3. Zanjani and Rocha, "Heart," 87–89.

4. Elliott, "Troubles," 378–79; Rocha, "Labor," 17–19.

5. Rocha, "Labor," 18–20; GC, Feb 25, 1908; GN, Feb. 21–22 and 24, 1908; and Zanjani and Rocha, "Heart," 91.

6. *Mining and Scientific Press* 95 (Aug. 3, 1907), 128.

7. Rice, *Adventures*, 130.

8. Zanjani, "Wingfield," 120.

9. Rice, *Adventures*, 128, 130; the GR, Aug. 12 and Nov. 22, 1907; GN, Nov. 22, 1907; and the daily stock quotations in the Goldfield press.

10. GN, Mar. 23, 1909. Figures on Goldfield Con dividends per share are from Shamberger, *Goldfield*, 210; also see Zanjani, "Wingfield," 121.

11. Zanjani, "Myers," 16CCC–17CCC; on Taylor, see the *GDT*, Mar. 3, 1907. On the sale of the Combination Fraction, see the GC, July 11, Aug. 12, and Sept. 19, 1908, and Shamberger, *Goldfield*, 191.

12. GC, Nov. 28, 1908. Also see the GR, Oct. 5, 1907.

13. GN, Aug. 3, 1907, Feb. 21, 1908, and June 2, 1909.

14. Francis L. Bosqui, "Letter," *Mining and Scientific Press* 92 (May 26, 1906), 342, and "Milling vs. Smelting in the Treatment of Tonopah–Goldfield Ores," in the same journal (Mar. 31, 1906), 217; and Thomas A. Rickard, "Goldfield, Nevada—V," in v. 96 of the same journal (June 20, 1908), 841–43.

15. GN, Mar. 23, 1909. Also see Shamberger, *Goldfield*, 205, 209, 211.

16. GC, Jan. 27 and Feb. 5, 1908; Shamberger, *Goldfield*, 190; Thomas A. Rickard, "Goldfield, Nevada – II," *Mining and Scientific Press* 96 (May 16, 1908), 667.

17. Thornton, "Wingfield," 9. On the stock option, see the GN, Dec. 14, 1907.

18. Rice, *Adventures*, 149. Nixon to Christopher B. Zabriskie, June 23, 1904, Nixon papers; Wingfield to George K. Edler, Mar. 31, 1909, Wingfield papers; GN, Mar 30, 1909.

19. GN, Mar. 23, 1909. Also see Zanjani, "Wingfield," 121-22.

20. *Mining and Scientific Press* 96 (Dec. 21, 1908), 758-59.

21. Shamberger, *Goldfield*, 201; Albers and Stewart, "Geology," 68; the Goldfield Con annual report in the GN, Dec. 14, 1907; and Thomas A. Rickard, "The Great Gold Mines – II," *Mining and Scientific Press*, 96 (Feb. 1, 1908), 161.

22. Zanjani, "The Mike Smith Case: A Note on High Grading in Goldfield, Nevada, 1910," *Labor History* XXIV (Fall, 1983), 580-87. On Hayes and Monnette, see the GR, Oct. 19, 1907; GC, Jan. 30, 1908; GN, Dec. 1, 1906.

23. Rickard, "Goldfield, Nevada – II," 666. Rice's nefarious career is summarized in Lilliard, *Challenge*, 272, and his newspaper in Richard E. Lingenfelter, *The Newspapers of Nevada: A History and a Bibliography* (San Francisco: John Howell – Books, 1964), 154. Also see Rice, *Adventures*, 165-78 and the GC, Nov. 11, 1907.

24. Goldfield Mohawk Mining company v. Frances-Mohawk Mining and Leasing Company, District Court, *Nevada Reports* 33 (1910), 494. Also see the GN, Mar. 18, 1909.

25. Zanjani and Rocha, *Conspiracy*, 147. A useful summary of Wingfield's career appears in "George Wingfield's Political Machine: A Study in Historical Reputation," by Elizabeth C. Raymond, *Nevada Historical Society* Quarterly 32 (Summer, 1989), 98-101.

NOTES TO CHAPTER V

1. Phillip V. Mighels, "Camps;" Helen D. Croft, *The Downs, the Rockies – and Desert Gold* (Caldwell: Caxton, 1961), 108 (Coloradan); Roberta Childers, interview with author, May 9, 1988, Fallon, Nevada.

2. GDT, Apr. 18, 1907.

3. Wheeler, *Report*, 45-46; GR, Aug. 31, 1905 (Bonfils). Also see Richard and Jacob Rabkin, *Nature in the West: A Handbook of Habitats* (New York: Holt, Rinehart and Winston, 1981), 181-84.

4. GN Sept. 18, 1905; Jack McCloskey, interview with author, Aug. 19, 1982, Hawthorne, Nevada.

5. *Goldfield Gossip* (GG), July 1, 1907; on pack rats, see the GDT, July 12, 1907.

6. GN, June 26, 1909. On the Goldfield climate, see Albers and Stewart, "Geology," 4.

7. Zanjani, *Rail*, 114; GR, July 27, 1907; TB, July 22, 1905; GDT, Nov. 16, 1907.

8. GN, June 28, 1909.

9. GN, Nov. 24, 1905. On Goldfield winters, also see the GDT, Jan. 16 and 26, 1907, and Zanjani, *Rail*, 100.

10. Anne Ellis, *The Life of an Ordinary Woman* (Lincoln: University of Nebraska Press, 1980), 253. Also see Zanjani, *Rail*, 100.

11. GDT, Feb. 2, 1907 and GC, Sept. 24, 1907.

12. GC, Nov. 18, 1908.

13. GN, Nov. 3, 1906; GG, Oct., 1906 (Kent); Shamberger, *Goldfield*, 95, 117–19, 217; Paher, *Towns*, 149–55.

14. GDT, Nov. 16, 1907. Also see Shamberger, *Goldfield*, 117, 149–55 and Paher, *Towns*, 392.

15. Sewall Thomas, *Silhouettes of Charles Thomas: Colorado Governor and United States Senator* (Caldwell: Caxton, 1959), 160. Also see the GN Oct. 6, 1905 and Nov. 3, 1906.

16. GDT, June 13, 1907. On the Hayes and Bragdon homes, see the GN, Nov. 3, 1906.

17. GN, Oct. 6, 1905 (De Wolf). Also see the GDT, July 19, 1907 (Rogers), and Shamberger, *Goldfield*, 95.

18. GG, Oct., 1906 (Kent); GDT, June 14, 1907.

19. GN, Sept. 22 and Oct. 6, 1905.

20. GDT, Apr. 23, 1907; Shamberger, *Goldfield*, 119.

21. TB, Mar. 26 and June 11, 1904; GR, Dec. 21, 1907; GN, Dec. 28, 1907; Fox v. Myers, 169–87 and Phenix v. Frampton, 306–20, both Nevada Supreme Court cases in *Nevada Reports*, 29 (1907). On title disputes in other camps, see Rohrbough, *Aspen*, 77–78, and Odie B. Faulk, *Tombstone: Myth and Reality* (New York: Oxford University Press, 1972), 76–79.

22. GDT, Jan. 30, 1907. Also see the GR, July 6, 1905 and GN, Nov. 24, 1906; the GDT, June 3, 1907; GG, June, 1907; and the GDT, Feb. 21 and Jan. 30, 1907.

23. GDT, June 28, 1906, Apr. 20 and June 2, 1907; GR, May 11, 1907; and Shamberger, *Goldfield*, 33.

24. Ellis, *Life*, 251–52. Also see Glasscock, *Gold*, 224 and Shamberger, *Goldfield*, 33–35, 67.

25. GG, Oct., 1906 (Kent). On Hilton, see the GDT, June 13, 1907.

26. GC, May 2, 1908; Shamberger, *Goldfield*, 35–45; GN, Sept. 15, 1906, July 12 and Oct. 5, 1907; GG, Oct., 1906; GC, Oct. 5, 1907. In different sources, the price of the water system varies from three hundred thousand dollars to five hundred thousand dollars.

27. GC, Aug. 1, 1908; GN, May 31, 1909; Shamberger, *Goldfield*, 67–68.

28. GN, Oct. 27, 1905.

29. Shamberger, *Goldfield*, 65–66.

30. *Ibid.*, 97. On early autos, also see the TM, July 4, 1903 and GDT, Feb. 17, 1907.

31. Martin C. Duffy, *Goldfield's Glorious Past* (Sparks: Western Printing and Publishing Company, 197?), 39–40; GN, Aug. 11, 1905; TM, Dec. 12, 1904; GR, June 29, 1905; Elliott, *Boom*, 31–34; and Shamberger, *Goldfield*, 66.

32. GDT, Apr. 17, 1907. Also see the June 20 issue, the GC, July 16, 1908, and Shamberger, *Goldfield*, 97.

33. Thomas A. Rickard, "Goldfield, Nevada – IV. Rich Ore and Its Moral Effects," *Mining and Scientific Press* 96 (June 6, 1908), 777; Phillip I. Earl, "Railroaders Staged Steamy Struggle for Nevada Lines," *Reno Gazette-Journal*, Aug. 7, 1986, 2E; Elliott, *Boom*, 30; GN, Dec. 1, 1905 and June 16, 1906; GDT, June 14, 1907.

34. GR, Nov. 16, 1907 (Pierce); GDT, Nov. 23, 1907; GN, Dec. 1, 1906; and Shamberger, *Goldfield*, 117–18.

35. GR, May 4, 1907; GC, Jan. 30, 1908.

36. Phillip I. Earl, "The Beer That Saved Goldfield," *Record-Courier*, Aug. 8, 1985, 11A; GN, July 14, 1905; GDT, May 7, 1907.

37. John Koontz with Willa Oldham, "John Koontz: Boy of Old Goldfield," *The Nevadan*, n.d., Central Nevada Historical Society, Tonopah, Nevada; Shamberger, *Goldfield*, 71–78.

NOTES TO CHAPTER VI

1. *GN*, Apr. 25, 1908 (Eddy); *GN*, Apr. 15, 1905 (De Wolf); *GDT*, Apr. 18, 1907 (Wamsley).

2. *TB*, Nov. 26, 1904; *GN*, July 14, Sept. 21, and Dec. 29, 1905; *GR*, Mar. 2, 1907.

3. Letters to *News* editor James F. O'Brien are from: Earl L. Taylor, Nov. 22, 1904; Lewis Brewins, Sept. 16, 1904; and John Stuart, Nov. 18, 1904, all in the O'Brien papers.

4. *GN*, July 13, 1907.

5. United States decennial censuses of 1910 and 1920; *GN*, Apr. 20, 1908.

6. John Koontz, interview with author, Apr. 26, 1988, Carson City, Nev.; Shamberger, *Goldfield*, 15.

7. *GDT*, July 5, 1907.

8. *GN*, Dec. 29, 1906. Also see the *TB*, Dec. 24, 1904, *GC*, Feb. 2, 1909, and *GN*, Apr. 8, 1909; Phillip I. Earl, "No Justice for the Chinese Murdered in Tonopah in 1903," *Record-Courier*, Dec. 6, 1984; and on the Chinese in the Rocky Mountains, Duane A. Smith, *Rocky Mountain Mining Camps: The Urban Frontier* (Bloomington: Indiana University Press, 1967), 29–34, 87, and Rohrbough, *Aspen*, 76, 132–33.

9. *GC*, June 17 and Aug. 6, 1908; *GDT*, Mar. 3 and Aug. 18, 1907; Elmer R. Rusco, "*Good Time Coming?" Black Nevadans in the Nineteenth Century* (Westport, Conn.: Greenwood Press, 1975), esp. 124, 173–75, 211–12; Minnie Blair, "Days Remembered of Folsom and Placerville, California; Banking and Farming in Goldfield, Tonopah, and Fallon, Nevada," Oral History Program, University of Nevada, Reno, 1966–67, 30.

10. E. W. Lucas, "Letter," *GDT*, July 1, 1907.

11. *GN*, Mar. 26, 1909; decennial censuses. Wilbur Shepperson points out that Nevada's large foreign born population was notably heterogeneous and rarely congregated in ethnic enclaves, see *Restless Strangers* (Reno: University of Nevada Press, 1970), 3–20.

12. Elliott, *History*, 229.

13. *GR*, May 25, 1907. Also see the *GN*, Oct. 13, 1906 and July 27, 1907.

14. Henry W. Miles, "Recollections of Goldfield, Nevada" (1948 ms, Nevada Historical Society, Reno); *GC*, Sept. 24, 1907.

15. Miles, *loc. cit.*; *GN*, Apr. 15, 1905 (De Wolf).

16. *GC*, July 1, 1908.

17. *GN*, Apr. 15, 1905.

18. *GDT*, Apr. 2 and 12, July 12, 1907.

19. *GC*, Oct. 17, 1907, Apr. 7 and 20, 1908, Feb. 15, 1909.

20. *GC*, Sept. 17, 1907. Also see the *GDT*, July 19, 1908 (McDevitt) and Elliott West, "Heathens and Angels: Childhood in the Rocky Mountain Mining Towns," *Western Historical Quarterly* XIV (Apr., 1983), 145–64.

21. *TB*, Aug. 27, Sept. 3 and 10, 1904; *WLB*, Sept. 9, 1904 and Jan. 6, 1905; *TM*, Aug. 27, 1904; *GC*, July, 18, 1908; *GN*, Mar. 26, 1909; Nevada Historical Society, "First Woman in Goldfield," *Apple Tree*, Nov. 13, 1977; Shamberger, *Goldfield*, 20; and Williams letter to Jeanne E. Weir, Nov. 4, 1908, Nevada Historical Society. On the proportion of women, see the 1910 decennial census and the *GC*, May 12, 1908.

22. *GC*, Dec. 19, 1908; Ellis, *Life*, 246–47; Loftus to O'Brien, Mar. 21, 1904, O'Brien papers.

23. Emmett L. Arnold, *Gold-Camp Drifter 1906–1910* (Reno: University of Nevada Press, 1973), 72; Claude Inman, unpublished and undated memoir, Central Nevada Historical Society, 19, 22.

24. Catherine McKenna, interview with author, Aug. 19, 1982, Hawthorne, Nev.; Arnold, *loc. cit.*; Zanjani, *Rail*, 129, 152–56.

25. GN, July 28, 1906 (Miller); *TB*, Dec. 24, 1904 (Ferris); *GDT*, Feb. 10 and Apr. 28, 1907; GN, Oct. 6, 1905 and June 30, 1909.

26. [Anonymous Woman], "Letter," GC, Jan. 7, 1909.

27. In the later phases of the California gold towns, Mann found that women "lived more traditional lives" and the proportion of working women declined; apparently Goldfield's women professionals and mining entrepreneurs had no counterparts in these towns, see Mann, *Rush*, 107–12, 162–65, 203. Especially helpful references from the large literature on American women were: Julie R. Jeffrey, *Frontier Women: The Trans-Mississippi West 1840–1880* (New York: Hill and Wang, 1979); Joan M. Jensen and Darlis A. Miller, "The Gentle Tamers Revisited: New Approaches to the History of Women in the American West," *Pacific Historical* Review XLIX (May, 1980), 173–213; Susan Armitage, "Women and Men in Western History: a Stereoptical View," *Western Historical Quarterly* XVI (Oct., 1985), 381–95; and Page Smith, *Daughters of the Promised Land: Women in American History* (Boston: Little, Brown and Company, 1970).

28. GR, June 29, 1905 (Phenix); GN, Apr. 10, 1909 (Jones and Harris); *GDT*, Jan. 10, 1907 (Archibald).

29. GN, Apr. 13, 1909; Merrill, *Tenderfoot*, 11–12.

NOTES TO CHAPTER VII

1. Arnold, *Drifter*, 61–66.

2. GC, May 12, 1908.

3. *Ibid.*; Thomas, *Silhouettes*, 102.

4. Zanjani, "Looking for Mr. Goldbar," *Nevadan* 29 (Feb. 18, 1990), 12S–13S.

5. *Ibid.*

6. Frank Crampton, *Deep Enough* (Norman: University of Oklahoma Press, 1956), 43–55. On tenderloin marriages, see Blair, "Days," 34.

7. *Goldfield Sun* (GS), July 28, 1906. Also see the *TB*, Sept. 13, 1907 and *TM*, Sept. 21, 1907. Marion S. Goldman also found widespread domestic violence on the Comstock, see *Gold Diggers and Silver Miners: Prostitution and Social Life on the Comstock Lode* (Ann Arbor: University of Michigan Press, 1981), 45.

8. GC, Dec. 10, 1908 (protective teenager); *GDT*, Nov. 11 and 13, 1908, GC, Nov. 10 and 11, 1908 (Sheridan).

9. GN, Oct. 28–30, and Nov. 2, 1909; *GDT*, Oct. 29–30, 1909.

10. Though not all divorces were reported in the Goldfield press and not all newspapers have been preserved, sixty divorce suits covered in the press between Nov. 3, 1905 and Sept. 18, 1909 provided useful information on boomtown divorce. Especially see: the GC, Dec. 3 and 4, 1908 (national statistics); GC, Sept. 24, 1907 (Stoneburner); and the *GDT*, June 18, 1907 (Gallini).

11. GC, Feb. 8, Dec. 28, 1908. On frontier divorce generally, see: Jeffrey, *Women*, 144; Robert L. Griswold, "Apart But Not Adrift: Wives, Divorce, and Independence in California, 1850–1890," *Pacific Historian* XLIX (May, 1980), 265–83; and Paula Petrik,

"If She Be Content: The Development of Montana Divorce Law, 1865–1907," *Western Historical Quarterly* XVIII (July, 1987), 261–91. Cruelty and adultery had substantially declined as grounds for divorces since the 1867–86 period analyzed by Goldman in *Diggers*, 49.

12. GC, Oct. 12, 1908.

13. GC, Sept. 28, 1908 (Phenix); GC, Jan. 30, 1908 (Stimler); GC, Jan. 7, 1909 (Davis); GN, Sept. 2, 1909 (Johns).

14. May Wingfield v. George Wingfield, Third District Court, Aug. 13, 1906, in the Patrick A. McCarran papers, Nevada Historical Society; personal records of May Baric, Wingfield papers; Jerome E. Edwards, *Pat McCarren: Political Boss of Nevada* (Reno: University of Nevada Press, 1982), 10.

15. Glasscock, *Gold*, 48.

16. Crampton, *Deep Enough*, 48; TB, Dec. 10, 1904; GDT, Apr. 20, 1907.

17. Ellis, *Life*, 254; Guy Louis Rocha, "Regulating Public Health in Nevada: The Pioneering Efforts of Dr. Simeon Lemuel Lee," *Nevada Historical Society Quarterly* 29 (Fall, 1986), 205. The death records in the Esmeralda County courthouse, Goldfield, covering 779 deaths during the period Sept. 29, 1904 to Feb. 11, 1909, were analyzed in Zanjani, "To Die in Goldfield: Mortality in the Last Boomtown on the Mining Frontier," *Western Historical Quarterly* 21 (February, 1990), 47–69. On health on the frontier generally, see George W. Groh, *Gold Fever: Being a True Account, Both Horrifying and Hilarious, of the Art of Healing (so-called) During the California Gold Rush* (New York: William Morrow & Company, 1966); Robert H. Shikes, *Rocky Mountain Medicine: Doctors, Drugs, and Disease in Early Colorado* (Boulder: Johnson Books, 1986); and John E. Bauer, "The Health Factor in the Gold Rush Era," *Pacific Historical Review* 18 (February, 1949), 97–108.

18. Ellis, *Life*, 247, 260, 290–91; Rocha, "Health," 207; Zanjani, "Mortality," 48–50.

19. Arnold, *Drifter*, 68; Zanjani, "Mortality," 55.

20. Ellis, *Life*, 267; Zanjani, "Mortality," 55–56.

21. Mark Wyman, *Hard Rock Epic: Western Miners and the Industrial Revolution 1860–1910* (Berkeley: University of California Press, 1979), 84–92, 115.

22. Wyman, *loc. cit.*; Zanjani, "Mortality," 57–59.

23. Brian Shovers, "The Perils of Working Underground: Industrial Fatalities in the Copper Mines, 1880–1920," *Montana The Magazine of Western History*, 37 (Spring, 1987), 26–27; Wyman, *loc. cit.*; Zanjani, "Mortality," 59–60.

24. Zanjani, "Mortality," 60.

25. *Ibid.*, 60–62.

26. *Ibid.*, 62–63; GDT, Feb. 11–12, 1908.

27. Roger D. McGrath, *Gunfighters, Highwaymen & Vigilantes: Violence on the Frontier* (Berkeley: University of California Press, 1984), 253–55; Zanjani, "Mortality," 63–64.

28. Zanjani, "Mortality," 64–65; on suicide generally, see Jack P. Gibbs and Walter T. Martin, *Status Integration and Suicide* (Eugene: University of Oregon Books, 1964), 202–25.

29. John H. Gilbert and John T. Saunders, "Letter," *Miner's Magazine* 8 (Nov. 14, 1907), 13; Richard B. Taylor, *The Nevada Tombstone Record Book*, I (Las Vegas: Families Project, 1986), 149–76; Ellis, *Life*, 274–83; Zanjani, "Mortality," 65–67.

Notes to Chapter VIII

1. Crampton, *Deep Enough*, 35–38; Rice, *Adventures*, 116–17; GN, Aug. 11, 1906. Also see: Phillip I. Earl, "King of the Matchmakers," 26–28, Steven R. Nicolaisen, "The Battle of Goldfield," 28–30, and Guy L. Rocha, "Boomer Fights," 31, all in *Nevada* 40 (Sept./Oct., 1980).

2. Crampton, *Deep Enough*, 38; Nicolaisen, "Battle," 30; GC, Feb. 26, 1909.

3. GDT, Feb. 4, 1907; GC, Feb. 26, 1909. Aso see Nicolaisen, "Battle," 30; Zanjani, *Rail*, 94, 100; and the GS, Sept. 3, 1906.

4. GC, Jan. 2, 1908. Also see the GN, Sept. 1, 1906.

5. GDT, June 21, 1907. Also see Shamberger, *Goldfield*, 81 and the GN, Sept. 22, 1905.

6. GC, Sept. 26, 1907.

7. GN, Mar. 18, 1909.

8. GDT, June 10, 1907; GC, Nov. 23, 1908; and Thomas, *Silhouettes*, 126.

9. GR, Oct. 2, 1907. On the hunt club, see the GC, Nov. 18, 1907.

10. Arnold, *Drifter*, 68–72; Thomas, *Silhouettes*, 161.

11. Dan De Quille (William Wright), *The Big Bonanza* (New York: Alfred A. Knopf, 1947), 295–96. Also see: David Courtwright, "Opiate Addiction in the American West, 1850–1920," *Journal of the West* XXI (July, 1982), 23–31; and Zanjani, "Hop Fiends' Gulch," *Nevadan* 28 (July 2, 1989), 10AAA–11AAA.

12. Inman memoir, 43–44. Also see: Henry O. Whiteside, "The Drug Habit in Nineteenth-century Colorado," *Colorado Magazine* 55 (Winter, 1978), 46–68; Justin Kaplan, *Mark Twain and His World* (New York: Crescent Books, 1974), 30; and Zanjani, "Gulch."

13. Inman, *loc. cit.*; Zanjani, "Gulch;" and Albert Bradshaw, interview with author, Nov. 5, 1988, Tonopah, Nevada.

14. GG, May 18, 1907.

15. W.P. De Wolf "Sidelights on the Camp," GN, Sept. 29, 1905; Arnold, *Drifter*, 55.

16. Glasscock, *Gold*, 108, 165.

17. Paher, *Towns*, 400–401; Joseph Fuetsch, interview with author, Dec. 8, 1986, Walnut Creek, California; Ellis, *Life*, 257.

18. De Wolf, "Sidelights." Also see Thomas, *Silhouettes*, 161; Zanjani, "Colorful Gamblers Helped Build Goldfield," *Nevadan* 29 (Aug. 26, 1990), 10T–12T.

19. De Wolf, "Sidelights;" Zanjani, "Gamblers."

20. *Ibid.*

21. A. M. Jr., "The Arizona Lid," GC, Oct. 31, 1907.

22. Zanjani, "Gamblers." On gambling past and present, see: Smith, *Camps*, esp. 224–27; and A. D. Hopkins, "High Rollers: The Suite Life," *Nevada* 45 (Sept./Oct., 1985), 30–38.

23. Glasscock, *Gold*, 40–41; Duffy, *Past*, 45–48 (Rickard); Zanjani, "Gamblers."

24. Duffy, *Past*, 48 (Rickard); Phillip I. Earl "Veiling the Tiger: The Crusade Against Gambling, 1859–1910," *Nevada Historical Society Quarterly* XXIX (Fall, 1985), 175–204; Jerome E. Edwards, "Nevada: Gambling and the Federal-State Relationship," *Halcyon*, 11 (1989), 237–54; Zanjani, "Gamblers."

25. Shamberger, *Goldfield*, 149–54; the GN, Apr. 29, 1904 and Sept. 24, 1904 (Jews), and Apr. 28, 1909 (Salvation Army); GR, Dec. 14, 1907 (Union Mission); GC, Feb. 28 and Apr. 16, 1907 (Christian Scientists), and Oct. 14, 1907 (Sacred Heart dedication).

26. Father Dermody was recalled in: Ellis, *Life* 271; Zanjani, *Rail*, 139–140; Crampton, *Deep Enough*, 30; and Croft, *Downs*, 135, 138–39.

27. Wallace Stegner, *Joe Hill* (New York: Doubleday & Company, 1964), 11, 13.

28. GC, Dec. 12, 1908; Catherine McKenna interview. Rohrbough notes that dances also loomed large in Aspen's social life, see *Aspen*, 48.

29. GN, May 6, Oct. 12, 1909.

30. GN, July 28, 1905; GC, Jan. 16, 1908.

31. Shamberger, *Goldfield*, 128–29; GDT, May 16, 1907; GN, Dec. 27, 1905.

32. GN, Feb. 22, 1906, Mar. 27, 1909; Thomas, *Silhouettes*, 102.

33. Zanjani, "Hailing Halley's," *Nevada* 46 (March/April, 1986), 14–16. Also see the Fuetsch interview, Shamberger, *Goldfield*, 101, and the GN, July 1, 1909.

34. Mining camp cuisine is covered in Joseph R. Conlin, *Bacon, Beans, and Galantines* (Reno: University of Nevada Press, 1986). Also see the GC, Sept. 25, 1908 (Casey Hotel dinner) and GC, May 25, 1908 (Goldfield Hotel Grill breakfast). Throughout American history, affluent times have meant sumptuous menus, see the *New York Times*, Jan. 23, 1991, B1, B8.

35. Glasscock, *Gold*, 158; GC, Oct. 12, 1907.

36. GG, Oct., 1906 (Kent); GDT, July 8, 1907 (Walters).

37. Ellis, *Life, 258*; GDT, June 2, July 15, 1907.

38. GN, May 19, 1906, May 15, 1909; Ellis, *Life*, 258. On the Comstock, see Margaret G. Watson, *Amusements of the Mining Frontier in Early Nevada 1850–1864* (Glendale: Arthur Clark Company, 1964).

39. GN, Oct. 13, 1905; GDT, May 12–13, 1907; GC, Apr. 22, 1908.

40. Koontz interview.

41. *Ibid.*; Fuetsch interview.

42 Crampton, *Deep Enough*, 37; James McKenna, interview with author, Aug. 19, 1982, Hawthorne, Nev.

43. GC, Mar. 28, 1908.

44. Ellis, *Life*, 256; GC, Dec. 19, 1907; GN, Aug. 25, 1905.

45. Zanjani, "Goldfield's Last Hurrah," *Nevada* 50 (Nevada, July/August, 1990), 24–25.

46 Jack Merriman, "Way Back East," GR, Oct. 12, 1907.

NOTES TO CHAPTER IX

1. Aston, "Esmeralda," 864–68; Mann, *Rush*, 19, 138; GN, Aug. 4, 1906.

2. *San Francisco Examiner*, Mar. 27–28, 1906.

3. Reports of the Nevada State Controller in the *Appendix to the Journals of the Senate and Assembly*, 1905, 1907, and 1909; report of the Nevada State License and Bullion Tax Collector in the 1909 *Appendix*.

4. *Ibid.*; GN, Dec. 8, 1905; GDT, Apr. 28, 1907; GC, July 11, 1908; *City Directory of the City of Goldfield—Columbia, Diamondfield, Jumbo Town, Mill Town Nevada, 1907–1908*, (Chicago: National Directory Company, 1907), 303–04; Parker, *Deadwood*, 63, 228; Elliott West, *The Saloon on the Rocky Mountain Mining Frontier* (Lincoln: University of Nebraska Press, 1979), 121–22.

5. De Wolf, "Sidelights;" Arnold, *Drifter*, 78–81, 85; Faulk, *Tombstone*, 122.

6. Fuetsch interview; Duffy, *Past*, 45.

7. Rice, *Adventures*, 83–89; Mark Twain, *Roughing It* (New York: New American Library, 1962), 255; GDT, Mar. 2, 1907.

8. Earl, "Matchmakers," 27.

9. GG, Nov., 1906; *Directory*, 242–307.

10. *Directory*, 302; Fuetsch interview; Shamberger, *Goldfield*, 60–61.

11. GG, Nov., 1906. Also see *Directory*, 272–73 and the 1908 License and Bullion Tax Collector's report.

12. Lena Hammond, "Memories of Austin, Bodie and Goldfield, 1900–1910," in "Women, Children and Family Life in the Nevada Interior, 1900–1930's," Oral History Program, University of Nevada, Reno, 1987, 10–12. The shopping tour is from the GC, Dec. 20, 1907.

13. Manager, *Denver Mining Record* to O'Brien, Sept. 16, 1904, O'Brien papers; Lingenfelter, *Newspapers*, 127; Wells Drury, "Journalism," in Davis, ed., *History*, 490; Glasscock, *Gold*, 107–08.

14. Lingenfelter, *Newspapers*, 127–30; GG, Mar. 9, 1907; GN, Apr. 20, 1909.

15. Lingenfelter, *Newspapers*, 128; Drury, "Journalism," 490–91; Zanjani and Rocha, *Conspiracy*, 110.

16. GC, Sept. 24–25, 1907, Jan. 14 and Feb. 26, 1909; Lingenfelter, *Newspapers*, 129.

17. Drury, "Journalism," 492; Lingenfelter, *Newspapers*, 127; Davis, *History* v. II, 1243–44.

18. Drury, *loc. cit.*

19. GC, Sept. 16, 1907; Shamberger, *Goldfield*, 98. On Truax, see the GR, May 4, 1907.

20. GN, Mar. 16, July 12, Aug. 21, 1909.

21. GR, May 4, 1907.

22. Smith, *Comstock*, 62–63. Also see Marian V. Sears, *Mining Stock Exchanges, 1860–1930: An Historical Survey* (Missoula: University of Montana Press, 1973), 10, 110, 180; GN, Nov. 10, 1905; GDT, July 9, 1907.

23. GN, Aug. 17, 1907. Also see: Sears, *Exchanges*, 110; Mann, *Rush*, 89–90; and on the visiting San Francisco brokers, the GN, July 21, 1905.

24. Glasscock, *Gold*, 180; Rice, *Adventures*, 85; Miles recollections; GDT, June 20, 1907.

25. Miles recollections.

26. Loftus to O'Brien, Dec. 7, 1903, O'Brien papers.

27. Lilliard, *Challenge*, 264–65; Rice, *Adventures*, 47–55, 79, 121, 165–67; Elliott, *Boom*, 91–93.

28. Rice, *Adventures*, 56–82; Delos Dunbar to Frank Ish, Mar. 25, 1904, O'Brien papers. Also see Elliott, *Boom*, 77 on reasons for speculation.

29. Prospectus, O'Brien papers; GR, Apr. 27, 1907.

30. Rice, *Adventures*, 176; Ellis, *Life*, 250, 255.

31. Loftus to O'Brien, Jan. 4 and Feb. 10, 1904; GR, Nov. 16, 1907 (American Mining Congress recommendations).

32. Loftus to O'Brien, Dec. 7, 1903; Rice, *Adventures*, 92–93.

33. GC, Oct. 21, 1907; GN, Dec. 1, 1906. Also see Smith, *Comstock*, 222–23, and Elliott, *Boom*, 86–89.

34. GDT, Apr. 4, 1907; Loftus to O'Brien, Feb. 20, 1904, O'Brien papers; GN, Apr. 13 and Oct. 20, 1906.

35. GC, Nov. 12, 1908; also see the Aug. 24, 1907 issue.

36. Lilliard, *Challenge*, 265–66, 271–72.

37. GC, Jan. 22, 1909; on Stanton, see the GN, Apr. 12, 1909.

38. Sears, *Exchanges*, 110; Parker, *Deadwood*, 65; GDT, Apr. 14, 1907; Shamberger, *Goldfield*, 115, 136.

39. Shamberger, *Goldfield*, 136–37.

40. Zanjani, *Rail*, 107–08.

41. Zanjani and Rocha, *Conspiracy*, 138. Also see Shamberger, *Goldfield*, 133–35.

42. GC, Oct. 13, 1908; Richard E. Lingenfelter, *Death Valley & the Amargosa: A Land of Illusion* (Berkeley: University of California Press, 1986), 303–04; Elliott, *Boom*, 93; Zanjani and Rocha, *Conspiracy*, 165.

43. GC, Dec. 10–12, 1907; Rice, *Adventures*, 52; Shamberger, *Goldfield*, 135–36.

44. Aston, "Esmeralda," 875; GDT, June 13, 1907.

45. Albert S. Watson to E. C. Brown, Oct. 16, 1905, Goldfield Mining Company, miscellaneous records, Bancroft Library, University of California, Berkeley; also see Smith, *Comstock*, 66–67.

46. Glasscock, *Gold*, 169; Zanjani and Rocha, *Conspiracy*, 140; Zanjani, *Rail*, 138; GC, Dec. 12 and 14, 1908.

47. Zanjani, *Rail*, 146–47; on trials as frontier entertainment, also see Frank R. Prassel, *The Western Peace Officer: A Legacy of Law and Order* (Norman: University of Oklahoma Press, 1972), 14–15.

48. GDT, June 23, 1907.

NOTES TO CHAPTER X

1. Ellis, *Life*, 250; Glasscock, *Gold*, 121; GC, Dec. 18, 1907; GR, Dec. 28, 1907 (Inman's raid); Zanjani, "Smith Case," 581.

2. GC, Sept. 18, 1907 ; GR, Dec. 28, 1907; Zanjani, "Smith Case," 583.

3. Inman memoir, 19–20; GR, Dec. 28, 1907; Zanjani, "Smith Case," 583. In Deadwood, by contrast, Parker suggests that tolerance of highgrading by management contributed to peaceful labor relations, see *Deadwood*, 115–16.

4. Thompson and McCabe v. State, Nevada Supreme Court, *Nevada Reports* 31 (1909), 226–27; Thomas, *Silhouettes*, 116; Zanjani, "Smith Case," 584–85.

5. Catherine and John McKenna interviews; GC, Nov. 22, 1907, June 10, 1908; Zanjani, "Smith Case," 585–86.

6. Zanjani, "Smith Case," 587. Also see Rocha, "Labor," 15–16, and Rickard, "Moral Effects," 777.

7. Reports of the Nevada Attorney General in the *Appendix to the Journals of the Senate and Assembly*, 1905–1907; the GR, Oct. 19, 1907; TS, June 6, 1907; GC, Nov. 12, 1908; McGrath, *Gunfighters*, 248–50.

8. GC, Nov. 29, 1907, Jan. 4, 1908, Feb. 1, 1909; Zanjani, *Jack Longstreet: Last of the Desert Frontiersmen* (Athens: Swallow Press/Ohio University Press, 1988), 106.

9. Inman memoir, 30–33; GDT, June 24, 1907 (auto theft); GN, Dec. 17, 1910 (Enright).

10. Thomas, *Silhouettes*, 127.

11. *Ibid.*, 129–30; Zanjani, *Rail*, 100–01, Zanjani and Rocha, *Conspiracy*, 25–26, 50, 134, and David R. Grover, *Diamondfield Jack: A Study in Frontier Justice* (Reno: University of Nevada Press, 1968).

12. GN, Oct. 20, 1905 and Jeffrey M. Kintop and Guy Louis Rocha, *The Earps' Last Frontier: Wyatt and Virgil Earp in the Nevada Mining Camps, 1902–1905* (Reno: Great Basin Press, 1989); Thomas, *loc.cit.*

13. GC, Nov. 14, 1907.

14. *Ibid.*; Inman memoir, 21–22; *TB*, Nov. 15, 1907; *Reno Evening Gazette*, Nov. 13, 1907.

15. GC, Sept. 23, 1907.

16. GC, Oct. 7, 1908, Jan. 27, 1909 (Rickey); Zanjani and Rocha, *Conspiracy*, 165; *GDT*, July 12, 1907 (O'Farrell); on Vortrees, see Zanjani, *Rail*, 129–31.

17. Bessie Beatty, *Who's Who in Nevada* (Los Angeles: Home Printing, 1907) n.p., GC, Apr. 9 and June 26–27, 1908, GC, Aug. 14, 1908, GN, Dec. 7, 1910, and State v. Weber, Nevada Supreme Court, *Nevada Reports* 31 (1909), 385–95.

18. GC, Oct. 31, 1907. Also see the *GDT*, Feb. 28, 1907.

19. Esmeralda County Commissioners, *Records* I (Feb. 6, 1905), 281; Zanjani and Rocha, *Conspiracy*, 105; and Koontz interview.

20. GC, June 30 and Nov. 25, 1908; GN, June 12, 1904. Also see McGrath, *Gunfighters*, 161.

21. GC, Nov. 6, 1907. Also see: Bell v. District Court, Nevada Supreme Count, *Nevada Reports* 28 (1905), 280–99; *TB*, Apr. 1, 1905; *WLB*, Apr. 14, 1905; and the GC, Sept. 11–13, 1907.

22. GC, Sept. 11–13 and 24, 1907; GR, Dec. 28, 1907.

23. *GDT*, Apr. 3 and 23, 1907.

24. GC, Sept. 13, 1907.

Notes to Chapter XI

1. Croft, *Downs*, 122; GN, Dec. 15, 1905 (Bell); GR, Nov. 2, 1905 (fusillades).

2. McGrath, *Gunfighters*, 251, 254; *New York Times*, Aug. 13, 1989, 15. Sources for Goldfield homicides were the newspapers and the *Death Records* previously cited.

3. Angel, *History*, 340–41.

4. GR, July 27–28, 1905 (Dixon-Moore); GS, Sept. 11, 1906 and GR, Sept. 13, 1906 (Kieran).

5. Angel, *History*, 341–58; *Reno Gazette-Journal*, Aug. 12, 1985, 1; McGrath, *Gunfighters*, 251.

6. *GDT*, June 24–25, 1908 ; GC, June 23–25, 1908; Glasscock, *Gold*, 170–71.

7. Zanjani and Rocha, *Conspiracy*. On feuds elsewhere, see: Faulk, *Tombstone*, 129–59; McGrath, *Gunfighters*, 160–61, 251; and C. L. Sonnichsen, *I'll Die Before I'll Run* (New York: Devin-Adair Company, 1962), esp. 118–24.

8. Lawrence M. Friedman and Robert V. Percival, *The Roots of Justice: Crime and Punishment in Alameda County, California 1870–1910* (Chapel Hill: University of North Carolina Press, 1981), 26–35; Charles E. Silberman, *Criminal Violence, Criminal Justice* (New York: Vintage Books, 1980), 40–42, 294–95; Prassel, *Legacy*, 6–7.

9. GN, Feb. 11, 1907. Also see the *New York Times*, Apr. 17, 1989, A10 and GR, Nov. 2, 1905.

10. GN, Sept. 2, 1909. On St. John, see Zanjani and Rocha, *Conspiracy*, 112–13; on Casey, see the GN, Aug. 17, Oct. 28–29, Nov. 1, 1909.

11. TS, Mar. 9 and 11, 1907.

12. Richard M. Brown, " 'Meet Anyone Face to Face' and Keep the Bullet in Front," *Montana The Magazine of Western History* 37 (Summer, 1987), 74–76; Zanjani, *Rail*, 145.

13. Zeb Kendall, "Letter," *TB*, Aug. 6, 1904. Also see the *TB*, Apr. 16, 1904, and *Proclamations Book* I (June 23, 1906), Nevada State Division of Archives and Records. The Nevada governor eventually posted a reward for Sharp, but by then Sharp had faded from the scene.

14. Pierre Berton, *The Klondike Fever* (New York: Carroll & Graf, 1985), 318–19.

15. W. Foster-Harris, *The Look of the Old West* (New York: Viking Press, 1955), 117–18.

16. *GDT*, Jan. 4, 1907. Also see Nevada Attorney General, "Report," in the *Appendix to the Journals of the Nevada Senate and Assembly* (1907), 54.

17. Thomas, *Silhouettes*, 127.

18. *GC*, Nov. 7, 1907. Also see: the July 17–18, 1908 issues; *GDT*, Oct. 8, 1907; and on the role of Southerners in frontier violence, W. Eugene Hollon, *Frontier Violence: Another Look* (New York: Oxford University Press, 1974), 115–16.

19. Inman memoir, 24–27; Thomas, *Silhouettes*, 118.

20. Laura A. White, "History of the Labor Struggles in Goldfield, Nevada," Master's thesis, University of Nebraska, 1912, 67, 69, 89; Zanjani and Rocha, *Conspiracy*, 15, 16, 26, 129–34; Zanjani, *Rail*, 148–52.

21. *New York Times*, Oct. 22, 1984, 6; Ted R. Gurr, "Drowning in a Crime Wave," *New York Times*, Apr. 13, 1989, A19; Robert R. Dykstra, *The Cattle Towns* (New York: Alfred A. Knopf, 1968), 132–48; McGrath, *Gunfighters*, 199.

22. *GC*, Dec. 26, 1907.

23. W. Turrentine Jackson, *Treasure Hill: Portrait of a Silver Mining Camp* (Tucson: University of Arizona Press, 1963), 60; Silberman, *Violence*, 294–95.

24. *GDT*, Nov. 7 and 9, 1906.

25. Zanjani and Rocha, *Conspiracy*, 21–26.

26. *GN*, June 15 and 25, 1909. Also see Zanjani and Rocha, *Conspiracy*, 112–13 (Mullaney) and the *Carson City News*, Nov. 13, 1907 (Foley).

27. Angel, *History*, 341; Zanjani and Rocha, *Conspiracy*, 152–53; McGrath, *Gunfighters*, 256–57; Zanjani, *Rail*, 149–51. On Oakland, see Friedman and Percival, *Justice*, 36–38.

28. *GC*, Oct. 26 and 29, 1908, Jan. 9, 1909. On plea bargaining, see Silberman, *Violence*, 344–45, 377.

29. *GN*, Aug. 17 and Oct. 29, 1909; Nevada State Prison Warden, "Report," *Appendix to the Journals of the Senate and Assembly* (1911), 48.

30. Zanjani, "'Twixt Wife and Husband," *Nevadan* 29 (May 27, 1990), 10T–11T.

31. *Ibid.*; *GDT*, Oct. 5, 1907. On temporary insanity pleas in American courts, see Charles E. Rosenberg, *The Trial of the Assassin Guiteau: Psychiatry and Law in the Gilded Age* (Chicago: University of Chicago Press, 1968), 53–55.

32. Zanjani, "'Twixt." On recent physiological explanations for violent crime, see the *New York Times*, July 17, 1987, 13.

33. *GC*, Sept. 26, 1907; Miles recollections (Arctic brotherhood); Zanjani, *Rail*, 148–52 (Gibson); *GC*, Apr. 25, 1908; *GN*, Mar. 20, 1909 (Hughes).

34. Zanjani, *Rail*, 148–52.

NOTES TO CHAPTER XII

1. Aston, "Esmeralda," 866–67. As Jackson noted in *Treasure Hill*, 93–94, in the late 1860s and early 1870s, mining camp democracy quickly became politically passive and self interested. Since few voted, a small minority gained control.

2. *TB*, Aug. 1, 1905; *GN*, July 21, 1905. On the town board system, see Elliott, *Boom*, 58–62; on mining camp politicians generally, see Mann, *Rush*, 22.

3. *GDT*, Jan. 25 and 30, 1907. Also see the *GN*, Sept. 29, 1905, Jan. 19 and Feb. 2, 1906, and *Carson Appeal*, Jan. 26, 1907.

4. *GDT,* Feb. 8, 1907; GC, Oct. 12, 1907 (Millard).

5. GN, June 8, 1907; also see the July 20, 1907 and Mar. 9, 1909 issues.

6. GN, July 13, 1907; GC, Sept. 17 and 25, 1907.

7. GC, Sept. 24, 1907. Also see: the Oct. 5–6, 1908 issues; Elliott, *Boom,* 68; the recurrent reports on auction sales in Esmeralda County Commissioners, *Records* v. K (e.g., Aug. 4, 1910); and the GN, Oct. 13, 1909.

8. Dykstra, *Towns,* 126; GN, Jan. 26, 1906; *GDT,* Jan. 2–3, 1907.

9. GN, Oct. 12, 1907; Commissioners, *Records* v. I (May 2, 1906), 140, v. K (Aug. 3, 1909), 190; GN, Dec. 15, 1905. Also see Rohrbough, *Aspen,* 201.

10. *GDT,* June 19–20, 1907.

11. Commissioners, *Records* v. I (Aug. 7, 1905), 326–37 (Mar. 6, 1906), 445; v. K (Oct. 5, 1909), 291. Also see: Mann, *Rush,* 57–60; Parker, *Deadwood,* 211–12; and on the Comstock, Goldman, *Diggers,* 35. Goldman is on shakier ground, however, when she suggests that the gratifications of vice forestalled the development of militant labor unions (31).

12. Commissioners, *Records,* v. I, (Mar. 6, 1906), 467–68; (May 12, 1906) 488–89. Also see Zanjani, *Rail,* 132–38.

13. Russell v. Esmeralda County, Nevada Supreme Court, *Nevada Reports* 32 (1909–1910), 305; Tilden v. Esmeralda County in the same volume, 324; Bradley v. Esmeralda County in the same volume, 166; Aston, "Esmeralda," 868; and the *GDT,* Feb. 21, 1907.

14. *GDT,* Feb. 21, 1907. The Nevada legislature altered the salaries and fees of Esmeralda County officials in 1905 and 1907 but did not abolish the fee system, see Nevada Legislature, *Statutes,* (1905), 210–11, (1907), 98–99.

15. WLB, Oct. 21, 1904; GC, Dec. 7, 1907, Oct. 28, 1908; *GDT,* May 30, 1907.

16. Goldfield Business Men's and Mine Owners Association ledger, Central Nevada Historical Society, 13; William E. Burrows, *Vigilante* (New York: Harcourt Brace Jovanovich, 1976), 8; Zanjani and Rocha, *Conspiracy,* ch. 2.

17. Association ledger, 12–13, 17, 27, 36, 53, 57. On the union downfall, see Elliott, "Troubles."

18. Richard M. Brown, *Strain of Violence* (New York: Oxford University Press, 1975), 22; Zanjani and Rocha, *Conspiracy,* 27–29, 118–20; and Burrows, *Vigilante,* 18–20, 160–92.

19. Zanjani and Rocha, "Heart," 76–78; *Conspiracy,* by the same authors, 12–14, 18–19.

20. Zanjani and Rocha, "Heart," 81–82.

21. *Ibid.,* 82–84, 90–91.

22. Zanjani and Rocha, *Conspiracy,* 59; also see 149–50, the GC, Nov. 16, 1906, and John Koontz, *Political History of Nevada,* 5th ed. (Carson City: State Printing Office, 1965), 188. Grant Miller's Goldfield victory in 1914 suggests that moderate Socialism had strong appeal to the town's electorate during the declining years.

23. Bell v. District Court; Russell v. Esmeralda County, 304–15; WLB, Sept. 23, 1904; TB, Apr. 1, 1905; Zanjani and Rocha, *Conspiracy,* 59.

24. GN, July 21, 1905; Zanjani and Rocha, *Conspiracy,* 11–12, 135, 137.

25. *GDT,* Oct. 15 and Nov. 8, 1906; Zanjani and Rocha, *Conspiracy,* 183–84; Wilbur S. Shepperson, *Retreat to Nevada: A Socialist Colony of World War I* (Reno: University of Nevada Press, 1966), 52; Zanjani "A Theory of Critical Realignment: The Nevada Example, 1892–1908," *Pacific Historical Review,* XLVIII (May, 1979), 277.

26. GN, May 28, 1909; Phillip I. Earl, "Nineteen-eight Vote Won Esmeralda Fame and a Mule," *Reno Gazette-Journal,* Aug. 28, 1988, 2E.

27. Zanjani, "Realignment," 262–64, 271–77. Despite partisan trends, Republicans won in Goldfield in 1910, but in the four succeeding elections, Democratic candidates for higher office were more often victorious.

28. GC, June 18 and 22, Oct. 27, 1908; Zanjani, *Rail*, 132–38.

29. Zanjani, "Losing Battles: The Revolt of the Nevada Progressives, 1910–1914," *Nevada Historical Society Quarterly* 24 (Spring, 1981), 21; also see 17–26. On Nevada Progressivism from the top down, see William D. Rowley, "Senator Newlands and the Modernization of the Democratic Party," in the same journal, XV (summer, 1972), 25–34.

30. Fred L. Israel, *Nevada's Key Pittman* (Lincoln: University of Nebraska Press, 1963), 24; Zanjani, "Battles," 17–25, 35–38.

31. Zanjani, "Battles," 26–38.

32. Though it is believed that controversial material has been purged from the Wingfield papers, a few hints of Wingfield's political activities during 1910 remain. See: N. H. Mix to Wingfield, Oct. 19; unsigned to J. W. Finlay, May 4; Finlay to Wingfield, July 1 and Aug. 3; Finlay to J. H. MacKenzie, Apr. 23.

33. Zanjani and Rocha, *Conspiracy*, 147. Also see: Raymond, "Machine," 100–01; Wingfield to W. J. Bell, Aug. 28; Wingfield to Lindley C. Branson, May 19; unsigned to W. S. Johnson, Sept. 2; unsigned to V. L. Ricketts, Sept. 2; and unsigned to W. J. Bell, Sept. 2, all from 1910, Wingfield papers.

34. Zanjani, *Rail*, 322; also see Jerome E. Edwards, "Wingfield and Nevada Politics — Some Observations," *Nevada Historical Society Quarterly* 32 (Summer, 1989), 129–31; Howdy Wilson, interview with author, Sept. 14, 1989, Reno, Nev. For a different interpretation of Wingfield's political activities, see Raymond, "Machine."

35. Edwards, "Wingfield," 128.

NOTES TO END OF THE LAST GOLD RUSH

1. Thomas, *Silhouettes*, 163–67.

2. Prospectors of later years were recalled in the Koontz, Fuetsch, Bradshaw, and McKenna interviews. On the return to leasing, see Elliott, *Boom*, 159–60.

3. Koontz interview; Shamberger, *Goldfield*, 75. Also see: Phillip I. Earl: "Did Bootlegger Start Fire?" *Record Courier*, June 16, 1988, 8A; and Catherine McKenna interview.

4. Earl, "Fire;" on the Sprague house, see the GN, Nov. 3, 1906.

5. Many excellent mining camp histories offer a basis for comparison. Especially see: Berton, *Klondike*; Faulk, *Tombstone*; Jackson, *Treasure Hill*; Mann, *Rush*; Parker, *Deadwood*; Paul, *California*; Rohrbough, *Aspen*; and Smith, *Comstock*.

6. Smith, *Camps*, 248.

7. Richard H. Peterson, *The Bonanza Kings: The Social Origins and Business Behavior of Western Mining Entrepreneurs, 1870–1900* (Lincoln: University of Nebraska Press, 1977), 122ff, 142; Arnold, *Drifter*, 86.

8. Paul, *California*, 339.

9. Richard W. Etulain, "A Conversation with Wallace Stegner," *Montana The Magazine of Western History* 40 (Summer, 1990), 10.

10. Shamberger, *Goldfield*, 201; Rice, *Adventures*, 128.

11. Patricia N. Limerick, *The Legacy of Conquest: The Unbroken Past of the American*

West (New York: W. W. Norton, 1987), 77; on recent Nevada gold mining, see the *Reno Gazette-Journal*, Mar. 31, 1990, 7.

12. Jerome E. Edwards, "From Back Alley to Main Street: Nevada's Acceptance of Gaming," *Nevada Historical Society Quarterly* 33 (Spring, 1990), 18–20.

13. On the enduring appeal of the Western myth, see Robert G. Athearn, *The Mythic West in Twentieth-Century America* (Lawrence: University Press of Kansas, 1986), esp. 272–75.

14. Zanjani, "Myers," and Millie Robbins, "The Ups and Downs of a Goldfield Tycoon," *San Francisco Chronicle*, Nov. 5, 1964, 2.

15. GC, Nov. 10, 1908; *GDT*, Mar. 5, 1907; Wingfield to Ramsey, Feb. 21, 1910, Wingfield papers.

16. GN, Nov. 17, 1906 (Kernick); GN, Mar. 26, 1909 (Williams).

17 Zanjani, *Rail*, 289, 292–95, 320.

18. Earl, "Matchmakers," 26–28; Fuetsch interview.

19. *Carson City Appeal*, May 28, 1920.

20. Zanjani, *Rail*, 148–52, 236–37.

21. Grover, *Diamondfield*, 107–108, 169–76; Fuetsch interview.

22. Richard Johnston, letter to author, Nov. 11, 1981; Zanjani and Rocha, *Conspiracy*, 47–48, 82–84, 132–34.

23. Zanjani and Rocha, *Conspiracy*, chs. IX–XI.

24. *New York Times*, May 15, 1987, 11.

25. Zanjani and Rocha, "Heart," 89–90.

26. Edwards, "Observations," 134; Zanjani, *Rail*, esp. chs. 17–19.

27. Zanjani, "George Wingfield: Nevada's 'Napoleon,'" *Nevadan* 29 (Apr. 8, 1990), 12T–13T; Edith Thorn, interview with author, Genoa, Nevada, Aug. 16, 1984; Blair, "Days," 42; Raymond, "Machine," 100–01.

28. Zanjani, "'Napoleon;'" Wilson interview.

29. Zanjani, *Rail*, 360; *Nevada State Journal*, Aug. 14, 1976.

30. TB, June 16, 1938; Eason interview.

31. Douglas interview; Childers interview; Shamberger, *Goldfield*, 229; Elton Garrett, "Nuggets of Nevada Color," *Las Vegas Review-Journal*, Aug. 28, 1931; the Aug. 18 issue of the same newspaper; and Glasscock, *Gold*, 90.

32. GDT, Jan. 24, 1923; Zanjani, "Prospectors," 53–55; Glasscock, *Gold*, 66–67.

33. GC, Apr. 25, 1908.

34. Arnold, *Drifter*, 87.

35. *Ibid.*; Zanjani, *Rail*, 360.

Bibliography

ARTICLES AND PAMPHLETS

Albers, J. P., and J. H. Stewart. "Geology and Mineral Deposits of Esmeralda County, Nevada." *Nevada Bureau of Mines and Geology Bulletin* 78 (1972): 1–80.

A. M. Jr. "The Arizona Lid" (poem). *Goldfield Chronicle*, Oct. 31, 1907.

[Anonymous Woman]. "Letter." *Goldfield Chronicle*, Jan. 7, 1909.

Armitage, Susan. "Women and Men in Western History: A Stereoptical View." *Western Historical Quarterly* XVI (Oct., 1985): 381–95.

Aston, M. B. "Esmeralda County." In *The History of Nevada*, edited by Sam P. Davis, V. II. Los Angeles: Elms Publishing Company, 1913: 847–87.

Bauer, John E. "The Health Factor in the Gold Rush Era." *Pacific Historical Review* 18 (February, 1949): 97–108.

Bosqui, Francis L. "Letter." *Mining and Scientific Press* 92 (May 26, 1906): 342.

_____. "Milling vs. Smelting in the Treatment of Tonopah-Goldfield Ores." *Mining and Scientific Press* 92 (March 31, 1906): 217.

Brown, Richard M. " 'Meet Anyone Face to Face' and Keep the Bullet in Front." *Montana The Magazine of Western History* 37 (Summer, 1987): 74–76.

Courtwright, David. "Opiate Addiction in the American West, 1850–1920." *Journal of the West* XXI (July, 1982): 23–31.

De Wolf, W. P. "Sidelights on the Camp." *Goldfield News*, Sept. 9, 1905.

Draper, M. D. "The Goldfield District, Nevada." *Mining and Scientific Press* 90 (Mar. 11, 1905): 150–51.

Drury, Wells. "Journalism." In *The History of Nevada*, edited by Sam P. Davis, V.I. Los Angeles: Elms Publishing Company, 1913: 459–502.

Dubofsky, Melvyn. "The Origins of Working Class Radicalism, 1890–1905." *Labor History* 7 (Spring, 1966): 131–54.

Earl, Phillip I. "The Beer That Saved Goldfield." *Record-Courier* (Gardnerville), Aug. 8, 1985, 11A.

_____. "Did Bootlegger Start Fire?" *Record-Courier* (Gardnerville), June 16, 1988: 8A.

_____. "Killer of Nye County Lawman Never Captured." *Reno Gazette-Journal*, June 14, 1987, 2E.

_____. "King of the Matchmakers." *Nevada* 40 (Sept./Oct., 1980): 26–28.

_____. "Nineteen-eight Vote Won Esmeralda Fame and a Mule." *Reno Gazette-Journal*, Aug. 28, 1988, 2E.

_____. "No Justice for the Chinese Murdered in Tonopah in 1903." *Record-Courier* (Gardnerville, Dec. 6, 1984.

_____. "Railroaders Staged Steamy Struggle for Nevada Lines." *Reno Gazette-Journal*, Aug. 7, 1986, 2E.

_____. "Veiling the Tiger: The Crusade Against Gambling, 1859–1910." *Nevada Historical Society Quarterly* XXIX (Fall, 1985): 175–204.

Edwards, Jerome E. "From Back Alley to Main Street: Nevada's Acceptance of Gaming." *Nevada Historical Society Quarterly* 33 (Spring, 1990): 16–27.

_____. "Nevada: Gambling and the Federal-State Relationship." *Halcyon* 11 (1989): 237–54.

_____. "Wingfield and Nevada Politics—Some Observations." *Nevada Historical Society Quarterly* 32 (Summer, 1989): 126–39.

Elliott, Russell R. "Labor Troubles in the Mining Camp at Goldfield, Nevada 1906–1908." *Pacific Historical Review* 19 (Nov., 1950): 369–84.

Etulain, Richard W. "A Conversation with Wallace Stegner." *Montana The Magazine of Western History* 40 (Summer, 1990): 2–13.

Garrett, Elton. "Nuggets of Nevada Color." *Las Vegas Review-Journal*, Aug. 28, 1931, 10.

Gilbert, John H. and John T. Saunders. "Letter." *Miners' Magazine* 8 (Nov. 14, 1907): 13.

Griswold, Robert L. "Apart But Not Adrift: Wives, Divorce, and Independence in California, 1850–1890." *Pacific Historian* XLIX (May, 1980): 265–83.

Gurr, Ted R. "Drowning in a Crime Wave." *New York Times*, Apr. 13, 1989, A19.

Hatch, Willard P. "Fireman's Night." *Goldfield News*, July 28, 1905.

Hopkins, A. D. "High Rollers: The Suite Life." *Nevada* 45 (Sept./Oct., 1985): 30–38.

Jensen, Joan M., and Darlis A. Miller. "The Gentle Tamers Revisited: New Approaches to the History of Women in the American West." *Pacific Historical Review* XLIX (May, 1980): 173–213.

Keeler, P. E. "Nye County." In *The History of Nevada*, edited by Sam P. Davis, V. II. Los Angeles: Elms Publishing Company, 1913: 960–72.

Kendall, Zeb. "Letter." *Tonopah Bonanza*, Aug. 6, 1904.

Koontz, John, with Willa Oldham. "John Koontz: Boy of Old Goldfield." *The Nevadan* (n.d.), Central Nevada Historical Society Collection.

Lucas, E.W. "Letter." *Goldfield Tribune*, July 1, 1907.

Merriman, Jack. "Way Back East." *Goldfield Review*, Oct. 12, 1907.

Mighels, Phillip V. "Nevada's New Camps." *Tonopah Sun*, Mar. 26, 1905.

Myrick, David F. "Introduction." *The Newspapers of Nevada 1858–1958: A History and a Bibliography*. By Richard E. Lingenfelter. San Francisco: John Howell, 1964.

Nevada Historical Society. "First Woman in Goldfield." *Apple Tree*, Nov. 13, 1977.

Nicolaisen, Steven R. "The Battle of Goldfield." *Nevada* 40 (Sept./Oct., 1980): 28–30.

Petrik, Paula. "If She Be Content: The Development of Montana Divorce Law, 1865–1907." *Western Historical Quarterly* XVIII (July, 1987): 261–91.

Raymond, Elizabeth C. "George Wingfield's Political Machine: A Study in Historical Reputation." *Nevada Historical Society Quarterly* 32 (Summer, 1989): 95–110.

Rickard, Thomas A. "Goldfield, Nevada—II." *Mining and Scientific Press* 96 (May 16, 1908): 664–67.

_____. "Goldfield, Nevada—III. Geological Notes." *Mining and Scientific Press* 96 (May 30, 1908): 738–42.

_____. "Goldfield, Nevada—IV. Rich Ore and Its Moral Effects." *Mining and Scientific Press* 96 (June 6, 1908): 774–77.

_____. "Goldfield, Nevada—V." *Mining and Scientific Press* 96 (June 20, 1908): 841–43.

_____. "The Great Gold Mines—II." *Mining and Scientific Press* 96 (Feb. 1, 1908): 161–64.

Robbins, Millie. "The Ups and Downs of a Goldfield Tycoon." *San Francisco Chronicle* (Nov. 5, 1964): 2.

Rocha, Guy L. "Boomer Fights." *Nevada* 40 (Sept./Oct., 1980): 31.

_____. "Radical Labor Struggles in the Tonopah-Goldfield Mining District, 1901–1922." *Nevada Historical Society Quarterly* 20 (Spring, 1977): 3–45.

_____. "Regulating Public Health in Nevada: The Pioneering Efforts of Dr. Simeon Lemuel Lee." *Nevada Historical Society Quarterly* 29 (Fall, 1986): 201–9.

Rowley, William D. "Senator Newlands and the Modernization of the Democratic Party." *Nevada Historical Society Quarterly* XV (Summer, 1972), 25–34.

Searles, Fred, Jr. "A Contribution To the Published Information on the Geology and Ore Deposits of Goldfield, Nevada," *University of Nevada Bulletin* XLII (Oct., 1948): 3–21.

Shovers, Brian. "The Perils of Working Underground: Industrial Fatalities in the Copper Mines, 1880–1920." *Montana The Magazine of Western History* 37 (Spring, 1987): 26–39.

Spilman, Charles F. "Two Men Met under a Joshua Tree." *Goldfield Chronicle*, Sept. 14, 1907.

West, Elliot. "Heathens and Angels: Childhood in the Rocky Mountain Mining Towns." *Western Historical Quarterly* XIV (Apr., 1983): 145–64.

Whiteside, Henry O. "The Drug Habit in Nineteenth-century Colorado." *Colorado Magazine* 55 (Winter, 1978): 46–68.

Zanjani, Sally. "Alvah Myers: Fast-living Father of Goldfield." *Nevadan* 28 (Sept. 24, 1989): 16CCC–17CCC.

_____. "George Wingfield: The Goldfield years." *Nevada Historical Society Quarterly* 32 (Summer, 1989): 111–25.

_____. "George Wingfield: Nevada's 'Napoleon.'" *Nevadan* 29 (Aug. 26, 1990): 10T–12T.

_____. "Goldfield's Last Hurrah." *Nevada* 50 (July/August, 1990): 24–25.

_____. "Hailing Halley's." *Nevada* 46 (March/April, 1986): 14–16.

_____. "Hop Fiends' Gulch." *Nevadan* 28 (July 2, 1989): 10AAA–11AAA.

_____. "Indian Prospectors." *Nevada* 46 (November/December 1986): 53–55.

_____. "Looking for Mr. Goldbar." *Nevadan* 29 (Feb. 18, 1990): 12S–13S.

_____. "Losing Battles: The Revolt of the Nevada Progressives, 1910–1914." *Nevada Historical Society Quarterly* 24 (Spring, 1981): 17–38.

_____. "The Mike Smith Case: A Note on High Grading in Goldfield, Nevada, 1910." *Labor History* 24 (Fall, 1983): 580–87.

_____. "A Theory of Critical Realignment: The Nevada Example, 1892–1908." *Pacific Historical Review* XLVIII (May, 1979): 259–80.

_____. "To Die in Goldfield: Mortality in the Last Boomtown on the Mining Frontier." *Western Historical Quarterly* 21 (February, 1990): 47–69.

_____. "'Twixt Wife and Husband." *Nevadan*, 29 (May 27, 1990): 10T–11T.

Zanjani, Sally S., and Guy L. Rocha. "A Heart for Any Fate: Vincent St. John in Goldfield." *Nevada Historical Society Quarterly* 27 (Summer, 1984): 75–91.

BOOKS

Angel, Myron., ed. *The History of Nevada*. Oakland: Thompson and West, 1881.

Arnold, Emmett L. *Gold-Camp Drifter 1906–1910*. Reno: University of Nevada Press, 1973.

Athearn, Robert G. *The Mythic West in Twentieth-Century America*. Lawrence: University Press of Kansas, 1986.

Beatty, Bessie. *Who's Who in Nevada*. Los Angeles: Home Printing, 1907.

Berton, Pierre. *The Klondike Fever*. New York: Carroll & Graf, 1985.

Brown, Richard M. *Strain of Violence*. New York: Oxford University Press, 1975.

Burrows, William E. *Vigilante*. New York: Harcourt Brace Jovanovich, 1976.

Caruthers, William. *Loafing along Death Valley Trails*. Palm Desert, California: Desert Magazine Press, 1951.

City Directory of the City of Goldfield—Columbia, Diamondfield, Jumbo Town, Mill Town Nevada, 1907–1908. Chicago: National Directory Company, 1907.

Conlin, Joseph R. *Bacon, Beans, and Galantines*. Reno: University of Nevada Press, 1986.

Coolidge, Dane. *Death Valley Prospectors*. New York: E.P. Dutton, 1937.

Crampton, Frank A. *Deep Enough*. Norman: University of Oklahoma Press, 1956.

Croft, Helen Downer. *The Downs, The Rockies—and Desert Gold*. Caldwell: Caxton, 1961.

Davis, Sam. P., ed. *The History of Nevada*. 2 vols. Los Angeles: Elms Publishing Co., 1913.

De Quille, Dan (William Wright). *The Big Bonanza*. New York: Alfred A. Knopf, 1947 reprint.

Duffy, Martin C. *Goldfield's Glorious Past*. Sparks: Western Printing and Publishing Company, 197?.

Dykstra, Robert R. *The Cattle Towns*. New York: Alfred A. Knopf, 1968.

Edwards, Jerome E. *Pat McCarran: Political Boss of Nevada*. Reno: University of Nevada Press, 1982.

Elliott, Russell R. *History of Nevada*. Lincoln: University of Nebraska Press, 1973.

———. *Nevada's Twentieth-Century Mining Boom: Tonopah, Goldfield, Ely*. Reno: University of Nevada Press, 1966.

Ellis, Anne. *The Life of an Ordinary Woman*. Lincoln: University of Nebraska Press, 1980 reprint.

Faulk, Odie B. *Tombstone: Myth and Reality*. New York: Oxford University Press, 1972.

Foster-Harris, W. *The Look of the Old West*. New York: Viking Press, 1955.

Friedman, Lawrence M., and Robert V. Percival, *The Roots of Justice: Crime and Punishment in Alameda County, California 1870–1910*. Chapel Hill, University of North Carolina Press, 1981.

Gibbs, Jack P., and Walter T. Martin. *Status Integration and Suicide*. Eugene: University of Oregon Books, 1964.

Glasscock, Carl B. *Gold in Them Hills: The Story of the West's Last Wild Mining Days*. New York: Grossett & Dunlap, 1932.

Goldman, Marion S. *Gold Diggers and Silver Miners: Prostitution and Social Life on the Comstock Lode*. Ann Arbor: University of Michigan Press, 1981.

Groh, George W. *Gold Fever: Being a True Account, both Horrifying and Hilarious, of the Art of Healing (so-called) during the California Gold Rush*. New York: William Morrow & Company, 1966.

Grover, David H. *Diamondfield Jack: A Study in Frontier Justice*. Reno: University of Nevada Press, 1968.

Hollon, W. Eugene. *Frontier Violence: Another Look*. New York: Oxford University Press, 1974.

Hulse, James W. *The Nevada Adventure: A History*. Reno, University of Nevada Press, 1961.

Israel, Fred L. *Nevada's Key Pittman*. Lincoln: University of Nebraska Press, 1963.

Jackson, W. Turrentine. *Treasure Hill: Portrait of a Silver Mining Camp*. Tucson: University of Arizona Press, 1963.

Jeffrey, Julie R. *Frontier Women: The Trans-Mississippi West 1840–1880*. New York: Hill and Wang, 1979.

Kaplan, Justin. *Mark Twain and His World*. New York: Crescent Books, 1974.

Kintop, Jeffrey M., and Guy L. Rocha. *The Earps' Last Frontier: Wyatt and Virgil Earp in the Nevada Mining Camps, 1902–1905*. Reno: Great Basin Press, 1989.

Koenig, Louis W. *Bryan: A Political Biography of William Jennings Bryan*. New York: G.P. Putnam's Sons, 1971.

Koontz, John. *Political History of Nevada*. 5th ed. Carson City: State Printing Office, 1965.

Lilliard, Richard G. *Desert Challenge*. Lincoln: University of Nebraska Press, 1942.

Limerick, Patricia N. *The Legacy of Conquest: The Unbroken Past of the American West*. New York: W.W. Norton, 1987.

Lingenfelter, Richard E. *Death Valley and the Amargosa: A Land of Illusion*. Berkeley: University of California Press, 1986.

———. *The Newspapers of Nevada: A History and a Bibliography*. San Francisco: John Howell Books, 1964.

Mann, Ralph. *After the Gold Rush: Society in Grass Valley and Nevada City, California 1849–1870*. Stanford: Stanford University Press, 1982.

McGrath, Roger D. *Gunfighters, Highwaymen, & Vigilantes: Violence on the Frontier*. Berkeley: University of California Press, 1984.

Merrill, Orin S. *"Mysterious Scott" The Monte Cristo of Death Valley and Tracks of a Tenderfoot*. Chicago: Orin S. Merrill, 1906.

Ostrander, Gilman M. *Nevada: The Great Rotten Borough, 1859–1964*. New York: Alfred A. Knopf, 1966.

Paher, Stanley W. *Nevada Ghost Towns & Mining Camps*. Berkeley: Howell-North Books, 1970.

Parker, Watson. *Deadwood: The Golden Years*. Lincoln: University of Nebraska Press, 1981.

Paul, Rodman W. *California Gold: The Beginning of Mining in the Far West*. University of Nebraska Press, 1947.

Peterson, Richard H. *The Bonanza Kings: The Social Origins and Business Behavior of Western Mining Entrepreneurs, 1870–1900*. Lincoln: University of Nebraska Press, 1977.

Prassel, Frank R. *The Western Peace Officer: A Legacy of Law and Order*. Norman: University of Oklahoma Press, 1972.

Rabkin, Richard, and Jacob Rabkin. *Nature in the West: A Handbook of Habitats*. New York: Holt, Rinehart and Winston, 1981.

Rice, George G. *My Adventures with Your Money*. New York: Bookfinger, 1974, orig. published 1913.

Rohrbough, Malcolm J. *Aspen: The History of a Silver-Mining Town 1879–1893*. New York: Oxford University Press, 1986.

Rosenberg, Charles E. *The Trial of the Assassin Guiteau: Psychiatry and Law in the Gilded Age*. Chicago: University of Chicago Press, 1968.

Rusco, Elmer R. *"Good Time Coming?" Black Nevadans in the Nineteenth Century*. Westport, Conn.: Greenwood Press, 1975.

Sears, Marian V. *Mining Stock Exchanges, 1860–1930: An Historical Survey*. Missoula: University of Montana Press, 1973.

Shamberger, Hugh A. *Goldfield*. Carson City: Nevada Historical Press, 1982.

Shepperson, Wilbur S. *Restless Strangers*. Reno: University of Nevada Press, 1970.

———. *Retreat to Nevada: A Socialist Colony of World War I*. Reno: University of Nevada Press, 1966.

Shikes, Robert H. *Rocky Mountain Medicine: Doctors, Drugs, and Disease in Early Colorado*. Boulder: Johnson Books, 1986.

Silberman, Charles E. *Criminal Violence, Criminal Justice*. New York: Vintage Books, 1980.

Smith, Duane A. *Rocky Mountain Mining Camps: The Urban Frontier*. Bloomington: Indiana University Press, 1967.

Smith, Grant H. *The History of the Comstock Lode 1850–1920*. University of Nevada Bulletin, Geology and Mining Series, No. 37. 1st. revised ed. Reno: Mackay School of Mines, 1974.

Smith, Page. *Daughters of the Promised Land: Women in American History*. Boston: Little, Brown and Company, 1970.

Sonnichsen, C.L. *I'll Die Before I'll Run*. New York: Devin-Adair, 1962.

Stegner, Wallace. *Joe Hill*. New York: Doubleday & Company, 1964.

Taylor, Richard B. *The Nevada Tombstone Record Book*. V. I. Las Vegas: Families Project, 1986.

Thomas, Sewall. *Silhouettes of Charles S. Thomas: Colorado Governor and United States Senator*. Caldwell: Caxton, 1959.

Twain, Mark (Samuel L. Clemens). *Roughing It*. New York: New American Library, 1962 reprint.

Watson, Margaret G. *Amusements of the Mining Frontier in Early Nevada 1850–1864*. Glendale: Arthur Clark Company, 1964.

West, Elliott. *The Saloon on the Rocky Mountain Mining Frontier*. Lincoln: University of Nebraska Press, 1979.

Wyman, Mark. *Hard Rock Epic: Western Miners and the Industrial Revolution 1860–1910*. Berkeley: University of California Press, 1979.

Zanjani, Sally, and Guy L. Rocha. *The Ignoble Conspiracy: Radicalism on Trial in Nevada*. Reno: University of Nevada Press, 1986.

Zanjani, Sally. *Jack Longstreet: Last of the Desert Frontiersmen*. Athens: Swallow Press/Ohio University Press, 1988.

————. *The Unspiked Rail: Memoir of a Nevada Rebel*. University of Nevada Press, 1981.

NEWSPAPERS AND PERIODICALS

Carson City Appeal

Carson City News

Goldfield Chronicle

Goldfield News

Goldfield Gossip

Goldfield Review

Goldfield Sun

Goldfield Daily Tribune

Inyo Independent

Las Vegas Review-Journal

Miners' Magazine

Mining and Scientific Press

Nevada State Journal

New York Times

Reno Evening Gazette

Rhyolite Daily Bulletin

San Francisco Chronicle

San Francisco Examiner

Tonopah Bonanza

Tonopah Miner

Tonopah Sun

Walker Lake Bulletin

MANUSCRIPT COLLECTIONS AND UNPUBLISHED MATERIALS

Blair, Minnie P. "Days Remembered of Folsom and Placerville, California; Banking and Farming in Goldfield, Tonopah, and Fallon, Nevada." Oral History Program, University of Nevada, Reno, 1966–1967.

Burke, Frank. Letter to author, Mar. 31, 1985.

Fisherman, Veltha. Letter to author, Jan. 19, 1985.

Goldfield Business Men's and Mine Owners Association ledger. Central Nevada Historical Society, Tonopah.

Goldfield Mining Company. Miscellaneous Records. Bancroft Library, University of California, Berkeley.

Hammond, Lena. "Memories of Austin, Bodie and Goldfield, 1900–1910," in "Women, Children and Family Life in the Nevada Interior, 1900–1930's." R.T. King, editor. Oral History Program, University of Nevada, Reno, 1987

Inman, Claude. Unpublished and undated memoir, Central Nevada Historical Society, Tonopah.

Johnston, Richard. Letter to author, Nov. 11, 1981.

McCarran, Patrick A. Papers. Nevada Historical Society, Reno.

Miles, Henry W. "Recollections of Goldfield, Nevada." 1948 manuscript, Nevada Historical Society, Reno.

Nixon, George S. Papers. Nevada Historical Society, Reno.

O'Brien, James F. Papers. Nevada Historical Society, Reno.

Thornton, Barbara C. "George Wingfield in Nevada from 1896 to 1932." Master's thesis, University of Nevada, Reno, 1967.

White, Laura A. "History of the Labor Struggles in Goldfield, Nevada." Master's thesis, University of Nebraska, 1912.

Williams, Frances. Letter, Nov. 4, 1908. Nevada Historical Society, Reno.

Wingfield, George. Papers. Nevada Historical Society, Reno.

GOVERNMENT DOCUMENTS

Bell v. District Court, Nevada Supreme Court. Nevada Reports 28 (1905): 280–99.

Bradley v. Esmeralda County, Nevada Supreme Court. Nevada Reports 32 (1909): 159–69.

Death Records, 1904–1909, Esmeralda County courthouse, Goldfield, Nevada.

Deeds. Esmeralda County 1902–1906, Books Y and Z, Esmeralda County courthouse, Goldfield, Nevada.

Esmeralda County Commissioners. Records, vols. I and K, Nevada Historical Society, Reno.

Ford v. Taylor, U.S. District Court, Nevada District. Federal Reporter 137 (1905): 149–51; 140 (1906): 356–61.

Fox v. Myers, Nevada Supreme Court. Nevada Reports 29 (1906): 169–87.

Goldfield Mohawk Mining Company v. Frances Mohawk Mining and Leasing Company, District Court. Nevada Reports 31 (1909): 348–59.

Jumbo Mining Co. v. District Court, Nevada Supreme Court. Nevada Reports 28 (1904–1905): 253–64.

Nevada. [reward notice for Howard Sharp]. Proclamations Book I (June 23, 1906), Nevada State Division of Archives and Records, Carson City, Nevada.

Nevada Attorney General. "Report." Appendix to the Journals of the Senate and Assembly, 1905–1907.

Nevada Legislature. Statutes, 1905, 1907.

Nevada Secretary of State. "Report." Appendix to the Journals of the Senate and Assembly, 1903–1911.

Nevada State Controller. "Report." Appendix to the Journals of the Senate and Assembly, 1905–1909.

Nevada State License and Bullion Tax Collector. "Report." Appendix to the Journals of the Senate and Assembly, 1909.

Nevada State Prison. Records, Nevada State Division of Archives and Records, Carson City.

Nevada State Prison Warden. "Report." *Appendix to the Journals of the Senate and Assembly,* 1911.

Phenix v. Frampton, Nevada Supreme Court. *Nevada Reports* 29 (1907): 306–20.

Russell v. Esmeralda County, Nevada Supreme Court. *Nevada Reports* 32 (1910): 305–15.

State v. Thompson and McCabe, Nevada Supreme Court. *Nevada Reports* 31 (1909): 209–27.

State v. Weber, Nevada Supreme Court. *Nevada Reports* 31 (1909): 385–95.

Tilden v. Esmeralda County, Nevada Supreme Court. *Nevada Reports* 32 (1910): 319–27.

United States Bureau of the Census. Decennial reports, 1900–1920.

Wheeler, George M. *Preliminary Report Concerning Explorations and Surveys Principally in Nevada and Arizona.* Washington, D.C.: Government Printing Office, 1872.

INTERVIEWS

Childers, Roberta, May 9, 1988, Fallon, Nevada.

Bradshaw, Albert, Nov. 5, 1988, Tonopah, Nevada.

Douglas, Robert, Mar. 30, 1988, Reno, Nevada.

Eason, Kenneth, May 24, 1990, telephone, Tonopah, Nevada.

Fuetsch, Joseph, Dec. 8, 1986, Walnut Creek, California.

Koontz, John, Apr. 26, 1988, Carson City, Nevada.

Littlebeaver, Curtis, May 26, 1990, Tonopah, Nevada.

McCloskey, Jack, Aug. 19, 1982, Hawthorne, Nevada.

McKenna, Catherine, Aug. 19, 1982, Hawthorne, Nevada.

McKenna, James, Aug. 19, 1982, Hawthorne, Nevada.

Nay, Charlotte Stimler, undated oral history tape, Nevada Historical Society, Reno.

Thorn, Edith, Aug. 16, 1984, Genoa, Nevada.

Wilson, Howdy, Sept. 14, 1989, Reno, Nevada.

Index

T R I B U N E 1907

A Note About the Author

Sally Zanjani is associated with the political science department at the University of Nevada, Reno. She is the author of several books, including *Jack Longstreet: Last of the Desert Frontiersmen*, and more than thirty articles on the West. *The Ignoble Conspiracy: Radicalism on Trial in Nevada*, written with Guy L. Rocha, was largely responsible for the posthumous pardons granted to Goldfield union radicals Morrie Preston and Joseph Smith in 1987, eighty years after their conviction. In 1906 Zanjani's father, the late George Springmeyer, joined the great rush to Goldfield.